Christmas Evans

The Life and Times of the One-Eyed Preacher of Wales

This reproduction is from a colour portrait of Christmas Evans by Stuart Mantell, and is used with his kind permission.

Christmas Evans

The Life and Times of the One-Eyed Preacher of Wales

Tim Shenton

EVANGELICAL PRESS
Faverdale North Industrial Estate, Darlington, DL3 0PH, England

Evangelical Press USA
P. O. Box 84, Auburn, MA 01501, USA

e-mail: sales@evangelicalpress.org

web: www.evangelicalpress.org

First published 2001

British Library Cataloguing in Publication Data available

ISBN 0 85234 483 X

Index compiled by Edmund Owen

Portrait and maps by kind permission of Stuart Mantell

Printed and bound in Great Britain by Creative Print & Design Wales, Ebbw Vale

Contents

Dedicated to
Ma and Iola,
and to every other Welsh person,
high or low, rich or poor,
in the north or in the south of Wales,
who seeks first God's kingdom and his righteousness.

Acknowledgements

It is with a deep sense of gratitude that I acknowledge the debt I owe to the following: Dr Eifion Evans, for his practical advice and encouragement, and for the judicious remarks he made on my MS; Dr Densil Morgan and Dr Noel Gibbard, for the time and trouble they spent reading through and commenting on my work; Dr Stuart Olyott, for writing the foreword; Iola Thomas, Prydwen Jenkins, Eluned Evans, Jane Earnshaw and Bill Jones for the many hours of translation work done on my behalf; Stuart Mantell, for drawing two maps of Wales and for painting a colour portrait of Christmas Evans, along with his willingness to help in whatever way he could; Trisa Mantell, for her support and hospitality in Wales; Richard Lewis of the National Library of Wales, Aberystwyth; Susan Mills and Jennifer Thorp of the Angus Library, Regent's Park College, Oxford; Mary Margaret Benson of the Northup Library, Oregon; Earle Havens of the Yale University Library, Connecticut; S. J. Taylor of the Evangelical Library, London; my mother, for her unfailing support; my father, for his companionship on my 'research travels' and for proof reading the final draft; and most of all my wife, whose suggestions for improving the MS have been invaluable.

Tim Shenton

Foreword

In this book you will meet a man who was possibly the greatest preacher that God has ever given to Wales. It is over 160 years since he died and, although he has not been forgotten, his memory is fading fast. There are fewer and fewer people who have any reliable and detailed information about him and even fewer who understand what his life and ministry have to teach us in the twenty-first century. We are so grateful therefore to Tim Shenton for the enormous amount of time and labour that he has spent in writing this new biography of the one-eyed preacher. His extensive, thorough and well-documented research has produced the most accurate work on Christmas Evans that has ever appeared; it is certainly going to be the standard work for many years to come. This does not mean that the book is dry, or in any way uninteresting. It is written in a style that everyone can enjoy, and with a spiritual insight that makes every page worthwhile.

But it is not only Christmas Evans that you will meet in this book. As the early nonconformist preachers of Wales are revealed through the pages, you may be surprised to discover that some of them were martyrs. You will be helped to understand the spiritual situation when Christmas Evans came onto the scene, and into what heritage he entered. You will also meet the men who deeply influenced him at different stages of his life, and especially during his early years. In addition, you will get to know many others who worked for Christ during the same period, as well as those who opposed him. In those days the Spirit of God was wonderfully at work in Wales. Great numbers were coming to Christ throughout the Principality. You will be permanently enriched as you learn about how Christ's cause marched forward in the face of open hostility, and despite the countless faults and errors to be found within the professing church.

So what sort of man was this Christmas Evans who preached with such uncommon power, whose unforgettable sermons attracted and thrilled vast crowds, and by whose ministry so very many came to receive and rely upon the Lord Jesus Christ alone for salvation? Tim Shenton does not hide anything from us. He faithfully traces the considerable disadvantages under which Christmas Evans laboured; he specifically identifies twenty or so flaws in his character and actions and he focuses on the Christ-like fruit that was so abundantly evident in his consecrated life. An ordinary and always imperfect man became filled with love for God and for others! He gave himself to the simple preaching of Christ and his cross, and set about it with imagination and flair. He understood the intimate connection between the blessing of the Spirit on his preaching and his own personal life of prayer. How do we explain all this? How did such a man become so very useful? Mr. Shenton's book points us to the answer: the *grace of God* made him what he was.

In this twenty-first century every nation on earth could do with a modern Christmas Evans. A lot of what passes for preaching today is not preaching at all. Where are the impassioned earnestness and love that characterized the one-eyed preacher? Where are his spirit of self-sacrifice and his example of hard work? Where is the divine anointing, 'the grand inward secret'? Where are the preachers who put eyes into their hearers' ears?

Where are the sermons that *never fail* to portray Christ as crucified and to set him forth as risen, exalted and reigning? Where are the congregations who are moved, thrilled and subdued by the preached Word of God? Where are the men, women, young people and children who can honestly say that nothing, but nothing, makes such an impression on them as the sermons they hear?

May our Lord be pleased to use this fine book to light a fire and to restore such preaching to us!

Stuart Olyott,
The Evangelical Theological College of Wales,
Bryntirion,
Bridgend.
September 2001.

Preface

I was surprised during the course of my research into the life and times of Christmas Evans how many Christian people, having been told the name of my subject, looked at me blankly and said, 'Christmas who?' At one of the first evangelical libraries I visited, when I asked the librarian if there were any biographies on Christmas Evans in the library, he replied, 'If there are, they are still on the shelves,' implying that our preacher was so little known that few would be interested in reading about his life. As I travelled in the Principality, where once his name was a household word, I was conscious of an ignorance among Christians of this great man, who, in the previous century, was acknowledged by many as 'the greatest preacher that God has ever given to Wales'.[1] Many who had heard the name Christmas Evans seemed to be unaware of the details of his life and the influence he had on Wales, and particularly the Baptist denomination, during the late eighteenth and early nineteenth centuries. I spoke to one man outside Bethesda Chapel, Swansea, where Christmas Evans is buried. He told me he had done some research on the churches in that area, so I mentioned Christmas Evans to him, expecting him to be a mine of information. 'Oh yes, Christmas Evans,' he replied thoughtfully. 'He was a missionary to China, wasn't he?', confusing him no doubt

with Griffith John (1831-1912), who was born in Swansea and
became a missionary in China.

Thomas Raffles (1788-1863), the Independent minister of
Great George Street Chapel, Liverpool, and himself a celebrated
preacher, acknowledged Christmas Evans to be 'the mightiest
preacher of the age'; the British prime minister, David Lloyd
George, whose knowledge of Welsh preachers was quite extensive, said, 'One of the things that I should like to enjoy when I
enter paradise is a preaching festival with John Elias, Christmas
Evans, Williams of Wern and others occupying the pulpit. That
is how these fathers of Nonconformity appeal to me;' D. M.
Lloyd-Jones, who needs no introduction to evangelical Christians, speaks of 'the great Christmas Evans, who, some would
say, was the greatest preacher that the Baptists have ever had
in Great Britain — certainly he and Spurgeon would be the two
greatest';[2] and the *Freeman*, a widely read nineteenth century
English Baptist journal, after observing that 'The coming of Mr
Spurgeon to any city, town or village, either in England, Wales
or Scotland, is an event which moves the entire population,
Church and Nonconforming, rich and poor, church-going and
non church-going,' summed up by remarking: 'No other
preacher in this age wields such power, and it may be questioned whether anyone else has ever done it in these islands
save John Knox in Scotland and Christmas Evans in Wales.'[3]

So why is Christmas Evans not as well known in this present
century, especially among English-speaking Christians, as he
deserves to be? One reason must be attributed to the general
decline in religious instruction and of interest in religious
subjects among the Christian community. In many areas secu-
larism has invaded the church, and left little room for the popu-
larisation of men who carried forth the gospel of Christ in bygone
years. We must also take into account that his *Works* are in
Welsh, though some of his sermons have been translated into
English. This language barrier is sufficient cause for many to

search no further into his life. Recent English biographies have been disappointing. E. Ebrard Rees's *Christmas Evans* (1935) fails to do justice to its subject, while B. A. Ramsbottom's (1984) work is only a short introduction. The latter appears to have been heavily reliant on D. M. Evans, *Christmas Evans: A Memoir* (1863), a biography, useful for its quotable anecdotes, but with a tendency to lean more to the sensational than to the factual.

Another cause of Christmas Evans's slide into oblivion is the denomination to which he belonged. The most recent interest and writings in English about Welsh preachers have centred on those connected with Calvinistic Methodism, men like Howel Harris, Daniel Rowland and John Elias, and the revivals within that denomination; whereas Christmas Evans was a Baptist. These reasons taken together have caused a generation of English-speaking Christians to grow up knowing little of *The One-eyed Preacher of Wales*, who has become, as one biographer calls him, 'The Forgotten Christmas'.[4]

I am indebted to five authors in particular. The first is David Phillips, whose biography *Memoir of the Life, Labors, and Extensive Usefulness of the Rev. Christmas Evans* (1843) is mainly extracted from the Welsh memoir by William Morgan that was published in the Principality soon after Christmas Evans's death. The author was acquainted with Christmas Evans for some thirty years, and has added to the Welsh memoir a variety of incidents well known to him. With respect to the translation of Christmas Evans's writings, which occur throughout the work, he has rendered them 'in language as nearly as possible to that which Evans would have used himself had he written in English'.[5] This work I prize above all others for its simple and honest delineation of Christmas Evans's ministerial usefulness and eminent piety.

The second author is David Rhys Stephen, a Baptist minister, who was entrusted by his 'venerable friend' Christmas Evans to write his biography (1847). The whole was written with the

aim of putting 'the reader in a position to understand and know
the great preacher for himself'.[6] Then there is Jonathan Davis,
whose book *Memoir of the Rev Christmas Evans: A Minister of
the Gospel in the Principality of Wales* (1840) is very rare. I
obtained my copy from the Northup Library, Oregon, having
been unable to find it anywhere in the UK. Davis was
well-acquainted with Christmas Evans, travelling and preaching with him, frequently for weeks and months at a time, from
the year 1810 to the year 1828. The fourth author is Joseph
Cross. His work *Sermons and Memoirs of Christmas Evans*
(1856) was at one time so rare that libraries held it under lock
and key and book dealers valued it highly. Thankfully it was
reprinted in 1986 by Kregel Publications. Finally, Densil Morgan,
whose biography *Christmas Evans a'r Ymneilltuaeth Newydd
(Christmas Evans and the New NonConformity)*, published in
1991, makes full use of the most recent research in the field.

Wherever possible during the course of the work, I have
allowed Christmas Evans to speak for himself, which means,
inevitably, there are some extended extracts of his writings. I
have not in any way attempted to conceal or minimise his failings, which, as with most men, were obvious and not a few;
nor have I for effect exaggerated his gifts, but have portrayed
them with the restraint that honesty demands. Although I have
devoted a chapter to various extracts from his sermons, I have
also inserted further extracts at various points to publish more
fully his views and exemplify his style. It must be understood
that it is an impossible task to reproduce the animation and
effect of Christmas Evans's delivery on the printed page. Some
of his most powerful sermons appear quite ordinary in black
and white; it is therefore left to the reader to imagine the fiery
oratory and power that accompanied them.

Wherever necessary, but particularly in the early chapters, I
have taken the liberty of sketching the lives and ministries of
other Welsh preachers, who either influenced or were associated

with Christmas Evans. My aim has been to inform the reader, as far as possible, of some of the great men who have served the Principality with that wholehearted devotion to the cause of Christ that was so prominent in the life of Christmas Evans. I hope these short digressions do not deflect attention away from the main subject of this biography.

Finally, I must mention the spellings of Welsh place-names, notoriously difficult for monoglot Englishmen. If there has been any doubt or confusion over the correct spelling, I have referred to *A Gazetteer of Welsh Place-Names (Rhestr o Enwau Lleoedd)*, published by University Press of Wales (Cardiff, 1967) and edited by Elwyn Davies, which is regarded as the standard guide.

Abbreviations and Select Bibliography

A   R. E. Williams (Translator), *The Allegories of Christ-
        mas Evans* (G. M. Evans, Aberdare, 1899).
CENN   D. Densil Morgan, *Christmas Evans and the New Non-
        conformity (Christmas Evans a'r Ymneilltuaeth
        Newydd)*, (Gomer Press, Llandysul, 1991).
DBMW   D. Densil Morgan, *The Development of the Baptist
        Movement in Wales Between 1714 and 1815* (Unpub-
        lished thesis, University of Oxford, 1986).
DME   D. M. Evans, *Christmas Evans: A Memoir*, The Bunyan
        Library, vol. IX (J. Heaton &Son, London, 1863).
DNB   *The Dictionary of National Biography* (Oxford Uni-
        versity Press, London, 1956-1960).
DP   David Phillips, *Memoir of the Life, Labors and Exten-
        sive Usefulness of* the *Rev. Christmas Evans* (M. W.
        Dodd, New York, 1843).
DWB   *The Dictionary of Welsh Biography Down to 1940*
        (London, 1959).
ER   E. Ebrard Rees, *Christmas Evans* (The Kingsgate Press,
        London, c.1935).
EWH   David Davies, *Echoes from the Welsh Hills* (Passmore
        and Alabaster, London, 1888).

GHJ   Geraint H. Jenkins, *The Foundations of Modern Wales 1642-1780* (Oxford University Press, Oxford, 1993).

GPW   Owen Jones, *Some of the Great Preachers of Wales* (Passmore & Alabaster, 1885), (Reprinted by Tentmaker Publications, Clonmel, 1995).

HW   John Davies, *A History of Wales* (Penguin Books, London, 1994).

HWB   J. Davis, *History of the Welsh Baptists* (D. M. Hogan, Pittsburgh, 1835), (Reprinted by Church History Research & Archives, Gallatin, 1982).

JD   J. Davis, *Memoir of the Rev. Christmas Evans, A Minister of the Gospel in the Principality of Wales* (J. Davis & S. Siegfried, Mount Pleasant, 1840).

PH   Paxton Hood, *Christmas Evans: The Preacher of Wild Wales* (Hodder & Stoughton, London, 1888).

RS   David Rhys Stephen, *Memoirs of the Late Christmas Evans of Wales* (Aylott and Jones, London, 1847).

SM   Joseph Cross, *Sermons and Memoirs of Christmas Evans* (Leary & Getz, New York, 1856), (Reprinted by Kregel Publications, Grand Rapids, 1986).

SVS   J. Davis (Translator), *Sermons on Various Subjects by Rev Christmas Evans* (Beaver, 1837).

TMB   T. M. Bassett, *The Welsh Baptists* (Ilston House, Swansea, 1977).

TR   Thomas Rees, *History of Protestant Nonconformity in Wales* (John Snow and Co., London, 1883).

I, Christmas Evans, do solemnly declare in the presence of Almighty God that I am a Christian and a Protestant and as such that I believe that the Scriptures of the Old and New Testament commonly received among the Protestant Churches do contain the revealed will of God and that I do receive the same as the rule of my doctrine and practice.

The oath of allegiance taken by Christmas Evans when he was licensed to preach in 1805.

Other countries have had their philosophers, poets, statesmen, and social reformers, but in Wales the preachers supplied the highest stimulus to the national life. They were philosophers and theologians; they were eminent in sacred poetry and hymnody; they were reformers of the moral and social condition of the poor; they were the organisers of national education. Very largely they created the literature of modern Wales, and they have steadily cultivated the national sentiment. No land has owed so much to its preachers.

C.Silvester Horne.[1]

Introduction
'A Great Cloud of Witnesses'

'O! highly favoured country!' wrote a minister from England to Thomas Charles in 1785. 'I believe that you have more of the spirit and simplicity of the primitive Christians, among the rocks of Wales, than there is anywhere else in this day throughout the whole world.'[2] It was the 'spirit and simplicity of the primitive Christians' — a sound theology, a commitment to prayer, a life of piety, a courageous faith — that invigorated the great preachers of Wales, enabling them with the words of heaven to set the land of Cambria on fire. By the influence of the Holy Spirit inflaming their love for Christ and igniting a passion for the souls of men, they transformed the Principality from a stronghold of drunkenness, immorality and superstition, into 'one of the most scripturally enlightened, loyal and religious nations on the face of the earth'[3] — a nation where men and women embraced a Christianity that was 'at once fervent, doctrinal and practical'.[4] These men are the heritage of the Welsh people of whom Christendom is justly proud. It is our privilege, before we turn our attention to Christmas Evans, their successor, and in setting the scene for him, to review some of their histories.

A prince among these heralds of the kingdom and the pioneer of Welsh non-conformity was John Penry (1563-1593), a 'talented, courageous and eminently pious man'. He embraced

Presbyterianism while a student at Cambridge. From 1586 he was at St Alban's Hall, Oxford, where he soon distinguished himself as 'a *famous preacher* in the university'.[5] After his conversion, the chief purpose of his life was to work and devise plans for the evangelization of Wales. He believed that only the pure gospel, preached energetically and without compromise by holy men of God, could remedy the degradation and ignorance into which his countrymen had fallen.[6] In 1589, because of his links with the printing press that produced the Marprelate Tracts,[7] he fled to Scotland, where he was warmly received. Three years later he set up home in London, and allied himself with the Separatists there. The following March (1593), when barely thirty years of age, he was recognised by Anthony Anderson, vicar of Stepney, arrested and subjected to a trial before the Court of High Commission, which, in the words of Sir Thomas Phillips, 'disgraces the name of English justice'.[8] His private papers and public writings were used against him, and, for his Puritan and separatist convictions, seen as dangerous and treasonable in the reign of Queen Elizabeth I, he was condemned to death. Just a week later, on 29 May, he was hanged at St Thomas a Watering, Surrey, at five o'clock in the afternoon.

His words to Lord Burghley, written seven days before his execution, are a fitting testimonial: 'I am a poor young man, born and bred in the mountains of Wales. I am the first, since the last springing up of the Gospel in this latter age, that laboured to have the blessed seed thereof sown in those barren mountains... And being now to end my day... *I leave the success of my labours unto such of my countrymen as the Lord is to raise after me, for the accomplishing of that work which, in the calling of my country unto the knowledge of Christ's blessed Gospel, I began.'* [9]

One man who planted more of 'the blessed seed' was Rhys Prichard (1579-1644), a distinguished preacher for thirty years

and one who forthrightly proclaimed the 'inestimable efficacy
of Christ's blood-shedding'. Huge congregations gathered when
he preached in the parish churches of Llandovery and Llanedi.
When he officiated at St David's Cathedral, 'It is said that he
was obliged to erect a movable pulpit in the churchyard, as
even the venerable Cathedral Church itself could not hold the
vast multitudes that thronged to hear him.'[10] His sermons produced a lasting and widespread effect. However, he is best
remembered as the author of *The Welshman's Candle (Canwyll
y Cymry)*, a set of homely poems full of biblical allusions and
practical advice that came to be known affectionately as *The
Vicar's Book*. It was intended as a popular handbook of sound
Protestant theology that would 'hammer furiously at the gates
of Satan's kingdom and convert sinners out of the world'.[11] It
did incalculable good, with fourteen editions being published
between 1658 and 1730, which were circulated in part or in
whole. There was a time when nearly every literate family in
Wales possessed a copy.

Among the men whom the Lord raised up 'for the accomplishing of that work' was the Puritan cleric William Wroth
(1576-1641), rector of Llanfaches, near Chepstow. The story
behind his transformation from an apathetic, pleasure-seeking
clergyman to a minister of fervour and industry is striking.

A certain nobleman in Mr Wroth's parish, having occasion
to go to London to attend a law-suit, and having been successful, as soon as the news reached home that he had
gained the victory, Mr Wroth the vicar, being very fond of
music, bought a new violin, for the purpose of joining the
nobleman and his friends on their return, in feasting, music
and dancing. The time was appointed, great preparations
were made, and the vicar, with his new violin, ready to
receive him, when the news came that he was dead; so that
their great rejoicings were turned to bitter lamentation and
mourning.The vicar immediately fell upon his knees, and

for the first time in his life he prayed. Yes, he prayed from
his heart; he most earnestly and fervently prayed, that the
Lord would bless that solemn event to them all; that the
widow, the fatherless children, himself, and all their friends,
relatives and connections, might consider the frailty of life,
the vanity of the world, the certainty of death, and the
importance of eternal things...

   He then began to study the word of God, and preached
with power and energy, as one having authority. Now he most
earnestly endeavoured to glorify God, to exalt the Saviour
of sinners, and to save precious and immortal souls.[12]

His popularity grew to such an extent that in summer he was
obliged to preach in the churchyard to accommodate the crowds.
Some of Wroth's contemporaries, because of his saintly character, earnest preaching of a simple evangelical creed, and
unique position as the first minister of the first Independent
Church in Wales, called him an 'apostle' and regarded the church
at Llanfaches 'as an Antioch amidst a Gentile country'.[13]

   A prolific writer of poetry was Morgan Llwyd (1619-1659),
who was converted at Wrexham in 1635 under the ministry of
Walter Cradock. He was a Puritan saint and mystic, and a
preacher of 'compelling artistry', who, it is said, 'terrified his
hearers with flamy eloquence and allured them with his songs'.[14]
As an itinerant he made North Wales the main sphere of his
extensive labours and was the first ray of light to find its way
into Caernarfonshire. He is remembered chiefly for his literary
works, especially *The Book of the Three Birds (Llyfr y Tri
Aderyn)*,[15] published in 1653, 'one of the greatest Welsh prose
classics and the most mature and complex fruit of the Puritan
muse'.[16] On the night of his premature death, 3 June, 1659, a
strange uneasiness took hold of the Welsh Puritan Vavasor
Powell, causing him to exclaim, 'Tonight the brightest star in
Wales went under a cloud!'[17]

   One of the foremost influences for good in the Principality

was the theologian Walter Cradock (1606?-1659), an unusually talented preacher and a man of heroic temperament,
who represented the moderate wing of the Puritan movement.
He was converted under the ministry of William Wroth and
became curate to William Erbery at St Mary's, Cardiff, where in
1634 his licence was revoked by the bishop of Llandaf because
of his Puritanical beliefs.[18] He moved to Wrexham, where his
ministry was singularly blessed, many were converted, and
where he preached so vigorously against drunkenness and sin
that many taverns and carnal amusements were deserted.
Consequently many rose up against him. Undeterred he continued to preach faithfully and perseveringly in the town and
the country around for about a year, not only laying the foundation of the Nonconformist interest in that part of the Principality, but creating such an impression that the North Wales
Puritans became known as 'Cradockians'.

From 1639 he was a member of the Puritan congregation at
Llanfair Waterdine, in Herefordshire, under the patronage of
the member of Parliament Sir Robert Harley. Towards the end
of that year he moved to Llanfaches, where he assisted William
Wroth in organising the first Independent church in Wales,
becoming its minister after the death of Wroth, and raising up
and establishing seven or eight ministers, all of whom became
men of renown in the church of God. On 26 June, 1641, he
supported a petition to Parliament praying for more preachers
for Wales, and in the following five years brought considerable
pressure to bear on Westminster to provide a more effective
ministry for the Principality. Two years later, on account of the
Civil War, he joined the church of *All Hallows the Great* in
Thames Street, London.

According to Geraint Jenkins, Cradock was 'much revered
by his contemporaries as a riveting preacher of the gospel,
capable of presenting the essentials of the Christian faith in simple, intelligible language. His warm piety and elegance

of both tongue and pen won him universal admiration. He was deeply sensible of the spiritual needs of Wales and worked assiduously to create an effective preaching ministry and to encourage religious toleration.'[19] In the view of many he 'did more than any other, save perhaps Vavasor Powell, for the evangelization of his country'[20] and its neglected people. His delight was found in winning souls for Christ, and with help from two of his converts, Morgan Llwyd and Powell, the gospel spread over the mountains like 'fire in the thatch'. He was among the principal originators of the 'Act for the Better Propagation of the Gospel in Wales' (1650), under which he became one of the twenty-five examiners appointed to inquire into the suitability of preachers who sought to minister in Wales. He was also largely instrumental for getting the New Testament translated into Welsh and then printed, two editions of which were published in 1646 and 1647.

Few men have done more for Wales, either for its religion or for its language, than Stephen Hughes (1622-1688), a man who rarely preached without melting into tears. With Thomas Gouge (1605?-1681), he established a number of schools in Wales during the course of the seventeenth century and published new editions of the Bible, many hundreds of which were distributed gratuitously to the poor throughout the Principality.[21] He possessed an all-consuming energy, and whatever tended to uplift and educate his countrymen he laboured at with courage and perseverance. He is to be remembered, not only as an apostle of Nonconformity, but as one of the men who began to persuade the masses to preserve the Welsh language.

In 1649 the Welsh Puritan leader John Miles (1621-1683), after being baptised by immersion at Glass House Baptist Church, Broad Street, London, was sent back to Wales to spread Baptist principles among his countrymen. His determination and energy soon bore fruit. He established the first Baptist church within the borders of Wales at Ilston, near Swansea, and he supervised others that emerged at Hay (1650), Llanharan (1650), Carmarthen (1651) and Abergavenny (1652). He was a godly man, with a great gift of organization, who, among other things, initiated throughout south-west Wales a well-organised campaign against evil. In his time he was the leading minister of the Baptist denomination in Wales. His respected position among Welsh Puritans is confirmed by his appointment as an 'approver' under the Propagation Act. After the restoration of Charles II he fled with his family to New England.

Vavasor Powell's (1617-1670) tireless energy, holy charac-ter and indomitable courage, rank him among the first of the great Welsh Puritans. After the intense and prolonged spiritual agony of his conversion that 'forms the prologue to his dynamic contribution to the Christianity of his generation',[22] he became an indefatigable and active instrument in propagating the gospel among his countrymen. For thirty years he capti-vated Wales with his fiery preaching. 'He very often preached two and three times the same day, and was seldom two days in the week, throughout the year, without preaching. He ... preached at fairs, markets, in fields and on the mountains, and wherever he could find ... people willing to listen. It is impossi-ble to form an adequate idea of the extent of his labours in Wales from the year 1646 to 1660.'[23]

No one was more active in clearing Wales of incompetent ministers or more energetic in promoting the success of the Propagation Act. He published some thirteen works, the best known of which *The Bird in the Cage, Chirping* (1661)[24] he wrote in prison; yet he remarked, 'I would not neglect, for the printing of a thousand books, the preaching of one sermon.'[25] He was a man of unbending resolution, with a mind that remained unshaken amidst the severest persecution. On many occasions his life was endangered in North Wales — at

Machynlleth, Dolgellau, Newtown and Montgomery. Once he was stopped on his way to a meeting by a Mr Trevor of Treuddyn, who, without realising to whom he was talking, proceeded to explain how he was on his way to a church service to murder the preacher Vavasor Powell. When they arrived at the place of the service Mr Trevor was amazed to see his travelling companion mount the pulpit steps and begin to preach. So powerful was the sermon that as soon as it was over Mr Trevor rushed up to the preacher, confessed his sin and begged for forgiveness.

His uncompromising stand and zealous preaching, regarded as irregular and too theocratic in tone by some, brought him into conflict with the authorities, and with the collapse of the Puritan ascendency he became a marked man. In 1660, two years after the death of Cromwell, King Charles II returned to England and in July of that year Powell was imprisoned. For the next ten years, apart from twenty-four days in 1660 and a ten month period in 1667-1668 when he renewed his evangelistic labours, he remained in jail. During his confinement he was held in thirteen prisons, the conditions of which were often rigid and offensive and the treatment he received exceptionally bad. Thus his health was impaired, bringing his life to a premature end in Fleet Prison, London. It is said that at the sight of death and eternal glory he rejoiced with joy unspeakable. He was buried in Bunhill Fields. The inscription on his tomb reads:

> Vavasor Powell lyes here enterred, who was a successful teacher of the past, a sincere witness of the present, and a choyce example of future ages; who, in the defection of many, found mercy to be faithful; for which, he being called to several prisons, he was there tryed and found faithful, would not accept deliverance, expecting a better resurrection, in hope of which, he finished his life and testimony together, in the eleventh year of his imprisonment, and in the fifty-third year of his age, October 27,1670.[26]

'His crusading zeal, his ability to communicate warmth, spontaneity and vigour, and his willingness to uphold orthodox Calvinism against all challengers' [27] are among his most prominent virtues. It was his 'dedication to the task of preaching the gospel', says Tudur Jones, 'his passionate concern for the welfare of the Welsh people, and his patient suffering of imprisonment', that make him 'one of the outstanding Christian leaders of the seventeenth century'. [28]

After a period of 'indifference' among the clergy and a time when the laity were generally sunk in ignorance, superstition and immorality, and utter unconcern about spiritual things, God raised up other men of noble faith, deep devotion and irresistible power. Through them he transformed the religious, social, educational and literary character of Wales. First among these reformers was Griffith Jones (1683-1761), [29] a 'popular preacher of rare quality and boundless energy'. [30] He was ordained deacon by the Bishop of St David's, George Bull, on 19 September, 1708, and priest by the same prelate on 25 September the following year. He served for some time as curate of Laugharne, Carmarthenshire, before being appointed in 1711 rector of Llandeilo Abercywyn. At both places he became known as a great preacher, and thousands gathered to hear him from all parts of South Wales. He was promoted to the rectory of Llanddowror in 1716 by his patron and subsequent brother-in-law Sir John Philipps, a leading figure in the religious and philanthropic movements of the day.

Griffith Jones was regarded by his contemporaries as the finest preacher in the Principality and it is said that he rarely delivered a sermon that did not result in conversions. Often he preached with tears rolling down his cheeks to large and excited congregations, either in churches or, when they were too small or their pulpits denied him, in graveyards. [31] With a puritanical zeal he denounced the influences of fairs and wakes, and terrified the ungodly with his portrayals of the evil and

danger of sin. Then, by unveiling the atoning sacrifice of Christ,
he persuaded them to flee to God. 'None but Christ, nothing
but Christ's blood' was the motto of his ministry. A fitting
memorial to him in Llanddowror Church reads: 'In his preaching he inculcated the plainest and most obvious duties of Christianity, which he enforced upon the minds of his hearers with a
truly Christian zeal, and in so interesting a manner, that none
could depart unaffected or unedified.'[32]

A description of his preaching has been left by one who had
personal knowledge of him:

> His pronunciation and manner of speaking in the beginning
> was tranquil and easy ... As he advanced, his subject fired
> him more and more. How spirited was his utterance! His
> hearers could feel their blood thrill within them. One could
> plainly see the various passions he would inspire by turns
> rising in his own breast, and working from the very depth of
> his heart. One while, he glowed with ardent love to his
> fellow creatures; anon, he flamed with a just indignation at
> the enemies of their souls. Again he swelled with a holy dis-
> dain at the turpitude of sin; then melted with grief and fear
> lest some of his hearers should neglect their day of grace
> and thereby perish eternally. Every feature, nerve, and part
> of him were intensely animated...
>
> There was a noble pomp in his description; clearness
> and strength in his reasoning; his appeals to conscience were
> close and pointed; a surprising force and abruptness in his
> interrogations; a divine pathos in his address, worthy the
> imitation of every preacher...
>
> In refuting, remonstrating and reproving, he assumed the
> tone of conviction and authority; but when he came to the
> application, he entered upon it with solemn pause. He
> seemed to summon up all his remaining force; he gave way
> to a superior burst of religious vehemence, and, like a flam-
> ing meteor, bore down all before him. His voice broke
> silence, and proceeded with a sort of dignified pomp. Every
> word was like a fresh attack, and carried with it a sort of
> triumphal accent. No wonder that his hearers wept, when

the preacher himself burst into tears. No wonder that he was
so successful in the conversion of sinners, when it was the
divine Spirit that made the Word effectual.[33]

It was this powerful preaching, along with his educational pro-
grammes, that prepared the way, albeit unintentionally on his
part, for the advent of Methodism. It was he who secured the
conversion of Daniel Rowland. William Williams readily
admitted that the 'fruitful soil in which Methodism grew had
been prepared by the rector of Llanddowror',[34] while those who
opposed him accused him of being 'the Methodist Pope'. In a
very real sense, because of his endeavours, Llanddowror was
as much a cradle of Methodism as Llangeitho and Trefeca.
Deservedly he has received the title 'The Morning Star of the
Revival':

> He had been labouring in the ministry for seventeen years
> before John Wesley, and for twenty-nine years before George
> Whitefield, received deacon's orders; he had been carrying
> on his Circulating Schools, and ... had circulated thousands
> of Bibles, Prayer Books and useful religious publications,
> among his monoglot countrymen, and had preached in many
> parts of the neighbouring countries, before Daniel Rowland
> commenced his itinerant ministry, or Howel Harris his field
> preaching; he had established three hundred and twenty-nine
> schools, and, by their means, had helped to instruct 19,139
> of the poor in the truths of the Gospel, when ... William
> Williams and Peter Williams commenced their ministry; and
> he had entered into rest before Thomas Charles was six
> years old.[35]

Of the three men who were to become great leaders of Welsh
Methodism, William Williams (1717-1791) of Pantycelyn, 'The
Sweet Singer of Wales', is probably the best known. He was
converted one Sunday morning at Talgarth, Brecknockshire, in
1738, after hearing an 'unusually terrifying' sermon from Howel

Harris. 'It was a morning,' he wrote many years later, 'which I shall always remember, for it was then I heard the voice of heaven; I was apprehended as if by warrant from on high.'[36] From 1744, because the bishop refused to ordain him as priest, he dedicated himself to the Methodist movement and became a tireless itinerant preacher, travelling some 150,000 miles between 1744 and 1791, and drawing vast crowds from one end of Wales to the other. He is not regarded as one of the Principality's greatest preachers, yet at times his eloquence was quite overpowering. It was his genius as a hymn writer for which he is immortalized, 'the greatest of them all', according to Martyn Lloyd-Jones. He began to print hymns of 'supreme craftsmanship' in 1744 and in all wrote over 850,[37] many of which are remarkable for 'their imagery, intensity, and lyrical quality, and which were sung with great joy and fervour by Methodist brethren'.[38] Much of the success of Welsh Methodism must be attributed to their sound theology and deep experiential nature. His monument stands in the gallery of the 'Heroes of Wales' in Cardiff City Hall.

The energetic and useful services of Williams and others such as Howel Davies (1716-1770) were blessed by God, but it was the preaching of Howel Harris (1714-1773) and Daniel Rowland (1713-1790) in particular that roused the people of Wales. Immediately after his conversion in 1735 at Talgarth, Harris visited the sick and aged, and gathered his neighbours together into his mother's home and read religious books to them. Within a few weeks the house was crowded with expectant hearers. Soon, because of the size of the congregations, he was compelled to preach in the open air, and before long the whole countryside was talking of the fervent exhorter. With fire kindled in his soul, and clothed with heavenly power and authority, he thundered against sinners in 'the most dreadful manner', pleading with them to flee from the wrath to come, 'and fear and terror would be seen on all faces'.[39]

As his reputation grew he received invitations from all parts of the country. On his travels he preached to crowded and expectant congregations, frequently six or seven times each day, riding 150 miles a week over hills and mountains, through floods, ice and snow, and sleeping on average for only four hours a night. Sometimes he fell asleep while travelling and dropped from his horse utterly exhausted. Hundreds were converted and with his exceptional organizational skills he formed them into Societies, the first of which was established in 1736. Within six or seven years he had awakened the Principality from the sleep that was paralysing its national vigour, revived public and private worship, and fairly destroyed many of the vicious sports and festivals of licentiousness that darkened the country. Inevitably opposition arose, and as a result of 'irregular preaching', he was refused ordination on four separate occasions by Nicholas Claggett, bishop of St David's.

Harris possessed almost superhuman energy, a thunderous voice, and, it is said, a gift of preaching impromptu from anywhere in the Bible for up to four hours. In fact, some of his services continued without a break for six hours! Charles Wesley, in a striking account of his preaching, says, 'O what a flame was kindled! Never man spake, in my hearing, as this man spake. What a nursing-father has God sent us! He has indeed learned of the good Shepherd to carry the lambs in his bosom. Such love, such power, such simplicity was irresistible. The lambs dropped down on all sides into their shepherd's arms.'[40] He responded to the call of duty with a consuming passion, 'taxing and spending himself to the glory of God and the salvation of souls, until the iron constitution seemed ready to burst'.[41] He was 'a man on fire, a torch in the hand of the Almighty to kindle in others the incandescent flame that began in his own soul'.[42] In his elegy to Harris, William Williams describes him as full of sparks and flaming fervour.

He is known affectionately as 'The Apostle of Jesus Christ to the Welsh People'. Thomas Rees calls him 'the most successful preacher that ever ascended a pulpit or a platform in Wales', and sums up the effects of his ministry by remarking: *'He was an extraordinary instrument raised by Providence, at an extraordinary time, to accomplish an extraordinary work.'* [43] R. T. Jenkins, a Welsh historian and an authority on eighteenth century Wales, writes: 'It is difficult to believe that Howel Harris was not the greatest Welshman of his century.' One of his biographers, Griffith T. Roberts, says of him: 'This powerful revivalist, able organiser, and great Methodist was God's gift to Wales, and very few men have so deeply and so permanently influenced the religious life of the Principality as Howel Harris.'[44] Arnold Dallimore, in his biography of George Whitefield, comments on Harris's influence:

> He was the pioneer of Methodist field-preaching, the originator of its itinerant evangelism and the first to form a number of Societies and link them together in a permanent organization. Wesley's work was patterned after him, and Whitefield was deeply indebted to his stalwart example. Among certain persons of the present day whose knowledge is such as to lend authority to their opinion, Harris is regarded as the greatest Welshman of that day and, indeed, as among the greatest men that Wales has ever produced.[45]

A final comment on Harris from Hugh J. Hughes, who, in his *Life of Howell Harris*, introduces his subject by saying:

> Towering head and shoulders above all who went before or have come after, stands the name of Howell Harris... From the time he first appeared upon the stage with his fire and indomitable zeal, the awakening of the nation takes its date. He stands, therefore, pre-eminent amongst the benefactors of his country, and the very sound of his name has become amongst the people of his own nation the synonym for all

that is brave and unconquerable, and of the nature of true heroism. It would not be an exaggeration to say that children have been spell-bound by the narratives of his gigantic deeds, that old men have lingered with fondness upon the memory of his fame, and that young pressed forward by the score to swell the ranks of the gospel ministry, excited to ambition and emulation, and supported amidst the difficulties of their calling, by the charms of his matchless renown.

Howell Harris, in fact, has been looked upon by the Welsh people as the special creation of the Almighty, he has been regarded as a comet flashed out suddenly into the darkness of a midnight sky; he is the Luther of Wales, the Elijah of the Principality, sent forth to level the fortifications of darkness, and himself as an army of chariots and horsemen to mow down the devotees of sin.[46]

Daniel Rowland, the other giant of the Welsh pulpit to awaken the slumbering people of Wales, was, according to William Romaine and Thomas Jones (Creaton), 'the greatest minister in the whole world'.[47] Jones, who attended his ministry on many occasions, exclaimed 'that he never heard but *one Rowland* '.[48] Other contemporary opinions were just as enthusiastic. After ten years of his evangelical ministry one admirer said of him, 'In his pulpit he is a second Paul.' David Jones (Llan-gan), writing in 1773, claimed, 'Surely he is the greatest preacher in Europe.'[49] The estimate of so many who knew him was that 'There was loftiness and grandeur, and every other excellency in his endowments: profound thoughts, strength and sweetness of voice, clearness and lively energy in proclaiming the deep things of God to the astonishment and effectual arousing of his hearers.'[50]

Rowland was converted under the ministry of Griffith Jones during the winter of 1734-35 and from that time began to preach with depth and fervour. Soon large congregations assembled at Llangeitho, which became the natural centre of Welsh Methodism. For half a century he exercised a profound influence

over his countrymen and proclaimed the gospel with such extraordinary spiritual success that few preachers have enjoyed
since the days of the apostles. Over two thousand used to
attend his monthly communion services and more than one
hundred ministers of the gospel acknowledged him as the means
of their salvation. It is said that seven revivals occurred during
his life-time. In one of these revivals, as reported by his son,
'The whole chapel seemed as if it was filled with some super-
natural element, and the whole assembly was seized with
extraordinary emotions; hundreds of them, with tears streaming down their faces, some evidently from excess of sorrow,
others from the overflowing of joy; some broken and contrite
with penitence, and others rejoicing with the hope of glory.'[51]

The extraordinary power that accompanied his sermons,
which were constructed with the utmost care and precision and
delivered with compelling urgency; his melodious voice and
theatrical gestures, along with a sweet spirit and magnetism,
gripped his hearers, many of whom would 'tremble fearfully,
leap joyfully, or weep unashamedly',[52] sometimes for hours on
end. On one memorable occasion it is reported that he preached
for six hours without intermission to a spellbound multitude.
One Sunday morning, in the middle of summer, he preached
with amazing effect and the service continued until four o'clock
in the afternoon. We are told that as many as 800 became
members of churches after that sermon.

George Whitefield, on a visit to South Wales, reported that
'The power of God at the sacrament, under the ministry of Mr
Rowland, was enough to make a person's heart burn within
him.'[53] Similarly, Howel Harris, writing to his 'dearest brother
Whitefield' on 1 March, 1743, comments:

It is very common when he preaches, for scores to fall down
by the power of the word, — pierced and wounded by the
love of God, and by a sight of the beauty and excellency of

> Jesus — and lie down on the ground, nature being over-
> come by the sight and enjoyment of God given to their
> heaven-born souls so that they cannot bear any more — the
> Spirit almost bursting the house of clay to go to its native
> home! Some lie there for hours; some praising and admir-
> ing Jesus Christ and free grace, others wanting words to
> utter their minds![54]

Such were the scenes that accompanied the preaching of
Rowland. When he died on Saturday 16 October, 1790, at the
age of 77, many throughout Wales viewed and felt his death as
a great loss. He was buried the following Wednesday at
Llangeitho church cemetery. There is a monument to his
memory at Llangeitho inscribed with words first uttered by him
in a time of revival, and which epitomise his 'burning passion
to bring men to Christ, saints to heaven, and glory to God': 'O
Heaven! Heaven! Heaven! Your mansions would be empty
enough if Zion did not nurture children for you on earth!'[55]

We have sketched the histories of a few of the 'great cloud
of witnesses', who laboured to transform Wales into that 'highly
favoured country', where, as one writer notes in 1835, 'The
religion of Christ has been and now is so flourishing, and where
it has had such an universal effect.'[56] At the end of this long line
of eminent men stands Christmas Evans, who, as we shall see,
carried on their noble tradition of preaching the gospel with
'uncommon power'. We could say that he was an after-fruit of
the great evangelical awakening in Wales. He certainly used to
regard himself as the successor of men like Daniel Rowland
and Howel Harris, whom he described as 'children of the rising
sun'. Once he prayed, 'As thou didst prosper Bunyan, Vavasor
Powell, Howel Harris, Rowland and Whitefield, O do thou prosper me.' Harris, to cite but one example of this succession, was
'a firebrand who has since been matched by none save Christmas Evans'.[57] To a new generation he held aloft the same torch
of grace that had inflamed these stalwarts of faith, with a zeal

for God's glory and a passion for saving souls. In his hand that torch burned as brightly as in former days. With it he published the glad tidings to sinners — that 'Christ died for sins ... and is now able to save unto the uttermost all that come unto God by him' — and urged the contrite in heart, without delay, to 'Fly to the throne of grace.'[58] We now turn our attention to this great man.

Christmas Evans is the connecting link between the beginning and the ending of the eighteenth century. He has the light, the talent and the taste of the beginning, and has received every new light that has appeared since. He was enabled to accompany the career of religious knowledge in the morning and also to follow its rapid strides in the evening. In this he is unlike every other preacher of the day: the morning and evening light of this wonderful century meet in him. He had strength to climb up to the top of Carmel in the morning and remain there during the heat of the day, and see the fire consuming the sacrifice and licking up the water; his strength continued, by the hand of the Lord, so that he could descend from the Mount in the evening, and run without fainting before the king's chariot to Jezreel.

A Congregational minister, who was well acquainted with him.[1]

Had Christmas Evans enjoyed the advantages of education, the high natural powers of the Welsh preacher and his Christian graces, would have enabled him to have blended the impassioned declamation of Whitefield with something of the imperial opulence and pomp of fancy that distinguished Jeremy Taylor.[2]

David Phillips, who knew him well and often sat under his ministry.[3]

1
Troubled Youth and Conversion

William Edwards concludes his biographical sketch of Christmas Evans with the comments, 'Christmas Evans was a Paul in labour, a Bunyan in imagination, and a Whitefield in eloquence. He stood on the highest pinnacle of fame as a preacher; but more than this — his record is on high as an indefatigable, earnest, successful winner of souls, and as a burning and shining light that helped to fill the Principality with the radiance of the pure Gospel.'[4] Robert Hall, a distinguished preacher himself and a contemporary of Christmas Evans, regarded him as the first great pulpit genius of the age; and Thomas Phillips of Cardiff, in a lecture on Christmas Evans, opens by remarking, 'When a person arouses our sympathies by a display of extraordinary powers and achievements, in a corresponding degree he awakens the desire to know the particulars of his personal history.'[5] In the course of our study it will be increasingly evident that *The One-eyed Preacher of Wales*, as he was affectionately known, was a man of 'extraordinary powers and achievements' whose career, moulded by hardships and poverty, awakens in us the 'desire to know his personal history'.

Christmas Evans was born on December 25, during the stormy winter of 1766,[6] in a small cottage called Esgair Wen, located in the Dyffryn Llynod valley near the village of Tre-groes

An oak tree planted in Tre-groes to mark the site of
Christmas Evans's birth.

The sign attached to the trunk of the tree.

in the parish of Llandysul.[7] The nearby village of Llandysul, lying on the banks of the River Teifi and set in the picturesque Cardiganshire hills, consisted of only a few homes in the middle of the eighteenth century; and the surrounding district, with its wooded slopes and bleak pastoral uplands, was barely accessible to outsiders. The population of Wales was about 500,000 and 'Its people were mostly small farmers and labourers, living in thinly-populated, isolated communities, with few towns or centres of population. Most of them were illiterate or barely literate, and too poor to be able to buy books. Being mainly monoglot Welsh speakers, they tended to be sealed off by their language against outside influences.'[8]

Christmas was the middle child of Samuel and Joanna Evans, who named him Christmas either after the day of his birth, or after Samuel's brother, who must also have been born on Christmas Day. At birth he was so frail and small that he could fit snugly into a quart container. His mother, because of his size, did not expect him to survive. Nothing is known about his older sister and there is little information concerning his younger brother John, who grew up to be a 'solitary self-contained man, leading an objectless, semi-vagrant life, in the poorest circumstances, with little to comfort him except the reflected greatness of Christmas, of which he availed himself in his wanderings'.[9] As adults he and Christmas looked very much alike. Both were tall, bony and not very good-looking, and both had only one eye, John having lost his in some accident or fight. Christmas helped his brother considerably in life and was very sorry that he was so unfortunate, but it appears that such philanthropy arose more out of pity than from a deep brotherly affection, as the two were not particularly close. There is no mention of his brother or sister in any of Christmas's writings.

Samuel Evans and Joanna Lewis were married on 19 December, 1761, in the parish of Llandysul. Joanna was illiterate and marked her name with a cross in the register.

Samuel was a shoemaker from Llangeler who, for most of his life, fought against ill health. His sister married Evan James and their son John James (1779-1864), who became a schoolmaster, was the first Unitarian minister in Cardiganshire. Samuel's brother Christmas, a farmer in the locality, became an elder and trustee of Penrhiw Chapel, Dre-fach, a branch of the Arminian chapel at Llwynrhydowen. Daniel, Samuel's other brother, was also a shoemaker. He was the father of the Methodist preacher Daniel Evans, who in turn became the grandfather of Evan Phillips (1829-1912), 'one of the greatest preachers of his age'.[10]

Joanna came from a respectable family of freeholders in the parish, who offered Christmas little financial assistance during his poor and troubled youth. However, he did not hold them accountable for his hardships, as in after years, when well-known throughout the Principality, he visited them, preached in their houses and in return was treated by them with great respect. One of Joanna's relatives, James Lewis (1674-1747), a staunch Calvinist, was the Independent minister of Pencader Church and Pantycreuddyn Chapel. He became a prominent leader in the area and in 1743 his son John Lewis was ordained to assist him. After upholding the Calvinistic tradition for twenty-three years, John Lewis died in the same year as Christmas Evans was born.

Little is known about Joanna's character and faith, partly due to her son's reticence to speak of his family, except that she urged him, when a boy, to consider spiritual matters, especially his eternal welfare and destiny. One of his few references to her is in a sermon on *The Parable of the Prodigal Son*, in which he comments, 'I remember my godly mother saying to me, "Christmas, my boy, think of your soul;" and I would say jeeringly, "Do you hear how mother can preach?"'[11] His parents were very poor and unable to offer him or his brother and sister any formal education.

During his childhood some remarkable deliverances from misfortunes and accidents occurred in which he saw the protecting hand of God. The first of these took place when he was eight years old. He went into the fields to plough on the back of a very wild horse, which suddenly bolted down a hill and towards the stable. Without slowing it galloped through the stable door with Christmas still clinging to its back. Amazingly, its terrified rider was not injured. Years later, when he examined and measured the stable door, he was unable to fathom how he had escaped without injury, remarking, 'It was through God's good providence that I was not struck dead at the entrance door.'[12] When aged nine 'He climbed up into a tree with the intention of cutting down a branch. He had his knife open in his hand, and was resting upon one branch and taking hold of another in order to cut it, when one of the branches broke, and he fell down from a great height. He remained there on the ground until the afternoon, when he was discovered in a state of unconsciousness.'[13] When he remembered this accident he wondered how he had not been killed, or at least why his bones had not been broken, concluding that God was keeping him for some special future work.

These incidents had a profound effect on him, alerting him to the perils and fragility of life, and, no doubt recalling his mother's exhortations, to the closeness of eternity. But it was another more devastating occurrence that was to change the course of his life. In 1775 his father died, leaving Joanna destitute and wholly dependent on the support of the parish and any kind-hearted friends of the family, whose hearts were far larger than their fortunes. From his father's funeral he dates his first religious impressions, when he was 'much terrified with the fear of death, and of the day of judgement', which caused him great anxiety, especially at night, and induced him 'to make some kinds of prayers'; yet 'These thoughts of terror were not of long continuance — they vanished, and recurred now and

again.'[14] Near the end of his life he said, 'I was disturbed by
certain operations of mind, which, I believe, were not common,
from my ninth year upwards. The fear of dying in an ungodly
state especially affected me, and this apprehension clung to me
till I was induced to rest upon Christ. All this was accompanied
by some little knowledge of the Redeemer; and now, in my
seventieth year, I cannot deny that this concern was the dawn
of the day of grace on my spirit, although mingled with much
darkness and ignorance.'[15]

Joanna Evans, bound by the straits of poverty, struggled to
bring up her children on her own. Before long, to relieve the
pressures at home and with the intention of securing a more
prosperous future for Christmas, who had already been helping with the family finances for over a year, she sent him to her
brother James Lewis, who owned a farm at Bwlchog in the
nearby parish of Llanfihangel-ar-arth. Uncle Lewis was a 'cruel,
selfish and drunken man',[16] who, in spite of his promise to feed
and clothe Christmas in return for his labours on the farm, treated
his nephew with contempt, working him ruthlessly. He refused
him any schooling, and gave him no moral or religious instruction, so that when he left four years later he could not read a
single word, knew nothing of books or the Bible, and had spent
the formative years of his life witnessing the drunkenness of a
family member.[17]

It was while working at Tynewydd Farm in
Llanfihangel-ar-arth that he experienced another remarkable
escape. He was about twelve years old and walking in a field
through which a rapid river flowed and in which there had just
been a great flood. He drew near to inspect a deep whirlpool
which the flood had formed. Suddenly the ground gave way
beneath him and he was thrown into the water. There was no
one nearby and no branch or post onto which he could cling.
Somehow, after a great struggle, he managed to scramble out.
He could never say how his life was saved, as it had seemed
impossible for him to pull himself out of the swirling waters.

During these miserable years working for his uncle mainly as a shepherd, 'He was not wanted anywhere. He was an outcast. He was denied the amenities of the farm kitchen and the comfort of a decent bed. He lived among the beasts of the field by night as well as by day, for no human desired his company.'[18] Understandably all his recollections of his youth, and particularly of James Lewis, were painfully bitter. In later life he said of his uncle, 'It would be difficult to find a more unconscionable man than James Lewis in the whole course of a wicked world.'[19] When he finally left Bwlchog, he was a poor, homeless, friendless teenager, whose 'very condition in life condemned him into association with whatever was rude, unreflecting and brutal in his neighbourhood',[20] and whose prospects for usefulness appeared pitifully poor.

After Bwlchog he worked for several farmers successively in his native parish of Llandysul. At Pen-yr-allt Fawr his standard of living improved slightly, and at Glancletwr near Pont-siân he was shown kindness and respect, though food supplies were meagre. At Glancletwr, when he was about fifteen, he was one day out on the mountain watching the sheep, when 'A dispute arose between him and another shepherd; and in the contention, this other shepherd drew out his knife and stabbed him in the right breast; the knife, however, touching a bone, and glancing off without inflicting any mortal injury.'[21] He also worked at Castell Hywel on a farm that was owned by the Arian minister David Davis (1745-1827), who was to exercise such a deep influence on him. At this period he was still illiterate and described as 'remarkable even among his fellows for uncouthness and rusticity, and bore about him an awkward, ponderous individuality, which might, according to circumstances, develop into some sort of notoriety or distinction — a large-boned, muscular, much-brooding and somewhat passionate young man'.[22] He was given to frequent meditations, and possessed a lively imagination, although there was no hint of the genius that would soon captivate Wales.

In 1783, when Christmas Evans was sixteen and perhaps an occasional churchgoer, a religious revival occurred in the Arminian Presbyterian Church at Llwynrhydowen, an important church as far as early Welsh Nonconformity is concerned and the first Arminian church in Wales. It was built in 1733 on his own land by Jenkin Jones, a blacksmith's son and a popular preacher, who was originally a member of the Independent Church at Pantycreuddyn. In 1720 he joined the Carmarthen Academy, which was the centre of 'liberalism in theology', especially in the early years of the century. While there Jones was recognised as one of Thomas Perrot's brightest pupils. During Perrot's 'liberal' tenure of the Academy, 'Men of considerable learning and strength of mind were openly advocating unorthodox theological views,'[23] and many of his pupils subsequently drifted into heterodoxy. Jones emerged as the 'apostle of Arminianism' when he established the first Arminian congregation in the Principality in a farmhouse at Pen-y-banc in 1726. By the time of his death in 1742 there were six Arminian churches in his neighbourhood.

At Llwynrhydowen Jones was 'for some years the only public advocate of Arminianism in Wales, though many of the younger ministers and Carmarthen students were probably in secret sympathy with him'.[24] According to David Williams 'Under Jenkin Jones's ministry and that of his successors, David Lloyd[25] and David Davis, Castell Hywel, the church moved towards Arianism ... and the foundations of these beliefs were firmly laid in this locality. Less than twenty miles away at Llangeitho, Daniel Rowland threw vast crowds into paroxysms of fear and exaltation by expounding the redemptive powers of Christ, but on this solid core of Arianism his passionate eloquence had no effect whatsoever.'[26]

At the time of Christmas Evans the church at Llwynrhydowen was almost Unitarian[27] in its beliefs. Its pastor, David Davis, from the Carmarthen Presbyterian College, was ordained

under an old oak tree at Llwynrhydowen on 15 July, 1773, and
noted, among other things, for his prodigious size. It is said that
on account of his gigantic stature and bulk his neighbours were
reluctant to lend him their small Welsh ponies in case they
collapsed under his weight. After his death, his tailor, who
counted it a privilege to have fashioned his clothes, claimed
'that he was, without exception, the biggest man he ever worked
for in his life'.[28] His size, along with a crop of unkempt,
shoulder-length flaxen hair and the loose-fitting garments he
used to wear, made him an unforgettable character.

But he is remembered for more than just his eccentric
appearance. Paxton Hood describes him as 'an Arian, an
eminent bard, a scholar, an admirable and excellent man, who
has left behind him a very honourable reputation'.[29] He was
certainly a renowned bard, whose Welsh translation of
Thomas Gray's *Elegy Written in a Country Churchyard* in 1789
is said by competent judges to be at least worthy of the stately
original. He was also a classicist, competent in both Latin and
Greek, and in 1782 the founder of the Academy at Castell
Hywel, which thrived for thirty years. Thomas Rees esteemed
him as 'the most celebrated and successful teacher of youth in
the Principality'.[30] He educated many of the clergy and
dissenting ministers of that part of Wales, especially those who
could not afford to study at university, and boys from all over
the locality came to study in his school.

However, Davis had very indefinite views on Christian
doctrine, and leaned towards Arianism. In both politics and
religion his strongest held conviction was that man should obey
his own reason and conscience before any external authority
— a view that echoed the ideals of the French Revolution. Once,
when he heard a sermon on, in his view, a doubtful doctrine,
by the great William Williams of Wern, he exclaimed, 'If that
sermon be true, it will be a dark lookout for a great many of
us!'[31] In a letter to a friend he reveals his doctrinal broad-

mindedness, writing, 'I am perfectly satisfied in my own mind that [the Unitarian] Dr Priestley, and others of his party, may be good and pious Christians; I have also the same opinion of John Calvin, Dr Crisp, and their disciples. I would cheerfully sit in the same communion with them, with the delightful hope of being in their company for ever in heaven.'[32] It was this departure from conservative theology, coupled with some unusual pulpit habits, such as closing his eyes for long periods during his sermons, that restricted his usefulness as a preacher.

In spite of these theological weaknesses, David Davis was a generous and benevolent man, whose liberal views sprang more from a desire not to be critical or exclusive than from an independent spirit of unorthodoxy. Rhys Stephen writes:

> Mr D. Davis was the very soul of kindness and fine feeling; and wherever you meet one of his old pupils, be he clergyman or dissenting minister, there is a kind and admiring word for the Patriarch of Castell Hywel... While, in mind, he lived with the old Greeks and the mighty Romans ... he ate, drank and lodged as did the small farmer of his district. With few wants, and less discontent — teaching all that were sent to his school; paid most moderately, indeed, by the richest of his neighbours, not at all by the poorer among them; breaking in upon the 'noiseless tenor of his way' only by the sermons on Lord's day, and occasionally at some house on week-day evening, when, especially if he referred to the Prodigal Son, which he was much addicted to, he would weep profusely, affected by his own teaching; at once the cause of his own felicity, and the source of whatever power he exerted upon others.[33]

He was particularly accommodating to the youth in the church, allowing them scope and freedom in discussion, and encouraging them to discover the truth for themselves. He can rightly be called Christmas Evans's first instructor, philosopher and friend. The revival of religion at Llwynrhydowen, which Christmas

Evans soon heard about and participated in, spread throughout the church and many in the congregation, particularly among
the young, turned to Christ.

> Religion became the only thing that mattered. It was the
> only topic of conversation... Services at the chapel and else-
> where were continued for endless hours during the day and
> night. When the ecstasy began to wane among the older
> folk it was rekindled among the young. The second flame of
> fire was more captivatingly furious and thorough than the
> first, and many who had not felt the first in its heat and warmth
> came into contact with the second and were caught by it. Its
> warmth changed them. They were as helpless as others who
> had passed through similar experiences. They had to sub-
> mit to a higher power that drove them to surrender to God.[34]

During the revival a great change for good came over Christmas Evans. He became very serious in manner and outlook,
prayed much, vowed to lead a better life, and, along with the
other converts, joined the church. However, his early 'Christian
experience was evidently very imperfect. He had a conviction
of the evil of sin, and a desire to flee from the wrath to come,
but no evidence of acceptance with God, and a very limited
knowledge of the plan of salvation. Yet his religious impressions were not entirely fruitless. They produced, at least, a partial reformation of life, and led to many penitential resolutions.
He thought much of eternity, and was frequent in secret prayer,'[35]
a habit he was to maintain for the rest his life. In a sermon he
later preached on *Justification by Faith* he highlights the day of
salvation and all the memories that are attached to it, perhaps
partially reflecting his own experiences at this time:

> We recollect the heavy burden that pressed so hard upon
> us, and how it fell from our shoulders at the sight of the
> cross. We recollect the time when the eyes of our minds
> were opened to behold the evil of sin, the depravity of our

hearts, and the excellency of our Redeemer. We recollect
the time when our stubborn wills were subdued in the day of
his power, so that we were enabled both to will and to do of
his good pleasure. We recollect the time when we obtained
hope in the merit of Christ, and felt the efficacy of his blood
applied to our hearts by the Holy Spirit. And we shall never
forget the time when we first experienced the love of God
shed abroad in our hearts. O, how sweetly and powerfully it
constrained us to love him, his cause and his ordinances!
How we panted after communion and fellowship with him,
as the hart panteth after the water-brooks! All this, and a
thousand other things, are as fresh in our memory as ever.[36]

After this spiritual awakening he realised more and more that
the Christian must have 'a rock in the merits of the Redeemer
to rest upon', and that that rock is a 'place of refuge and a
covert from the storm and the rain'. In an ever-increasing measure 'the spirit of energetic supplication' was poured out on him,
although, according to his own testimony, such a spirit was
accompanied by fear and ignorance:

Earnestness in prayer grew with me, though I frequently
feared it would become extinct. Still, it was not entirely
extinguished, even in those days of darkness when I but
barely perceived the merits of Christ were the only plea,
without reference to anything of our own. After I came to
know and feel that the righteousness of Christ formed the
only ground to be depended on before God, I was able with
every sense of unworthiness to approach him with a stronger
expectation.[37]

As has been mentioned, he had at this time a confused knowledge of the way of salvation and a rather shallow experience
of it in his heart, but he earnestly desired to read the Bible,
which he accomplished with very little aid. He also studied other
branches of learning in order to try to make up what was lacking
in his education. His pastor, David Davis, who was very keen

to promote the intellectual standing of his congregation and who noticed his desire to progress in this area, took a keen interest in him and invited him to his school, which was the only formal education he ever received. His learned teacher maintained that he never had a young man who made so much progress in so short a time, and under such disadvantageous circumstances. He soon became a popular pupil with the whole Davis family. 'He was a very sober man,' said David Davis's second son Timothy, '... always with us during our prayer meetings. I remember him carrying me in his arms to the chapel at Llwynrhydowen.'[38] Recollecting this time much later in life, Christmas Evans says:

> During a revival which took place in the church under the care of Mr David Davis, many young people united themselves with that people, and I amongst them. What became of the major part of these young converts, I have never known; but I hope God's grace followed them as it did me, the meanest of the whole. One of the fruits of this awakening was the desire for religious knowledge that fell upon us. Scarcely one person out of ten could, at this time, and in those neighbourhoods, read at all, even in the language of the country. We bought Bibles and candles, and were accustomed to meet together in the evening, in the barn of Penyralltfawr; and thus, in about one month, I was able to read the Bible in my mother tongue. I was vastly delighted with so much learning. This, however, did not satisfy me, but I borrowed books and learnt a little English. Mr Davis, my pastor, understood that I thirsted for knowledge, and he took me to his school, where I stayed for six months. Here I went through the Latin Grammar; but so low were my circumstances that I could stay there no longer.[39]

There is an interesting story connected with Christmas Evans's entry to his pastor's school. One evening he asked the senior farm hand, John, if he could go to church the following Sunday to hear David Davis preach. John agreed and promised to take care of the farm animals while he was away. On the Sabbath morning he arrived at the church in a serious mood, and throughout the whole service sat with his head in his hands and his elbows resting on his knees. As soon as the service was over, without saying a word, he hurried home. David Davis had noticed the young man's strange behaviour and after dinner sent for John to see if he could explain it. John asked his pastor to follow him and together they crept into a field to find Christmas standing before a congregation of cows, horses and sheep! He had erected a shelter of branches near the hedge for his protection and fashioned a pulpit out of twigs. As they approached they witnessed him commence a 'mock' service that was almost identical to the morning service in the church: he announced a hymn and sang it; he read the Scriptures and then preached, practically word for word, David Davis's sermon; afterwards he prayed and sang a concluding hymn, during which the two humans in the congregation quietly escaped from the hallowed ground.

On the way home Davis asked John if he knew of another young man who could replace Christmas on the farm so he could take the budding preacher into his school. That evening John told Christmas he was no longer needed on the farm and that Davis wanted to speak with him. Christmas, fearing the worst, thought he was about to be dismissed for some misdemeanour and began to weep, but his anxieties were soon dispelled when he heard his pastor say, 'You are to come to my school to be educated free of charge.'

Llwynrhydowen, the first Arminian church in Wales, where
Christmas Evans was converted.

Castell Hywel, where Christmas Evans went to
school for six months.

Wales has produced many able preachers, but none greater than Christmas Evans. At the height of his fame, no chapel in Wales was large enough to hold the thousands who flocked to hear him. It is not an exaggeration when writers of his time say that many people followed him from village to village, for twenty to thirty days. Were it not for the fact that his sermons exist largely in the Welsh language, barring a few that were translated into English in 1837 and 1856, his fame as a preacher would be second only to that of Wesley and Whitefield.

F.R.Webber.[1]

2
Early Pilgrimage

The early Christian experiences of Christmas Evans were soon followed by a desire to preach the gospel. After joining the church at Llwynrhydowen he was called upon to pray in public and in the various prayer meetings. Noticing his gifts, some of the congregation asked him to say a few words to them by way of exhortation. 'To this,' he says, 'I felt a strong inclination, though I was, as it were, *a heap of spiritual ignorance.*'² His first performance was well received so he was inclined to continue. His first full sermon was preached at Tybedw, Pentre-cwrt, in a cottage belonging to a kind tailor, David Hughes, who gave singing lessons in the neighbourhood and who helped the young men to read. Cottage preaching was very important in those days and the congregations that assembled were knowledgeable and discerning. According to his own confession, this sermon, preached 'at a prayer meeting which was held in a house in the parish of Llangeler', Carmarthenshire, was not original, but taken from a book he had probably borrowed from his pastor. He also owns up to another instance of plagiarism:

> My first sermon was a translation of one of Bishop Beveridge's from *Thesaurus Theologicus*.³ One of my hearers ... said, 'Had

Mr D. Davis heard it, he would be ashamed to preach himself.' But I had no faith in myself — I knew my poverty. I
remember, too, securing a copy of the seven published sermons of Mr Rowland of Llangeitho. In later years I learned
that he also had borrowed them. I memorised one of these
sermons and preached it near Llwynrhydowen, where Mr
Davies of Gamnant was listening. He was surprised to hear
such a mighty sermon from such a young preacher. But within
a week the praises vanished like Jonah's gourd, for Mr Davies
had secured a copy of the volume that contained the seven
sermons. 'But,' said he, 'I believe there is something great
in the son of Samuel the shoemaker, for his prayer was equal
to his sermon.' But that was no praise to me, for I knew that
the prayer was memorised word for word from the prayer
book of the Rev. Griffith Jones of Llanddowror. I had begun
before I had gathered knowledge, and before *the vessels
were opened*, as it were, to receive information.[4]

This 'art' of memorising sermons, and especially of translating
and adapting English sermons, became quite common in Wales
in later years, a practice Christmas Evans came to deplore. His
excuse at this time was that he was too ignorant to preach or
pray in any other way. His subsequent protestations against
plagiarism of this type brought down on him anonymous criticism which greatly wounded his feelings. In a paper he wrote
on this subject for a Welsh Baptist Magazine, he says in a characteristic and forthright style:

There are many in connection with every religious denomination who get their sermons ready-made for them in the
English market.These preachers are very much like the
nail-merchant; they have never beaten out for themselves a
single nail heated with the fire of their own meditation, but
some Englishman has manufactured every nail in their possession. If it be so, it is high time to reform. These English
eightpenny nails split up our Welsh boarding, and will never
suit our purpose in the country... It would be a poor excuse
for a fisherman to say, 'I had a better net than any of them

(made probably by some Englishman), and I cast it in in beautiful style, but somehow caught nothing.' It would have been quite as well if the poor fellow's net had been left spread on an English hedge to this day. If we don't *catch* with our nets, they are worth very little.[5]

Alluding to the same subject he was once heard to advise a young minister, somewhat flippantly, 'You may steal the iron, brother, if you like, but be sure you always make your own nails; then, if needs be, you can swear they are your own property.' He then humorously compared two well-known contemporary preachers who made use of other men's sermons, 'G — goes to Llandovery fair, sees his chance, runs away with a horse, and at the first smithy gets it newly shod, docks the mane and tail, and transforms the animal as much as possible; W — goes to the fair, steals a horse too, but leaves it precisely as he found it: the consequence is, that W — is caught as a thief, while G — passes for an honest man.'[6]

After his first sermon he received a few invitations to preach in the neighbourhood, but found it very hard to earn enough money to support himself. At most of the chapels he visited he was given the nominal fee of one shilling, which meant that, in spite of his pastor's generosity, he could only stay in school for six months. To relieve these financial straits he journeyed in the autumn of 1784 or 1785 to Herefordshire to work during the harvest, a common enough venture for Welsh agricultural labourers, who wanted to supplement their purses. Probably his original intention was to earn enough money to return to school. However, while he was in England he fell into a state of spiritual indifference and, tempted to pursue a secular employment, contemplated leaving school and turning his back on the ministry. School, to his mind, was unaffordable, and the ministry offered only a life of hardships and toil.

While considering the matter he was set upon one night by

a group of ruffians — an attack he interpreted as a divine chas-
tisement: 'I thought of relinquishing the work of the ministry,
and the school altogether, and of engaging again in secular
pursuits; but for this I was sharply reproved. A man, in connection with four or five others, agreed to waylay, overpower and
stone me to death; one of them struck me on my right eye with
a cudgel, so that I lost it on the spot. I was also violently beaten
on the head, which utterly deprived me of my senses, and I lay
for some time as dead.'[7]

The above incident, along with his dispute with a shepherd
some years earlier, has led some to report that he was for awhile,
in his youthful and unconverted state, a notorious boxer who
enjoyed fist fights, and that he lost his eye in one of these bouts;
but this is a mistake. He observes in his diary: 'It is true, that I
had my eye struck out by some young men who attacked me in
the night, but that I was a noted boxer is incorrect, for I never,
as such, fought a battle in my life.'[8] 'Indeed,' says his biographer Rhys Stephen, 'he was by no means a man of great physical
courage; he was too much a man of imagination, while his
habits were the simplest, the least offensive, and the most yielding that can be conceived.'[9]

His one eye was often the focus of attention, provoking comments from all sorts of people. Once when someone was making fun of Welsh preachers before Robert Hall, an eloquent
English Baptist preacher and a shrewd apologist for Christianity, upon mentioning Christmas Evans, the jester said, 'And he
only has one eye!' 'Yes, sir,' answered Robert Hall, 'but that's a
piercer; an eye, sir, that could light an army through a wilderness in a dark night.'[10] On another occasion the same preacher
described his contemporary as 'the tallest, the stoutest and the
greatest man I ever saw; that he had but one eye, if it could be
called an eye; it was more properly a brilliant star — it shone
like Venus!'[11] Jan Morris in *The Matter of Wales* calls Christmas
Evans 'the one-eyed Baptist virtuoso of Llandysul in Dyfed,

who was said to make his congregation tremble just by his Cyclopian glare';[12] another says that his one eye was 'large and bright enough for two. It had a peculiarly penetrating glance; and when kindling under the inspiration of the pulpit, added wonderfully to the effect of his eloquence.'[13] A number of other witnesses also mention the quite remarkable fiery and piercing glare of his one large eye, especially when he was animated, or, as the Welsh say, *in the hwyl* (full sail).

The night he lost his eye he 'saw in a dream, that the day of judgement was come, and I beheld Jesus on the clouds and all the world on fire; and I was in great fear, yet crying earnestly, and with some confidence, for his peace. He answered and said, "Thou thoughtest to be a preacher, but what wilt thou do now? The world is on fire and it is too late!" This restored me from my backsliding, and I felt heartily thankful when I awoke that I was in bed.'[14] This dream left a deep impression on his mind, as did many dreams throughout his career, and he remembered it for a considerable time. In later years he reasoned that some of the most important intimations of his life had been given to him through dreams, 'and it was utterly vain to attempt to persuade him to the contrary'.[15]

He determined to return to God and to the calling that was upon his life. He started to read the Bible regularly and to observe seasons of prayer, much to the annoyance of his fellow haymakers, who beat him in order to drive religion from him; but their cruelty served only to strengthen his resolve to continue in the ministry. He returned to Wales and began to preach with new energy and success. Those who heard him delighted in what he said and encouraged him to continue. His friends predicted that he would yet 'become a great man, and a celebrated preacher'.[16]

He received considerable encouragement at this stage from William Perkins,[17] an Independent minister at Pantycreuddyn and Pencader, who frequently opened his pulpit to the young preacher, offered him friendship and understanding, and even placed his library at his disposal. Perkins was an 'able, eloquent and popular preacher, but addicted to intemperance. His churches failed to induce him to mend his ways, and majority decisions inhibited him from his ministry.'[18] There is a tradition connecting Perkins and Christmas Evans:

> About this time the late W. Perkins of Pencader, a well-known minister in that neighbourhood, having engaged to preach at a certain funeral, failed to fulfil his appointment; a prayer-meeting was therefore about to be held; whereupon a person present suggested that 'the lad Christmas, Samuel the shoemaker's son', was in the cottage, who had, to his knowledge, a stock of sermons in hand, and would preach as well as Mr Perkins himself. 'The lad Christmas', then eighteen or nineteen years old, undertook to preach at this short notice, and went through the service to the satisfaction of his audience. The Baptist and Independent ministers of the locality encouraged him, invited him occasionally to occupy their pulpits, and he soon found himself engaged as a monthly 'supply' by some of the neighbouring churches.[19]

One of the churches he visited every month was a branch of Llwynrhydowen at Mydroilyn about ten miles north of Llandysul. He was well received by the small congregation at Crug-y-maen and at Pantycreuddyn, where, it is said, he was the last to preach before the church moved to Horeb in 1783. The pulpits of the Methodists of Cefn Llanfair and the Baptists at Pen-y-bont, Llandysul, where he preached on many occasions, were also open to him. Of the latter congregation he speaks very highly, noting that there were men and women 'who were eminent for their experimental knowledge of the grace of God', and whose conversations were 'a blessing to me'. In particular he mentions a relative, 'Mr Lewis, Cwmhyar, whose family showed me great kindness; they contributed very much toward my support, and lent me some valuable books, and amongst them Mr

Aberduar Baptist Church.

Pen-y-bont Baptist Church, Llandysul, where
Christmas Evans preached on many occasions.

Evans's Dictionary, by the aid of which, I began to understand the works of English authors, which has been of great benefit to me through the whole course of my ministry.'[20]

It is astonishing that two of the greatest Welsh preachers, Christmas Evans and David Davies of Swansea, whose religious convictions were informed and strengthened under the ministry of William Perkins, were admitted into membership of the same church on the same evening, and preached their first sermon within a week of each other in the same cottage! Unfortunately, at least as far as Welsh Presbyterianism is concerned, there was a law in the church stating that no member would be permitted to preach without first passing through a college course, an impossible demand for Christmas Evans as he was extremely poor and without the assistance of influential friends. Consequently both Evans and Davies left the church in order to preach the gospel, the former joined the Baptists and the latter the Independents. Their pastor always regretted this train of events as it deprived his church of the two most eminent ministers it had ever produced.[21]

Although his early ministry was blessed of God and the responses of those who heard him favourable, Christmas Evans lacked confidence in preaching and, for the next three years, was somewhat confused about his beliefs. He had little peace with God and was often tormented by feelings of guilt and inadequacy. He doubted his own salvation and became more and more dissatisfied with the life of the church and his pastor's preaching, which tended to induce self-righteousness, thereby contradicting his own experience and further exasperating his muddled state of mind. His heart, to use his own expression, was 'a *little hell* within him'.[22] Yet, as he records, he was gratefully preserved from Arminianism and Socinianism, doctrines that were upheld by several men of exceptional talent at that time and which prevailed fairly extensively in what was called the most 'rationalistic' part of Wales.

He had obvious affection for his pastor, but he could not help noticing that many of the other preachers he heard had distinct and more Biblical views of the gospel than David Davis, and that the worship at Llwynrhydowen was formal and cold, unlike the warm and fervent worship of the Baptist Church at Aberduar, which he occasionally visited. He found himself increasingly attracted to Christians who held Calvinistic doctrines and was impressed by their godliness and knowledge of the Word. As he studied the Bible for himself, he realised that the Calvinistic Baptists were much nearer the truth than the Arminians with whom he worshipped.

It was during this period of uncertainty that he became unsettled about baptism, a doctrine he had not seriously considered before. He says, 'I had always regarded the Baptists as Anabaptists, as *re*-baptizing, and from my infancy had always heard them called Anabaptists; nor had I ever understood that any man of my condition had searched the Bible for himself, to ascertain what baptism it enjoined.'[23] Evan Amos, who had left Llwynrhydowen for the Calvinistic Baptist Church at Aberduar, where he had been baptised by Timothy Thomas (Amos later joined Pen-y-bont), challenged him on the matter and eventually he was convinced about 'the necessity of obeying the baptism instituted by Christ':

This man paid me a visit one day, when I attacked him with some severity upon the errors of the Anabaptists, but Amos silenced me very soon. I thought that his vanquishing me so easily was owing to my ignorance and unacquaintedness with the New Testament. I commenced reading, beginning in Matthew, in order to prepare myself with a sufficient number of Scriptures to meet Amos at the next interview. After having gone through the whole of the New Testament, I could not find one passage substantiating the rite of infant baptism. I frequently met with passages in the Old Testament, and some in the New, referring to the circumcision of

children, to the naming of children, and to the training of
children up in the nurture and admonition of the Lord; but
not one for the baptising of children. I found about forty
passages which gave their testimony in the plainest and most
unhesitating manner for baptising on a profession of faith.
They spoke of conscience, and convinced me of the necessity of obeying the baptism instituted by Christ, who required
me to yield personal obedience to him. After a little struggling between flesh and spirit, between obedience and disobedience, I went to the Baptist Church at Aberduar, in the
parish of Llanybyther, in the county of Carmarthen. I was
cordially received there, but not without a degree of dread
on the part of some, that I was still a stout-hearted Arminian.[24]

Friends suggested to him that he ought to be baptised and
furnished him with relevant books on the subject. After a strict
examination before the church, he was baptised, with nine
others, by Timothy Thomas, one of his new pastors, in the
River Duar in the summer of 1788 and admitted to the
communion of the church. He was twenty-one years old.

'Mr Timothy Thomas was the illustrious man who, in the first place, discovered and turned into the right channel the exceptional gifts of his still more illustrious disciple. Had he done nothing more he would have accomplished something well worth living for in befriending and imparting an inspiration to the greatest giant of the Welsh pulpit, while as yet his grand soul had not developed its resources or revealed its strength. Ah, we shall never have the like of Christmas Evans again.'

'No, it's not very likely that we shall,' added another minister. 'He was a man specially raised by God for a great work.'[1]

3
Inspired but Depressed

Although Daniel Rowland and Howel Harris were converted in 1735, the evangelical awakening in Wales did not really influence Baptist and Independent congregations until the mid 1770s. At the time Christmas Evans joined the Baptists, the denomination was about to enjoy its second period of growth and spiritual renewal. One of the churches to share in this revival was Aberduar, where 'Scores were awakened to a sense of the state of their souls, a great degree of religious rejoicing was experienced, and the sound of praise was heard through the whole neighbourhood.'[2] These new converts were filled with an 'inexpressible and glorious joy' that manifested itself in ecstatic bodily movements, arm-wavings, and enthusiastic singing and laughing, called *Welsh Jumping* [3] by those who disapproved. At first, notes Christmas Evans, 'Such life and animation in divine worship greatly surprised me, for I knew nothing of religious enjoyment heretofore. I had experienced some taste of it whilst preaching on one occasion [at Cefn Llanfair], with one of the Calvinistic Methodists, and the relish of it remained with me asleep and awake for some days; but now, among my new friends, I could not help viewing myself as a speckled bird, not feeling what they felt, until my mind was filled with very low and dejected thoughts of my state and condition.'[4] It was about a year later, after he had studied much and been fervent in prayer, that he experienced an inner release of the Spirit.

His new pastor, Timothy Thomas 'II' (1754-1840), was a nephew of John Thomas and the son of the teacher and writer Timothy Thomas 'I' (1720-68), a prominent Baptist, who produced one of the ablest theological works of that period *The White Robe (Traethiad am y Wisg-Wen Ddisglair)* (1759), as well as other widely read and useful publications. Thomas 'I' started to preach before he was twenty and was ordained in 1743 as minister of his mother-church at Aberduar, Carmarthenshire, where he stayed until his death. This church had been constituted in 1742 after members left Glandŵr, and in that year it had a membership of between seventy and eighty. The firstborn son of his second marriage, Timothy Thomas 'II', was a Welsh gentleman, who began preaching ten years after his father's death and was ordained as one of the ministers of Aberduar five years later. This proved to be his only pastorate. At the time of his father's premature demise he was only fourteen, but his response to his mother's plea was an indication of future resourcefulness. After the funeral his distraught mother cried, 'The family altar is fallen, and there is no one to raise it again: I shall feel this deeply.' Timothy immediately replied with the firmness and determination that were to mark his ministry, 'No, it shall not fall, I will do what I can.' That night he stood in his father's place at family worship.[5]

He inherited the extended lease of a beautiful farm in the vale of Teifi, the running of which he superintended. There was only a nominal rent to pay so he was able to preach and conduct all the duties of a pastor without remuneration. In his old age the lease expired and he found himself dependent on his children for daily sustenance. Rhys Stephen, who knew him personally, speaks of his 'gallant bearing, his ingenuous spirit, his more than princely magnanimity' which was combined 'with the lowliness of his spirit before God, and the earnestness of his administration of the divine ordinances'.[6] 'It would require,' he says, 'a small volume to do justice to his merits and his memory. His services to his generation were not more distinguished by their length, than by their assiduity, zeal, efficiency and disinterestedness. His time, his robust health, his active and untiring mind, his invincible courage, his all, he devoted not only ungrudgingly, but most cheerfully and joyfully, to serve God in the gospel of his Son.'[7] John Williams of Trosnant, who knew him well, exclaimed in admiration, 'Oh, that I could but pray like him! I have tried, and must confess that I have failed.'[8]

Thomas was a man of strong and clear faith, whose fervent preaching had a profound influence on many, including Christmas Evans. Because of the plurality of ministers at Aberduar (his three co-pastors were Zechariah Thomas, his uncle; David Davies, Brynllo; and David Saunders, afterwards of Merthyr Tudful) Timothy Thomas could spend on average two Sundays a month, as well as weekdays, preaching the gospel in neighbouring churches. At the time of the revival he preached to large congregations and such was the effect that many spontaneously broke out in prayer and rejoicing. During a church meeting, when his uncle tried to quench the enthusiastic spirit of the young people, he stood up and boldly cried, 'Brother, can you be so presumptuous as to attempt to extinguish the fire which God has lit up in Zion? You cannot do it! All the floods of the devil cannot do it!'[9] On another occasion, in Brecknockshire, after his sermon had greatly excited the congregation and 'Another minister present having offered the concluding prayer, Mr Thomas again stood up and pealed forth, in his most thrilling tones, the one word *Bendigedig* (wonderful, blessed). The excitement was renewed; another prayed, and another; seventeen prayers were offered in succession, and the meeting broke up only when the day dawned.'[10]

There are other anecdotes, some amusing, others alarming, that exhibit the earnestness and intrepidity of spirit that compelled

him to go into the world and preach the gospel, baptising believers in the name of the Father, the Son and the Holy Spirit.
Sometimes he rode thirty or forty miles on a Saturday afternoon to the remotest parts of Carmarthenshire and
Cardiganshire in order to be ready on the Lord's Day to baptise believers in the open air, a somewhat dangerous occupation in those days owing to the mobs that were ready, by all
possible means, to interrupt the service. Once he was invited to
a district where baptism by immersion was unknown, except to
the few Baptists who had recently taken up residence there.

> The people of the neighbourhood were there in full expecta-
> tion of the Administration; some of them fully prepared for
> mischief, with the instruments of insult and offence in their
> hands; when suddenly a well-dressed gentleman, mounted
> on a noble horse, drove over the village bridge, hastily
> alighted, gave his bridle to a by-stander, and walking briskly
> into the middle of 'the little flock' on the water's edge.
> Instead of dispersing them, as the lookers-on — having no
> doubt that he was a county magistrate at least — exultingly
> expected him to do, he took a candidate by the hand, walked
> down into the stream, booted and spurred as he was, and
> before the mobility present had closed their gaping mouths,
> he had done his work; after which he stood on the brink, and
> with his wet clothes about him, he preached to them one of
> his most ardent discourses: conciliated their esteem, and
> actually persuaded them that 'the Dippers' had, at least, one
> respectable man.[11]

There were times when he was unashamed of using a form of
'muscular Christianity' if it meant protecting members of his
family. While travelling to a preaching engagement, four strong
men attacked his brother and his wife who were following in a
gig. Upon hearing their cries for help, he 'spurred his horse,
rode back as fast as he could, and, stick in hand, soon floored
two of the ruffians, and the others were, ere long, disposed of

by the energies of all combined'. But by this time, other men from the nearby public house had joined 'the ranks of the enemy'. Unfortunately, Thomas had broken his weapon in his first defence, so 'He dashed at a fence just opposite, pulled out a prodigious stake, and was again going forth to victory, when the innkeeper, having a wholesome fear of law before his eyes, interposed, and put an end to the struggle.'[12]

Such acts of aggression, however, were rare. Thomas was for the most part a gentle and sympathetic man, warm in his humour and capable of displaying a praiseworthy catholicity of spirit. One Sunday morning in summer he was preaching near Llandeilo to a huge congregation, and baptising, when he received an urgent message that the rector of the parish had been detained for an hour, unable to pass by to his church because of the crowd. In those days obstructing the roadway with a congregation was deemed a serious offence. Immediately upon hearing the message he addressed the people with simplicity and tact, 'I understand that the respected clergyman of the parish has been listening patiently to me for the last hour; let us all go to church and return the compliment by hearing him.' The church and the churchyard were soon crowded, much to the rector's delight, and nothing more was said of the matter, except a word of appreciation for Thomas's catholicity. A few weeks later Timothy Thomas returned to the neighbourhood to baptise several members of the original congregation who had been affected by his sermon.

Thomas was also a strong church disciplinarian, who dealt firmly, yet graciously and wisely, and sometimes humorously, with any member of his congregation whose behaviour was contrary to the Christian faith. This often meant excommunicating the offender. One instance of his dry wit and straightforwardness is seen in how he dealt with a member of the church at Aberduar, who was brought before him at the 'preparatory meeting' accused of deliberately knocking down a Unitarian.

The preparatory meeting, in which the spiritual state and daily conduct of the communicant were examined and any necessary discipline administered, was usually held the day before the communion Sunday:

'Let us hear all about it,' said the pastor.

'To tell you the truth about it, sir,' said the culprit, 'I met Jack the miller at the sign of the Red Dragon, and there we had a single glass of ale together.'

'Stop a bit,' said the minister. 'I hope you paid for it.'

'I did, sir.'

'That is in your favour, Thomas,' said the pastor. 'I cannot bear those people who go about tippling at other people's expense. Go on, Thomas.'

'Well, sir, after a little while we began quietly talking about religion, and about the work of Jesus Christ. Jack said that he was only a man, and then he went on to say shocking things, things that it was beyond the power of flesh and blood to bear.'

'I daresay,' said the pastor, 'but what did he say?'

'He actually said, sir, that the blood of Christ had no more power in it than the blood of a beast. I could not stand that anymore, so I knocked him down.'

'Well, brother,' said the minister, 'I cannot say that you did the right thing, but I quite believe that I should have done so too. Go and sin no more.'[13]

Such was the man who welcomed Christmas Evans into the Baptist Church and, with patience and power, helped him to become more settled in his beliefs and more forthright in his preaching. He died on 21 January, 1840, at Cardigan, the home of his son Joshua Morgan Thomas, when eighty-six years old, and was buried at Aberduar. In his later life, when asked how many he had baptised, he would answer abruptly, 'About two thousand!' Sometimes he replied: 'I have baptised at least two thousand persons. Yes, thirty of them have become ministers of the gospel; and it was I who baptised Christmas Evans.'[14]

With all the godly influences around him, and experiencing a new environment of enthusiasm and zeal for the things of God, Christmas Evans received much spiritual good, and was greatly helped to embrace, albeit slowly, the Calvinistic doctrines and to form more definite views of the person of Christ. His understanding of the scheme of salvation was still somewhat confused, but it must not be supposed that he was wholly ignorant of the method of grace in the redemption of sinners through Jesus Christ. 'He himself observes, that joining the Baptists was of great benefit to him — bringing him to behold the righteousness of Christ imputed to him that believeth, and the blood of Jesus Christ "purifying the conscience from dead works to serve the living God" — and also, that hearing some of the most eminent ministers of the day, of different denominations, was greatly blessed, to lead him to consider the doctrine of the grace of God through a Mediator, without any human merit.'[15]

Two men whom he heard and derived great benefit from were T. Davies of Neath, and David Morris (1744-91), Lledrod, a Calvinistic Methodist exhorter and a hymnwriter of some distinction. Morris was one of the biggest men who ever entered a Welsh pulpit, and one who possessed 'perhaps the sweetest and most melodious voice that ever rang in the Welsh hills'.[16] In his preaching he displayed 'fire and dramatic action', along with superior oratorical powers, which must have had a profound effect on Christmas Evans. So many assembled to hear him that he often preached out of doors to accommodate the crowds. It is said of him that he never preached a sermon that did not result in the conversion of souls.

On his evangelistic tours, which, because of his debilitating size, were not as frequent as some of his contemporaries, he preached two or three times every day. On one occasion, when preaching at Rippont Bridge, Anglesey, he realised, with sudden and almost unbearable force, that many before him were lost; so with a deep and agonised cry, he exclaimed, 'Oh, you people of the great loss! The great loss!' The congregation was so moved by what he said that they swayed before him like reeds in a storm, as the sermon was imprinted on their hearts.[17] Owen Jones, quoted above, goes on to say that his greatness as a preacher was due, not to the sound of his voice, beautiful though that was, but to 'his thorough grasp of gospel truths, his deep pathos, and his enthusiastic fervour in preaching'.[18] Daniel Rowland thought of him very highly and always invited him to preach one of the sermons of the great Communion Sunday at Llangeitho. He died at Carmarthen after a life of dedicated service in the ministry. His son, Ebenezer Morris (1769-1825), was one of the ablest Calvinistic Methodist preachers of his day and, like his father, owned a voice of almost matchless melody, over which he exercised perfect mastery. John Elias regarded Ebenezer Morris as 'one who was renowned, valiant, faithful and laborious in the work of his Lord, one of the first three in the army of our spiritual David'.[19]

Another preacher Christmas Evans heard was David Jones (1736-1810), Llan-gan, who worked in close association with Daniel Rowland for twenty years. He was born at Aberceiliog, Llanllwni, Carmarthen, and was ordained a deacon and then a priest by the bishop of St David's in 1758 and 1760 respectively. By reading the works of John Flavel, the English Puritan, his preaching underwent a dramatic change. He travelled extensively in North Wales and everywhere he went he was condemned by his superiors for his fervent and evangelical proclamation of the gospel and for the purity of his life. Numerous complaints were made against him to Barrington and Watson, successive bishops of Llandaff, for preaching outside his parish and in unconsecrated places. Once, when confronted by Bishop Barrington for preaching in 'unholy places', he answered, 'No, never, my lord; for when Mary's son put his foot on this earth he consecrated every spot of it; without that no consecration of yours, my lord, could do much good.'[20]

People travelled from miles around, sometimes in atrocious weather, to hear him preach, and he often had to move into the churchyard because of the crowds that attended his ministry. The preacher Robert Roberts, Clynnog, who, as we shall see, had such a deep influence on Christmas Evans, was converted under his ministry. He was highly esteemed by Lady Huntingdon and was admitted to the living of Llan-gan by one of her titled friends. The countess also employed him as often as possible to supply her chapels, especially at Spa Fields in London, where on her death he preached a funeral sermon on 3 July, 1791. He also preached at the graveside of Daniel Rowland when his text was Revelation 14:13. In 1775 he built a meeting-house three miles away from his parish church, and it was there that he ministered, making it a centre of Methodism second only to Llangeitho, and experiencing some extraordinary visitations of God's Spirit. After Rowland's death he became the virtual leader of the Methodist movement.

Many have noted his tender, gracious and meek spirit. Christopher Bassett, at one time curate to William Romaine, said of him: 'I have never seen one who appeared in the pulpit imbued to such a degree with the spirit of the gospel. His ministry seemed to me singularly adapted to conciliate enemies to the truth, to strengthen the weak, and to decide the wavering. He was well-skilled in administering the "Balm of Gilead" to the wounded conscience.'[21] *The Dictionary of National Biography* makes a similar comment: 'Jones occupied a unique position among the Welsh preachers of his day: his amiable and cheerful countenance, his sweet and musical voice, soothed hearers who had often been driven nearly frantic by the violent oratory of other revivalists.'[22] According to Williams, Pantycelyn, he could 'melt the rocks with his warmth and make the stoutest oak tree bend as humbly as the reed'.[23]

A third man whose sermons Christmas Evans heard at this time was Peter Williams (1723-96), a fine preacher, Bible scholar, author and poet. He was converted at Carmarthen on 14 April, 1743, under the ministry of George Whitefield, whose text on that occasion was Isaiah 54:5. At the time Williams was in his twentieth year and studying at the local Grammar School. The clergyman schoolmaster, who despised Whitefield's evangelical doctrines, warned his pupils to beware of the Englishman's flaming oratory. Ignoring his teacher's advice, Williams, with three other students, secretly attended the meeting and was converted. In his own words, he says:

> The dayspring from on high visited me. The time of my conversion was accomplished. All my sins in thought, word and deed were brought to my remembrance, as though a floodgate had been opened and the angry flood poured furiously upon me; so that my soul was overwhelmed with fear and confusion. Everything around me appeared strange and uncouth, nay, the neatest building was no more to me than a nauseous dunghill; I had no more any delight in heathen authors; I went to school, but could not collect my thoughts to study my lesson.[24]

Two years after his conversion he obtained deacon's orders in the Church of England and became a curate to the notorious John Evans, who, in 1752, wrote 'one of the most scurrilous and vulgar pamphlets ever issued by the British press',[25] in which he tried, unsuccessfully, to ruin both the character and the work of Griffith Jones. Williams worked tirelessly in his new charge at Eglwys Gymyn, which was the neighbouring parish to Llanddowror,[26] and then, after his expulsion, successively at Swansea, Llangrannog and Llandysiliogogo, but he did not receive 'complete' Anglican orders on account of his Methodism, whose ranks he formally joined in 1747. A curious incident led to his dismissal from his own curacy:

When he was delivering a carefully written discourse one Sunday morning, he was disturbed by the bad behaviour of some young people in the church, whom he proceeded to remonstrate with, and in doing so, he lost his place in the manuscript. He had to make the best he could of an awkward situation, and rather than terminate abruptly, he finished with a few extemporised words, which, he confesses, had no particular reference to the subject of the sermon. The wife of the rector, who happened to be in the congregation that morning, wrote to inform her husband that his curate was now unmistakably convicted of being a Methodist, as he had preached extempore. The rector gave him notice to leave on the charge of 'preaching original sin, justification by faith, and the absolute necessity of regeneration'. The incriminated curate tried to defend himself, but his irate rector was inexorable. He went to the bishop, but it was of no use. His Lordship accused him of preaching in two churches outside his own parish, but told him that, if he behaved well for three years, he would grant him full ordination. 'How can I subsist, my Lord,' was the reply of the astonished curate; 'I cannot dig, I am ashamed to beg.' 'Live as you can,' was the bishop's rejoinder; and the curate left the palace without the offer of meat or drink.[27]

Williams wrote 'voluminously on doctrinal matters, and on his missionary tour in 1747 was the first Methodist minister to penetrate into Anglesey'.[28] He was not well received by the North Walians, being imprisoned for the night in the Wynnstay dog-kennels by Sir Watkin Williams Wynn. In the 1750s his 'great contribution was to supply, in some measure, the itinerant ministry of preaching and counselling the societies which Harris had previously fulfilled'.[29] He visited the less evangelized parts of Wales and her borders, and, with the exception of Harris, suffered perhaps more persecution than any of his contemporaries. His greatest achievement was to publish a Welsh family Bible, with expository notes on every chapter, issued in shilling parts on a bimonthly basis from 1768. It was the first

Welsh commentary on the whole Bible ever issued, and the first to be printed in Wales. It was very popular for several generations, and thirty-eight editions were published between 1770 and 1900. In 1773 he circulated a concordance to the Welsh Bible under the name *Mynegeir Ysgrythurol*.

Overall he worked faithfully and diligently for the Methodist cause for forty-six years before being expelled in 1791 because of an alleged connection with Sabellianism. The controversy, set to rage for twenty years, arose because of some comments he made on John 1:1, which suggested an inclination towards Sabellianism. By 1791 other factors had aggravated the situation, such as his publication of a Welsh edition of John Canne's *Little Bible* (1790),[30] and he was expelled from Methodist ranks at an association held at Llandeilo Fawr on 25 May, chiefly at the instigation of Daniel Rowland's son, Nathaniel. The deaths of Daniel Rowland in 1790 and William Williams, Pantycelyn, in January the following year, two supporters of Peter Williams, probably account, at least in part, for the action taken against him for comments made twenty years previously. According to *The Dictionary of National Biography*, 'He was guilty of nothing worse than a confused mysticism with reference to the doctrine of the Trinity, and the cruel treatment meted to him after his unrivalled services to Welsh Methodism stands out as the darkest passage in the history of that body.'[31]

John Thomas of Tremain, upon hearing both Daniel Rowland and Peter Williams, said: 'These two men strike exactly the same chord, namely, God is everything; man, and all to do with him, is nothing; God is eternally exalted and glorious, and man down in the dust as dung underfoot, with all the best that belongs to him. This is the chord that all the saints have ever struck; my spirit feels it, too, and its sound is exceedingly sweet.'[32] Another calls him 'a great preacher and an exemplary man' who did tremendous work to 'cultivate religious literature in Wales'.[33]

There is little doubt that Christmas Evans was aroused and inspired by these fine men and fed 'manna from heaven', but they had another salutary effect on him. He started to compare himself with them, and with other preachers of his new denomination, and found them 'altogether better and godlier preachers than I was'.[34] 'I entertained,' he said, 'the highest thoughts of every other preacher, but none of myself. I conceived that every person who was born again, and had believed, was endowed with much better light in divine things than I possessed.'[35] This led him to entertain depressing views of his own Christian character and ministry. He imagined he was not endowed with the necessary gifts for ministry, despaired every time he heard his own voice, and, conscious of his appearance, entered the pulpit with dread, thinking that the mere sight of him was enough to cast a gloom over the service and cloud his hearers' minds. When he looked back over the years he had been preaching, he could not ascertain that he had been the means of salvation to a single soul. These feelings of inadequacy caused him such overwhelming distress that he sometimes rolled himself on the floor in the deepest agony of mind.

This experience and the adoption of a different method of preaching, he himself describes:

I could feel no influence, no virtue in my own sermons. It occurred to me that this might be owing to my habit of committing my sermons carefully to memory, and that I thus superseded the Divine aid; while I supposed other preachers had theirs direct from heaven. I accordingly changed my plan, and would take a text and preach from it without preparation, saying whatever would come uppermost at the time; but if it was bad before, it now was still worse, for I had neither sense, nor warmth, nor life; but some weakly intonation of voice that affected no one. It was painful to me to hear my own voice in prayer or in preaching, as it seemed to proceed from a hard heart. I travelled much in this condition, thinking every preacher a true preacher but myself; nor had I any confidence in the light I had upon Scripture. I considered everybody to be before myself, and was frequently tortured with fears that I was still a graceless man. I have since seen God's goodness in all this, for thus was I kept from falling in love with my own gifts, which has happened to many young men, and has been their ruin.[36]

These battles with depression, recurring as they did throughout his life, were aids to prepare him for usefulness as a pastor and preacher, and to keep his spirit in humble dependence on God in the midst of great success. His own account of these early trials, according to Rhys Stephen, not only proves that the religious teaching he had received up to this point, excellent though some of it must have been, had failed 'to inspire [in him] Christian hope and confidence', but

... exhibits early and significant intimations of his own peculiar idiosyncrasy, which subjected him throughout his whole life to mental suffering for which the most spiritually-minded of his friends could see no cause. He was often sad when God would not have him to be sad. His prolific imagination, excited by a sense of infinite unworthiness before God, would become excited, and would 'body forth' forms of calamity that had no real existence, but were not the less torturing to the mind that conceived them. It also impressively shows, how it is possible for a society of believers to be in a state of high religious enjoyment, while ... *he*, whom the Head of the church was now preparing for a course of protracted and extensive labour in his vineyard, and who afterwards, for half a century, preached the gospel with zeal, ability and power unsurpassed in his day, went and returned with heaviness of spirit and a wounded heart.[37]

To make matters worse he had 'no friend under the sun, to whom I could open my mind, and disclose the plague of my heart; I dared not unbosom myself, for I thought if any knew how it was with me, they would at once conclude that I was an unconverted man, and expose me to the whole world'.[38] Though he entertained such depressing views of himself and was unconscious of the power of God on his ministry, all who knew him thought him to be an excellent Christian and had full confidence in his piety.

The ministry of the gospel, through the instrumentality of Welsh preachers, has produced a most wonderful effect, which is visible in the ornament of evangelical knowledge, and the beauty of that morality, that broidered garment of pure gold in which the Principality is clothed. Notwithstanding many of her ministers go out to preach ... by the influence of the Holy Spirit of God inflaming their gifts, and firing their zeal and love to Christ and the souls of men ... There is no portion of the terrestrial globe, of its size and containing the same number of inhabitants, where ... the flowers of morality decorate its hills and dales, and ungodly and heathenish customs are flying away, like the demons of Gadara before the Son of God in the days of his flesh, as the Principality of Wales.

J. Davis in 1835.[1]

4
The Gospel in North Wales

At this stage in his career, Christmas Evans had no idea that he was about to depart for the North, where he would labour so effectively for over forty years. His ministry in that part of the Principality, as we shall see, was singularly blessed of God, producing a lasting impact on the Baptist denomination there and, with the help of his contemporaries, on society as a whole. Coupled with his yearly tours to the South, his success in the North made him one of the most popular and powerful preachers of all time.

In many senses Christmas Evans's ministry in the North was a pioneering work, although it is true to say that the ground had been prepared for him by the leaders of the great evangelical awakening in Wales. These men were all born and bred in South Wales, within a radius of about thirty or forty miles from Llanddowror, the home of Griffith Jones. As the move of God spread in the southern counties, its principal advocates began to look north, realising their responsibility to preach Christ throughout Wales. The difficulties, though, of evangelizing the North were considerable: the distance between each isolated hamlet, the various northern dialects of the spoken Welsh language, the mountains and hills that had proved such an effective barrier against invading armies, and the opposition they

were bound to meet, all tended to increase the size of their task
— a task that was far from complete at the close of the century.

Howel Harris began his mission to North Wales in 1738 when
the state of religion in that part of the Principality was very low.
The people were 'steeped in ignorance', he informs us, and 'A
spiritual darkness and torpor was spread over the land.' Bibles
were scarce, the customs of the country were corrupt and
immoral, and the clergy were as indifferent and dead as the
people themselves: 'Gluttony, drunkenness and licentiousness
like a torrent overran the land; nor were the doctrines and
precepts of the churches but dark and feeble to counteract these
evils. From the pulpit the name of the Redeemer was hardly
ever heard.'[2]

As the southern reformers made inroads into new territory
with the gospel the expected hostility towards them was severe.
At Machynlleth Harris was stoned by a mob and one of his
attackers discharged a pistol at him. In January 1741 he was
fortunate to escape with his life from Bala, where he was
besmeared with mire and beaten by his enemies 'with their fists
and clubs, one of them striking him in the face, others pelting
stones and inflicting such wounds that his path could be marked
in the street by the crimson stains of his blood'.[3] On another
occasion, with the mob vowing his death, Harris 'was five times
for [his] life in North Wales in one journey'.[4] In March 1742 he
wrote: 'Last week I saw some of our brethren come home from
North Wales, where they escaped very narrowly with their lives.
Some they sent from one prison to another, one they struck
[as] dead, another they followed for many miles in order to
execute their rage on him.'[5] These experiences so affected him
that he came to believe that the people of the North lived 'like
brutes'. However, he was undeterred when it came to proclaiming the gospel, promising, 'I'll preach of Christ till to pieces I
fall.'[6]

Many of his brethren suffered similar receptions, at times

being hunted down and treated 'as if they were ravenous beasts'. On one of Daniel Rowland's northern excursions 'A threat was made that if he opened his mouth to preach his bones would be ground so small as could be put in a bag.'[7] John Owen (1698-1755), vicar of Llannor near Pwllheli, and the chancellor of Bangor, was a 'barbarous persecutor'. He was nicknamed 'the Bonner of the eighteenth century' and, because of the absence of a resident bishop, was able to incite both clergy and populace, throughout the diocese of Bangor, into a persecuting rage.

> It was his practice, in which the clergy generally followed his example, to lead a mob to every place where he found that Nonconformists or the Methodists intended to hold a meeting. The inoffensive worshippers were abused most mercilessly, pelted with stones, wounded with swords or knives, shot at; men and women were stripped naked in the presence of the crowd; able bodied men were pressed for the army or navy, and driven away from their families and friends, like cattle, to different parts of England.[8]

One man we must mention again, this time in connection with the gospel in North Wales, is Griffith Jones (1683-1761), a farmer's son from the Teifi Valley, and considered by more than one historian as the greatest Welshman of the eighteenth century. As we have noted, he was a powerful preacher, whose 'very presence was like the ringing of the Sabbath bells for the people to come and hear'.[9] Among the 'many burning and shining lights' of the Principality, Jones, according to George Whitefield, 'shines in particular'.[10] Ever since his own conversion, saving souls had been the ruling passion of his life and with that aim in mind he established a network of circulating schools, which he first launched in 1731. Their purpose, he wrote, 'is not to make gentlemen, but Christians and heirs to eternal life'.[11]

These schools, in addition to 'saving souls', were designed

to teach his countrymen, ninety per cent of whom were illiterate before they were first established, to read the catechism
and the Bible in their own language. Initially they were vigorously opposed, hindering their progress north. Up to 1742, apart
from the odd exception, they were confined to South Wales
and it was not until 1746 that they reached much beyond
Montgomeryshire and were first established in Anglesey. After
that their move northwards was rapid. In the Annual Report for
1747-48, Jones notes the encouraging advance of his charity
schools, saying that they 'have now spread themselves so far
over the Principality, that some of them are set up in every
county of South and North Wales, the county of Flint only
excepted'.[12] By the time of Jones's death in 1761 the schools,
3225 of which had been established in nearly 1600 different
locations in Wales, had reached the farthest limits of Anglesey,
as well as the mountainous districts of Merioneth and Caernarfon, and some 250,000 students — more than half the population of Wales — had been taught to read fluently in them.

'With enormous passion and perseverance,' says Geraint
Jenkins, 'Griffith Jones had launched and sustained a national
system of schools and turned it into a truly Welsh institution.
Even after his death, the schools continued to flourish under
Madam Bevan's benevolent and watchful eye … The peak year
was 1773, when 242 schools were set up and 13,205 scholars
received instruction.'[13] It is no exaggeration to say that these
schools paved the way for the great evangelical awakening and
were the principal means behind the erecting of Welsh Sunday
schools. Because of them Griffith Jones is regarded as one of
the pioneers of Welsh popular education on an extensive scale.
In the words of Thomas Phillips, it was to him 'in great part
owing that the Bible has been so generally found and read in
the Welsh cottage'.

Before the 1770s only a small percentage of the population
of North Wales had been touched by Methodism, and no

distinctive organization was established there until Thomas
Charles (1755-1814), a native of Carmarthenshire, settled in
Bala in 1784, five years before Christmas Evans travelled north.
According to Daniel Rowland, Charles was 'the gift of God to
North Wales'. He was the first to spread the Methodist movement in that part of the Principality and it was through his indefatigable labours and earnestness that true Christianity
flourished. He was born a few miles from Llanddowror on 14
October, 1755, six years before Griffith Jones's death. After
studying at the Carmarthen Academy under Jenkin Jenkins he
went to Jesus College, Oxford, where he was trained for the
Church. He was converted at the age of eighteen after hearing
a sermon by Rowland — 'a day much to be remembered by
me as long as I live', enthused Charles. 'Ever since that happy
day I have lived in a new heaven and a new earth ... I had such
a view of Christ as our High Priest, of his love, compassion,
power, and all-sufficiency, as filled my soul with astonishment,
with joy unspeakable and full of glory.'[14] After being ejected
from three curacies because of his links with Methodism, he
finally joined that society in 1784 and became a powerful and
influential leader.

Shocked by the prevalent ignorance of the Scriptures among
his people, Charles decided to revive Griffith Jones's circulating schools, which had lapsed six years earlier after the death
of Jones's patron, Madam Bridget Bevan of Laugharne, 'an
active and selfless philanthropist', and because of the long
legal wranglings over her will.[15] Soon, however, partly because
of lack of teachers and of support, and partly because the inac-
cessibility of so many villages in North Wales made it difficult
for the people to attend, Charles realised that more could be
achieved through Sunday Schools, which he organised
successfully from about 1789.[16] The aim of these schools, he
states, 'was to teach the children to read their native language
correctly, and to train them in the principles of Christianity, and

nothing else. As the salvation of their souls was the only purpose in view, we exclude from our little schools everything that does not have a direct tendency to facilitate that significant end.'[17] The schools were attended by adults as well as children, and became a powerful means of religious instruction in Wales, particularly in the Methodist Societies of North Wales, and in 1791 (the year Christmas Evans moved to Anglesey) a great revival radiated from Bala throughout North Wales as a result of them.

They also stimulated a great interest in the Bible, for which there was an urgent need.[18] This demand for Welsh Bibles, along with the ignorance and impiety of the common people, and especially the dedication of young Mary Jones, who walked barefoot twenty-five miles from her home in Llanfi-hangel-y-Pennant, across Cadair Idris, to Bala in order to pro-cure a Bible, persuaded Charles to act.[19] In 1804, he joined members of the Clapham sect, a group of wealthy Anglican evangelicals who proposed the idea to the Religious Tract Society in London, in founding the British and Foreign Bible Society. Their aim was to encourage the wider circulation of the Holy Scriptures, without note or comment, and to that end they made available vernacular translations of the Scriptures to people of all races at a price they could afford.

On Wednesday 6 June, 1827, at an association of ministers and messengers in Pontypool and afterwards at a missionary meeting, Christmas Evans preached a sermon on the *Messiah's Kingdom* (Daniel 2:44-45), in which he adds further details of the founding of the BFBS, before urging 'Welshmen!' to support its cause liberally:

> In the year 1802, the Rev. Mr. Charles of Bala ... deeply impressed with the preciousness of the Bible, and aware of the scarcity of copies throughout the principality, felt that some measures ought to be adopted to furnish it at a

reduced price, and circulate it gratuitously among the poor. He wrote concerning it to his countryman, the Rev. Mr. Owen, an Episcopal clergyman in London. The subject was subsequently introduced to a circle of Christian gentlemen, who had met to transact other business. It elicited much conversation, and excited a lively interest.

The Rev. Joseph Hughes, a Welshman and Baptist minister at Battersea near London, suggested that Wales was not the only part of the world that felt a want of the Bread of Life; and that it was desirable to awaken, if possible, a more extensive interest on the subject among Christians of every name; and stir them up to the adoption of some measure, which might lead to a general circulation of the Scriptures. The suggestion was heartily entertained and warmly supported by the rest of the company; and its discussion led to those incipient efforts, which, in 1804, issued in the organisation of the British and Foreign Bible Society. The little spring of Bala soon became a stream large enough for a man to swim in; and now it widens and deepens into a great river, on which float the merchandise of Zion, and the navies of God.

Welshmen! it is your privilege and honour, as well as your duty, to sustain this excellent institution. It is a native of Wales, born in your northern mountains. It is your own child, and you are bound to protect and support it to the extent of your ability. I call upon you as Welshmen, to aid an institution originating in Welsh philanthropy. I call upon you as Welsh Baptists, to help forward an enterprise which sprang from the heart of a Welsh Baptist minister.[20]

At the first meeting of the BFBS, £700 was subscribed and, owing to the exertions of Thomas Charles and others, the contribution in Wales amounted to nearly £1900, most of this sum consisting of the subscriptions and donations of the lower and poorer classes. In July 1806 the first copies of the Welsh Bible, printed at the Society and prepared for the press by Charles himself, were distributed, much to the delight of many in North Wales, who could hardly wait to lay their hands on them. When the first load arrived in a cart the Welsh peasants hurried out to meet it, 'welcomed it as the Israelites did the ark of old, drew it into the town, and eagerly bore off every copy as rapidly as they could be disposed of. The young people were to be seen consuming the whole night in reading it. Labourers carried it with them to the fields that they might enjoy it during the intervals of their labour and lose no opportunity of becoming acquainted with its sacred truths.'[21]

Within four years of the formation of the Society 60,000 copies of the Welsh Bible and 45,000 copies of the New Testament were published. Three years later in 1811 Thomas Charles enthusiastically wrote: 'The whole country is, in a manner, emerging from a state of great ignorance and ferocious barbarism to civilisation and piety ... Bibles without end are called for and read diligently, learned out by heart, and searched into with unwearied assiduity and care. Instead of vain amusements ... we have now prayer meetings. Our congregations are crowded and public catechising has become pleasant, familiar and profitable.'[22]

Paxton Hood pays a fitting tribute to Charles when he writes: 'All his works and words, his inward and his outward life, show the active, high-toned saintliness and enthusiastic holiness of the man. There is, perhaps, no other to whom Wales is so largely indebted for the giving direction, organisation and usefulness to all religious labour, as to him.'[23]

For most of the eighteenth century the Baptist denomination in Wales was a small and ecclesiastically insignificant body. In 1714 there were only eleven Welsh Baptist churches with 600 or so members. These churches were characterised by a strict and ordered churchmanship and a Calvinistic theology, and restricted to the southern counties. By 1735, a crucial year in the denomination's life and the year that Daniel Rowland and Howel Harris started to preach evangelical doctrines, 'There existed seventeen Baptist churches ... throughout Wales, the largest at Llanwenarth having a complement of 100 members.'[24] There were some early contacts between Baptist church members and Howel Harris, but these meetings did not prevent the denomination remaining impervious to the evangelical awakening for some forty years, due to a separate ecclesiology, doctrinal differences, and a deep-rooted suspicion of emotionalism. By 1770 evangelism was gaining power and moving northwards, and in 1774 the denomination reached a turning point. New life was breathed into many assemblies and from that point growth was considerable.[25] Baptist numbers soared from about 1600 in 1760 to over 7000 in 1794, 'And they grew faster again in the first thirty years of the nineteenth century ... Two hundred or so ministers were produced between 1775 and 1800, as compared with only 60 or so between 1750 and 1775.'[26]

In 1776 Thomas Llewellyn (1720?-83), a learned Baptist minister, who is best remembered for his efforts to supply and distribute Welsh Bibles to his fellow-countrymen, with monetary assistance from the Particular Baptist Fund in London and under the auspices of the Baptist Churches of South Wales, pioneered a missionary campaign for the evangelization of North Wales. This included the counties of Merioneth, Caernarfon and Anglesey in which the Baptists had no place of worship. In part of Denbighshire too the Baptists were comparatively unknown, although they did have three meeting houses (Wrexham, Cefn-mawr and Glyn Ceiriog), where numbers were small.

David Evans, pastor of Dolau in Radnorshire, made an exploratory journey in May of that year and brought back an optimistic report. He was encouraged to return to the North, which he did in August with a friend Morgan Evans, minister of Pentre. He made another two journeys in May and August 1777. Finally his efforts were rewarded in April 1779 when he baptised by immersion two candidates, Robert Williams and

William Edwards, 'the first persons who were baptised within the last century in Anglesey'.[27] By this time other missionaries from the South were visiting the North, commonly two at a time. Ten more were baptised in Anglesey on 20 June, 1779, and on that day the first church was established on the island. This congregation met in the home of Grace Powell at Lower Trefollwyn in the parish of Llangefni. A second meeting place was soon licensed at Clwchdernog Hir. A proper chapel building, which was named Ebenezer, was opened two years later, and in 1791 Christmas Evans became its pastor.

Two more churches were gathered at Beaumaris in 1785 and at Llanfachreth in 1787. Daniel Davies, Felin-foel, was an energetic servant in the mission from 1785, and Timothy Thomas, the former pastor of Christmas Evans, also participated. These men, along with others, were instrumental in leading many to Christ. They spent a month or two, without payment, preaching the gospel in villages and towns with some blessing, often returning to re-evangelize the same area, and baptising those who were converted. As a result of their labours the Baptist cause in the North slowly advanced.

These forays, however, were transient, much like the efforts of the revivalists. They collected congregations and established a few scattered preaching stations, but failed to deal with the internal problems that then existed among the North Wales Baptists, who remained peripheral to the life of the Baptist denomination as a whole. Thirteen years after the missionary endeavours of Llewellyn and his associates, the number of Baptist churches in Wales was still pitifully small, scarcely fifty, and of those only nine were in the North. The North needed a permanent ministry from experienced men who were prepared to plant and maintain churches, and to dedicate their lives to that part of Wales. Instead, many of the ministers were young and often showed an immaturity hardly conducive to the stability of their churches. Many soon returned to the larger congregations of the South. An indigenous ministry was not achieved in the North until the second decade of the nineteenth century. However, with the ministry of Christmas Evans about to commence in that part of Wales, the cause of religion, and in particular the Baptist cause, was to receive a considerable boost.

Brethren in the ministry, this is our consolation. The Spirit that blessed the labours of David Jones, Daniel Rowland and Howel Harris, still 'dwelleth with you, and shall be in you'. O let us seek his aid in our holy work, and pray for his outpouring upon our congregations!

Delegates of the different churches, be of good courage! You may not have seen as many additions lately as in former times; but the Holy Spirit has not yet departed from the faithful. You have heard of wonderful revivals in America, as well as in some parts of Wales. The 'Comforter' is yet at work. The illuminator of souls is yet at hand. The office is yet open. The blessing is yet offered. O let us all pray for the Holy Spirit! Let us look for his coming! Let us wait for his salvation!

Christmas Evans preaching on John 14:16-17.[1]

5
Lleyn: A New Man and a New Ministry

On 9-10 June, 1789,[2] after the harvest, the Baptist churches of
South and West Wales assembled at Maes-y-berllan chapel in
Brecknockshire for an Association meeting, and 'The chief matter
under discussion on the practical and administrative side was
the evangelization of North Wales. Reports of the work already
accomplished were presented, but they all agreed that a settled
ministry was the great need of the land.'[3] Christmas Evans
walked all the way from Aberduar and arrived on the Tuesday
afternoon at Maes-y-berllan, prepared to read the churches'
letters and in the hope of being sent North to preach the gospel, a hope he had before occasionally entertained. This was
the first Association meeting he attended.

The ministers appointed to preach at the Association were:
William Williams of Ebenezer, near Cardigan, who preached
on Wednesday morning from Nehemiah 7:21; Caleb Evans,
head of the Academy at Bristol, who preached in English (Acts
15:9); George Rees, a minister of the old cause at Rhydwilym,
who preached on Thursday afternoon (1 Timothy 6:6); and
Benjamin Francis, Horsley, a prince among Baptist preachers,
who also spoke on Thursday afternoon on Romans 6:15. The
latter preached in English but gave a synopsis of his sermon
in Welsh. These four men were among the greatest Baptist

preachers of the time in Wales and Christmas Evans must have
profited from their ministries. He also heard David Evans, the
minister at Maes-y-berllan, on the Thursday morning.[4]

During the meeting Christmas Evans met several preachers
from North Wales, including Thomas Morris of Anglesey; little
William Roberts of Galltraeth, Lleyn; and the man who in years
to come was to exercise such an influence over him, John Richard Jones, a powerful orator and a follower of Sandemanianism
later in the century. These men explained to him the field of
labour open in the North and the great shortage of gospel
preachers. On the recommendation of his pastor Timothy Thomas and of others who had heard glowing reports about his
preaching, they urged him to return with them. With much trepidation, but without a thought of returning home to bid farewell
to his friends, he consented to accompany them. They went
through Merionethshire, where J. R. Jones left the party, and
then into Caernarfonshire, where he preached in Cricieth with
Williams of Cheltenham. He arrived at the extreme corner of
the country called Lleyn in July 1789. All was not well though,
for in spite of a pleasant journey, with opportunities of preaching in the different churches along the way, 'The heavy burden
that lay on his mind, like the burden of Bunyan's pilgrim,
continued to oppress him.'[5]

Lleyn, in the north western part of Wales, is a wild, remote
but beautiful tract of country, about twenty-five miles long and
from five to ten miles broad, and surrounded by impressive
hills and overhanging mountains. In the latter part of the eighteenth century its inhabitants — described as 'ignorant, glutton-
ous, drunken and licentious', and 'religiously indifferent and
morally lawless' — were poor, illiterate and primitive in their
existence, making homes in huts and hovels, and following many
superstitious customs.

The Baptist cause in Lleyn, formed about five years before
Christmas Evans's arrival, was feeble and disorganised. The

mother church was Salem Ty'ndonen in the parish of Botwnnog, with branches at Llangïan, Rhoshirwaun, Galltraeth and Nefyn. There had been no minister at these places since David Morris left in 1785 for the church at Porth Tywyll in Carmarthen, and their small congregations were eager to receive the new preacher from the South. At each of the stations there was a place of worship and every Sunday, in an effort to preach throughout the peninsula, Christmas Evans travelled on foot from one to another. In the week he preached at midday or in the afternoon, as well as in the evening, so long as there was a congregation, large or small, ready to listen. He had few books to aid his preparations: the Bible, a borrowed Welsh-English dictionary, a Welsh translation of Bunyan's *Pilgrim's Progress*; and William Burkitt[6] on the New Testament, which he would study in bed at night, looking up the more difficult words in his dictionary, and which became so important to him that the residents renamed it Christmas Evans's *Barcud*.[7]

Within a month of his arrival he was ordained at Salem Ty'ndonen as missionary preacher to itinerate among the small churches. The public service was traditional, with the two officiating ministers, John Evans and Thomas Morris, at the time the only available ministers in the neighbourhood, laying on hands. Such an appointment was regarded by the few Baptists in the area as highly significant and indicative of God's blessing towards them.

From the beginning of his ministry in Lleyn he was invigorated and inspired, and brought into the light and liberty of the gospel. It was as if a new day had dawned upon his personal religion. His confidence in prayer grew and he experienced a deeper sense of rest and peace in Christ. He started to enjoy the Christian life, to judge religious matters for himself, instead of relying too heavily on the opinions of others, and to understand more fully his calling to preach Christ, although the old doubts continued to surface every so often. Through the study of the Scriptures, 'the last vestiges of Arminianism disappeared from his theology' to be replaced by the Calvinistic doctrines of grace. In a note on the margin of his MS, he adds, 'I then felt that I died to the law; abandoned all hope of preparing myself to apply to the Redeemer; and realised the life of faith and dependence on the righteousness of Christ for my justification.'[8] From that position he was pushed by a later controversy to adopt an extreme Calvinistic view before following the more evangelical stance propagated by Andrew Fuller.

A new power attended his preaching, which was to rest on him for the whole of his life, though it was obscured for a time during his involvement with Sandemanianism. He was vibrant and full of passion in the pulpit, with a strength and conviction in his ministry, overflowing with love, and anxious for the salvation of souls. His congregations, said one of his converts, Evan Evans of Llanarmon, would 'weep, cry out and jump up and down as though the world was bursting into flames around them'[9] and a revival of religious feeling awoke wherever he went. 'A breeze from the New Jerusalem,' he wrote many years later, 'descended upon me and on the people, and many were awakened to eternal life.'[10]

In a relatively short time the religious life of the district was changed from a cold deadness to life and power in Christ. He himself was surprised by the fruit of his labour, especially when those who came before the church as candidates for membership attributed their conversion to his ministry, 'because,' as he observes, 'I had been for three years preaching, and never had received any intimation that one sinner had been converted, and also on account of the old feelings of despondency and fear which yet occasionally troubled me; still I was obliged to believe, and it was wondrous in my eyes.'[11] His own ministry there, so he thought, was owned of God to as great an extent as any other place in which he subsequently laboured, perhaps with the exception of Caerphilly. It was to this period he constantly referred throughout his life. In a paper he contributed to the memoir of Simon James, which appeared in the *Welsh Baptist Magazine* for April and May, 1827, he compares his own spiritual renewal in Lleyn with the dramatic changes that took place in James's ministry, and explains why both of them received 'new power ... in the most discouraging place the Baptists have in Wales':

> It was in Caernarfonshire the great increase took place in his [Simon James's] understanding of theology, and in his power of preaching; and thus it should be considered a new era in his ministry ... It was in the midst of poverty and discouragement that the red leaves of the rose of James's ministry were unfolded; and it is marvellous to the writer to remember that it was in the same place, twenty-eight years before, that the Holy Spirit was pleased to insert the colour, to fix the form, and to mature the fruit of his own ministry. Whatever growth has taken place since, the form and the colour of the flower have remained the same... It was there the Holy Spirit put the cause of Christ in the heart, till we became distressed for the salvation of souls and the establishment of the Redeemer's kingdom upon earth. It is in proportion as we love Christ, and are jealous for his name, and have love to the souls of men, as two unquenchable flames burning in our bosoms, that we shall pray and wrestle with God for his blessing to give strength and authority to our preaching, and that grace shall be poured upon our lips until our words descend as dew on the tender grass.[12]

It was while at Lleyn that he had frequent opportunities of hearing several godly men, whose manner and spirit of preaching deeply affected his own ministry and prepared him, as a servant of God, for greater and more universal usefulness. He had always held in high esteem men such as Vavasor Powell, David Jones of Pontypool,[13] Daniel Rowland and Howel Harris, considering them as very able ministers raised up by God for the benefit of his church in Wales. He read the histories of Powell and Harris[14] and heard Jones and the aged Rowland preach, and they exerted 'a considerable influence upon his mind, and prepossessed him to a great degree in favour of a powerful, zealous and Scriptural ministry'.[15]

One major influence at this time was the renowned and learned Evan Richardson (1759-1824), a schoolmaster and 'practically the founder of the Calvinistic Methodist cause at Caernarfon'.[16] He was converted under the ministry of Daniel Rowland, and thereafter became a peculiarly tender preacher in his denomination. He was ordained at the first Calvinistic Methodist ordination at Bala, 1811. His short sermons, though soundly evangelical, were remembered more for their beauty and sweetness. Once, when he was preaching in Welsh at the Association at Bala, the whole congregation was bathed in tears as they listened to his address. John Elias was there, crying like a child, and Mark Wilks, who had come to the Association on behalf of the London Missionary Society, lifted up his hands in admiration, with tears streaming down his cheeks, though he understood not a word of the Welsh language! At Brynsiencyn, when Elias was 'pouring forth his vehement and dreadful words, painting the next world in very living and fearful colours, his audience all panic-stricken and carried along as if they were on the confines of the darkness, and the gates opening to receive them, a man, in the agony of his excitement, cried out, "Oh that I could hear Evan Richardson of Caernarfon but for five minutes!"'[17]

Another of these godly men was John Jones (1761-1822), Edern, a strong character of an original turn of mind, with a ready but rather satirical wit. He was converted after hearing David Morris at Amlwch and began to preach with the Methodists in 1784. When he was thirty-five years of age he married Mary Williams, the heiress of Pen-y-bryn, Edern, where he lived comfortably for the rest of his life.

Thomas Richards said of him that he never saw a man who looked so dignified and authoritative as John Jones. He was tall and of a strong build, of great power and readiness of speech, full of wit and humour, and of the most cutting and sweeping sarcasm... At times, when his wit tended to levity, he would suddenly check it, and the bright tear would twinkle in his eye, and he would bring the truth home to the breasts of his hearers with such power that many who came there for curiosity and pleasure left under deep convictions of sin. The first time he went to preach to Aberffro, Anglesey, 189 were added to the church. This was published and questioned by some. Upon this one of the converts himself came forward, and proved that the number was not 189 but 190.[18]

The man who most influenced Christmas Evans during his Lleyn ministry, especially his style of preaching, was Robert Roberts (1762-1802), 'one of the brightest stars of the Welsh pulpit'.[19] He was an extraordinary preacher, with extraordinary powers of oratory, and remarkable for the authority and effects that attended his ministry. It is said that he was capable of riveting the attention of his hearers simply by reading his text. He possessed great physical energy, a beautiful and penetrating voice, a fine memory, and a keen grasp of the truth, all of which were combined with wonderful dramatic and imaginative powers. Michael Roberts says that 'The most wonderful characteristic he possessed was the fiery enthusiasm of his spirit during delivery; the unction, the Divine light, and the downpour of the Holy Spirit, who fell upon himself and hearers; the fashion of his countenance, so suited to the words that his power was quite irresistible at the moment to every one in the place. I have often seen the congregation weeping, even to a man.'[20]

Griffith Solomon, who heard Roberts preach on many occasions, said of him: 'He was a bright, fiery star; in his ministry were thunder, lightning, rain and dew; he was a clear thinker and an able orator; his sermons were burning ones, and the

unction of heaven was in and upon them. Looking at his preaching in general, I almost believe that he excelled all the preachers I ever heard in this respect, though indeed, at times, some
could equal him in burning eloquence.'[21] Ebenezer Morris, a
powerful Methodist preacher of his time and a man who had
heard Daniel Rowland, enthused: 'If I had died without hearing Robert Roberts, Clynnog, I should have gone to the grave
without ever having fully seen the glorious splendour of the
gospel.'[22]

Here is a fine account of one of Roberts's sermons, written
by an old man to John Jones, Talsarn, in which the preacher
describes the final battle between Christ and the devil:

> Roberts had taken his position at the foot of Mount Calvary;
> he was looking at the champions in mortal fray, and as he
> looked he described to his hearers what was taking place.
> Gradually the sky blackens, the sun is hidden, and a cloud
> of darkness surrounds the combatants. Suddenly a deep
> gloom comes over the preacher himself; alarm and anxiety
> are traced upon his face, for he feels that the salvation of
> the world hangs upon that dread hour. He would ask the
> Saviour a question; but there is such a weight pressing heav-
> ily upon his spirit that he cannot think of asking him a word.
> 'Satan,' said he, 'what is the fate of the combat?'
>   'Fallen together!' he replies.
>   'Ah,' said Robert Roberts, 'Jesus still holds his ground,
> though the powers of hell are against him. Mighty Jesus!
> Mayst thou conquer, for our life depends upon the fortune of
> this day. Satan,' he asks again, 'what of the conflict now?'
>   'Fallen together again!' is the answer, but in a harsh tone,
> which the preacher imitates.
>   'Oh, thanks be to God! Our Jesus still holds his ground;
> and I almost think that the tide of the battle is on his side;
> and I gather from that gruff, grumbling voice that Satan is
> losing the day.'
>   Then he went on to show again what boundless interests
> hung upon the result of the struggle, and how a cloud of

deep anxiety had spread over the heavens, and what an absorbing, anxious interest Abel, Enoch, Noah, Abraham, Moses, David, and the prophets felt in the combat of the champions on Calvary. The hearers also had forgotten everything in their riveted attention, and they became anxious themselves to know the fate of the day. The preacher shouted again, 'Satan, is the victory thine?' But there was no reply. 'Satan, Satan! Take but a single second to tell me how the tide of battle turns.' But there was neither voice, nor any to answer.

By another sudden turn of alarm the preacher asked: 'What! is there none to answer? Have the two champions slain each other? Jesus, I am sorry to trouble thee for an instant, but tell us — art thou still alive? How does the victory turn?'

Upon this, Jesus cried with a triumphant voice: 'It is finished; I have trodden the winepress alone, and of the people there was none with me!'

Then the preacher gave a sudden shout of joy. 'Glory be to God — there is life eternal for me!' The congregation also responded with one accord.[23]

The dramatic effect of this kind of preaching is portrayed vividly in an account of what happened at Brynyrodyn when Roberts was describing, by means of an illustration of the sea, the alluring and enticing pull of sin, and how it creeps up on men unawares:

The day was fine and beautiful, the sands gleamed in the sun, and the tide was out far in the distance. A number of men, full of joy and glee, come upon those sands to play some wild game; they play on; the interest in the game increases; the players become more deeply engrossed; their enthusiasm is higher, and they are quite absorbed; they forget altogether that they are playing on the sands, and that the rolling ocean is not far away; the tide has already turned, and the lashing of the loud-sounding waves comes nearer and nearer. But they do not hear it; the tide rises and the sea has at last surrounded them, except at one point, where there is a narrow tract over which they may yet escape. Upon this a man upon the shore beholds their danger, and shouts with all his might, 'The sea is around you — escape by the tract of sand on your right! Quick, or it will be too late!'

By the vividness of the above description the hearers forgot the time, the place, and the circumstances altogether; they imagined that the tide was actually coming, and that the waves were rolling in upon them. They thought there was not a moment to lose; they rose in their places and ran through the doors. Many of them soon returned, however, and the preacher applied the above to the spiritual danger they were in, and exhorted them to receive Jesus Christ as their Saviour.[24]

It was the dramatic effect of Roberts's sermons, coupled with his bold and original imagination, that moved Christmas Evans to adopt a new style of preaching. Once, when he heard Roberts in a certain place, 'where he drew one of his graphic pictures, and made a bright light to play upon it, until the eyes of all the people were riveted in attention', he exclaimed after the sermon, 'I also could preach in that manner, but I never ventured; I shall try from henceforth.' He did try, and as a 'natural consequence of this change in tone and manner of his preaching, [even] great[er] success followed his efforts'.[25]

During his time in Lleyn he lost no opportunity of hearing Roberts, and in subsequent years, when asked about his own unusual way of preaching, he was always ready to explain:

I had the ideas before, but somehow couldn't get at them. When I was in Lleyn, the Methodists had a preacher of the name Robert Roberts of Llanllyfni, who was very popular, and there was a great deal of talk about him. Well, I went on one Sunday afternoon [to Rhydyclafdy] to hear him. He was one of the most insignificant-looking persons I ever saw — a little hunchbacked man;[26] but he neither thought nor said anything like other people; there was something wonderful and uncommon about him. This Robert Roberts gave me the key.[27]

Referring to these men, particularly Evan Richardson and Robert Roberts, Christmas Evans said, 'I reaped much advantage from hearing them, especially as it regarded my manner of preaching. Their ministry conveyed to me some spiritual taste, which I highly appreciated, and prayed for assistance to retain. Mighty powers accompanied them.'[28] He always spoke about them in this way. In a letter to his Methodist neighbour David Jones, dated September, 1834, he again acknowledged the debt he owed them: 'Perhaps you have not heard what I have said a hundred times to my brothers in the denomination to which I belong ... that it was by listening to Robert Roberts, Evan Richardson and John Jones (my friends) that I grasped ... the doctrine ... of grace founded on the merit of Jesus, the one through whom the powerful act of God did benefit and does benefit the souls of men.'[29] He thought that when able and anointed ministers such as these were called home, the churches were responsible to pray that the mantle of their gifts should be passed to others, as Elijah passed his cloak to Elisha; thus he said, 'These were my contemporaries, children of the same age; but they have been called home early, and I am still left on the field.'[30]

It was during the first year of his ministry on the Lleyn peninsula, which he often referred to as the most important of his life, that he met and fell in love with Catherine Jones, a poor and illiterate member of the same church. Catherine was born at Pwllheli in 1766 and converted when she was about nineteen. From the time of her conversion she experienced a deep sense of her own corruption, saw the 'indispensible necessity' of the merits of Christ for salvation, and realised the need for the renovating influence of the Holy Spirit in her life. She joined the Baptist church at Lleyn and was baptised by Daniel Davies of Llanelli, Carmarthenshire. She married Christmas in the church at Bryncroes on 23 October, 1789, in the twenty-third year of their ages and the people of the area gave them £15 as a wedding present. Christmas, in a tribute he wrote after her death, comments, 'In her the designation *help-meet* was signally verified. Her husband must long remember her affectionate kindness in straits and difficulty.'[31]

It is alleged by some that on his journey north Christmas Evans consulted a fortune teller, who, having been informed by one of his travelling companions of his bachelor status, prophesied that he was moving north in search of a church and a wife, whom she described in great detail. Catherine Jones, according to the story, fitted the gypsy's description.[32] Whatever the truth of this tale, his new wife proved a faithful and compatible soul mate, prepared to endure every hardship occasioned by her devotion to Christ and to her husband. She was kind, thoughtful and generous in her dealings with others, in spite of subsisting on meagre rations of oatmeal, buttermilk and potatoes. 'It is almost incredible,' says Christmas in his tribute, 'that she should have been so extensively charitable, when her husband's income never surpassed *thirty* pounds a year. What food she gave away to poor children and needy folks! Garments to poor members of the church! Money and bread to thousands of Irish labourers, who passed her door on their way to and from the English harvests! Her house was always open to itinerant ministers, and she readily administered to them with her own hands.'[33] Once Christmas responded playfully to her promptings to tend the garden by saying, 'Catherine *fach*, you never mind the potatoes; put your trust in Providence and all will be well.' She calmly replied, exhibiting her strong common sense, 'I tell you what we'll do, Christmas. You go and sit down on top of Moel y Gest, waiting for Providence, and I'll go and hoe the potatoes; and we shall see to which of us Providence will come first.'[34] Needless to say, after such a gentle rebuke, he hurried to perform his duty.

After his marriage the ministerial responsibilities of the churches increased markedly. These extended over a large area and kept him from home night after night. He often preached five times on the Sabbath, walking in all weathers from Llangïan to Ty'ndonen and from Ty'ndonen to Nefyn, and home again from Nefyn to Ty'ndonen, a journey of twenty miles. The Baptist cause in those parts, hitherto very weak, was greatly strengthened by his constant labours, which were rewarded with so little remuneration that he could barely exist. During his first year he baptised fifty people of all ages, but mostly poor, at Ty'ndonen, and eighty sought church membership the second year, though many of these actually joined the Calvinistic Methodists and some the Independents. Many years after he had left Lleyn one of the stewards of the Calvinistic Methodists there, testifying to the lasting change for good wrought in the lives of many through his ministry, told him at Nant, 'Your spiritual children are with us in great numbers in our societies unto this day.'[35] Eventually the strain of the work told and in the second year of his settlement in Lleyn he suffered exhaustion and ill health. His friends feared consumption, but he was spared.

Surprisingly, in this weakened condition, he embarked in 1791 on a long preaching tour to South Wales, hoping the journey and a different sphere of labour among old friends would benefit his health. He could not procure a horse for the journey, as the societies he served were very poor, so he set out on foot, preaching at least once a day, often twice and occasionally three times, in every town and village through which he passed. He probably followed the usual practice of the time and notified beforehand the churches along his route about his visit. Though he preached acceptably at these stations, there is no report of any extraordinary effects accompanying his ministry until he reached South Wales.

While he was heading for Beddgelert, somewhere between Pont Aberglaslyn and Maentwrog, probably on his first journey to South Wales, the following incident occurred. It is not possible to determine exactly when it happened, except to say that it took place while he was living in Lleyn, for it was in Lleyn that his preaching was so thoroughly transformed. The horse that is mentioned was probably borrowed by him somewhere along the way:

> He was starting upon a distant journey to preach the gospel, and he was greatly pained in his mind by the thought that he had not been called by heaven to the great work of the ministry. He was going on thus when this anxious fear pressed upon him heavier and heavier, so that, at last, he ... retired into the field to pray and to wrestle with God. After the struggle was over he felt himself a new man. Great peace and consolation took possession of his mind ... he preached with great delight and with new power.[36]

Some years later, while passing the spot where God had met him and dissolved his fears, he described the incident to his friend and travelling companion, Manuel Evans, a Calvinistic Methodist preacher, who observed, 'The effect of this holy conversation abode on my spirit during the whole of my journey, and yet recurs at times.'[37] Christmas Evans looked back and said:

> Although I had the gift of speaking, and was thirsting for knowledge that I might be able to teach others, and multitudes were eager to hear me, my fears pressed so heavily upon me that I dismounted, fastened my horse, and went into a field close by, which I will just now point out to you; for as I draw near the place I recollect it more vividly. Whether anyone saw me I heeded not, because the end of all things, as it were, had come upon me. However, God had mercy on my poor soul, and I received Jacob's blessing, dear brother; yes, I saw, as it were, the heavens open. When I arose, I

started on my journey, and the smiles of the Heavenly Spirit
lighted up my way for the space of two months. I have since
that occasionally had my doubts and fears; but the fear I
had not been called to the ministry never afterwards so troubled me. I have not the slightest doubt but that it is my duty
to put forth all my power in the ministry as long as I live.[38]

During the tour he visited Aberystwyth, Newcastle Emlyn,
Cardigan, Pen-parc and Blaen-waun, as well as Newport,
Fishguard and Tabor in Pembrokeshire. Many had never heard
of him, yet they were amazed at the power and authority of his
message, and the doctrines he preached with such rousing and
stirring effect. Old acquaintances regarded him as a new man,
and stood dumbfounded as a great awakening followed wherever he went, especially in the neighbourhood of Cardigan,
where the churches enjoyed larger congregations for a year
afterwards.[39] If it was announced he was preaching, thousands
would gather, filling chapels and graveyards, with many following him from one service to another for many miles. Scores
were converted, and the power of the preached Word and the
effect it had on the crowds was extraordinary, as he himself
describes:

I now felt a power in the word, like a hammer breaking the
rock, and not like a brush. I had a very powerful time at
Cilfowyr, and also pleasant meetings in the neighbourhood
of Cardigan. The work of conversion was progressing so
rapidly and with so much energy in those parts, that the ordinance of baptism was administered every month for a year
or more, at Cilfowyr, Cardigan, Blaen-waun, Blaen-y-ffos,
and Ebenezer, to from ten to twenty persons each month.
The chapels and adjoining burying grounds were crowded
with hearers of a weekday, even in the middle of harvest. I
frequently preached in the open air in the evenings, and the
rejoicing, singing, and praising would continue until broad
light the next morning. The hearers appeared melted down
in tenderness at the different meetings, so that they wept

streams of tears, and cried out in such a manner that one might suppose the whole congregation, male and female, was thoroughly dissolved by the gospel. 'The word of God' was now become as 'a sharp two-edged sword, dividing asunder the joints and marrow', and revealing unto the people the secret corruptions of their hearts.

Preaching was now unto me a pleasure, and the success of the ministry in all places was very great. The same people attended fifteen or twenty different meetings, many miles apart in the counties of Cardigan, Pembroke, Carmarthen, Glamorgan, Monmouth, and Brecknock. This revival, especially in the vicinity of Cardigan, and in Pembrokeshire, subdued the whole country, and induced people everywhere to think well of religion. The same heavenly gale followed down to Fishguard, Llangloffan, Little Newcastle, and Rhydwilym, where Mr Gabriel Rees was then a zealous and powerful preacher. There was such a tender spirit resting on the hearers at this season, from Tabor to Middlemill, that one would imagine, by their weeping and trembling in their places of worship, and all this mingled with so much heavenly cheerfulness, that they would wish to abide for ever in this state of mind.[40]

It was common for him after the sermon to close the services with a short prayer and a single verse from a well-known hymn, usually written by Williams of Pantycelyn, which he gave out from memory. He would then remain standing during the singing before dismissing the crowd. As he had originally hoped, the tour to South Wales revitalised his soul and invigorated his body. With the effects for good that accompanied his preaching and partly because these tours became an annual event, it did not take long for his fame to spread throughout the Principality, and in a short time he acquired a greater popularity in Wales than any other minister of his day.[41]

He returned to Lleyn with great strength and confidence in God, yet the work among the Baptists there did not progress as quickly or as smoothly as he had hoped. Many who were blessed under his ministry decided not to join the Baptists, preferring to attach themselves to the flourishing, older and more established Calvinistic Methodist chapels, which discouraged their 'spiritual father' considerably. This decision by the majority of his converts was partly because many of them were either the children of Methodist parents or servants in Methodist families, so it was only natural for them to join that denomination; and partly because, as Christmas Evans himself admits, in his zeal for evangelism, he 'neglected to consolidate them into specifically Baptist congregations. Only later did he emphasise a separate denominational ecclesiology.'[42] If the reasons above are coupled with his own inexperience and autocratic style of leadership, the disunity and confusion that prevailed among the few Baptist churches of that district, and 'the dogmatic, angry and unevangelical manner in which they defended their distinctive principles',[43] it is evident that not only was his tender spirit badly affected, but his influence for good restricted; thus, prompted by the leading of God, he began to search for a wider and more prosperous field of labour.

Many years later, in his *Autobiographical Sketches*, he refers to his departure from Lleyn:

I must now refer to my departure from Caernarfonshire. I thought I saw symptoms of the Divine displeasure on the Baptists there. It cannot have been on account of new doctrines preached among them; for those were the same as the Methodists maintained, and they were numerous and orderly in that county. The difference referred to baptism only; and there, in my conscientious judgement, we had the advantage; and I believe the Lord was not displeased with us for administering baptism aright and in the name of the Trinity...

The following three things have borne down our interest in Caernarfonshire: The want of practical godliness in some of the preachers that have been there; the absence of an humble and evangelical taste (spirit) in the ministry, and the

prominence of a sour, condemnatory temper, burning up
everything, like the scorching heat of summer, until not a
green blade is to be seen; and, lastly, serious defects of
character, both as to mind and heart, in many of the leading
members.[44]

So after two years in Lleyn he moved to Anglesey. Looking
back to his time in Caernarfonshire, he acknowledged, with a
deep sense of gratitude to God, the development of his own
ministry in that place and the many sinners who were converted
under his preaching: 'The form and taste of my ministry has
never been changed since I left Lleyn, despite all the revolu-
tions I have passed through. I highly prize the recollections now,
in my sixty-third year ... It is probable I never had the favour of
being the instrument to convert so many sinners, during the
same period of time, until 1829, at Caerphilly.'[45]

Salem, Ty'ndonen, where Christmas Evans was ordained.
During the first year of his ministry in Lleyn he baptised fifty
people at Ty'ndonen.

Where Druids dwelt, immersed in tenfold night,
Here the bless'd Gospel shed its heavenly light.
In Anglesey great CHRISTMAS EVANS woke,
And the strong chains which bound his soul were broke.

Forgive, good man, if I presume to trace
Thy former life, to magnify his grace
Who found thee fighting in Apollyon's field,
While Satan bid thy pride disdain to yield.

He saw thee madly breaking all his laws,
His mercy flew t'engage thee in his cause:
He saw thee half deprived of earthly sight,
And poured upon thy soul celestial light!

How vast the change! new clad in arms divine,
While grace and love his ardent zeal refine:
Though earth and hell his arduous way oppose,
Undaunted still the faithful champion goes.

With sin, eternal war he dare proclaim,
And hopes to conquer in his Captain's name:
Yet in the garden of the Church he's seen,
A towering Hollycock, bland and serene.

Long may he live to run the Christian race,
A striking trophy of victorious grace.

By a Lady.[1]

6
Anglesey: Pastor of 'The Dark Isle'

For some time before he removed to 'The Dark Isle', during the problems at Lleyn, Christmas Evans had looked for another field of labour, and, as he admits, 'prayed that God would send me to Anglesey in particular'.[2] He also received, what he calls, a 'providential intimation' that he should move to the island and serve the Baptist Church there, when a farmer by the name of John Jones, coincidentally a Baptist deacon at Llangefni, invited him and his wife to the island. As expected, he did not hesitate to go with him. He commenced the journey on horse-back, with his wife sitting behind him and their few personal belongings hanging from the side of the animal, on his twenty-fifth birthday, Christmas Day, 1791. His first Welsh biographer at this point notices his total separation from the entanglements of this world, which are but obstacles to a travelling preacher, and the submissive and faithful attitude of his wife:

> I cannot help perceiving the hand of the Lord, in keeping Mr Evans without the incumbrance of this world's goods, that he might respond with greater facility to his Master's call, wherever his work was assigned him. He was but as a pilgrim, without an inheritance in this world, which rendered

it a matter of very little inconvenience for him to take up the
furniture of his tent and follow his Leader, like Israel of old
the pillar that went before them. He was also blessed with a
companion particularly suited to his circumstances, always
willing and ready to accompany him wherever he was called
to labour.[3]

According to his own account 'The way was long and the wind
was cold ... it was a very rough day of frost and snow.' Some
time later he humorously referred to this journey as similar to
attacking the North Pole! With the Caernarfonshire mountains
and Snowdon on the right, watching over him all the way, and
the sea and the Menai Strait ebbing and flowing on the left, he
boarded the ferry to Anglesey and arrived, 'by the good hand
of God', in the evening of the same day, tired and worn, at
Llangefni, where he was to remain for thirty-five years.

In 1791, the island of Anglesey, a stretch of land twenty-nine
miles long and twenty-two miles wide, was regarded as one of
the most heathen parts of Wales with its exceptionally low moral
and religious condition. It would be no exaggeration to say that
iniquity flooded the land while a black cloud enveloped its
inhabitants in spiritual darkness and ignorance. The sin of
fornication was rife among the young of the lower classes, and
many illegitimate sons and daughters were born; drunkenness
prevailed; quarrelling and fighting were commonplace; and the
Sabbath was broken without any sense of shame. It was
particularly infamous for smuggling and for the earnestness with
which the locals plundered the cargoes of shipwrecked vessels,
pouncing upon the spoils like hungry beasts of prey.[4] It had
been little affected by the great evangelical awakening, and the
ministers, who were meant to be the shining lights of Anglesey,
joined the follies and corruptions of the age.

By the time Christmas Evans arrived on the island there were
among the Baptists ten preaching stations: two houses of
worship (Llangefni and New Chapel) and eight private houses

(Holyhead, Llanfachreth, White Chapel, Amlwch, Llanfair, Beaumaris, Pencarneddi and Llannerch-y-medd). There were a few members at each of these places, and all were members of the mother church at Llangefni; that is, all the Baptists in Anglesey formed one church. The members around Beaumaris had been constituted into a church in 1785, appointing Richard Michael as their pastor, and the church at Llanfachreth was received into the assembly two years later. With Christmas Evans's arrival the Llanfachreth church gave up its independence by joining with Cil-dwrn (Llangefni) as part of a single multi-branch Baptist church on the island. The church at Llangefni was gathered together by David Jones of Pen-y-garn and Stephen Davies of Carmarthen after a number of converts had been baptised by David Saunders (Aberduar). It is said that Jones and Davies celebrated communion at Trefollwyn farmhouse in the neighbourhood of Llangefni.

> The new church was received into the Association at Llanwenarth in 1780, and in 1781 the Association undertook to help with the building of a chapel for them and adjured the churches [in the South] to direct their contributions to one of three, William Williams, David Evans or David Jones. The chapel was opened that same year and named 'Ebenezer'[5] out of respect for William Williams, minister of Ebenezer, Dyfed. This was of course the church which met at Cildwrn on the outskirts of Llangefni.[6]

The Baptist societies, though closely connected with each other, were in a lukewarm and chaotic condition, and distracted from their primary task of preaching Christ by theological arguments. From his base at Llangefni Christmas Evans endeavoured to restore order and unity to the whole island. The only other minister of note was Richard Michael, already mentioned. According to Christmas Evans, he was 'extremely industrious and faithful ... and was considered by many to be a good man'.[7]

Cil-dwrn Chapel, Llangefni.

Plaque on the front of Cil-dwrn Chapel.

Unfortunately he departed for Pennsylvania at the end of the century. Six other Baptist leaders were mentioned by Christmas Evans: 'One joined the Methodists, another left the island, two were unpopular and ineffective preachers, and the remaining two lost their positions because of apostasy.'[8]

Llangefni itself was made up of only a few scattered houses, each consisting of just one room, where the members of the family lived and died. In this one room 'All the washing, cooking, baking, weaving, spinning and dyeing were done. Hidden away in corners were the few belongings necessary to live, while under the rafters hung dried fish, salted meat and bacon, and the herbs so necessary to flavour the meals.'[9] Cil-dwrn chapel, with its small pulpit perched on top of narrow stairs, stood on a bleak and exposed piece of ground, with a good view of the surrounding neighbourhood. Adjoining the chapel was a small cottage or, more properly, a hut for the minister and his wife. It contained several pieces of ageing and broken furniture: a table, two chairs and a bed that had to be supported by stone slabs. Some of the floorboards had rotted away and in their place lay a pile of bare stones. The door through which the couple entered the cottage was old and decayed, and afforded little shelter from the wind and rain, and the frugal congregation saved the expense of a new door by nailing a tin plate across the bottom of it for added protection against the elements. The roof was so low that the master of the house, who was of commanding stature, could barely stand upright and he often knocked his head. The stable, which housed the preacher's horse, was slightly separated from the cottage, and on Sundays it was used by those members of the congregation who rode to the meetings.

The first permanent Baptist minister of Cil-dwrn was Seth Morris from Newcastle Emlyn in the South, a godly and humble man, who was accounted by many in Wales as 'a man of sterling worth and a zealous and powerful preacher'.[10] He was appointed pastor of the new converts in 1783. (Until that time the island's congregations had been served by missionaries from the South.) Matters were going well until he invited Thomas Morris, also from South Wales, to serve as his assistant. 'A more gifted man than the pastor, Thomas Morris's popularity alienated one faction among the members, who saw his success as a threat to their pastor's authority. Polarisation occurred and much acrimony, which led, his faction claimed, to Seth Morris's death in 1785.'[11] Christmas Evans says that 'Mr [Seth] Morris died soon, as it is thought, of a broken heart; owing to another minister ... occasioning great confusion, and ultimately dividing the church. This was like the nipping frost in the month of May, and effectually checked the growth for a season.'[12] It was a wound to the cause of Christ that 'required more than ten years to heal, besides a great deal of fasting and prayer'.[13] After the pastor's death, the field was free for Thomas Morris. He married in 1787, accumulated heavy debts thereafter, and was forced to leave the island. He emigrated to America, where he died. The congregation fell away and the spiritual progress made under the ministry of Seth Morris evaporated, leaving a dismal state of affairs. In later years, after he had established 'unity in the church between the factions', Christmas Evans referred to his 'many ... labours to restore peaceful relations between the various groups and put an end to the disputes ... whose memory and impressions remain like smallpox scars on the face of the cause'.[14]

It was into this atmosphere of partisanship and conflict, that had driven away many hearers and brought the work into disrepute, that Christmas Evans set about his task with vigour and earnestness. One of his first initiatives was to appoint a day of humiliation for the unhappy divisions in the churches and to fast and pray for God's favour and peace, and the restoration of his blessing. The meeting was held at Llannerch-y-medd, where the preaching services were usually held. 'We confessed our sins, which had dishonoured the glorious Name, and we had strength in some degree to give our hearts to God, and to lay hold of his covenant. The consequence was, that God's merciful hand was upon us, and we received into fellowship twenty or more persons every year for some time afterwards.'[15] Some, who had previously been reticent to get involved, were heard to say, 'We will go with you, for we have heard that the Lord is with you.'

Christmas Evans proceeded to divide the island into four districts so that by preaching in three places every Sabbath, each of the congregations would have at least one Sabbath service a month. During weekdays he preached and held a conference meeting in each district every two weeks. This method he pursued for about twenty years and thereby doubled the number of preaching stations. He also encouraged each congregation to hold a weeknight *seiat*, or fellowship meeting, believing that 'The particular fellowship of the saints is a special means of strengthening by corporate prayer and delighting together in the things of God. These kinds of meetings are highly valued by those who love the presence of God and the powerful effects of godliness.'[16] He was often away from home for up to five nights a week conducting these meetings. In addition, he found time to attend to church affairs, to visit the needy, and, when the membership increased, he explored the possibility of building chapels to accommodate the growing numbers.

For all his work he was paid only £17 per annum, although this was raised to £30 in later years. In his MS he notes his salary without any additional comment, happy as he was to 'serve Anglesey' in poverty. Occasionally, because of his extreme poverty, he received a small gift from his friends in South Wales when he was on a preaching tour in that part of the Principality, but it was rarely enough.

> The ... preacher could hardly keep body and soul together, and had it not been for frugality and patience exercised by his good wife, it would have been much more hard upon them to eke out an existence. This giant in the church of Christ in his journeyings would receive a little help through kind friends for his own sustenance.... By this means the old patriarch could get a decent suit of clothes to appear in the pulpit, when if there had been half the religious charity exercised that was due, he would have kept above reach of the enemy *Want*, causing his heart to ache from time to time.[17]

Occasionally he wrote and printed a small pamphlet, which he was obliged to sell away from home to gain a little extra money for necessary expenses, and which became a mode of conveying knowledge to his countrymen. Once he reckoned 'He had published some twenty books which he and his wife used to cart around. He expected a profit of £20 from an edition of 2000 sixpenny books and £50 from a similar number of shilling books.'[18] Of the two principal benefits occasioned by these 'selling' trips, he remarks: 'One was the extension of my ministry, so that I became almost as well known in one part of the Principality as the other; and secondly, [God] gave me the favour and the honour to be the instrument of bringing many to Christ, through all the counties of Wales, from Presteigne to St David's, and from Cardiff to Holyhead. Who will speak against a preacher's poverty, when it thus spurs him to labour in the vineyard?'[19]

From 1792-1826 he served many congregations and preaching stations, but when these became too numerous for him to shepherd single-handedly, he endeavoured to place resident pastors over some of them while remaining as general supervisor over all. Some of the pastors and congregations did not take kindly to this new form of imposed government and, as shall be seen, they stirred up considerable trouble for him, which eventually led to his departure from Anglesey.

During his Anglesey pastorate, whether at home or on a

preaching tour, Christmas Evans read constantly, and would take up with delight any interesting volume that came his way, sometimes meditating on it for hours while cutting peculiar marks on his chair with a penknife. At times these meditations were so intense and concentrated that he was oblivious to everything else. After he had learned to read English, the books in that language were avidly read by him. 'His authors were selected with prudent discrimination and pursued with earnest attention, indicating an intense desire to be thoroughly furnished for his work ... He was extensively acquainted with the best theological writers of the age and quoted them frequently in his discourses.'[20]

Although he read theological works from all schools, his favourite authors were John Owen, the Reformed theologian, whose works he admired to the end of his days; and John Gill, the Baptist minister and Biblical scholar. The former helped to shape his theology, the latter influenced his ideas about the exposition of Scripture. Once, when talking to Robert Hall[21] about the copiousness of the Welsh language and his admiration for John Gill and his works, he wound up by expressing a wish that Gill's works had been written in Welsh. Robert Hall, who did not share his brother's admiration, replied, 'I wish they had, sir; I wish they had with all my heart, for then I should never have to read them. They are a continent of mud.'[22] Robert Hall's comments did not affect Christmas Evans's enthusiasm unduly, for he went on, with Joseph Harris and Titus Lewis, to translate part of Gill's *Commentary on the New Testament* into Welsh. Lewis, the editor and corrector of the proof-sheets, died after *Acts* was completed and so no more appeared.[23]

Christmas Evans's own library was never large but his choice of reading, which he used to good effect in his sermons, was broad and imaginative. He was keenly interested in Oriental manners and customs, became well acquainted with the various movements in African and American life, and, in later years especially, possessed a good grasp of Egyptian, Greek, Roman, Asiatic and European history. He was familiar with Welsh hymns, the songs of William Williams, Pantycelyn, being among his favourites. He enjoyed Welsh poetry, occasionally tried his hand at an *englyn* (a Welsh alliterative stanza), translated Shakespeare, Milton, Cowper and Young, modelled his language on the lines of the renowned lexicographer and grammarian William Owen Pughe, and was particularly fond of tracing the rise and fall of empires. In a sermon on Daniel 2:44-45, while stressing the eternal nature of the Messiah's kingdom, he cried:

> Where now are the illustrious empires of Babylon and Persia and Greece and Rome? Where are the Pharaohs, the Ptolemies, the Alexanders, the Caesars, the Napoleons, whose voice terrified nations, and whose tread shook the world? Where — with all their power and splendour, their iron sceptres and golden crowns? Gone; mouldering in the dust; and their magnificence nourishes the worm. They are utterly demolished, and shall rise no more. But the King of Zion liveth through all time … 'His kingdom is an everlasting kingdom, and of his dominion there shall be no end.'[24]

He rated Robert Haldane's *Exposition of the Epistle to the Romans* as one of the best commentaries he knew and unhesitatingly recommended it to other ministers. He enjoyed the commentaries of the American scholar, Moses Stuart, and one of his most treasured possessions, which he learned to use in both languages when he was about forty, was *A Greek and English Lexicon to the New Testament* by John Parkhurst, in the back of which he wrote: 'Gracious smiles of Divine Grace in the life of publick worship. O let us be favoured with them through our Divine Redeemer that we may go in.' In addition, 'T he writings of Andrew Fuller modified the rigidity of his earlier Calvinism, and he was very appreciative of the *Essays* of John Foster … As we should expect, he greatly admired the work and was a diligent student of John Bunyan ... Nor must we forget that he achieved a working knowledge of Latin, Greek and Hebrew,'[25] a pursuit he only relinquished on account of advanced age. This insatiable desire he had for knowledge, ever urging himself on to learn more, was not simply for knowledge's sake, but to achieve more accuracy in teaching and greater power in the pulpit. He was never completely satisfied with what he attained, and every attainment was the subject of much after-reflection.

In old age he passed on the lessons and practices of a lifetime to other less experienced ministers, advising them to develop their own spiritual habits. To Rhys Stephen, a young man who was just entering the ministry, he spoke a word of caution:

All the ministers I have ever known, who have fallen into disgrace or into uselessness, *have been idle men*. I never am much afraid of a young minister when I ascertain that he can, and does, *fairly sit down to his book*. There is Mr —, of whom we were talking just now, a man of such unhappy temper and who has loved for many years to meddle in all sorts of religious disputes and divisions. He would have long ago been utterly wrecked had not his habits of industry saved him. He has stuck to his book and that has kept him from many dishonours which, had he been an idle man, must have by this time overwhelmed him. An idle man is in the way of every temptation; temptation has no need to seek him; *he is at the corner of the street ready and waiting for it.* In the case of a minister of the Gospel, this peril is multiplied by his position, his neglected duties, the temptations peculiar to his condition, and his own superior susceptibility. *Remember this — stick to your book.*[26]

He was eminently a man of one book, the Bible, which he valued as supremely important and beyond the usefulness of all others. To him the Bible was 'a most wonderful book. It came to us from heaven, and is stamped with the Spirit and the character of heaven ... It is the sword of God, by which he conquers the nations — the instrument of his grace, by which he renovates the world ... it is more than a match for the cunning and prowess of the Prince of Darkness and his hosts.'[27]

He searched the Scriptures for hours in preparation for preaching, and his sermons are full of Biblical quotations, sometimes filling whole paragraphs, and 'even that lofty imagery which constituted the peculiar charm of his ministry was ordinarily but an amplification of Scriptural tropes [metaphors] and descriptions'.[28] In a sermon he prepared for the press he describes, with his usual imagery, how he 'trembled' before the word and how the 'two-edged sword ... penetrated into my heart':

> Though thou hast slain me, thou hast given me hope. Thou art the cause of terror to me, yet thou givest joy. As a sentinel from the eternal world thou standest over me with a drawn sword in thine hand; thou wanderest through every chamber of my mind, and all my hidden paths and ways are open before thee; I cannot continue in one sin, or omit any duty, but that I see the flash of thy sword. In my garden and my vineyard no weeds shall grow, and no grace shall wither without thy censure. Thus thou followest me like an invisible angel; when everyone is gone, thou art still with me. When I am on my journey, or when I am sitting and resting, thy naked sword alarms me; and yet, Oh Word of God, thou hast all the tenderness of a dear mother; thy wine cheers me, thy milk and honey feed me, and thy treasures enrich me. Blessed am I because thou art true; though I tremble, yet all my hope is in thee, and without thee I am in despair and cannot live.[29]

His love for the Bible, and hunger for knowledge in general, influenced those who sat under his ministry, as the testimony of David Owen (Brutus), a harsh critic of the Welsh nonconformist pulpit, bears out: 'The congregation of Cil-dwrn ... were, while under the oversight of Christmas Evans, very knowledge-able in the Scriptures. They had an excellent grounding in the Word generally, and were able to reason readily and proficiently on the various articles of the Christian faith. They were thirsty and seeking hard after knowledge ... They were great readers, with broad understanding. They were faithful, kind and ex-tremely amiable; simple and godly. They were Christmas Evans's people.'[30]

His great respect for the Bible included a desire for it to be read properly in public. In 1793 he was present at a monthly meeting at Cefnmaes, near Bangor, when a young man named Richard Jones was invited to read the Scriptures before the assembly. Jones read Psalm 24, but without feeling or empha-sis. After the service some ministers, who had accompanied Christmas Evans to his host's farm, asked him for a word of advice, and he instructed them not to neglect the public read-ing of Scripture. 'I was hurt,' he went on, 'to hear that young man butchering that Psalm tonight. He paid no attention to stops and no respect to sense. Brethren, stop him from leaving home until he has learned to read properly.' Before he could say any more someone nudged him and indicated that the young man was in the room. 'If he's present, bring him here, and put the Bible on the table.' For the next hour Christmas Evans carefully taught Jones how to read the Bible and advised him to attend a Sunday School class. Though Jones was somewhat embarrassed, he learned his lesson and in due course became a good preacher.[31]

In the early days of his Anglesey ministry, he found it hard to govern the Baptist assemblies with the tact and patience they demanded, tending to be overbearing and too dogmatic in his views. This, along with the opposition that inevitably arises when the Lord begins a work, brought him into conflict with others. His character was attacked and various rumours that cast doubt on the integrity of his purpose began to circulate. One of these rumours alleged that he was paid half a crown for each person he baptised. 'This falsehood he squashed in his own inimitable way. The opportunity arose when he was to baptise the wife of a farmer of some social standing. A large crowd had gathered for the occasion. Lifting up his voice the preacher exclaimed, "They say I receive half a crown for each person I baptise. That is not true. I receive a crown — not half a one. They shall be my crown of joy and rejoicing in the great day."'[32]

With characteristic boldness he was able to answer his critics and continue with his work. Slowly but surely he managed to re-introduce the habit of prayer among the members of his congregations, to establish a form of order under which the churches could operate, and, to some degree, succeeded in restoring public confidence in the Baptist denomination, which had been shattered by 'the Morris affair'.

The Associations had a greater effect upon Wales than the Grecian games had upon Greece. People from all parts of the country came to those games, it is true; and good opportunities for traffic were afforded to the merchants; and artists and literary men had the best means for making their works known. But they had no Gospel to infuse into the minds of the multitude; people could hear the poets sing of the exploits of heroes; they could see the pictures of painters, and other noble works of art. There was, however, no strong force present in these meetings, which, entering into the souls of the people, could work a thorough change upon them. Poetry and philosophy, art and learning of all kinds, have proved themselves in all ages utterly insufficient for such a task.

But in the Associations of Wales the Gospel was preached, that Gospel to which is mainly due the present state of civilisation in Great Britain and Europe. Christ and Christ crucified, and the doctrines of the Reformation, were the great themes of these Associations.

Owen Jones.[1]

7

Associational Preaching

With some satisfaction at the progress made on the island Christmas Evans embarked on his second journey to South Wales, preaching along the route as he had done before. On his arrival he found that the religious aspects of the churches and hearers had changed considerably. The enthusiasm and fervour that had marked his previous visit had been replaced by a dry and critical spirit due to a series of doctrinal contentions that had arisen. The principal agitator was the Welshman William Richards of Kings Lynn, in Norfolk, a General Baptist minister and a 'theological and political controversialist',[2] who fairly frequently visited his homeland. Having abandoned Calvinism quite early, he took every opportunity during his visits to propagate 'Pelagian or Arian sentiments, and at length succeeded in inducing several ministers and their congregations to secede from the Calvinistic Antipædobaptist Association, and set up a general or Arminian connexion'.[3] Christmas Evans remarked in a letter (8 January, 1813) to John Reynolds, minister of Felinganol, that 'There is a tendency in debating to turn *everything* into a debate, until it becomes Deism. I look upon W. Richards from Lynn and John Jones as men who have been led that way by contentious debate.'[4]

The disputes Richards introduced at this time compromised and engaged many of the ministers in the counties of Pembroke, Carmarthen and Cardigan, and produced among the people 'a habit of critical hearing', and a desire to learn more about the 'disputed points'. This censorious way of thinking was certainly not a favourable attitude with which to hear Christmas Evans, although, according to Rhys Stephen, the controversies 'proved most opportune and effectual means to recall attention to the fundamental truths of the gospel, as well as to modify and moderate the tone of preaching that was becoming rampant with high doctrines and an exclusive spirit'.[5]

Christmas Evans's expectations for the tour were greatly frustrated, but instead of losing heart he returned home all the more determined to revitalise the church in the North. To his surprise and obvious delight he discovered that while he had been away the Spirit of God had fallen on his people and stirred up within them a deeper interest in religious things, so that the meeting places, usually the district's farms, soon became too small to accommodate the growing numbers attending the services. Having seen the larger churches in the South, Christmas Evans decided to erect several chapels for his growing congregations, even though there was much ignorance among Baptists about chapel building and sufficient funds were not readily available. Economically it was not a good time to build. The island was in a state of depression, with soaring prices, especially the price of wheat, and fish was the only plentiful food. Many children were severely undernourished and disease was rampant. Nevertheless, at an Association meeting at Ebenezer, Anglesey, in 1794, a resolution was passed that 'Brother Christmas Evans be permitted to collect among the churches for a meeting-house at Amlwch'.[6] With his people's backing the pastor journeyed to the Association at Felin-foel, Carmarthenshire, in order to raise the necessary capital.

There were no more memorable days in the religious life of

the Principality than the days of the Association Meetings, which were held annually by all Dissenting bodies in Wales. Among the Independents and Baptists these meetings were unions of a number of churches in which on the first day, usually a Tuesday, doctrinal and practical issues were discussed, resolutions passed and proposals implemented. Only ministers and church members were allowed at these business meetings, which also provided opportunities for men from different parts of Wales to encourage one another in the work of the gospel and to explore ways of strengthening struggling churches. Christmas Evans, who 'believed passionately in the principle of assembling together and in the need for a close link between churches', regarded these meetings as opportunities for the members to affirm 'doctrinal accuracy and unity ... to counsel, teach and rebuke one another', and to enjoy fellowship.[7]

The whole of Wednesday was devoted to preaching, and the most popular preachers of the day were invited to speak. Up to 15,000 people, often including ministers from every denomination, gathered in a state of enormous excitement and expectation. To accommodate so many 'The church which invited the Association would take care well beforehand to set aside a field big enough to pasture 7-800 horses and keep it free of animals so that it would be well grassed.'[8] The services were usually held in the open air towards the middle of June and generally lasted for two days during which time no one worked. The preachers who attended prepared their sermons well in advance and used many opportunities to 'practise' them on their journeys to the chosen venue. Webber gives a good general description of these Association meetings and the preparations involved:

> For a week there were local services in all the churches. References were made in the sermons to the coming Association meeting and prayers were offered for it. Every house

in the village was put in order — rooms swept, windows washed, the exterior walls whitewashed, the thatched roof mended and flowerbeds weeded. Thresholds were scoured, hearthstones were whitened with chalk, and furniture was polished with beeswax. Every home was ready to welcome either the visiting clergy or else friends from nearby communities. A speakers' platform was built in a place where the sloping ground formed a natural amphitheatre ...

Wagons, carriages and farm carts filled the village market square, and the fields surrounding the village. Other people came on horseback and many came on foot. A preacher such as John Jones, of Talsarn, Herber Evans or William Davies could be depended upon to attract the entire population for miles around. It was not at all unusual to find three or four such preachers at an Association meeting and people walked as far as twenty miles to hear them, if a horse was not available ... There were often 10,000 to 20,000 people gathered at the preaching grounds ...

There were three sermons, any one of which could be a full hour in length. After an intermission at noon, there were three more sermons in the afternoon, and two or three more in the evening... These Association meetings were often unionistic, and Calvinistic Methodist, Baptist and Congregational clergymen all took an active part.[9]

In 1794, when the annual South West Baptist Association, comprising of about thirty churches, was held on 11-12 June at Felin-foel near Llanelli, there were only two or three Associations in the Principality. The South West was probably the largest among the Baptists, and there the churches had recently enjoyed a period of considerable growth, which had been aided by the adoption by many Baptist Churches of Methodist practices such as society meetings, an experiential hymnology and a new style of preaching. Christmas Evans had already preached at the Northern Association in 1791, the first to be held since the one Welsh Association divided, but there are no records of any unusual successes from his labours there. He had attended the Association in the South in 1792 and 1793, but it was in 1794, at Felin-foel, that he became a household name.

Although the distance was some 200 hundred miles, Christmas Evans set out on foot, preaching at various places along the way, and duly arrived on time. The meeting, which drew huge crowds from all over Wales, was held in the open air on a sloping field that commanded an extensive view of the surrounding country. It commenced at 10:00 on Wednesday morning — an 'oppressively hot' summer's day — with three consecutive sermons, a system that Christmas Evans later tried in vain to change. The first sermon was preached by David Evans, Maes-y-berllan, and the second in English by Benjamin Davies (Pembrokeshire). Christmas Evans, who was known only to the ministers present and in certain Baptist circles, was to speak last. The first two orators were long and rather tedious and 'the hearers seemed almost stupefied', which may partly be accounted for by the fact that a large proportion of the people in Carmarthenshire could not understand one word of English! Christmas Evans then rose and stood before the desk:

> His subject was the return of the Prodigal Son. With an abundant flow of beautiful language, with apt illustrations, and with great fervour and enthusiasm, he described, in a long strain, the mercy of God welcoming the sinner back to his home. The people, immediately after he began, collected together in a compact mass; those that were sitting on the ground at once stood on their feet. And with description after description of the return of the prodigal, the palace, the guest, the sumptuous feast, etc, a strong wave of emotion passed over the congregation; and there were tears and great joy, and loud praise; and these expressions of feeling continued for a long time after the preacher had finished his sermon.[10]

Another says that when he had spoken for about fifteen minutes, 'hundreds of the people, who were sitting on the grass, all at once sprang up as if they had been electrified', some weeping, some praising, some leaping and clapping their hands for joy, others praying in the greatest agony of mind. 'He was therefore under the necessity of giving over preaching, but the people kept up the meeting.' For the rest of the day and during the whole night, the voice of rejoicing and prayer was heard in every direction; and the dawning of the next day, awaking the few who had fallen asleep through fatigue, only renewed the heavenly rapture.[11]

Not everyone though welcomed this religious excitement. 'Job David, the Socinian,' who was present at the meeting, 'was highly displeased with this American gale,'[12] said the preacher afterwards to a friend; and a learned and judicious Baptist minister observed that he 'hoped he should never see Christmas on the second week in June any more'.[13] But the 'gale' was too strong and too heavenly to be counteracted or frustrated by prejudicious criticism. Instead, the outcome of this one sermon in so prominent a setting was that Christmas Evans became one of the most popular and well-known preachers in the Principality.

Although there is no written record of the sermon Christmas Evans preached on this occasion, it may interest the reader if a few extracts of a similar sermon on the same subject preached by him are presented. *The Prodigal Son* is considered by many as 'the masterpiece and most popular' of his sermons, and is included in *The Allegories of Christmas Evans*. It must be borne in mind that the written sermon is 'mainly a sketch and divisions, without the living details and the matchless similes, which its author produced when dealing with all subjects'. Neither is it possible on the printed page to 'convey to the mind of the reader an adequate conception of the burning oratory and the winsome voice that made Christmas Evans's hearers to lose themselves in ecstasy and praise',[14] though one example may aid the readers' imagination. Once when Christmas

Evans was preaching on *The Prodigal Son* and describing the bedraggled and wretched young man returning to his father, he suddenly pointed to a distant hill and exclaimed, 'There he comes!' Thousands of people in the congregation immediately turned to where he was pointing, fully expecting to see the 'lost son', in a 'rotten and tattered robe' that was 'not worth turning, washing or mending', and with shoes 'good for nothing but to be cast away',[15] trudging down the hillside.

Our extract from Christmas Evans's *Allegories* opens with the prodigal gathering all his possessions together and setting off into a far country: 'I imagine,' says the preacher, 'I can see him … going in search of a caravan to carry away his belongings, with horses and chariots, manservants and maidservants, starting from his father's pavement and bidding him farewell. The elder brother stood there decked in a one-breasted coat with a staff in his hand; and he in red-topped leggings, a vain fellow from tip to toe, extending a single finger to bid his father farewell.' He did not leave even 'a shirt button behind him, or any little box or trinket', but carried all away to a distant land. Soon the prodigal 'lost all'. He hired himself out to feed swine and hungered after the husks in the troughs. He had 'but one shoe to his feet, and a stocking on one leg, and an old cap on his head like a Turk's turban, as it had been picked up from the dunghill, and a one-sleeved coat about him; standing there with death-through-hunger engraved on his countenance'. In this miserable condition he received a letter from his father, 'which made him remember bygone incidents'. He trembled at the thought of opening it 'for fear his father swore in his anger that he should never be allowed to return to the old homestead'. Slowly he tore the seal. His father did not invite him to return home, but made it known that he was alive and that all the family were well-fed. 'Tears of joy trickled from his eyes, and fear and despair in the far country induced him to make up his mind to leave it.'

As his father looked out 'through the windows of the silver palace', he saw the prodigal a far way off, 'trying to get along against the wind and storm'. He cried out, 'I must go unto him or he will not reach home before the sun sets behind the walls of the city.' Oh! how nimbly his father skips over the hills and leaps over the mountains to meet him:

'I have sinned,' said the prodigal [upon their meeting].
'I know that,' said the father, 'and I can forgive and forget.'
'And I am no more worthy to be called thy son.'
'Your worthiness, my boy, is not required; I will do without it.'
'Make me as one of thy hired servants.'
'I will do as I please with thee, my son, far exceeding and beyond anything thou canst think.'
By this time his father had brought him to his door, ragged and wretched in appearance. It is probable, that he expected that one slice of the bread of life would have been given him as the first thing, for he was still in the pangs of hunger, but, as if the father said, you must come *into* the house and *to* the table, for it is not a custom of mine to bring bread outside ...

Before the son had a chance to protest further, his father summoned a servant, 'Go to the covenant jewel chest and seek a ring which will suit his finger, that will make him a king at once.' It is not necessary to measure his feet, for 'The shoes are ready in the garment house of the Gospel of peace.' They are bound to suit his feet, although they have 'broadened and swollen, in consequence of the cold and rough weather he experienced in the land of his prodigality'. 'Bring hither the fatted calf and kill it,' his father commands. 'Let us eat and be merry, for lo, here one of the heirs of life has been born again.'

Thanks or grace before the meal was said by the Father. A full dish was handed to the prodigal, saying, 'Eat unto satisfaction now.' I fancy he swallowed some bits with extraordinary relish, yea, even sweeter than the honeycomb. We see him wondering and his tears flowing; his father noticing his feelings said, 'Eat, my son.'

He raised his head, and gazed into his father's face, the tears continuing to trickle down his cheeks. 'Father!' said he.

'What now, my son?'

'I do not deserve this feast.'

'There is no need, my son, all is of grace.'

'I call to mind my disrespect towards you, father, in the far country.'

'All's well, eat now.'

'O, father, shall I remain with you for ever?'

'Who said otherwise to thee?'

'Wilt thou retain me here with a covenant and a rod, and the covenant without being broken?'

'Behold, I will, neither will I alter the thing that is gone out of my mouth...'

The prodigal tasted plenteously of the forgiveness of sins and peace with God, the remembrance of which is better than the wine of Lebanon, until the fear of the grave retreated from the room. Then the music and dancing began...[16]

It was this kind of preaching, all intertwined with gospel truths, that caused Christmas Evans's congregations to believe that they were actually watching the story unfold. They would see the prodigal leaving his father's house. They would follow him to the far country and return with him. They would see his father welcoming him home and, as eye-witnesses, partake of the feast, the joy, the singing and the dancing, forgetting all the while that they were merely listening to someone describing the events to them.[17]

Every summer Christmas Evans was one of the great preachers at the various Associations in Wales. From the records it appears that he was present at nearly all the meetings and as a result became honoured and loved by the masses, and the very mention of his name created great excitement. Between 1791 and 1836 he preached at the South Eastern Associations twenty-one times, and at the South Western Associations thirty-four times, as well as many times in the Northern Association, making in all a total of 163 public Associational sermons, which is more than any other of his countrymen. He has rightly been called 'the man for the whole of Wales'. Towards the end of his settlement at Cardiff, he wrote a letter to the Welsh Baptist magazine *Greal*, respecting the Associational Records that had been compiled at that time by W. Jones of Cardiff. In the letter he refers to his own Associational preaching in a relaxed and informal manner. After acknowledging the number of times he had preached, he humorously remarks, 'And if my brethren would present me with an Irish car, it may be that the Lord would strengthen me to preach at several more.' He continues: 'When I say all this, I do not glorify myself, nor do I "boast of things without my measure". It is wonderful to me, who am not deserving of the least mercy from God's hand, that I have run such a course.'[18]

In his day and as a result of his labours the Baptist Associations, particularly the one in Anglesey,[19] rose to great prominence and popularity, with the annual conferences becoming memorable occasions. It is true to say that 'He did not visit any part of Wales where he did not meet with some who claimed him as their spiritual father, the Lord having so extensively blessed his travelling ministry for the conversion of souls unto himself.'[20] Several of the most respected ministers that were ever known in the Principality came to the fore during this period[21] and 'He was in some measure, more or less, a blessing to all of them; he undoubtedly contributed to their vigorous and zealous exertions in the cause of religion.' One of these men justly observed, 'There is life and evangelical savour attending Christmas Evans, wherever he is.' 'None of us understand and comprehend the extent of Christmas Evans's usefulness,' said another.[22]

Presented below is an extended extract from another of Christmas Evans's Associational sermons, the *Demoniac of Gadara*, which in the course of his itineracy he repeated with considerable variations. It was heard at an Association held in the county of Carmarthen in 1817. Many sermons had already been delivered at the meeting, but with little effect. Christmas Evans then stood up and began to preach with the express desire of arousing the attention of the congregation. The result was astonishing. His text was: 'And when he went forth to land, there met him out of the city a certain man, who had devils a long time, and wore no clothes, neither abode in any house but in the tombs.'

He opened by describing the 'terrific' appearance of the demoniac, with his 'dreadful and hideous' screams, and his home among the tombs — 'not far from the turnpike road' — where, in the opinion of some, 'all witches, corpse candles and hobgoblins abide'. No one could clothe or tame him. He was the property of Satan, who 'thought the best plan would be to persuade him to commit suicide by cutting his throat'. So the poor demoniac was driven to find a sharp stone with which to end his life. It was during his search for such an article that he encountered the Son of God, who 'commanded the unclean spirit to come out of the man':

> When he saw Jesus, he cried out, and fell down before him, and with a loud voice said, 'What have I to do with thee, Jesus, thou Son of the most high? I beseech thee, torment me not.' Here is the devil's confession of faith. The devils believe and tremble, while men make a mock of sin and sport on the brink of eternal ruin ...
>
> Jesus commanded the legion of unclean spirits to come out of the man. They knew that out they must go. But they

were like Scotchmen — very unwilling to return to their own country. They would rather go into hogs' skins than to their own country. And he suffered them to go into the herd of swine. Methinks that one of the men who fed the hogs kept a better look out than the rest of them, and said, 'What ails the hogs? Look sharp there, boys — keep them in — make good use of your whips. Why don't you run? Why, I declare, one of them has gone over the cliff! There goes another! Drive them back.' Never was there such a running, and whipping and hallowing; but down go the hogs, before they are aware of it.

One of them said, 'They are all gone!'

'No, sure not all gone into the sea!'

'Yes, everyone of them, the black hog and all! They are all drowned! — the devil is in them! What shall we do now? What can we say to the owners?'

'What can we say?' said another.

'We must tell the truth — that is all about it. We did our best — all that was in our power. What could any man do more?'

So they went their way to the city, to tell the masters what had happened. 'John, where are you going?' exclaimed one of the masters.

'Sir, did you know the demoniac that was among the tombs there?'

'Demoniac among the tombs! Where did you leave the hogs?'

'That madman, sir —'

'Madman! Why do you come home without the hogs?'

'That wild and furious man, sir, that mistress was afraid of so much —'

'Why, John, I ask you a plain and simple question. Why don't you answer me? Where are the hogs?'

'That man who was possessed with the devils, sir —'

'Why, sure enough, you are crazy! You look wild! Tell me your story, if you can, let it be what it may.'

'Jesus Christ, sir, has cast out the unclean spirits out of the demoniac; they are gone into the swine; and they are all drowned in the sea; for I saw the tail of the last one!' The

Gadarenes went out to see what was done, and finding that
it was even so, they were afraid, and besought Jesus to
depart from them.

How awful must be the state and condition of those men,
who love the things of this world more than Jesus Christ!

The man out of whom the unclean spirits were cast, besought Jesus that he might be with him. But he told him to
return to his own house, and show how great things God had
done unto him. And he went his way and published throughout the whole city of Decapolis, how great things Jesus had
done unto him. The act of Jesus casting so many devils out
of him, was sufficient to persuade him that Jesus was God
as well as man.

I imagine I see him going through the city, crying, 'O yes!
O yes! O yes! Please take notice of me, the demoniac among
the tombs. I am the man who was a terror to the citizens of
this place — that wild man, who would wear no clothes, and
that no man could bind. Here am I, now, in my right mind.
Jesus Christ, the friend of sinners, had compassion on me.
He remembered me when I was in my low estate — when
there was no eye to pity, and no hand to save. He cast out
the devils and redeemed my soul from destruction.'

Most wonderful must have been the surprise of the
people, to hear such proclamation. The ladies running to the
windows, the shoemakers throwing their lasts one way and
their awls another, running out to meet him and to converse
with him, that they might be positive there was no imposi-
tion, and found it to be a fact that could not be contradicted.
O, the wonder of all wonders! Never was there such a thing!
— must, I think, be the general conversation.

And while they are talking and everybody having something to say, homeward goes the man. As soon as he comes
in sight of the house, I imagine I see one of the children
running, and crying, 'O, mother! Father is coming — he will
kill us all!'

'Children, come all into the house,' says the mother. 'Let
us fasten the doors. I think there is no sorrow like my sorrow!' says the broken-hearted woman. 'Are all the windows
fastened, children?'

'Yes, mother.'

'Mary, my dear, come from the window — don't be standing there.'

'Why, mother, I can hardly believe it is father! That man is well dressed.'

'O yes, my dear children, it is your own father. I knew him by his walk the moment I saw him.'

Another child stepping to the window, says, 'Why, mother, I never saw father coming home as he does today. He walks on the footpath and turns round the corner of the fence. He used to come towards the house as straight as a line, over fences, ditches, and hedges; and I never saw him walking as slow as he does now.'

In a few moments, however, he arrives at the door of the house to the great terror and consternation of all the inmates. He gently tries the door, and finds no admittance. He pauses a moment, steps towards the window, and says in a low, firm and melodious voice — 'My dear wife, if you will let me in, there is no danger. I will not hurt you. I bring you glad tidings of great joy.' The door is reluctantly opened, as it were between joy and fear. Having deliberately seated himself, he says: 'I am come to show you what great things God has done for me. He loved me with an eternal love. He redeemed me from the curse of the law and the threatenings of vindictive justice. He saved me from the power and the dominion of sin. He cast out the devils out of my heart and made that heart, which was a den of thieves, the temple of the Holy Spirit. I cannot tell you how much I love the Saviour. Jesus Christ is the foundation of my hope, the object of my faith, and the centre of my affections. I can venture my immortal soul upon him. He is my best friend. He is altogether lovely — the chief among ten thousand. He is my wisdom, righteousness, sanctification and redemption. There is enough in him to make a poor sinner rich, and a miserable sinner happy. His flesh and blood is my food — his righteousness my wedding garment — and his blood is efficacious to cleanse me from all my sins. Through him I can obtain eternal life; for he is the brightness of the Father's glory, and the express image of his person: in whom dwelleth all the fulness of the godhead bodily. He deserves my highest esteem and my warmest gratitude. Unto him who loved me with an eternal love, and washed me in his own blood, unto him be the glory, dominion, and power, for ever and ever! For he has rescued my soul from hell. He plucked me as a brand out of the burning. He took me out of the miry clay and out of a horrible pit. He set my feet upon a rock and established my goings and put in my mouth a new song of praise and glory to him! Glory to him for ever! Glory to God in the highest! Glory to God for ever and ever! Let the whole earth praise him! Yea, let all the people praise him!'

It is beyond the power of the strongest imagination to conceive the joy and gladness of this family. The joy of seafaring men delivered from being shipwrecked — the joy of a man delivered from a burning house — the joy of not being found guilty to a criminal at the bar — the joy of receiving pardon to a condemned malefactor — the joy of freedom to a prisoner of war — is nothing in comparison to the joy of him who is delivered from going down to the pit of eternal destruction. For it is a joy unspeakable and full of glory.[23]

On another occasion that Christmas Evans delivered this sermon his detailed descriptions of the scene were portrayed with such dramatic effect and illustrated so forcibly that his numerous hearers 'first became profoundly serious, then wept like mourners at a funeral, and finally threw themselves on the ground, and broke forth in loud prayers for mercy; and the preacher continued nearly three hours, the effect increasing till he closed'.[24] One who heard that astonishing sermon remarked that 'During the first half hour, the people seemed like an assembly in a theatre, delighted with an amusing play; after that, like a community in mourning, over some great and good man, cut off by a sudden calamity; and at last, like the inhabitants of a city shaken by an earthquake, rushing into the streets, falling upon the earth, and screaming and calling upon God!'[25]

It is hardly surprising that such preaching made him a household name throughout the Principality, moving men, in later generations, of the calibre of C.H.Spurgeon, to comment on how he 'aroused his audiences and flashed truth into their faces'. Spurgeon himself, at an early date in his career, so far succeeded in captivating the Welsh 'that one admiring ancient dame ventured the opinion that the London preacher only needed to be blind of one eye to take rank with Christmas Evans'.[26]

After the 1794 Felin-foel Association, the ministry of Christmas Evans flourished, and the Baptist cause advanced and prospered around him, blossoming 'beneath the genial showers of divine grace, like the garden of the Lord, and the sweet notes of the birds of paradise echoed cheerfully in all the plantations of King Jesus'.[27] All proceeded with heavenly blessing for a few years until, in the words of Christmas Evans, 'A black cloud arose on the churches of the North, and a destructive storm burst from it.'[28]

Those holding Sandemanian views are always opposed to warm, emotional preaching which has the effect of bringing people to a feeling, and a sensible knowledge, of the fact that they are sinners, and the terrors of the Law, and that they are to face a holy God, and that they have to be holy before they can face him. So it has this great influence at once upon evangelism and preaching.

D.M.Lloyd-Jones.[1]

In Wales J. R. Jones showed less concern for the lost after accepting the system. The same was true of Christmas Evans until his deliverance from it. Andrew Fuller believed that one sure mark of false religion was the concern to make proselytes rather than converts to Christ. Assessing the writings of William Braidwood he concluded there was no aim to promote the kingdom of Christ. This is in marked contrast to Christmas Evans, before and after his involvement with Sandemanianism.

Ian Childs.[2]

8

The 'Frigid Zone' of Sandemanianism

The 'black cloud' that Christmas Evans referred to was a controversy called Sandemanianism that was to shake the Baptist churches of North Wales. It had already spread its 'limping, unbalanced teaching'[3] among the Welsh Methodists in the 1760s, principally through the exhorter John Popkin, who had introduced the heresy at the Woodstock (Pembrokeshire) Association in May 1764. He was strongly opposed on that occasion by William Williams, Pantycelyn, who later compared Popkin and his followers to Lucifer, declaring, 'Proud Sandemanians, boasting their light and power, inflated like bladders with wind, until they burst and come to nothing.'[4] ·After disseminating his opinions in print, translating into Welsh the more important works of Glas and Sandeman, and, on his preaching tours, sowing discord and confusion in many of the societies, Popkin was expelled from Methodist ranks.

Sandemanianism is a set of doctrines named after one of its chief exponents, the Scottish minister, Robert Sandeman (1718-71), who was the son-in-law of John Glas (1695-1773), the founder of the sect; hence its followers are sometimes called Glasites. Glas was a devout and able man who taught that, as Christ is king of the church, magistrates and the state have no authority over her in matters spiritual, and therefore her civil officers have no right to prosecute people as heretics; that a national church has no warrant in Scripture; and that the two Scottish covenants, National (1638) and Solemn League (1643), lack Biblical support. *The Dictionary of National Biography* states that he opposed 'founding the church ... upon any act of Parliament, or covenant, formed by the wisdom of men', and supported the presbytery, who, he said, were 'subject to no jurisdiction under heaven'.[5]

In accordance with his literal interpretation of Scripture, Glas favoured separation of church and state, and a complete autonomy for each local congregation, though he regarded as utterly wrong any attempt to enforce uniformity in the church or to permit domination by individuals. In an effort to safe-guard the doctrine of justification by faith alone, he redefined faith as a bare intellectual assent to certain facts and discarded the Calvinistic doctrines of assurance and the final persever-ance of the saints, as well as the Methodist's view of conver-sion. He taught that the Bible does not authorize missionary endeavours, which inevitably led to a lack of evangelistic and missionary zeal among his supporters, and, in an attempt to return to the simplicity of Scripture, introduced into the life of the church some unusual practices.[6]

He expounded several of these doctrines in a major work entitled *Testimony of the King of Martyrs* (1727), which led to his deposition from the Church of Scotland the year after its publication. In 1733 he moved to Perth where he met Robert Sandeman, who in 1737 married his daughter Catherine. Two years later (22 May, 1739), as a tribute to his Christian charac-ter and service, the general assembly restored him to 'the status of a minister of Jesus Christ, but not to that of a minister of the kirk of Scotland, leaving him incapable of holding a charge in the church until he should have renounced such tenets as were inconsistent with its constitution'.[7] He had, however, become too settled in Congregational ideas to return to the Church of Scotland.

In spite of these unorthodox theological beliefs, Glas was a meek, gentle and cheerful man, who was not well-suited to controversy or to being the leader of the sect he had unwittingly founded. He never regretted leaving the national church, although the subsequent hardships he and his family of fifteen had to endure were sometimes severe. At such times he portrayed great fortitude of character. After the execution of the murderers of his son, his first thought was of the 'glorious instance of divine mercy, if George Glas and his murderers should meet in heaven'.[8] His writings are scholarly and gracious in spirit, although some of his extant correspondence shows that in later life he chose to be more controversial.

Unlike his father-in-law, Sandeman was an aggressive and contentious man, a born polemicist, who made a name for himself when he attacked James Hervey's book *Theron and Aspasio* (1755), a Calvinist evangelical work, in which the doctrines of the cross are illustrated and enforced in the form of dialogues. In his controversial reply *Letters on Theron and Aspasio Addressed to the Author*, which was published in Edinburgh in 1757, he not only set out his own position very clearly, especially with regard to faith — a position first propagated by Glas — but argued that Hervey's view made faith a work of man. He claimed that an intellectual assent to the work of Christ was sufficient for salvation and that all religious feelings or desires were unnecessary and to be shunned. He opposed all direct calls, warnings and invitations to the sinner to believe on Christ, teaching that faith is a mere passive reception of the truth: 'I would set before the sinner all the evidence furnished me by the gospel. Thus and thus only would I press, call, invite, exhort or urge him to believe.'[9] His main doctrine was that 'the bare death of Jesus Christ, which he finished on the cross, is sufficient, without a deed or a thought on the part of man, to present the chief of sinners spotless before God'[10] — a view that is summarised on his tombstone in America.[11] His work

The One Thing Necessary became the cornerstone of J. R. Jones's doctrine of faith.

A third man, notable because of his connection with Sandemanianism, is Archibald McLean (1733-1812), a one time member of Glas's church. In 1765 he left that sect and embraced Baptist principles. Although he rejected the label 'Sandemanian Baptist', he retained much of the Sandemanian teaching, writing in his treatise on the *Commission* (1786), 'Now when men include in the very nature of justifying faith, such good dispositions, holy affections, and pious exercises of heart, as the moral law requires, and so make them necessary to acceptance with God, it perverts the apostle's doctrine upon this important subject and makes justification to be at least *as it were* by the works of the law.'[12] 'A simple belief in the testimony of God about his Son' was his definition of faith, which he taught was 'an act of the mind ... and of that alone'. In practice he rejected calling sinners to faith and thought it was wrong to press repentance, though he did admit that if invitations were given, they should be given 'before and in order to believing'. He also supported the divisive proposition of uniformity of belief in the church, 'the concept that people of different judgements should not sit together at the communion table'.[13] He is regarded as 'the Father of all the Baptist Churches in Scotland' and, at least as far as seeking to re-establish the standards and practices of the Early Church are concerned, the principal influence on that denomination in Wales.

Although Sandemanians adhered to many of the orthodox Christian doctrines, they held erroneous views on the nature of saving faith, claiming that 'Faith in Christ was the revelation of truth to the understanding in which neither the will nor the affections participate; that the faith of Christians and devils differs only in its results, and that these arise from the nature of the truth believed.'[14] Their system, as it relates to the nature of justifying faith, was *the bare belief of the bare truth*. It regarded holy affections and pious exercises as 'works' and neglected the aspects of personal application of the truth to the heart and will. There was no need, in the Sandemanian view, for any sort of conviction of sin, because a mere unmoved acknowledgement of Jesus Christ as the Son of God was sufficient for salvation. 'Everyone,' says Robert Sandeman, 'who obtains a just *notion* of the person, and work of Christ, or whose *notion* corresponds to what is testified of him, is justified, and finds peace with God simply by that *notion*.'[15] In his book he writes that everyone who understands the apostolic report of Christ's finished work on the cross to be true, 'or is persuaded that the event actually happened as testified by the apostles, is justified and finds relief to his guilty conscience'.[16]

Christmas Evans, after his own deliverance from Sandemanianism, commented on the 'intellectual' character of this view of faith and its innate dislike of the life and spirit of true religion:

> I thought that its principal evil proceeded from the faith peculiar to it, which is faith in the intellect, without any spiritual grace communicated to the person by the regenerating influence of the Holy Ghost to produce this faith. The phrase 'believing with the heart' they would explain to mean simply the understanding. 'The design of this faith,' say they, 'is to exclude all the works of man in his justification before God.' Such faith views man believing in his carnal, ungodly state. That faith has taken place in the understanding — 'naked belief in the understanding', without grace in the heart. And yet the system acknowledges man, when believing, as having become really pious, and acceptable to God. Thus, faith in its effects, somehow changes man into a new creature: and man by some operation of his own, in his own intellect, constitutes himself a godly person.[17]

Christmas Evans then asked the question: 'Which is it that excludes human boasting, and magnifies divine grace the most?

Man, working himself by his naked understanding to believe, or the Spirit of God, enlightening him, and by its regenerating grace, imparting unto him a spiritual disposition to receive the testimony which God gives of his Son?' The Sandemanian faith is 'born in the head, contrary to the will, affection or heart; and ... it never loves to dwell in the chambers of holy joy, godly sorrow, flaming zeal, importunate prayer, and lawful exertion; but all of it is comprised in disputing in the head. It will dispute with all the Babylonians from morning till night, without being at all affected with a broken heart, and an afflicted spirit.'[18]

Inevitably Sandeman and his followers were against passionate preaching that excited congregations — the fire and the power of the Spirit were resisted and only the bare facts of the Christian faith, without emotion or warmth, were presented, leaving their hearers cold and unmoved. It 'chills one's feelings', says William Williams, 'until they despise heaven's pure breezes'.[19] A spirit of censoriousness and intolerance towards Christians of different persuasions developed, with the effect of dividing and subdividing churches into new communities. They became hard and exclusive in their attitude, and adherents of 'a religious ice plant, religion in an ice-house, a form chiefly remarkable for its rigid ritualistic conservation of what are regarded as the primitive forms of apostolic times, conjoined to a separation from, and a severe and cynical reprobation of, all other Christian sects'.[20]

At the time of the controversy Christmas Evans was the most accomplished and popular Baptist preacher in the North. The ablest theologian of that denomination, and one of the main proponents of the Sandemanian heresy, who assisted its spread to many parts of Wales, was John Richard Jones (1765-1822), a Baptist minister at Ramoth.[21] He was probably influenced by William Richards (1749-1818), Kings Lynn, who accepted Scotch Baptists' views about 1783. For most of the period 1795-1798 Richards resided in Wales, trying to battle through ill health and depression, and propagating the Sandemanian teaching. From 1799 to 1802 he lived at Parc-nest near Newcastle Emlyn. 'For at least twenty-four years before his death, Jones kept up correspondence with him, and when Richards died, Jones still possessed forty-four of his letters.'[22]

Jones had invited Christmas Evans to Anglesey and then risen with him to become the natural leader of the North Wales Baptists. There is little doubt that he was a man of outstanding ability and, even after his connection with Sandemanianism, 'There was,' according to Christmas Evans, 'a power and greatness in his utterance, which evinced him to be a person possessed of very respectable abilities.'[23] Robert Thomas, an Independent minister and tutor, calls him 'the greatest man ever nurtured in Merionethshire'.[24] *The Dictionary of Welsh Biography* says of him: 'To convince, to argue, to expound the Scriptures, to discipline the will — these were the outstanding characteristics of his teaching and preaching. It was in his nature to be positive, dogmatic, and certain of his own mind, but he was also strong in his convictions, self-sacrificing in his services to his people, and imbued with a profound piety.'[25]

However, Jones's intelligence was dry and hard, and too deliberately confrontational. 'If,' said he, 'every Bible in the world were consumed, and every word of Scripture erased from my memory, I need be at no loss how to live a religious life, according to the will of God, for I should simply have to proceed in all respects in a way contrary to the popular religionists of this age, and then I could not possibly be wrong.'[26] He was arrogant in tone and, in Christmas Evans's view, 'of a domineering disposition'. He 'could not brook opposition; his equal, much less his superior, could not have lived near him; Caesar-like in this respect, he would rather be a "sovereign in a village than a second in Rome itself"'. He quarrelled with his first and second colleague in the ministry 'because they presumed to oppose him in some of his dogmas', and it is likely

that he would have 'dissolved his connection with the Scotch
Baptists had he lived a little longer, because Mr W. Jones of
London dared to oppose his views of the Millennium, and the
personal reign of Christ with the saints on earth'.[27]

Between 1788 and 1793 Jones fully supported his denomination's efforts to evangelise the North, exhibiting no sign that
he was dissatisfied with the revivalist emphasis, and was well
on the way to becoming a popular preacher of the type he
would later despise. However, towards the end of that period
he began to feel increasingly uncomfortable at the emotional
scenes generated by revivalistic preaching, and so distanced
himself from the 'wild and lunatic passion' and 'the despicable
example of the Methodists', as he would later write. During the
North Wales Association at Glyn Ceiriog (June, 1793), he
became acquainted with Robert Roberts of Rhos-ddu, a
deacon at *The Old Meeting*, the Baptist church at Wrexham,
and an admirer of the works of Glas, Sandeman and McLean.
Roberts mentioned to Jones the anti-revivalist ideas held by
these Scottish nonconformists and helped him to acquire some
of their writings. At first he reacted cautiously to McLean's works,
but as he continued to examine them, he became 'very much
struck with them'. He 'read them again and again; lent them to
his friends, talked and preached their contents, and left nothing
undone to diffuse their influence, and gain converts to their
peculiarities'.[28]

The excesses of the revivalists, Jones believed, had infiltrated
the Baptists of the North and within no time he became an
outspoken critic of them. 'Now, which is the most dignified way
to teach men?' argued Jones. 'Is it by reasoning gravely and in
earnest with the understanding and conscience, or by ranting
and raving and drivelling and thumping the Bible like a
madman? I am absolutely convinced of the irrationality and
folly of such offensive practices.'[29] He was 'persuaded that Christianity was a minority religion and in order to retain its purity it

had to abstain from appealing to the indifferent multitude'. In a
letter to his cousin, David Richards, dated 3 December, 1794,
he writes: 'We should never expect the majority to respect or
accept our ministry for "the world loveth its own", and when a
preacher is acclaimed by the majority in general, we can be
certain that he is preaching something in addition to the truth.'[30]
By 1795 'His conversion from evangelical revivalism was
complete. He had accepted the Scottish doctrine in its entirety
and applied it to the church in his care,' attributing the cause of
this important change to 'the writings of our beloved brother
Archibald McLean'.[31]

On 19 January, 1796, Jones reported some success to David
Richards: 'The simple gospel of the New Testament is beginning to dawn in the numerous Baptist Churches in the North.
The deceit of Anti-Christ is being revealed and Babylon is starting to fall, and the leaven of truth is beginning to work all through
the dough.'[32] Later that year he opened a correspondence with
McLean, which lasted until the latter's death, and with William
Braidwood, McLean's co-pastor in Edinburgh, detailing the
progress of the new reforms in Wales and seeking additional
information on other aspects of their religious practices. The
first of these letters to McLean, written from Ramoth on
2 September, 1796, is given below in an abridged form:

DEAR BROTHER IN THE GOSPEL ...
   It happened to me about two years ago, under the direction of Holy Providence, to meet with some books published
by you ...
   In reading these books I was convinced in my mind, that
they had a tendency to lead the minds of men to the original
glory and simplicity of the gospel of our salvation; and I may
say, in truth, that they have been a great blessing to my
soul... I endeavoured to read and translate them to the
church... Now I have the pleasure to see the Great Head of
the church hath made them instrumental in a great many

instances, 'to draw the church's attention to that kind of Christianity which was at first propagated by the inspired apostles of our Lord Jesus Christ, according to the commission he gave them and which is transmitted to us in the New Testament...'

Our church meets every Lord's Day to observe the following institutions of Divine service, namely,

1. The public prayers according to the direction given in 1 Tim.ii.1,2,3.

2. The public reading of Scripture.

3. The singing of praise.

4. Preaching and expounding the word.

5. The mutual exhortation of the brethren.

6. The collection for the poor and other necessary uses.

7. The breaking of bread, or the Lord's supper. This we observe every Lord's day, instead of every month...

Please give me some instructions in your letter concerning the following things. They are not, as yet, solved among our church: —

1. *Washing feet*, according to John xiii.7-16. Some in our church think it a duty to be done one to another, and that only in case of necessity, according to 1 Tim.v.10; others think it an ordinance to be observed once by every member. What is right?

2. It does not appear that the seven churches of Asia had a plurality of elders. What do you think of that?

3. What do you think of anointing the sick *with oil*, according to James v.14-19?...

J. Jones.[33]

Jones devoted untiring energies to the propagation of these new principles and practices in an attempt to revert to the sacraments and rites of the Early Church; and the more firmly he embraced them, the more forthrightly he opposed the Methodist's view of salvation, which he claimed was a kind of justification by works, and the revivalism that had for years pervaded the country, especially the ecstatic *jumping* of the congregations. Being a man of learning, he exercised a profound influence within the Baptist denomination in the North. Between the years 1795 and 1798 he successfully infused 'the poisonous draught' into the minds of many of his brethren, both ministers and others, Christmas Evans included. He raged against the old Baptists, labelling them 'Babylonian' and 'servants of Anti-Christ', while declaring that 'All the false Christians are travelling an easy road to hell deluded by the popular preachers.'[34] Reformation, in his supporters' eyes, became more important than the salvation of sinners, preaching was used primarily to settle questions of church order and discipline, and bitter arguments of controversy erupted.

As the debate intensified and many rose in opposition to him, Jones complained that 'All the religious world began to calumniate my ministry as an heresy, charging the doctrine with some wicked and dangerous consequences.' He interpreted the outcry against him as an effort 'to work hatred and prejudice in the public against my ministry', so that no one would go and listen to him. 'The most general stigma fixed upon me,' he complained, 'was that of a *Sandemanian*, and the most successful too because that epithet in Wales has much the same import that the term *Samaritan* had among the Jews in our Lord's time; and is always used to frighten devout people, especially such as appear to be under any concern of mind about the doctrine, church order and discipline established by the apostles among the primitive societies of the saints.'[35]

Many churches were slow to act practically according to Jones's principles, so he urged those 'true to the faith' to 'come out of Babylon and separate themselves ... in order to have unity of spirit, and walk in brotherly love'.[36] Eventually, in the winter of 1798, along with the majority of the Baptists of Merioneth who were under his leadership, he separated himself from the 'Babylonian' Baptists of Wales. Soon churches from all over the North followed his lead,[37] and for the next 'twenty-four years he was his people's general, tirelessly walking

over his widespread *parish*, refusing on conscientious grounds
to accept any salary, and faithfully spreading the truth as he
saw it'.[38]

It appears that the Baptists of Wales did not want him to
divide from them, apparently willing to allow him to pursue his
own course within the denomination, but such a compromise
was untenable for this 'imperious man', and an open rupture
ensued. Christmas Evans recorded the events of that 'separation'
meeting at Ramoth, which had been called by Jones, 'from
which delusion so dangerous and fatal to spiritual views and
feelings proceeded'.[39] The object of the meeting was to find out
who wanted to 'reform' the church, and who preferred to
remain in the old Baptist community. Christmas Evans and
another minister preached in the morning.

At the afternoon conference, after rebuking his supporters
for their reluctance to make a stand,[40] J. R. Jones 'declared his
determination to separate from the Baptist body in Wales, and
unite himself to the Baptists of Scotland'.[41] He produced
several letters he had received from McLean and a large piece
of paper on which were written, in detail and in a neat hand,
numerous reasons why he had to separate from the Welsh Baptists. It was with feelings of peculiar sorrow and grief that some
listened as the articles of separation were read out, 'realizing
that the old Christian unity that had existed among us for some
years was about to be broken without any hope of reconciliation'.[42] Three of the articles were crucial, namely: 'error in
doctrine, defilement of the communion, and disobedience to
the commands of our Lord and Saviour Jesus Christ and to the
example given by the first apostolic church'.[43]

Christmas Evans, after admitting that he embraced several
of the Sandemanian doctrines, and partly because he was troubled by the threat to church unity, 'held a long dispute with Mr
Jones at that meeting on account of his precipitate separation',[44]
whereupon the latter

... became greatly agitated, and said 'that the Baptists had in them a quarrelsome spirit of contradiction, and I [Christmas Evans] along with them, though he had thought better things of me before'. Then he stood on his feet at the table in front of the pulpit, in a spirit of great perturbation, and in a very hasty manner took hold of the Bible, and said, *That he, in the name of the Lord, separated himself from the Babylonish Baptists of Wales, and that he conscientiously separated himself from their errors in faith and practice, — to the truth, and to the communion of the brethren in Scotland, who receive the truth.* He then sat down.

Many of the spectators looked upon him with astonishment, while he performed the ceremony of excluding himself from the Baptists of the Principality, and there were some who beheld the scene with trembling, and with tears, as if they saw a burning mountain emitting smoke and sparks of fire, which occasioned deep sighs to burst forth from hearts big with grief and sorrow. Others appeared as cheerful as if the trumpets of jubilee had begun sounding; or, like the thieves and robbers in the French revolution, who broke out in hopes of obtaining a booty for themselves in the destruction of others; and some appeared as if stupefied, not knowing what the end of these things would be. — The scene was dreadful![45]

The division was a heavy blow to a denomination that had barely found its feet, and as feared no reconciliation ever took place. To his account of the Ramoth meeting Christmas Evans attached a portraiture of J. R. Jones, in which he expresses his astonishment that a man of his 'capacity and education' should lay so much stress on Sandemanianism, regarding many of the fundamentals of Christianity of little value unless the 'holy kiss', the 'washing of feet' and other peculiarities of that sect were observed. Jones's exclusiveness led him to admit into his pulpit 'none but those who were the zealous advocates of these things', while 'He would not so much as even take off his hat, when he heard some of the most successful preachers in the conversion of souls to Christ, either preaching, or performing some other religious service.'[46]

This portraiture was written some time after the event, and probably after the breakdown of their relationship. However, it must be said that their affection for one another remained strong for several years after the Ramoth meeting, certainly up to the Llangefni Association of 1802, although Christmas Evans never became a member of the new association. In a letter dated 7 November, 1800, and addressed to his friend John Williams of New York, he refers to Jones as a 'wise, prudent, good, witty and intelligent man', though he considers him 'to have been too impulsive in forming an association with him [McLean] by breaking communion with his Welsh brethren at home'.[47] In another letter, two months later (11 January, 1801), it is clear that though still on speaking terms their doctrinal positions were diverging. Christmas Evans defended his right to receive financial support from the London Baptist Fund and to fellowship with Christians from other denominations — two 'rights' that Jones, in all conscience, could not support. The differences between them increased until the breach occurred at Llangefni the following year.

The effects of Jones's Sandemanianism on the Baptist churches in North Wales and on his friend Christmas Evans were devastating.

The effect of this teaching upon Christmas Evans was to rob him of the warmth and the feeling and the urgency which he had known, and to introduce this terrible coldness into him.

D.M.Lloyd-Jones.[1]

Christmas Evans is an example of a preacher who, having experienced extraordinary power and revival in his ministry, went right off course in doctrine and, inevitably, in practice.

Robert Oliver.[2]

9

'A Cold Heart Towards Christ'

The reason for mentioning J. R. Jones at such length is because of the extraordinary influence he had on Christmas Evans. Along with the writings of the Scottish Baptists and Christmas Evans's own 'craving for anything new', it was Jones who was primarily responsible for leading his ministerial colleague into Sandemanianism. Christmas Evans always admired men of strong convictions and forthright views and could be led astray by them if they expressed their beliefs in an eloquent and dogmatic fashion. His admiration for Jones as a theologian, and his readiness to submit to his superior intellect, blinded him to the errors of his teaching, and before long he was 'singing from the same hymn sheet', although in later years he was slow to admit any close attachment to the Sandemanian sect. Even in his account of the Ramoth separation meeting and his portraiture of John Jones, Christmas Evans implies that he only embraced several of the contended points of doctrine, a view that is upheld in his own papers and adopted by his Welsh biographer William Morgan; whereas from some of his own published letters and the passing references made to him in the memoirs of other ministers, it is evident that he was in complete agreement and full cooperation with Jones in his reforms for a considerable length of time.

In one of these letters, written to J. R. Jones, he treats Thomas Morris of Lleyn 'quite unmercifully'; and in another he unveils his Sandemanian bias when he criticises the orthodox doctrine of George Lewis, an Independent minister of Caernarfon and a theologian: 'I cannot understand what kind of doctrine George Lewis maintains when he states that God opens hearts to receive the word. Question: How? He answers: By the Holy Spirit. That cannot be, for the word is the only tool which the Spirit possesses by which he can open hearts. It is the sword of the Spirit. And no heart was ever opened except through the word.'[3]

Extracts from two other letters written by Christmas Evans in the same year as Jones wrote to McLean, 1796, show this involvement, and also point to other influences. The first, from which we quote only a few lines, was written to McLean in rather 'broken English' and outlines the progress of Sandemanianism in Anglesey, which appears more rapid than in Merionethshire. It is dated Llangefni, 28 November, 1796, and signed by Christmas Evans, Hugh Williams and Edmund Francis:[4]

> It happened about one year and a half ago, that some of your books fell into our hands — viz., McLean on the *Commission*, and H. D. Inglis's *Short Notes*; and the reading of them proved to be a greater blessing to us, through the Divine Spirit, than the golden mine of Peru to the Spaniards is...
>
> The believing of the truth makes us willing to obey Christ's commands in all things; we practise the kiss of charity, the feast of love, and washing the feet of one another, not only in case of necessity, but also as a commandment to every one of the members of the church according to the law of the institution ... Our ministers wear no canonical dress. We hate the priestcraft...[5]

The second letter, which reads like a confession of faith, is addressed to a church near Swansea, *The Engine*, so called because it met in an old engine house belonging to a copper works at Glandŵr. Many of its members, who originally joined together because of their dissatisfaction with other communions, later associated themselves with either the Quakers, the General Baptists or the Unitarians, and the church dissolved. The date of the letter is uncertain although it was 'about the year 1796'. We give an outline:

DEAR BRETHREN IN CHRIST...

In order to elicit your thoughts, I will send you my own, that you may know my understanding in the mystery of Christ. What I shall send you will be contained in the following fourteen particulars:

1. God's word, in the revelation which God gave of himself. I do not consider that word as saying one thing and meaning another. It does not contain two meanings, but one: that is what some call the literal meaning...

2. The faith of God's elect. This, wrought by the Lord, is no more than a belief of the Word of God as true; to believe the account of the life, death, resurrection, and ascension of Christ, in consonance with the great end — to satisfy the Father...

3. Hope is the believer's expectation of the fulfilment (verification) of the things which he has believed; and this is founded on the faithfulness of God... It is not on the ground of his own experience, but on that of the promise, he hopes.

4. No work produced in man before he believes is (to be regarded as) preparatory; it is not required as a condition of faith...

5. Love is but the spirit of truth, communicated by a belief of the truth...

6. The new principle (disposition) in the saints, then, is the indwelling of the word through the Spirit in their hearts, in all its truth, purity, and incorruptibleness...

7. The sanctification of the believer, the removal of guilt, the subjugation and mortification of our members which are on the earth, and the engagement of the affections to love spiritual things. This is effected by the Spirit, through the Word, and not apart from the Word...

8. The joy of the believer springs from the word believed, and increases in proportion to the growth and vigour of that belief ... Joy does not arise from some excitement of feelings (temper), but from faith, growing with confidence, and love flowing in conformity to the truth.

9. The believer's assurance... It is said, 'He that believeth hath the witness in himself;' that is, by the abiding of the Spirit in him — the love of God shed abroad in his heart — as though the Spirit had written the testimony which God hath borne to his Son in his heart...

10. Slavish fear, the fear that giveth pain, is no help to the watchfulness of the Christian, but it is cast out by perfect love, which is the only impelling principle of the saints...

11. I perceive that we ought to wash the feet of the disciples, as of old.

12. That we ought to partake of the Lord's Supper every Lord's Day.

13. That we should observe the holy kiss.

14. And that we should keep the love feast.

Your brother and fellow prisoner, &c.,

Christmas Evans [6]

These letters show the depth of Christmas Evans's involvement in the Sandemanian heresy and his close alignment with the movement's leader — an alignment that was destined eventually to fall apart as both men were concerned ultimately with different priorities: John Jones with the intricacies of his doctrinal system and in persuading all and sundry that his beliefs were the only ones in agreement with the apostolic practice; and Christmas Evans, naturally warm-hearted and ebullient, with the passionate proclamation of the Gospel and the conversion of sinners. However, before their separation, it is clear that Christmas Evans considered following Jones's lead and breaking away from the old Baptists if they did not submit to the Sandemanian viewpoint.

With the movement's rigidity and formality Christmas Evans soon lost the warmth and urgency of soul that had been a hall-

mark of his ministry. The spiritual enjoyment and zeal for God's
glory experienced by him at Lleyn evaporated and his prayer
life, usually free and overflowing, was stifled. In line with the
Sandemanian spirit, he became hard, censorious and peevish.
A spirit of infallibility possessed him. He knew something was
wrong and that he had lost something precious, but he did not
know what it was or how to regain it. His confidence plum-
meted, his spiritual life became imbued to an alarming extent
with the dryness of the system, and his usefulness as a preacher
was seriously curtailed. He suffered in this way for about five
years. Taking a retrospective view of the effects on his own
spirit and remarking that 'I shall be in eternity when this comes
before the reader's eye,' he wrote:

> The Sandemanian heresy affected me so much as to drive
> away the spirit of prayer for the salvation of sinners. The
> lighter matters of the kingdom of God pressed heavier upon
> my mind than the weightier. The power which gave me zeal
> and confidence and earnestness in the pulpit for the conver-
> sion of souls to Christ was lost. My heart sank within me,
> and I lost the witness of a good conscience. On Sunday
> night, after I had been fiercely and violently condemning
> errors, my conscience felt ill at ease, and rebuked me be-
> cause I had lost communion and fellowship with God, and
> made me feel that something invaluable was now lost and
> wanting. I would reply that I acted according to the Word.
> Still it rebuked me, saying that there was something of inestim-
> able value gone. To a very great degree had I lost the spirit
> of prayer, and the spirit of preaching.[7]

The Sandemanian dispute in the Baptist churches of North Wales
was vigorously and often bitterly conducted, causing great harm
to the small, recently formed congregations. These congregations, it must be remembered, were the fruit of sustained yet
temporary missionary endeavours rather than a settled ministry
and were therefore more vulnerable to the 'spreading conta-
gion' of 'Mr Sandeman's notion', as John Wesley had called it.

Instead of establishing these new believers in the fundamental doctrines of the Christian faith, the disputants highlighted questions such as 'Whether the administrator in the Lord's Supper was to take up the bread, or *break it on the table;*'[8] 'Whether faith was a pure and distinct act of the mind; whether a church, with all its members, however scattered and however remote from one another, should meet in the same place; whether perfect unity of opinion was essential to Christian fellowship; whether the right of private property ought not to be abolished; whether the holy kiss and the washing of feet should not be practised.'[9] These and other peripheral issues dominated the religious scene and were preached at every opportunity by both supporters and opponents, upon whom 'a spirit of infallibility and worldly wisdom fell ... until the weakest of them felt himself qualified to govern the church and the world'.[10]

The consequence of this wrangling was 'exceedingly prejudicial' to the Baptists in North Wales and it succeeded in 'checking their progress, in all probability, thirty or forty years'.[11] The large congregations fell away everywhere and some churches were lost; many localities, previously sympathetic to the Baptists and ready to bear much fruit, 'were blasted and withered, others were neglected, labourers from other denominations stepped into others, and reaped what they had not sown';[12] individual members opposed each other; ministers were divided; the Sunday School, which had been zealously promoted, came to nothing; and the cause of Missions and the Bible Society suffered. Many adherents of the new sect, says Christmas Evans, 'impeded the prosperity of the other Baptists, and kept an open door to receive the irregular and disaffected members of that body, which was the means of hardening the minds of evil disposed persons against true discipline, and of encouraging them in their opposition and insubordination'.[13] After J. R. Jones's withdrawal 'The Northern Association disappeared completely for a time although some monthly and Quarterly Meetings were held ... the link between North and South was broken for a period, and a brake placed on the growth of the denomination.'[14]

The effect on Christmas Evans's people as a religious body in the North was equally devastating. The 'pastor of Anglesey' summarises the effect: 'We lost in Anglesey nearly all those who were accustomed to attend with us;[15] some of them joined other congregations; and, in this way, it pulled down nearly all that had been built up in twelve or fifteen years, and made us appear once again a mean and despicable party in the view of the country.'[16]

There seems to have been only one Baptist minister at that time in North Wales known to the public who stood firmly and fearlessly against the prevailing doctrines of Sandemanianism and effectively resisted its influence. His name was Thomas Jones (1769-1850) of Glyn Ceiriog, Denbighshire, whose marvellous memory and extraordinary knowledge of the Bible caused Christmas Evans to exclaim, 'Wherever Thomas Jones was, no concordance would be necessary!'[17] He had been ordained, together with his neighbour John Edwards, as minister of Glyn Ceiriog in 1794. Two years later, partly on account of personal and family rivalries, and partly because of the Sandemanian controversy, there was a schism in the church; 'One party under the leadership of Thomas Jones remaining faithful to the Old Baptists, and the other under the guidance of John Edwards forming itself into a separate church within the connexion of John Richard Jones.'[18]

Although Thomas Jones was attacked viciously by his opponents, he did not respond in kind, remaining humble and courteous throughout the controversy, yet vigorous in his determination to uphold the truth of the Gospel. In 1802 at the resuscitated Association meeting at Llangefni, he preached so effectively against Sandemanianism that the heresy never recovered. During the final sermon on the Thursday afternoon, as Jones preached from 1 John 2:12, Christmas Evans, obviously gripped by what he heard, cried, 'You know, this Thomas Jones is a whale of a man!'[19] It was after this meeting that Christmas Evans turned his back on the Sandemanian position. In 1808 Jones was called away to Rhydwilym, Carmarthenshire, where he built up the church for nearly two generations. His departure from North Wales prompted John Elias to lament, 'Behold, the light of the North has been removed.'[20] However, he frequently returned to the North, and his was the first name on the list of preachers who attended the annual Anglesey Association.

> At these meetings Christmas Evans and Thomas Jones would 'fight their battles over again'; and in friendly parley, would go through many of the former passages of their history and experience. Mr Jones, eminent for a native politeness of spirit, would be most deferential in bearing; but as unyielding as the oak to the storm, when the veriest dogma of systematic theology was concerned. Christmas Evans, not yielding to him in zeal and kindliness of feeling, but unused to 'arts polite', would exhibit a sort of elephantine grace, returning kind word for kind word, and kindling at once his own spirit, and that of his ancient friend, by referring to former happy occasions of divine worship and public service. The latter would, indeed, not be very unyielding as to former points of dispute, admitting ingenuously, either that he had been in the wrong, or that, being right, he had not rightly conducted his cause. In these respects, his candour was the candour of a child, prompt and thoroughgoing. The noble-minded men would part with mutual esteem, and with augmented attachment to their common Lord and his work upon earth.[21]

Jones died in 1850 having lived a life 'of quiet beauty, which perhaps has never been surpassed'.[22]

It was Thomas Jones who was instrumental in rescuing Christmas Evans from Sandemanianism and encouraging him back to the spiritual warmth he had previously known. He also arrested, very effectively, the spread of that heresy in North Wales, so that five or six years after its initial outbreak, he had the satisfaction of welcoming several of the leading ministers back to their 'old' faith.

Coupled with the influence of Thomas Jones was Christmas Evans's own conviction that the callousness and severity that characterized Sandemanians were contrary 'to the two tablets of the law and to the kind and gracious nature of the Gospel, and to the nature of the graces or fruit of the Holy Spirit'.[23] He complained that the men of Ramoth, who were 'far more like the Pharisee in the parable than the publican', possessed 'no real pleasure in the exercise of religion and walking with God';[24] dismissed family devotions, which had been practised for years, as unscriptural; opposed prayer meetings, Sunday schools and missionary endeavours, stating that there were no specific instructions concerning them in the New Testament and therefore they should be abolished; and despised everything that savoured of experience and spiritual life. 'The signs of regeneration, a life of faith in the Son of God, moral character, evangelical gifts and usefulness in restoring sinners were, in their sight, worthless and deserving of no consideration.'[25] Religion to them was an external matter 'that did not affect the objectivity of the doctrine of faith and salvation', whereas, in the words of Christmas Evans,

> ... the spirit of Christ's kingdom is a spirit of prayer, yes, perseverance in prayer; the most important things in Christ's kingdom are righteousness, peace and joy in the Holy Spirit. But certainly that is not the spirit of the Scottish Baptists, rather it is hostility and resentment towards the good who appear like full-blown flowers among them. They have no desire to listen to a sermon or to pray, to seek to save their

ungodly neighbours and they have no tear to shed as they
see the world lying in ignorance of the knowledge of the only
Saviour.[26]

It was this Pharisaical spirit that caused him to reappraise his
own views.

Christmas Evans was also challenged by the writings of
Andrew Fuller (1754-1815), who was so strongly opposed to
the nature and tendency of the *system* that he wrote: 'For my
part, without deciding upon the state of individuals, I am
persuaded that these people, with all their professions of *clear
views, simple truth* and *simple belief*, have imbibed a corrupt
and dangerous system of doctrine... If we may judge from its
effects during the last fifty years, it would lead the Christian
world, if not to downright infidelity, yet to something that comes
but very little short of it.'[27] In 1785 Fuller had published *The
Gospel Worthy of All Acceptation*, an evangelical Calvinistic
work that provoked criticism from both hyper-Calvinists and
Sandemanians. The former accused him of Arminianism and
the latter of advocating justification by works. McLean's reply
The Commission of Christ, a translation of which was signed
on the title page by Christmas Evans, J. R. Jones and Edmund
Francis, was challenged by Fuller in an appendix to the 1801
edition of his original work, in which he again emphasized the
evangelical doctrine of saving faith. Christmas Evans read the
appendix, and began to re-examine and change his views
respecting 'Sandemanian faith'. He then read twice McLean's
Reply and in some degree reverted to his old beliefs. Soon
afterwards Fuller produced a more detailed exposure of the
system called *Strictures on Sandemanianism*, and Christmas
Evans, to use his own expression, 'saw the *Rhinoceros* of Edinburgh beginning to give way, notwithstanding the strength and
sharpness of his horn, before the *elephant* of Kettering, and confess that faith is of a holy nature'.[28] He understood the Scriptural

basis of Fuller's argument and became more established in orthodox beliefs.

On Fuller and his works Christmas Evans commented: 'He undoubtedly subverted Sandemanianism in its main point, namely, faith taking place in the soul, without the regenerating power of the Spirit, or the Spirit imparting light to the soul, as the cause of it. *The Strictures on Sandemanianism* are the principal of Mr F's works, which evince him to be the greatest man of his age in powers of mind.'[29]

Both Jones and Fuller, aided by the Spirit of truth, helped Christmas Evans to escape from the 'religious ice-house' of Sandemanianism, but it was a remarkable encounter he had with God that finally sealed his deliverance. He had been trapped in the controversy for about five years, destitute of all religious enjoyment and as cold and hard as ice — 'as dry as Gilboa' is how he pictures himself. Then one day, as he travelled by himself up a lonely road near Cadair Idris, he experienced a spiritual refreshing that changed the course of his life. God met with him and a new day dawned. He broke with the 'reformers' and their movement, and reverted to his old warm and powerful revivalism. He describes what happened and the subsequent blessing in his journal:

I was weary of a cold heart towards Christ, and his sacrifice and the work of his Spirit — of a cold heart in the pulpit, in secret prayer, and in the study. For fifteen years previously, I had felt my heart burning within, as if going to Emmaus with Jesus. On a day ever to be remembered by me, as I was going from Dolgellau to Machynlleth and climbing up towards Cadair Idris, I considered it to be incumbent upon me to pray, however hard I felt my heart, and however worldly the frame of my spirit was. Having begun in the name of Jesus, I soon felt as it were the fetters loosening, and the old hardness of heart softening, and, as I thought, mountains of frost and snow dissolving and melting within. This engendered confidence in my soul in the promise of the Holy Spirit.

I felt my whole mind relieved from some great bondage: tears flowed copiously, and I was constrained to cry out for the gracious visits of God, by restoring to my soul the joy of his salvation; — and that he would visit the churches in Anglesey that were under my care. I embraced in my supplications all the churches of the saints, and nearly all the ministers in the Principality by their names. This struggle lasted for three hours; it rose again and again, like one wave after another, or a high flowing tide driven by a strong wind, until my nature became faint by weeping and crying. Thus I resigned myself to Christ, body and soul, gifts and labours — all my life — every day and every hour that remained for me:— and all my cares I committed to Christ. The road was mountainous and lonely, and I was wholly alone, and suffered no interruption in my wrestlings with God.

From this time, I was made to expect the goodness of God to churches and to myself. Thus the Lord delivered me and the people of Anglesey from being carried away by the flood of Sandemanianism. In the first religious meetings after this, I felt as if I had been removed from the cold and sterile regions of spiritual frost, into the verdant fields of the divine promises. The former striving with God in prayer, and the longing anxiety for the conversion of sinners, which I had experienced at Lleyn, was now restored. I had a hold of the promises of God. The result was when I returned home, the first thing that arrested my attention was, that the Spirit was working also in the brethren in Anglesey, inducing in them a spirit of prayer, especially in two of the deacons, who were particularly importunate that God would visit us in mercy, and render the word of his grace effectual amongst us for the conversion of sinners.[30]

A turn around in faith and experience of this magnitude infuriated J. R. Jones, who represented Christmas Evans as a man hunting after applause and paving the way for his own glory and honour. 'I remember the time,' he said accusingly, 'when there was no one as zealous for what he calls the McLeanist tenets as Christmas Evans. But after that, he discovered that it was more advantageous for his popularity and pocket to resort to his previous creed and stick to his old mistress — *hwyl.*'[31] And to John Roberts, minister of Bryndeunydd, six years after his 'friend's defection', he said, 'You have seen, without doubt, Christmas Evans's letters to his friend,' in which he opposed Sandemanianism. 'The condition of those people,' continued Jones, 'who take such a man as their oracle must be serious and wretched.'[32] But criticism such as this from his former ally could not deter a man who had been locked for five years inside 'the coldness of death' by the rigidity and hardness of the Sandemanian system.

And so the old fires of love for Christ and the souls of men began to burn again in the heart of Christmas Evans, much to the benefit of the Baptist cause in North Wales. The unbending strictness that observed 'the letter that killeth' was replaced by the Spirit of life, inducing prayer and praise; and his feelings and imagination, stifled and suppressed for too long, were given the free reign they had formerly enjoyed.

Not that I have already attained, or am already perfected; but I press on, that I may lay hold of that for which Christ Jesus has also laid hold of me. Brethren, I do not count myself to have apprehended; but one thing I do, forgetting those things which are behind and reaching forward to those things which are ahead, I press towards the goal for the prize of the upward call of God in Christ Jesus.

Philippians 3:12-14.[1]

10

A Deeper Walk with God

Before the advent of that 'cold and sterile' Sandemanian spirit, the Baptist cause in Anglesey, and indeed throughout most of North Wales, was 'lifting up its head and wearing a promising and cheering aspect'. The general populace was more favourable towards the preaching of the gospel and many doors of opportunity were opening. 'The Baptist cause at Lleyn,' notes Christmas Evans in his diary, assumed a 'flourishing aspect' and at Cricieth, Garn, Llanllyfni and other places all appeared 'like the garden of paradise, compared with what has been seen there since'.[2] The doctrine preached was in line with the ministry of the first preachers who visited the North from South Wales. 'If any difference existed,' says Christmas Evans, it was 'in the unction and success which at that period attended the ministry to a considerable extent.'[3]

Although the Sandemanianism controversy caused considerable harm among the North Wales Baptists, and pulled down what had taken years of hard work to build, it also had a more salutary effect in checking some of the extravagances that had grown up in 'the garden of paradise', which was not quite as rosy as Christmas Evans infers. Before the dispute, preaching in the North, generally speaking, had deteriorated. Many sermons, with a tendency to ultra-Calvinism, were taken from obscure or short texts and applied with strange spiritualizations. John Prichard, principal and divinity tutor of the Baptist College, Llangollen, testifies that 'Instead of enlightening the mind by the faithful preaching of the truth as it is in Jesus, and dispensing it in its light, warmth and life, to convince the judgement, move the will, and kindle a holy fire in the affections; the greater number of preachers spent their talents, and their precious time, to feed the depraved fancies of their hearers, by curious preaching from curious texts.' After the controversy the preaching was observed to be less exaggerated in its handling of God's word, with a more gracious and experimental effect on the hearts of the hearers. The 'old Baptists' became much more 'sober in handling the word of life. The ministers of the gospel aimed more at purifying the heart, by informing the understanding of the truth of God in its glorious harmony, its melting love, and holy tendency.'[4]

These beneficial effects were also apparent in the ministry of Christmas Evans, whose involvement with Sandemanianism forced him to reassess his religious beliefs, which in turn deepened his knowledge and understanding of the true principles of Christianity:

> It shook my old system like an earthquake; so that I was obliged to search all the foundations, and repair some of the gates, and measure the whole by the measuring rod of the truth. It made me re-examine for myself according to the word, into every part of my religion. This enlarged my understanding, and established my mind the more in the truth...
>
> Were it not for this earthquake, I could not treat of several points of religion in a manner nearly equal to the small degree of power with which I can do it at present... I derived so much blessing from the rise of Sandemanianism, that made me descend into the mine-pit myself by the ropes to examine and see what was in it. It compelled me to prove,

search, and see for my own self, what saith the Lord in his
holy Scriptures.[5]

Some of the points raised by McLean in his *Works*, notes Christmas Evans, although not new, were 'illustrated in a method
more forcible and exhibited in a clearer light' than in the writings of some Welsh authors. Consequently, certain doctrines,
such as 'the finished work of Christ as the only ground of a
sinner's acceptance with God', were 'brought to my view ...
more clearly than I had ever seen them before'.[6] He became
better informed about the two covenants — 'that of grace and
that of works' — the former he saw as 'the gospel of peace'
and the latter as made on Sinai 'with the Jews only, not any of
the Gentiles, except the proselytes, concerned therein'.[7] By reading Henry David Inglis's *Short Notes* he came to a more complete grasp of Christ's pre-existence: 'He was the image of the
Father before his incarnation, and by assuming our nature he
became the representative of that image to us. And in the unity
of both natures he is properly called the Son of God.'[8]

These blessings — a sharpening of his critical skills, a more
rigorous intellectual discipline in his attitude towards theology
and its tenets, a greater substance and solidity to his preaching
— well-prepared him to counter another heresy making inroads
into the Baptists of Wales at this time, Sabellianism.[9] He spoke
out fearlessly against it, regarding it as both dangerous and
divisive, and incurred considerable opposition, especially from
some of the brethren in Monmouthshire, where Sabellianism
had taken a deep root. In 1802, when requested to write the
circular letter of the South West Baptist Association, held that
year at Pen-parc, Cardiganshire, he chose as his subject *Three
Equal Persons in the Undivided Essence of the Godhead*, and
wrote so effectively that, coupled with his frequent preaching
on the subject, the advance of Sabellianism among the Baptists
was considerably hampered.

He was sharply rebuked at several Associations for his stance against it, and in 1808 at the Nant Gwyn Association, upon hearing one of the oldest ministers present say in his sermon 'that he expected, when he should enter heaven, to see but ONE there', he replied, 'with all the infallibility of the Sandemanian spirit', that the good brother who had made this assertion, 'was not likely then to see as John and Stephen saw; the first of whom, saw ONE sitting on the throne, and a rainbow around the throne, and *another* like a Lamb that had been slain in the midst of the throne, and the *seven* Spirits of God proceeding out of the throne, like seven lambs of burning fire. And the last "saw the heavens opened, and Jesus standing on the right hand of the Father."'[10] For these remarks he was called to account in the conference and 'severely reproved'.

With firmness he stood his ground and 'ultimately succeeded in banishing the heresy from the Baptist body, and also, more or less, from other Christian bodies in the Principality'.[11] His accomplishment was due, so he thought, to the fact that 'Sandemanianism had cast a light upon, and stirred up a spirit to contend for, the doctrine of the Trinity, and that, if it introduced one error, it checked another, like one evil genius devouring another.'[12]

In later years, because of his experience with disputed points of theology, he was able to judge that individuals and congregations were often secretly united and moved more by the spirit they imbibed, than by the doctrines, ordinances or practices they embraced. Many people, he noticed, who had imbibed the spirit of Sandemanianism, united themselves to that party, though they did not understand the system; while others, who understood the matter more clearly, hesitated to join with them. His own practice, whenever any point of doctrine was discussed, was to inquire immediately, 'Of what spirit is it? Is the heavenly unction in it?'[13] Particularly during times of controversy he saw the necessity of understanding such expressions as 'the righteousness of God', 'Christ the end of the law for righteousness unto every one who believes', and 'made perfect by one sacrifice in the death of Christ'. A person, he thought, must possess a right view of the value of saving truths, especially that the justification of a sinner is wholly of grace through the merits of Christ. Otherwise, 'too little religion' will be preached by the bearers of the Gospel 'to save a sinner or to save themselves'.[14]

It was about this time, after his 'wrestling with God' near Cadair Idris and his deliverance from Sandemanianism, that he was guided and strengthened on his course by a series of dreams, which are remarkable for their peculiarity. These visions of the night, many of which he believed to be divinely inspired, were often as vivid, imaginative and dramatic as his sermons and invariably exalted 'the great and blessed Saviour' and his victory over Satan. In the one given below, he found himself

> ... at the gate of hell and, standing at the threshold, I saw an opening, beneath which there was a vast sea of fire in wave-like motion. Looking at it, I said: 'What infinite virtue there must have been in the blood of Christ to have quenched, for His people, these awful flames!' Overcome with the feeling, I knelt down by the walls of hell, saying, 'Thanks be unto Thee, O Great and Blessed Saviour, that Thou hast dried up this terrible sea of fire!'
>
> Whereupon Christ addressed me, 'Come this way, and I will show thee how it was done.' Looking back, I beheld that the whole sea had disappeared. Jesus passed over the place, and said, 'Come, follow me.'
>
> By this time, I was within what I thought were the gates of hell, where there were many cells, out of which it was impossible to escape. I found myself within one of these, and anxious to make my way out. Still I felt wonderfully calm, as I had only just been conversing with Jesus, and because He had gone before me, although I had now lost sight of Him. I got hold of something, with which I struck the corner of the place in which I stood, saying, 'In the name of Jesus,

open!' and it instantly gave way; so I did with all the enclos-
ures, until I made my way out into the open field. Whom
should I see there but brethren, none of whom, however, I
knew, except a good old deacon, and their work was to
attend to a nursery of trees; I joined them, and laid hold of a
tree, saying, 'In the name of Jesus, be thou plucked up by
the root!' And it came up as if it had been a rush. Thence I
went forth, as I fancied, to work miracles, saying, 'Now I
know how the apostles wrought miracles in the name of
Christ.'[15]

After fourteen years of ministry on the island a formal application for a preaching licence for the 'pastor of Anglesey' was
submitted to the Beaumaris magistrates. It was dated 5 October, 1805, and signed by twelve Cil-dwrn members: 'His majesty's subjects and protestant dissenters: Our lawful wish and
humble desire is that you should licence or grant a licence to
Christmas Evans who is now a settled minister among us, that
he may preach and administer ordinances without being
obnoxious to the penalty which the law threatens unlicensed
preachers.'[16] The Act of Toleration (1689), which granted freedom of worship to Nonconformists, required preachers to be
registered with the state authority. Failure to do so incurred a
penalty of £40. To receive his licence Christmas Evans, who
held the authority of the Crown in high regard, paid the man-
datory 6d and swore the oath of allegiance: 'I, Christmas Evans,
do solemnly declare, in the presence of Almighty God, that I
am a Christian and a Protestant and as such that I believe that
the Scriptures of the Old and New Testament commonly
received among Protestant Churches do contain the revealed
will of God and that I do receive the same as the rule of my
doctrine and practice.'[17]

During his ministry at Lleyn he had been able to read, with
interest and enjoyment, some of the best English authors — 'I
was particularly partial,' he says, 'to criticisms upon select

passages of Scripture, that is, if the authors were conversant
with the plan of salvation'[18] — but because of his constant
labours in travelling and preaching, it was not until he had
resided in Anglesey for about six years that he began to study
English grammar, which enabled him to preach more effectively
in that language. He also committed to memory most of Richard's *Dictionary*. On his visits to Liverpool, Bristol and other
parts of England, where he spoke in the Welsh churches, he
was 'begged earnestly' by his English friends to preach in their
churches, in 'broken English', which

> ... induced me to set about the matter in earnest, making it
> a subject of prayer, for the aid of the Spirit, that I might be, in
> some measure, a blessing to the English friends, for there
> appeared some sign that God now called me to this depart-
> ment of labour in his service. I never succeeded in anything
> for the good of others, without making it a matter of prayer.
> My English preaching was very broken and imperfect in point
> of language; yet, through the grace of Jesus Christ, it was
> made in some degree useful at Liverpool, Bristol, and some
> other places.[19]

He preached repeatedly at Byrom Street and Lime Street in
Liverpool, and always referred, with deep gratitude, to the kindness of the English brethren, many of whom, particularly the
members of the English churches in Liverpool, proved true and
fast friends to the end of his days, and did much to refresh and
cheer him in his declining years. He reports in a letter to John
Williams, 1 April, 1816, that he became 'well acquainted with
the most famous in England and they with me. They are far
better than the old English preachers of twenty-five years ago.
They want life in their sermons. I have had fellowship with
R. Hall of Leicester, Andrew Fuller of Kettering, Dr Ryland of
Bristol, Mr Roberts of Bristol, Mr Fisher of Liverpool: they are
spiritual, enthusiastic, fiery men.'[20] His best English friend was
Robert Hall.

Christmas Evans regarded the services he rendered to his friends in England as insignificant. However, it is true to say that the English sermons possessed 'the same energy of thought and the same boldness of imagery as those in Welsh; but in the power of his peculiar delivery, they were inevitably inferior. His brethren in England were delighted with his performances and said it was "no wonder the Welsh were warm under such preaching"; but his language was broken and hesitant, and they could scarcely have any conception of his animation and energy when he spoke in his vernacular tongue.'[21] He admitted some years later that if he had studied the English language 'attentively and perseveringly', he would have been able to overcome many of his difficulties.

Towards the end of the first decade of the nineteenth century Christmas Evans entered into a solemn covenant with God, in which he dedicated himself wholly to God and his service. It is a wonderful example of the strength and simplicity of his faith, his unwavering hope in the grace of God, and of the humility of spirit in which he lived; and was made, as he says, 'in hope and confidence in Christ, and nearness to God, under a deep sense of the evil of my own heart and in dependence upon the infinite grace and merit of the Redeemer'.[22] It is dated 'April 10, 18 —'. Unfortunately the last two digits are obliterated, but it must have been made during the close of the first decade of the nineteenth century, or soon after, as this coincides with the 'fifteen years' he had felt his heart burning within, 'as if going to Emmaus with Jesus'. This 'burning within' did not begin until after he had gone to Lleyn in 1789. If we add on the five years of Sandemanian coldness, we arrive at our conjectured date. The covenant itself is regarded by many as among the most intimate in Christian literature:

I. I give my soul and body unto thee, Jesus, the true God, and everlasting life—deliver me from sin and from eternal death, and bring me into life everlasting. Amen. — C. E.

II. I call the day, the sun, the earth, the trees, the stones, the bed, the table and the books to witness that I come unto thee, Redeemer of sinners, that I may obtain rest for my soul from the thunders of guilt and the dread of eternity. Amen.— C. E.

III. I do, through confidence in thy power, earnestly entreat thee to take the work into thine own hand, and give me a circumcised heart, that I may love thee, and create in me a right spirit, that I may seek thy glory. Grant me that principle which thou wilt own in the day of judgement, that I may not then assume pale facedness and find myself a hypocrite. Grant me this, for the sake of thy most precious blood. Amen.— C. E.

IV. I entreat thee, Jesus, the Son of God, in power grant me, for the sake of thy agonising death, a covenant interest in thy blood which cleanseth; in thy righteousness, which justifieth; and in thy redemption, which delivereth. I entreat an interest in thy blood, for thy blood's sake and a part in thee, for thy name's sake, which thou hast given among men. Amen.— C. E.

V. O Jesus Christ, Son of the living God, take for the sake of thy cruel death, my time, and strength, and the gifts and talents I possess; which, with a full purpose of heart, I consecrate to thy glory in the building up of thy church in the world, for thou art worthy of the hearts and talents of all men. Amen.— C. E.

VI. I desire thee my great high priest, to confirm by thy power from thy high court, my usefulness as a preacher, and my piety as a Christian, as two gardens nigh to each other; that sin may not have place in my heart to becloud my confidence in thy righteousness, and that I may not be left to any foolish act that may occasion my gifts to wither, and rendered useless before my life ends. Keep thy gracious eye upon me, and watch over me, O my Lord, and my God for ever! Amen.— C. E.

VII. I give myself in a particular manner to thee, O Jesus Christ the Saviour, to be preserved from the falls into which many stumble, that thy name (in thy cause) may not be blasphemed or wounded, that my peace may not be injured, that thy people may not be grieved, and that thine enemies may not be hardened. Amen. — C. E.

VIII. I come unto thee, beseeching thee to be in covenant with me in my ministry. As thou didst prosper Bunyan, Vavasor Powell, Howel Harris, Rowland and Whitefield, O do thou prosper me. Whatsoever things are opposed to my prosperity, remove them out of the way. Work in me everything approved of God, for the attainment of this. Give me a heart 'sick of love' to thyself, and to the souls of men. Grant that I may experience the power of thy word before I deliver it, as Moses felt the power of his own rod before he saw it on the land and waters of Egypt. Grant this, for the sake of thine infinitely precious blood, O Jesus my hope, and my all in all! Amen. — C. E.

IX. Search me now and lead me in plain paths of judgement. Let me discover in this life what I am before thee, that I may not find myself of another character, when I am shown in the light of the immortal world, and open my eyes in all the brightness of eternity. Wash me in thy redeeming blood. Amen. — C. E.

X. Grant me strength to depend upon thee for food and raiment, and to make known my requests. O let thy care be over me as a covenant-privilege betwixt thee and myself, and not like a general care to feed the ravens that perish, and clothe the lily that is cast into the oven; but let thy care be over me as one of thy family, as one of thine unworthy brethren. Amen. — C. E.

XI. Grant, O Jesus, and take upon thyself the preparing of me for death, for thou art God; there is no need, but for thee to speak the word. If possible, thy will be done; leave me not long in affliction, nor to die suddenly, without bidding adieu to my brethren, and let me die in their sight, after a short illness. Let all things be ordered against the day of removing from one world to another, that there be no confusion nor disorder, but a quiet discharge in peace. O grant me this, for the sake of thine agony in the garden! Amen — C. E.

XII. Grant, O blessed Lord, that nothing may grow and be matured in me, to occasion thee to cast me off from the service of the sanctuary, like the sons of Eli; and for the sake of thine unbounded merit, let not my days be longer than my usefulness. O let me not be like lumber in a house in the end of my days, — in the way of others to work. Amen. — C. E.

XIII. I beseech thee, O Redeemer, to present these my supplications before the Father: and O inscribe them in thy book with thine own immortal pen, while I am writing them with my mortal hand, in my book on earth. According to the depths of thy merit, thine undiminished grace, and thy compassion, and thy manner unto people, O attach thy name, in thine upper court, to these unworthy petitions; and set thine amen to them, as I do on my part of the covenant. Amen.

Christmas Evans
Llangefni, Anglesey, April 10, 18 —.[23]

In speaking of this solemn covenant and the sense of security it brought him, he subsequently wrote: 'I felt a happy degree of peace and tranquillity of mind, like unto a poor man who had been brought under the protection of the royal family, and who had an annual settlement for life made upon him; from whose dwelling the painful dread of poverty and want had been for ever banished away; or like the brood under the wing of the hen. This is to dwell under the shadow of the Almighty, and hide beneath the shadow of his wings until every calamity is overpast.'[24]

By 1812 the membership of the Anglesey church had risen to about 385, with many more occasional listeners. With these larger congregations Christmas Evans turned his thoughts to church discipline and how best to encourage members to live according to their high calling, a subject he had dealt with in the Northern Assembly of 1811, when he had tried to create conditions for 'effective and meaningful church discipline'. Private sins should be dealt with according to Matthew 18:15-18, he advised, while public sins were a matter for the whole church.

If the transgression was serious enough, excommunication should be exercised, without any possibility of restoration, for 'There is no hope of changing a wolf into a lamb even after forty years of discipline.' In the Llangefni letter of 1813 he listed four of the most common faults: a factious spirit, a disregard for church meetings — 'Your Saviour is calling you to a feast and he has promised to be present and to convey his blessing. If you do not come to meet him, he will interpret it as contempt' — a lack of love among the membership, and impropriety.[25]

Christmas Evans was quite prepared to expel any member who was guilty of these sins:

> Robert Williams, 'a lame man', who was baptised by Christmas Evans in Holyhead on 26 August, 1796, was excommunicated in 1804... On 12 April, 1818, William Roberts, Hugh Jones, Robert Jones and Elinor Williams were excommunicated for neglecting church meetings. On 9 January, 1820, Mary William was expelled for a second time for accusing Jane Roberts of unchastity. And on 9 April of the same year, John and Elizabeth Williams were punished for playing music and dancing late into the night on their wedding day against advice.[26]

These examples demonstrate Christmas Evans's determination to maintain order within the fellowship and to ensure that his members were living according to the purity of the New Testament.

After the 1814-15 revival Christmas Evans returned to the subject of church discipline in the Anglesey Assembly's letter of 1816: 'When an army is strengthened and increased,' he wrote, 'the first task for young soldiers is to undergo the king's regular discipline, in order to test them and teach them to face the dangers of war more courageously and hopefully.' Every effort must be made by young and old 'to avoid personal quarrels, errors in doctrine, public sins, neglect of corporate worship and disobedience to leaders'. The authors of contention are to be severely reprimanded, for 'Such people are religious Jacobites who oppose the king's government wherever they be.'[27]

Immediately prior to the revival the cause at Ebenezer was very low. The members had 'lost their religious zeal' and were displaying 'a carelessness in religion' that caused 'the gifted and hardworking Christmas Evans to lament greatly for their sakes'. In 1811 he had complained about a lack of dependence on the Holy Spirit among preachers, who were tempted to 'go through a sermon as a child reads its lesson, without the brightness of divine glory'. On the one hand, the great danger was to preach Christ 'without spiritual feeling', coldly and lifelessly, or to listen to the Gospel 'in a worldly spirit'; on the other hand, the great need of the hour was for God to pour out his power upon the church as he had done at Llanfachreth in 1805 and two years later at Brynsiencyn, where many had been awakened to eternal life.[28] Little did the pastor of Anglesey realise that his yearnings for a deeper experience of God's grace in the churches under his care and for the fields to be made 'white unto harvest' were about to be satisfied.

All the children of men are void and without form, while in a state of nature, before they are quickened by the influence of the Holy Spirit. It is by his operation they are convinced and converted to God; are made partakers of faith, and united to Christ their living Head, and are made conformable to his image.

I pray, God, that the Holy Spirit may move on our congregations, as in the days of Paul and Peter, Whitefield in England and Rowland in Wales, and as he does in many parts of America at present. Amen, from the bottom of my heart.

> Come Holy Spirit, heavenly dove,
> With all thy quickening powers;
> Come shed abroad a Saviour's love,
> And that shall kindle ours.

Christmas Evans preaching on 1 Thessalonians 5:23.[1]

Unless we are favoured with frequent revivals, and a strong, powerful work of the Spirit of God, we shall, in a great degree, degenerate, and have only a 'name to live': religion will lose its vigour; the ministry will hardly retain its lustre and glory; and iniquity will, of consequence, abound.

Thomas Charles of Bala on revival.[2]

11
Times of Refreshing

Although the prospects for a revival looked bleak in 1812-13, Christmas Evans continued to preach with zeal and energy until, in 1814, a spirit of prayer descended on the churches, creating a deeper solemnity towards the things of God, especially among some of his deacons, and a new earnestness for spiritual prosperity. The fervour and devotion of the congregations, previously lukewarm, were restored and many were invigorated with new life. In his own words, Christmas Evans says, 'The Lord was pleased, out of the abundance of his mercy, after much wrestling in prayer, and ardent longings after the enjoyment of divine influence, to bestow upon us the dew of heaven, which occasioned great awakenings, conviction and concern to take place among the people throughout many neighbourhoods in Anglesey.'[3] 'The wilderness and the solitary places now rejoiced, and the dreary desert blossomed as the rose. Zion's tent was enlarged, and the curtain of her habitation stretched forth.'[4]

At the beginning of the revival Christmas Evans felt compelled to visit the South, leaving the responsibility for the Anglesey church in the hands of his assistant preachers. Robert Williams was appointed to take charge of Cil-dwrn. 'On one midweek evening,' Williams observes, 'there broke out a revival so powerful and general that there were, before the close of the service, in Ebenezer, many on their knees in prayer, crying out for mercy ... and clear signs that the Spirit of the living God was applying the ministry to the hearts of the hearers unto salvation; and by the time of Mr Evans's return from his visit to the South, the congregation had multiplied greatly and a number of candidates were requesting baptism.'[5]

Within two years (1814-1815) the eleven preaching places on the island belonging to the Baptists increased to twenty-one; 600 converts were added to the several branches of the church for which Christmas Evans was responsible, bringing the total to more than 1000; at Cil-dwrn, where 'eighty members were added in the course of a few months',[6] a gallery was built in order to double the number who could attend the chapel;[7] men of like-mind arose to assist him in the ministry; several new chapels were erected to accommodate the larger congregations; and 'The voice of joy and praise was heard, because God was again building up the shattered walls of his church... The scene was enchanting, and all seemed to behold and enjoy it with peculiar pleasure. They continued to administer the ordinance of baptism summer and winter, amid the heat and the cold; and the churches, especially those at Llanfachreth, Llanrhuddlad, New Chapel, White Chapel and Llannerch-y-medd, were raised to a state of some eminence in those delightful times.'[8]

In a sermon on Zechariah 3:9 Christmas Evans may have been alluding to this period of revival and growth when he traced the work of God in 'building up Zion' from the day of Pentecost to the time of Luther, who, 'with the lamp of God in his hand', discovered the Scriptures and set them to work:

> Millions of lively stones have since been dug out, and sent up from the pit, to be placed in the walls of 'God's building'...
> Glory to God, that I have in my own possession the

register of hundreds, who have been hewn from the flinty rock, and raised from the horrible pit, to a place in the Lord's holy temple — from drunkenness to sobriety, from unbelief to faith in Christ, from enmity to reconciliation to God, from persecution to patient suffering for righteousness' sake, from disobedience to the filial temper of 'sons and daughters of the Lord Almighty'; and many of them I have seen going home, rejoicing, to their Father's house above!

Hark! What do I hear? The hammers and chisels of mercy all over the mountain of the militant church... Glory to God! I hear his footsteps today in this mountain; I see his hand in this congregation. Brethren in the ministry, we are workers together with him. Delightful work! How easy it is to preach, when the hand of God is with us! Let us labour on! The topstone will soon be brought forth with shouting, the sound of the building shall cease, and we shall receive our reward![9]

The revival in Anglesey was part of the growth and blessing experienced by the Baptist denomination during the years 1790-1815, when consolidation occurred with some 10,000 new converts, an expansion unthinkable a century earlier. 'Showers of blessing regularly fell on the churches; they fell like the showers of nature, in a sovereign way and quite invincibly. The awakening would affect scores in a short time, causing them to shake, weep and cry out "What must I do to be saved?" That would be accompanied by the spirit of intense prayer and seriousness... Sometimes hundreds would be added to single churches during a year... More of God's work is achieved during a single Sabbath of awakening than in years of preaching.'[10]

Such a revival in the religious life of the Welsh people, achieved by the faithful and anointed preaching of the gospel, caused Christmas Evans, a few years later, to write, 'Perhaps no other nation has ever been won over more totally to the hearing of the Gospel. Meeting houses have been built in all corners of the land[11] and most of the common people, nearly all of them in fact, regularly congregate to listen.'[12] Thus the

Baptists, revived and renewed, and somewhat removed from their old exclusivism, became part of the movement of Dissent that would, by mid-century, not only become the dominant form of Welsh Christianity, but would also transform the religious, social and cultural life of the Welsh people.

During the revival in Anglesey some remarkable instances occurred, one of which is recorded below. It was about 1815 that Christmas Evans became acquainted with a respectable young man from Bangor of the name of Parry, who had been brought up in Oxford and prepared for the ministry in the Church of England. Having completed his education he was about to be ordained by the Bishop, who was favourably disposed to him, when he approached Christmas Evans at Llangefni, 'apparently under deep conviction, and appeared dead to all earthly objects, as if the eternal world and its important realities, had absorbed his whole soul and body'. His reason for approaching the pastor of Anglesey was to be baptised by him in the river. After questioning the prospective candidate, whose views on baptism were perfectly Scriptural, 'I persuaded him to return home ... without being baptised.' Christmas Evans continues the story:

> He came to me afterwards on four different occasions, and on the fifth visit, I did all in my power to advise him to return home, and comply with his parents' intentions, urging him as a reason the expense they had incurred in training him up for the ministry of the Episcopal Church. To this he replied, 'Oh what an unhappy man I am! Brought up by my parents to earn a livelihood by false preaching, for which I have neither gift nor spirit! Oh that they had brought me up a tinker! I would prefer that.' He had now commenced undressing himself, with a view to change his clothes for baptism: I endeavoured again with all my power of reasoning (with what propriety I cannot say) to prevail upon him to relinquish the thought and obey his parents, for I could not find him clear in his knowledge of the righteousness of Christ, as the only foundation of a

sinner's acceptance with God. This address succeeded so
far that he buttoned his clothes; but the next moment unbut-
toned them again, uttering these expressions with all solemnity as of another world: 'Oh, my parents will not accompany
me to the other side of death, and they will not answer for my
disobedience in the judgement to come!'

Here I could not deny him any longer; — 'Come down to
the river,' said I, 'and I will baptise you at your own request.'
Accordingly, we repaired to the river opposite to Ebenezer
meeting-house. I read the account of Christ's baptism, and
prayed, and went with the young man into the river, without
any earthly spectator whatever, but my wife. When he came
up out of the water, he appeared as if he had cast off some
heavy burden from his shoulders, and his countenance
assumed fresh cheerfulness. He said, in the English language,
'Oh Lord! accept this poor sacrifice of mine.' He returned to
the house to change his clothes and to take some refreshments;
and went his way rejoicing towards Bangor, having offered a
sacrifice of obedience upon a watery altar in Llangefni
brook.[13]

Christmas Evans only saw Parry once after his baptism, and
that was in the parish of Llanllyfni, where he was curate. 'For
some years he lived morally and circumspectly, and always
conducted himself affectionately towards the Baptists,' but 'He
had no talent for preaching, and his mind was much exercised
that he sustained an office whilst he possessed neither spirit nor
skill to perform its duties.' At length he resigned from the curacy
and the ministry altogether, and 'betook himself to
school-keeping for his support'.[14]

After the revival the duties connected with so many branches
of the church increased considerably. The principal manage-
ment of affairs fell on Christmas Evans, including the oversight
of the construction of new places of worship and the procure-
ment of funds for the work; his itinerant ministry became more
arduous as he attempted to consolidate and teach the growing
numbers under his care; and all cases of church discipline were

dealt with by him, a time-consuming and often thankless task. There were ordained ministers and other auxiliaries to assist him in the administration of Christian ordinances, but these twenty-eight preachers, all of whom arose during the course of Christmas Evans's ministry on the island, were natives of Anglesey and committed to other occupations and worldly businesses, and therefore could not spare the time to offer more than a token assistance. They were also young and inexperienced, needing to be trained and encouraged themselves, and, in the course of their duties, heavily dependent on Christmas Evans for guidance. An administrative meeting with these preachers, plus one representative from each branch, was held on the first Tuesday of every month, in rotation, at several of the places of worship. It followed a public preaching service, which was conducted on the Monday night. At these 'more private assemblages for the transaction of business'

> ... all matters of personal difference and all questions of discipline were introduced as they arose. The independence of the several churches was but slowly recognised, and was more slowly acted upon. Many matters that should have been adjusted at home, were frequently brought, and for many years, to these monthly meetings; and themes of gravest difficulty, as well as of the utmost puerility, were, in their turn, investigated and pronounced upon. All this he endured with a fortitude and a fidelity which no provocation could disturb, and no irritation of temperament in himself, though frequently betrayed, could impair. It was *his duty, his work, his burden* — conscience incessantly told him so, and the Redeemer had placed him in this post; that, at once, and for good, settled the question of obedience...
>
> At these meetings he invariably presided... All the preachers he called by their Christian names, some of them by abbreviated ones; nor did they, by scarcely any chance, call him *Mr Evans* — Christmas Evans, before his face as well as behind his back, was the name always in the mouths of the

Anglesey Baptists. To master this familiarity, so as to keep it within the bounds necessary for the relative position of the parties, cost him, on many occasions, all his skill and all his energy. A humble brother would unwittingly speak a second time to the same question, or speak irrelevantly; the Moderator in the pulpit might be seen gathering up his ample forehead — a short cough, or kind of grunt, followed — and at last, in a husky voice, Christmas Evans would say, authoritatively, 'Richard, *bach*; you have forgotten the question before the meeting: hold your peace.' 'William, my boy, you have spoken before; have done with it.' Once, when a minister from South Wales, but a native of Anglesey, got up from his seat, and made as though he was going to speak, Christmas Evans, suffering no intrusion from the South, gave him his quietus at once, by crying out, 'Sit down, Dafydd.'[15]

The meetings were generally productive, 'and glorious times they often had together — the Lord was with them, and much good was done in his name'.[16]

Problems remained, though. Several of the churches, even after the revival, still suffered under the chilling influence of Sandemanianism — an influence that lasted in one form or another for the next fifteen years. Particularly during his early Anglesey ministry, obstacles to the work arose in the form of some individuals unnecessarily meddling in the political affairs of Wales, and the desire of others to emigrate to America in order to secure more prosperous futures. It was at this point, during the very poor harvests of 1799-1801, when food was both scarce and expensive, that Christmas Evans, in a letter to John Williams, who had earlier emigrated to America, expressed his desire to follow his friend to the 'land full of mercies where life is easy'. 'There is a restlessness,' he admitted, 'which follows me about going over there.' In the letter he asked many questions about the temporal and spiritual aspects of the country and the receptiveness of the people to the gospel, hoping that Williams would give him 'any exhortation for my coming

over'.[17] Later in life, after some of his sermons had been translated and published in America, various individuals, having read
the sermons, wrote to him, offering to pay his expenses and to
support him honourably and liberally all the days of his life, if
he would leave Wales and travel to America.

However, as the economic climate improved, he became
more settled and the desire to leave the Principality disappeared.
In fact, in later years, both these hindrances to the gospel —
emigration and politics — which contributed much to weaken
the churches in Anglesey and to dampen the spiritual ardour of
the ministers who were ensnared by them, greatly annoyed
Christmas Evans, who opposed anything that interfered with
the simple preaching of Christ. He called 'these two talkative
and gifted gentlemen, Mr Politician and Mr Going-to-America,
alias Mr Love-Riches', and accused them of 'cooling religious
zeal, depriving professors of the spirit of prayer, and at length
ending in total apostasy', and of causing 'much mischief in the
churches'. 'Few of those who went to America,' he claimed,
'have been of much comfort and usefulness in that country.'[18]
In a letter to John Williams in 1816, he said, 'Many useful members went over to America, where their usefulness was buried
for ever.'[19]

He had no objection to Mr Politician's theory of religion,
which he found was 'well versed in Scripture'. What infuriated
him was his apathy towards religious topics in comparison with
his unbounded enthusiasm for politics. 'He seemed to be
asthmatical when religion was the theme of conversation; let
politics, however, be on the carpet, and his voice was as clear
as crystal, and his very soul was engaged in it.' Mr
Going-to-America, on the other hand, saw 'nothing good on
earth but in America. To America he *would* go, and to America
he *did* go; and buried his religion, not in the Atlantic, but in the
ocean of love of wealth.'[20] If he had been more aware at the
time of the harm these two 'men' were causing to the Baptist

churches, he would have been 'more severe towards them',[21] and 'less inclined to lodge them'.[22]

Christmas Evans never engaged in violent political discussion, and was perhaps the most politically inactive of all the Baptist leaders, refusing to be sidetracked by pursuits that were not compatible with his holy calling. Instead of fighting 'battles political', he urged his colleagues to 'Set aside some time each week to pray together for the success of the gospel and other worthy causes, such as the health of the king and stability of the kingdom, so that we may live quietly under its rule.'[23] 'It appears clearly to be the duty of all,' he wrote in a letter to one of the island's magistrates on 4 March, 1817, 'to humble ourselves before the throne of the Almighty, imploring his mercy ... instead of imbibing a spirit of disaffection against our civil rulers.'[24] And again, in the same letter, written during the civil unrest that troubled Anglesey in that year, he stated: 'We do therefore undissemblingly avow our utmost hatred, and abhorrence to every species of intermeddling with political topics, and disseminating and fostering the seed of discord and sedition.'[25]

Along with the majority of Welsh Baptists, who had been strongly conservative for a century and a half, he was 'afraid of being associated in the least manner with those who would threaten their fragile and uncertain civil rights', and, when opportunity arose, would forthrightly speak out in favour of the king: 'May the whole world know that the Baptists of Great Britain submit, for conscience's sake, to the higher authorities (Romans XIII). We are bound to speak respectfully of the king, to pray for him, to pay tribute to him willingly: this is the duty of every true Christian.'[26] In the first article he ever sent to a magazine, in this case *Seren Gomer*, he wrote: 'How obvious and clear it is that to follow Jesus of Nazareth is far better than to follow Voltaire and his like; how beneficial it is to conform to the laws of Christianity; how sublime and excellent are these words, "Fear God, honour the king."'[27]

During the industrial dispute in Mynydd Parys copper mine, he and eight of his fellow Baptist ministers in Anglesey drew up a highly conservative declaration, with which most of the Welsh Baptists would probably have agreed:

'It is not the province of Christians,' says the declaration, 'to debate and discuss politics — but to behave humbly towards our superiors.' It continues, 'Sir, we do not feel the least interest in the great noise about universal suffrage, annual Parliaments, reform of Parliament, abolishing of the tithe and many other things ... from Agrarian Laws and Spencean principles, good Lord, deliver us. We do cordially hate the political leaven of Cobbett,[28] Tom Paine[29] and other radicals. Our duty is plain before us, namely, to fear God and honour the king.' They promised to excommunicate anyone who ventured to speak slightingly of the king and his government, and placed the blame for the dearth and distress, not at the door of the king and his government, nor at that of the gentry, but firmly on the shoulders of the Almighty himself, 'The supreme ruler of all sublunary events does tenderly smite us with his rod.' The declaration ends in these terms, 'How unbecoming, how vain and infatuating it is for the common people to engage in political debates.'[30]

In spite of his 'political shyness', he did speak out against the French Revolution (1789) — a revolution that 'struck terror into his heart'[31] — for a considerable length of time. It seems that the majority of Welsh Baptists were extremely anxious about the prospects of violent revolution, especially as they were dependent in some instances on industrial leaders and their officials. He dreaded Bonaparte and his 'company of terrible thieves' because they had 'killed the royalty and nobility of France in order to snatch and grab possessions for themselves'. 'The fate of France,' he declared, 'was a warning to those who insisted on upholding radicalism, for radicalism went hand in hand with atheism.'[32] The last thing he wanted was a similar revolution in Wales.

Foremost among these political protagonists was the Baptist minister Morgan John Rhys (1760-1804), a 'strange and complex man',[33] in whom 'the spirit of rebellion was very strong', according to Christmas Evans, who also accused his old friend of leading 'many to speak disparagingly of their religious and civil privileges'.[34] With determination and energy Rhys spread the social ideas of the French Revolution, which he regarded as 'the coming of the golden age, when tyranny and Popery would be no more', and thereby caused a great stir. He resigned his pastorate in 1791 and spent some time in Paris, where he secured a large hall as a Bible storehouse and preaching station. He returned to Wales when war was declared and in 1793 started a Welsh magazine, which became a platform for political, social and religious propaganda.[35] 'Disgusted with anti-liberalism in politics and religion in Britain,' he emigrated to America, the Promised Land in his eyes, in 1794.[36] Christmas Evans had 'no knowledge that he was greatly known as a preacher there, nor that he displayed much industry or faithfulness in the ministry. The thorns continue to strangle the seed.'[37]

Although Christmas Evans was not unduly concerned about the departure of Rhys, he was sorry to lose his 'beloved brother' John Williams (1768-1825), whom he had ordained as minister of Garn in 1791. Williams was influenced by the unrest caused by the French Revolution and in 1795 emigrated to New York with his brother. Three years after his arrival he was appointed pastor of an English church in Oliver Street and remained there until his death. According to Christmas Evans, he was one of the few emigrants who exercised a useful ministry in America. It was to John Williams that Christmas Evans wrote on 31 March, 1817, assuring him that his involvement with the politics of Wales had not affected his priorities or deflected him from preaching Christ: 'To dedicate myself to God, to live to his glory and labour unceasingly for the cause of Christ, is as important to me as ever, and the vigour of body and spirit has not waned even though I have expended myself much. Oh! that I could do something for the glory of Jesus Christ. All I have done seems but a dream.' And again, two years later, he wrote: 'Oh! for strength to endure to the end and to die in the faith.'[38]

During his busy ministry, which included almost constant travelling and preaching, he still managed to apply himself to that time-consuming occupation of writing for the press. His output was varied and valuable, ranging from letters and articles to expositions and sermons — he wrote eight Association letters, eight books and three sermons between 1800 and 1815 — and he is regarded as 'the most literary of all the great preachers of Wales'.[39] His *Works* were gathered together and edited by Owen Davies, Caernarfon, and published in three substantial volumes (over 2000 pages) in 1898. Below are listed some of his published works:

1. *The Unsearchable Riches of Christ*, considered in a sermon from Ephesians 3:8 (1803). This was the first sermon he published.

2. In the Llangefni letter of 1802 he discussed election; in the Amlwch letter of 1803 he looked at the relationship between the gospel and the law; in the Llangefni letter of 1805 particular redemption was the topic; and Antinomianism was the subject of the Amlwch letter of 1806.

3. *The Character of Sound Doctrine ... or An Antidote for the Poison of Arminianism* (1803).

4. *A Word in Season Containing a Response to the Doctrine that is Contrary to Sovereign Grace* (1803).

5. A sermon on Hebrews 5:9, *Christ, The Prince of our Salvation*, preached at the South West Association, Ffynnon in Pembrokeshire (1804).

6. *Mene Tekel: A Review of a Booklet by Mr Wesley Entitled 'A Blow at the Roots'* (1806).

7. *The Circular Letter of the South East Baptist Association in South Wales*, held at Llys-faen in Glamorganshire (1807). The theme of this letter is the need to foster a religious zeal. Also a defence of this letter *A Plea for the*

Scriptural Method or *Work of the Spirit in Regeneration* (1809) in reply to some *Strictures* that were made upon it by one who called himself Philalethes.

8. A sermon from Hebrews 7:22 entitled *Christ a Surety for his People in the New Covenant* to which are attached *Three Letters to a Friend*: 1. On the nature of the judgement that came by the sin of Adam, 2. On proving that Christ was a priest on earth, 3. On showing that the life as well as the death of Christ constituted the matter of a sinner's justification (1807). In these three letters he signs himself 'Christmas Samuel Evans' for the first and only time.

9. *A Letter of Counsel to the Baptists of Cefn-mawr, Denbighshire* (1809), the theme of which is that it is impossible for man to come to Christ unless the Father draw him.

10. *An Answer for the Hope that is set before the Christian in the Meritorious Atonement of Christ* as the only ground of his acceptance or his justification before God. It contains replies to the objections of Socinians (1810).

11. *Particular Redemption*, showing in what it consists (1811).

12. *The Form of Sound Words* or *The Voice of the Turtle in the Land &c.* (1811), which was intended to help the travellers of Zion to judge rightly of Antinomianism.

13. *Redemption within the Circle of Election* or *The Particularity of Redemption* in relation to the church only and this particularity in the atonement of Christ (1819).

14. *Sarah and her Son Casting Out the Bondmaid and her Son*, a treatise on believer's baptism in reply to a book by the ex-Baptist Peter Edwards of Portsea, Hants. Edwards's book *Candid Reasons for Renouncing the Principles of Antipaedobaptism* had been published in Welsh.

15. *A Letter from a few Members of the Body of People Called Baptists, in Answer to a Letter he* [Thomas Jones of Denbigh] *Wrote to us Concerning Mr Christmas Evans's Book on Particular Redemption* (1820). This is a defence of Christmas Evans's view and conduct, with an appeal to Jones to retract his criticism.

16. *The Second Letter and Defence in Response to Mr Thomas Jones, Denbigh, a Preacher with the Calvinistic*

Methodists, Concerning his Letter to the Baptists. Written by one of the Baptists (1820). It is a series of thirty-one points attacking Thomas Jones's theology, the inconsistency of his views, his prejudice against the Baptists, his malice and pride, etc.

17. *A Review of the Baptismal Controversy,* occasioned by the publication of several pamphlets on baptism (about 1822).

18. *Lectures on Revelation* published in 1835, during his ministry in Caernarfon.

19. An essay on *Total Abstinence* (1836).

He also wrote while at Cardiff about two hundred sermons on various subjects, which were published in numbers, and thirty numbers were issued from the press before his death.[40]

These books, many of which were sold all over Wales, together with his preaching journeys, made him very well-known and popular throughout the Principality. The love and warmth extended to him at the great Association meetings prove the genuine affection in which he was held. At these meetings, where for thirty years he was usually the third and main preacher, men such as John Elias, a frequent hearer, sat 'with his whole form in motion'. On one of these occasions at Llangefni, Elias and his wife were sitting in the crowd listening to Christmas Evans, who had captivated the huge congregation. The sounds of praise and weeping were heard as the preacher ascended to the heights of religious fervour and Elias was seen lifting his handkerchief to his eyes to wipe away the tears of joy.

His catholic spirit, so opposed to sectarianism, especially after his deliverance from Sandemanianism, meant that he was often engaged to preach at the large gatherings of other denominations, such as the Methodists, who took so much delight in claiming him as their own that the Baptists feared his removal to that body. However, it was for his own denomination that he worked tirelessly, promoting the Associations, held annually in Anglesey, to as great a height as any other Association in the Principality — it certainly became through his efforts as large and influential as the older ones in the South and as popular as the Calvinistic Methodists, and gave the Baptists a name and place among the bodies of North Wales, as well as an important part in the 'Nonconformist tide that was sweeping through Wales'. 'There is a very heavenly glow over our assemblies in the North,' said Christmas Evans to Thomas Thomas, minister of Nantglyn, on 20 January, 1812, 'so that they are enjoying an abundant unction, and there are signs that they are being especially blessed to raise the character of the [Baptist] cause in the country.'[41]

His concern for these meetings is manifest, not only from his incessant anxiety that 'all turned out well', which moved him to 'fervent and agonizing prayer', but from the way he meticulously arranged and ran them. 'In illustration,' says Rhys Stephen, 'I well recollect an incident he once related to me:'

> The jealousy of religious politicians in the island was in its strength, and it was the custom for 'certain other brethren' to describe the poor Baptists as disloyal and 'Jacobin'. So nervously anxious was Christmas Evans that no colour might be given to this charge at the Association, that he was accustomed to kneel out of sight behind the front of the scaffolding, near the minister who engaged in prayer at the commencement of the service, so that, in the event of his omitting to pray for the king and the royal family, he might suggest it to him *unseen of the people*. So fully alive, and so watchful, was the spirit of politico-religious bigotry for years in this island, that an omission of this nature, in any one of the public prayers, during a series of seven or eight services, would become a matter of grave and injurious reflection upon the whole body, and not improbably form the ground of formal criminal information.[42]

To further the Association's cause, when he travelled south in the summer, he returned with seven or eight of the ablest preachers in Wales, with whom he engaged in uplifting conversations and in this way became familiar with the work of God in many other parts of the Principality. During the course of their stay, he treated his guests 'with a respect and consideration that frequently astonished them',[43] and in return they often spent three to four weeks touring the North. This practice he continued for thirty-three years. It 'deserves notice', he remarked in recognition of their faithful services, 'that the spread of religion among us owes its origin to the labours of our dear brethren in South Wales. How much are we indebted to them as instruments!' Their annual visits to the Anglesey Associations achieved 'incalculable good'. 'May the Lord pour millions of blessings on their heads!'[44] On 1 April, 1816, he mentioned to John Williams how the blessing of God rested on the two assemblies in the North: 'God has done wondrous things. The annual assembly in Anglesey draws ten to fifteen thousand listeners and the great outpourings of the Spirit are upon them, which causes some wonder in general. May the name of Jesus Christ be praised.'[45]

Among the men who preached at the Anglesey Association between the years 1802 and 1827 were Thomas Jones, Glyn Ceiriog, who has already been mentioned for his forthright opposition of Sandemanianism in the North; Titus Lewis, well-known as a staunch defender of Calvinism and whose simple sermons carried deep conviction; and Samuel Breeze of Aberystwyth, one of the most popular preachers of his day. Christmas Evans regarded him as standing 'in the first ranks of the ministry':

> His preaching was something like a warm day, with dewy mists preparing the harvest for the sickle. He had the physical capacity to set forth his ideas to the greatest advantage; an affectionate, pleasant countenance; eyes that could flame forth, alternately and at will, either love or terror; and a strong, musical voice, to a great extent well-managed, although he could not be considered perfect master of it, because the

> excitement within urged on the words too fast for his tongue;
> still his voice served, to a good degree, as a fit vehicle for his
> fiery affections... He would begin in a calm, free and easy
> tone of voice, his face wearing a benignant expression, but
> when a little excited towards the middle, his voice became a
> clear, silvery tenor; while at the end, his eyes looking a-flame,
> his voice waxed into something like a lion's roar, or rather it
> sounded like a martial drum-beat calling men to arms! And
> most extraordinary were the effects often produced upon the
> people.[46]

Others who attended the Anglesey Association were Henry
Davies, Llangloffan, an exceptionally fine preacher and the man
who in 1788 baptised John Richard Jones; Abel Vaughan and
David Saunders; John Jones (Newtown), John Jenkins and
Robert Edwards; Daniel Jones, who was baptised by Timothy
Thomas in 1807, and who eleven years later, at Christmas
Evans's request, took charge of a small Welsh Baptist church
(twenty-eight members) in Liverpool, where he laboured with
great success for twenty-five years; John Herring, of whom
Christmas Evans said that he possessed 'more of the attributes
of a great preacher than anyone else in Wales';[47] Joshua Watkins,
a zealous missionary for the cause of Christ; Francis Hiley, 'a
mighty preacher of whom Christmas Evans said, on one occasion, that he would never preach after him';[48] and David Evans,
an eminent minister of Maes-y-berllan, who on behalf of the
Welsh Baptist Mission visited North Wales thirteen times. At the
latter's interment, Christmas Evans delivered an address in the
burying ground connected with the chapel at Maes-y-berllan. It
was subsequently published in *Seren Gomer*, November, 1821,
and provides a typical example of Christmas Evans's ability to
sketch the character of a godly man:

> The Lord had endowed him with a strong understanding; his
> memory was retentive; his imagination prompt and lively; his
> voice strong and manly; with a firmly compact person, and

good health... His library consisted principally of the Bible and Concordance; whence, by diligent study, he drew his sermons...

His distinguishing excellence, perhaps, consisted in his eloquent and powerful address, and in the variety of his tropes and metaphors, which always gave forth the sound and pursued the current of Scripture; though they were lively, prompt and abrupt, yet free from all fanaticism; and he set them forth with dexterity, warmth and power, so that he seldom failed to enter into the conscience, the judgement, and the affections of his hearers. His whole manner was clear to transparency, so that the weakest hearer found no difficulty in following or understanding him...

I apprehend no one present will charge me with extravagance when I say that his talents were of the highest kind, and made him worthy of a place among the mighty ones of Wales.[49]

John Philip Davies of Tredegar was another eloquent preacher who attended the Anglesey Association. He was a devoted evangelist, fully committed to the missionary movement, an acute thinker and an able controversialist. He was 'a very pattern of humility, while he was full of curiosity, and habitually actuated by an intense desire for useful and varied information'. In the later years of his life 'Christmas Evans regarded Mr Davies with more real deference than, perhaps, any other minister in the circle of his intimate acquaintance in the whole Principality.'[50] He is known as the 'apostle in Wales of Andrew Fuller's Calvinism', called by some 'doctrines of straw and hay'; but 'those who differed from him were literally captivated and overcome by his persuasive and powerful ministry'. On one occasion, Sammy Shon, 'a notorious old deacon, who detested the new views of the preacher', listened to him very suspiciously. Towards the close of the sermon, when Mr Davies was in the *hwyl*, 'The old deacon was fairly won over, and compelled to acknowledge himself convinced and vanquished.

He threw up his hat exclaiming, "Well, if thou art a Fuller, I am a Fuller too."'[51]

Joseph Harris, who died in 1825 at the age of fifty-two and whose name appears on Christmas Evans's memorial in Bethesda Chapel, Swansea, is another man of note who visited the Anglesey Association. He was a zealous and enlightened preacher, who kept alive the tradition of the revivalists, an ardent patriot and 'one of the greatest benefactors of his country in his day'.[52] As a writer he distinguished himself and may be regarded as the father of the Welsh newspaper, for his *Seren Gomer*, 1814-15, was the first all-Welsh weekly.[53] In comparing him with Christmas Evans, Rhys Stephen says:

Mr Harris was the most vigorous and self-possessed, while, in imagination, he was a dwarf in the presence of a giant. In absorbing devotedness to the cause of Christ they were equals; but, in the exercise of that devotedness, there were certain important differences. Christmas Evans was for present action and direct means — Joseph Harris was eminent for perspicacity and far-sightedness, and would readily forego a small present advantage for an extensive and *certain* future good. The former, full of zeal and instinct with living fire, must set to work at the place, and in a moment; the latter, while quite prepared to take his share of present labours, chiefly occupied his mind with the fitness of measures for future influences and remote results...

Both were alike characterized by fervent piety, and distinguished for active untiring beneficence. Mr Harris would leave Anglesey inoculated, in no small degree, with the chivalric godliness of Christmas Evans; while the 'Welsh apostle' bore with him, for many months afterwards, a profound recollection of Joseph Harris's enterprising but sober-minded and practical spirit.[54]

Then there was Simon James, a godly man, who was noted for his 'untiring labour and perseverance in preaching the Gospel'. He was ordained in 1812 as a missionary to Lleyn, and 'liked exceedingly' by Christmas Evans, who urged him to stay in the North. 'His sermons,' remarks his friend, 'were full of well-arranged evangelical truth. In listening to him, you would not be struck with any great penetration, but you were attracted by the fragrance of tender affection and love. You were ravished as with the sweetest sounds of the harp. The hearers would often forget themselves, borne away by a delicious, although not many-toned music, under the influence of which "Amens" broke forth from the heart, and the tears flowed freely.'[55] Evan Jones was also on the list of preachers. He was a long-standing and intimate friend of Christmas Evans and a 'man of rare genuineness and simplicity of character, and, compared with most of his brethren, of great and brilliant power. He was a bard of some eminence, and in his preaching his highest thoughts would often rise into wild and daring poetry.'[56] When Christmas Evans died, as a last act of admiration and respect, Jones published, at his own expense, a noble tribute to the memory of his dear brother in Christ.

With the help of these able ministers the Baptist cause in Anglesey flourished and, after the deadness of Sandemanianism, the life, vigour and unity of the churches was the ground of much praise and thanksgiving from their pastor, whose own ministry 'blossomed as the rose'. Many opportunities for preaching the gospel were arising, often beyond the boundaries of his native Wales, and his usefulness in the kingdom of God was becoming more and more apparent. There were arduous and self-sacrificing days ahead though, as the revival, with its influx of new converts, meant that larger and more expensive places of worship were needed on the island to accommodate them. The responsibility for their construction rested on the shoulders of Christmas Evans, and developed into one of the heaviest and most stressful burdens of his ministerial career.

Some of the heaviest trials of his life arose in connection with chapel debts, and many prayers, sighs and tears did they draw from him; he was compelled to leave home and take a preaching tour through South Wales, and that frequently in the very depth of winter, and lay his case before the churches, that he might have the means to meet pressing claims. True, much of this burden should have been shared by his members and hearers, but he tells us 'The people left all these things to me, as to their father', probably thinking that it would be more effectively done by him than by them. And who can but admire the self-denial, disinterestedness, zeal and devotedness which he evinced in undertaking and resolutely grappling with it.

R. Morris.[1]

12
'Begging' Tours

Christmas Evans now had the extra 'obligation' of paying for the new chapels that were being built on the island.[2] This obligation continually pressed on his heart and mind and significantly increased his labours, especially as it appears that he was the only man responsible for financing the constructions.

> Later in life Christmas admitted that not enough care had been taken in the building of meeting-places; there were too many of them and they involved more expense than the worshippers were able to meet. He admitted also that it was a mistake to appoint preachers, rather than representatives of the congregations, to be responsible for paying for them.
>
> The usual procedure was to open a meeting place in a certain neighbourhood, in a farmhouse or barn, and, after securing a regular congregation, to plan building a more permanent chapel. When a convenient site had been found, it was the responsibility of the preacher, Christmas himself more often than not, to secure a loan.[3]

The money for construction was lent on the integrity of his name and that of a friend, sometimes without his consent, thus making him personally responsible for repaying the loan. Within two or three years either the interest was due or the full amount demanded, placing the pastor of Anglesey under considerable pressure.

In order to meet these debts, which his own people had
incurred but were either unwilling or too poor to pay anything
towards, he visited once a year the stronger and more affluent
churches in South Wales or England, with the express purpose
of raising money. These special and exhausting 'begging' journeys, as some have called them, were usually undertaken in
winter, when the travelling conditions were particularly difficult;
they lasted from between six weeks and two months, and were
always on horseback. It must also be remembered 'that his
constitution was one of the most unhappily formed — expos-
ing him to all the horrors of a most excitably nervous temperament, as well as to all the inconvenience of a most capricious
appetite; add to this, that he was at all times incapable of taking
any efficient care of himself in dress, in health, or in travelling
arrangements; and it will be easily discerned that in every long
journey ... he endured two or three martyrdoms'.[4]

A letter he wrote from Fishguard on 18 September, 1820,
provides an example of the extent of his travels and the efforts
he made to secure funds:

> Yesterday I collected £6 7s 0d and a similar sum in Llangloffan
> the previous Sunday. I'm afraid I shall not be able to collect
> one hundred and fifty in this Association and I must go to Bris-
> tol towards the end of November to preach at a Missionary
> Meeting... I intend, if my health allows it, to go from Bristol to
> Birmingham — to raise funds — and from there to London, if
> possible ... I hope that these efforts of mine will be a more
> effective way of stirring the Anglesey folk to make a special
> joint-collection, than anything I could have impressed upon
> their minds while I was with them ... Oh! that the most promi-
> nent members among them would undertake this task.[5]

The distress he experienced over these debts is best understood
from his own comments: 'I humbly believe that the troubles of
our missionaries in India, or any other part of the world, were
not so great as those I had to bear with the debts of places of

worship; and, moreover, they had not, in the meantime, to care for their own support, as I had during all the time I was in Anglesey; for the London Committee cared for them.'[6] He worked hard to establish a penny-a-week contribution to help the cause, but admits, 'I did not succeed well in it.'[7] Disconsolate and in great need, he poured out his heart to God: 'In the depth of night, I have wrestled in prayer, and entreated God to preserve his cause from disgrace. The promises of the God of Jacob, in support of his cause, were often of great comfort to my soul. I would examine the promises which involve the care of God for his own glory, and would take and spread them before him in prayer, until, sometimes, I felt as confident as if I had seen the whole debt paid.'[8]

As late in his life as February, 1835, after fifty years in the ministry, a letter by him addressed to the Baptist churches in Wales was published in the *Welsh Baptist Magazine*. In it he gives 'full and free expression to the feelings of his heart, upon a subject that engrossed so much of his thoughts, and entailed so much labour on his body' — a body, says his first Welsh biographer, that 'sunk into the grave, bearing deeply the impress of the heat and burden of the day on his furrowed countenance'.[9]

He opens the letter by expressing his astonishment that although 'Almost every town in Wales has been rebuilt, improved and enlarged' over the last fifty years, 'the debt incurred in building meeting houses belonging to our denomination has not received due attention.' There are Bible, Missionary and Tract Societies; the Sunday School, Temperance and other worthy institutions, but 'where is our *Building Fund Society*?'[10] The Spirit of God has been poured out abundantly on the Baptists and 'It ought to be considered that the erection of regular places of worship is of the greatest importance in the extension of Christ's kingdom.'[11] Then, probably alluding to himself and other men, such as Simon James, whose efforts to collect for the chapels in Caernarfonshire, among other things, 'contributed greatly ... to the breaking up of his constitution',[12] he remarks, 'Some have laboured much and injured their health in collecting money to liquidate the debt incurred in building meeting houses, and have been under the necessity of leaving their flocks and their families destitute while they were begging from house to house, not for themselves, but for the cause of him who is the sole owner of all the silver and gold in the universe... Brethren, these things ought not to be.'[13] Now observe, he continues:

1. That our cause in North Wales commenced about the same time, or a little before, the Baptist Mission to India.

2. That the expense was incurred in the extension of the means of grace, with a view to glorify the Redeemer.

3. That the great burden of the present existing debt was incurred at the time of the planting of churches.

4. That such circumstances can never occur again; because the places of worship are fixed in different parts, so as to embrace the principal portions of the counties.

5. If the body of Baptists were to unite to liquidate the present debt, the congregations would then be able to build a house here and there, for the happy Millennium that is in expectation.

6. I can perceive no force in the frivolous objections that are common; such as, that needless expenses have been incurred...

7. There is a relation subsisting between the name of Jesus and our houses of worship; for it is to preach his doctrine, and to administer the ordinances of his kingdom, that they have been erected. He considers the debt that lies upon them as a debt upon *his name* in the world, and expects his disciples to liquidate it, and deliver him from such a prison...

8. There is no way for us to exonerate ourselves from this debt without leaving our denomination in disgrace; and because of its connection with the name of Christ, if we do not exert ourselves to discharge this debt, we do not *visit him* in his cause... The dread of this, and the care which it involves,

occasions sleepless nights to some on the verge of the grave.
Believe me, this ferment you perceive in me has been heated
in the golden pot of my heart before God — *And the ark of
the Lord was taken.*[14]

During his winter journeys to South Wales, and his summer
trips to the annual Associations, he collected ideas for the medical treatment of both men and animals, especially horses; gathered herbs; and, where necessary, sharpened the knives and
razors of his hosts and their friends. On some of his papers,
next to a note on a theological issue, are found scribblings on
topics such as 'cures for asthma' that he had picked up along
the way. Often he wrote in a 'book of cures' lists of medicines
for scurvy, winter coughs, catarrh, toothache and various other
ailments. He also read and meditated on the Word of God with
such intensity that sometimes he lost all consciousness of what
was going on around him. Once his thirsty horse wandered off
the road into a nearby river to drink, before leisurely devouring
the long grass that was floating on the surface. Christmas Evans,
unaware that the animal had strayed from the intended path or
that the water was nearly up to the top of his boots, carried on
reading until a chapel-goer alerted him to his watery surroundings. With delight he used to relate a story that highlights the
hazardous nature of the itinerant ministry:

In some parts of the country, when it was felt desirable to
extend the household accommodation, it was done by making a 'wattle and daub' addition to the cottage. The apartment
thus erected was, in this instance, fixed upon for the 'prophet's chamber'. It was so small that a 'prophet' of our preacher's stature could not fully extend himself in it without an
undue pressure of the feet against the decaying fencework,
which barely enclosed him from the road. He was woken in
the morning by the rumbling of a cart which sounded dan-
gerously near, and, to his horror, he found that his protruding foot had narrowly escaped a very disagreeable collison.[15]

While in the South he preached for over an hour at least once every weekday and twice on Sundays. In all, if his summer excursions are included, he travelled from North to South Wales and back *forty times*, making him one of the principal links between Christians throughout the Principality. He notes that he did not know of another minister, even among the Methodists, who had made the journey more than *fifteen times*. It has been calculated that during his ministry in Anglesey he was away from home for a total of seven years and preached for nearly three thousand hours.

His habit on these journeys was to notify, about a week in advance, the inhabitants of a farm conveniently situated on the route about his forthcoming visit. The farmer would enthusiastically invite his family and friends and make announcements in the neighbourhood, so that when he arrived a large crowd was expectantly waiting. The farm labourers would take the day off, some working the whole of the previous night in order to attend the service. Hospitality, very coarse in most places, was cheerfully offered, although preparations at more salubrious surroundings were occasionally too elaborate, embarrassing the travelling preacher, who preferred simple meals of bacon, porridge and milk.

Often, as a result of these journeys, a church was planted or a new preaching station opened, and the flagging spirits of ministers and members were invigorated with new vision and purpose. On 21 May, 1806, he preached at Llanwenarth when John Jenkins, later of Hengoed, was set apart for the work of the ministry. At Aberystwyth, where he ministered regularly on his travels, he was a channel of great blessing. After preaching there on 23 July, 1815, John James, the minister in that town, wrote in his diary: 'Christmas Evans preached and there was much unction — more unction than I have seen on a sermon in Ab. for 18 or 20 years.' A week later he made another entry: 'On Tuesday night Ch. Evans preached. The praise was loud.

Wednesday night a special fellowship meeting was held and I do not think I shall ever forget those occasions. The majority found them to be particularly pleasant and precious and doubtless God was breaking hearts there.'[16]

Some churches welcomed him annually and were prepared to support his cause. Others objected to his visits, regarding them as irregular and too frequent, and complaining that if he wanted to build *so many* places of worship, he should wait until the people of Anglesey could finance their own projects, instead of begging in the South. They argued, albeit unconvincingly, that they were poor themselves, with their own chapels to upkeep, and, because of the 'hard times' they were experiencing, did not possess the means to contribute. Some of the ministers who opposed him, perhaps jealous of the large crowds that were drawn by him, thought of themselves as 'above' the uneducated preacher from the North, as they lived in towns and were the pastors of more affluent churches. These objectors did not deter Christmas Evans. He either ignored them altogether and carried on regardless, or won them over with tact, kindness and eloquence. To their protestations he would reply:

> What can I do? The people crowd to hear us; it is our duty to accommodate them as well as we possibly can. All we have we give. To you much is given — you can give much. 'It is more blessed to give than to receive...' We are in great distress. All the burden of procuring this money rests solely upon me. Do let me appeal to the people this time; I know they will love to help me. *I will not come again in this irregular manner; and we will take care at home not to build again until we are justified, even in your estimation.*[17]

In spite of his promise 'not to come again in this irregular manner', he travelled south the following year, and urged the people to give liberally to the building work in the North.

On another occasion, when he spoke further on this subject of giving, he highlighted a reluctance among the Welsh Baptists to support generously the cause of religion. He pointed most of the blame at 'wealthy ministers', who 'in all their conduct, conversation and speeches, always opposed burdening the churches with continual collections'; and more especially at the deacons, who, without Scriptural warrant, held 'the helm of government' in their hands and thereby 'were the cause of this ungenerous conduct':

> They often withstood vigorously, and opposed with all their might, the making of collections towards meeting-houses; while at the same time they were not very liberal in support of the ministry among themselves. Many of the wealthiest churches (alias deacons) would send a message in the mouth of their minister to the Association, stating, 'that no collector could be permitted to visit them with a view of taking up collections that year, because they were about building a small house of worship themselves'. Also, the ministers in Wales have not had that leading influence in the churches, generally speaking, which the word of God assigns them, according to the Epistle to the Thessalonians, Timothy, and the Hebrews; but the helm of government is held in the hands of deacons, or frequently, *the deacon*, so that the more liberal-minded of the ministers cannot remove this crying evil.[18]

The way he collected money on these journeys is of interest though by no means original. After he had concluded the ordinary service, he preached again, with as much zeal and earnestness as before, on the pressing needs of the churches in the North. He then took off his hat and went and stood by the door. As the congregation filed out he held out his hat to receive contributions, which were usually very small. This method he employed for many years until finally, due to the pressures of the work, he delegated a friend to take his place at the door, but never without an apology to the congregation lest it be thought he was disrespectful or inattentive to the generosity of others. In this way he collected between £1000-£1700, a considerable sum in those days, especially as the churches were young and their congregations reluctant to contribute to causes that did not directly affect them. However, hundreds of pounds of debt still remained on houses that had been built without his consent.

His usual practice when coming to a new neighbourhood was to learn as much as possible about the place and then use the information to his own advantage. On one occasion, when he entered a remote district, he learned that the area was notorious for sheep stealing, so when the time came to urge the crowd to contribute, he spoke animatedly about this crime, saying that in such a large congregation it was certain that some of the perpetrators were present. He addressed the thieves solemnly and implored them *not* to give their *filthy lucre*. The result was dramatic. Those who had no money quickly borrowed from their neighbours so that, it is said, not one person left the meeting without making a contribution!

These 'begging' journeys are not only examples of his dedication to the Baptist cause in Anglesey, but reminders of his own poverty. He was so poor that some have conjectured that his wife Catherine must have inherited money on which they both lived. One of the causes of his poverty was the frugality of the Welsh, who loved to hear the most eloquent and powerful preachers, but at the time did little to support them. Usually Christmas Evans was content with his meagre salary, which was supplemented by itinerant fees, but there were occasions when, after preaching, he did not receive enough even to cover his expenses. On one of these occasions, a poor old lady spoke up, 'Well, Christmas Evans, *bach*, I hope you will be paid at the resurrection; you have given us a wonderful sermon.' 'Yes, yes, Shân *fach*,' replied the preacher, 'no doubt of that, but what am I to do till I get there? And there's the old white mare that

carries me, what will she do? For her there will be no resurrection.'[19] Sometimes, in order to increase his income, he advertised his sermons and booklets from the pulpit after preaching.

Few, it seems, appreciated his efforts in collecting money,
and his exhortations on the duty of contributing often fell on
deaf ears. Because of this want of liberality, complained Christmas Evans, 'Many of the ministers are kept in very limited, and
narrow circumstances, and are often obliged to engage in the
unpleasant task of going out to collect towards their houses of
worship; whereas, had there been a liberal co-operation among
those to whom God had given the means, matters might soon
be brought into a comfortable state.'[20] He went as far as to say
that those who failed to support the ministry and the Baptist
cause should be excommunicated: 'Although this is a painful
duty for church and minister, yet it is as necessary to implement
it as it is to amputate a gangrenous limb from a person's body.'[21]
A minister should be able to devote all his time to his sacred
office, he said, thereby freeing himself of all worldly business,
and be adequately supported for doing so. In a letter to John
Reynolds of Felinganol, dated 8 January, 1813, he stated that
a minister should 'live for the Gospel and by the Gospel', a
subject he reiterated in the *Letter* of the Northern Association
in 1817 and again in the *Letter* of the South-western Association in 1824. However, his ideal was not realised before his
death, as some argued that it was beneficial for a minister to
have other work 'to keep him from wandering from house to
house gossiping!'[22]

Looking back over half a century of 'travelling, preaching
and collecting', and having 'gained nothing of this world's
goods', although he thought he had 'endured more toil of body
and mind than a dozen of my contemporaries in the ministry',
he could see how God had turned all things for good:

I have nothing to depend upon but the kindness of my brethren, as the Lord may prompt them. In the face of all this, I have reason to be thankful that the spiritual blessings which I have received, have counterbalanced all the difficulties which I have experienced. It is a matter of wonder to me that my straitened circumstances have been a sort of incentive to my usefulness throughout Wales, as I have been frequently obliged to travel, mainly on account of my own poverty.[23]

I have reached the evening and the [revival] day is greatly cooled...
Beyond a doubt, the preaching of intricate points — something like
questions concerning the law, and endless genealogies, have been
the means of cooling the work and the workmen in the evening of
the day. They will now lift up their heads and talk to every traveller
that passes the field; and towards Merionethshire, they will inquire,
'Dost thou know anything about Sandemanianism?' and in other
districts they will ask, 'Dost thou know something about Williamsism
and Fullerism?' and in consequence you may see young doctors
many, springing up, talking like learned Lilliputians. 'Some say that
Christ died for all, and others that it was for his church he died; but
the truth is this,' said the Lilliputians: 'he did not die for any man,
but for the sin of all men.'

I was there also on the great platform of this period, but I dared
not condemn all systems by a sweeping sentence of infallibility, and
take the bagpipe under my arm, as some were disposed to do, and
cry down every new voice without proving it. 'Prove all things.'

Christmas Evans.[1]

13
Controversy

Although the Sandemanian spirit still influenced the lives of some of the Baptist congregations in Anglesey, causing their pastor no little distress and in many ways obstructing the advancement of religion on the island, it was another dispute, called by Christmas Evans 'Wesleyanism', that dominated his attention during the opening years of the nineteenth century. This controversy caused agitation throughout the Principality.

At the end of the seventeenth century, after the Arminian Baptists of Radnorshire had emigrated in 1683 to the outskirts of Philadelphia, the religious bodies in Wales — the Church of England, the Independents, the Baptists and the Presbyterians — were all Calvinistic in their doctrines. There appears only one preacher at that time left in the Principality who adhered to Arminian teachings, and he was Henry Gregory, 'who suffered much at the hands of his persecutors'.[2] He was a leader of 'the people of Hugh Evans', the General Baptist. This is substantiated by the report of Henry Maurice, a prominent Puritan leader and an orthodox Calvinist, who says that Gregory was 'a teaching elder of the Arminians of West Radnor and North Brecknock who had their meeting place at Cwm in the parish of Llanddewi Ystradenny, at the house of Peter Gregory'.[3] Henry Gregory died at the beginning of the eighteenth century.

After 1689 the spread of Arminian doctrines was 'encouraged by the emphasis placed by Dissenters on reasoned intellectual and theological discussions, by greater religious freedom in Britain, and by more adventurous speculation by contemporaries'.[4] Forty years later a dispute known as *The Great Arminian Controversy* began to rage in Wales and several dissenting ministers and churches fell under its withering and blighting effect. The Arminian doctrines were given impetus by Thomas Perrot, the tutor of the Presbyterian Academy at Carmarthen, not because of his own unorthodoxy, but because of his inability to control the large number of students at the Academy, who

> ... became open advocates of Arminian or rather Pelagian sentiments, and from the year 1735, up to which time there was but one church in the Principality professing those sentiments, the numbers of Arminian Churches began to increase, so that by the year 1742 there were six or seven influential ministers and congregations that had embraced those views, greatly to the detriment of Puritan seriousness and morals, and in the course of a few years further other ministers and churches ... had adopted the same tenets.[5]

These new doctrines, championed by Jenkin Jones, one of Perrot's ablest pupils and the man who influenced the minds of a new generation of intellectuals and ministers, were greeted with alarm by many Calvinists, who viewed them as a serious threat to Christian orthodoxy. The ensuing war of attrition was both ill tempered and widely spread as the two parties crossed swords from local pulpits and via the printing presses. Many churches were greatly agitated and Calvinistic congregations in north Carmarthenshire and south Cardiganshire were thrown into turmoil. The fears of Calvinists were not unfounded, for the Arminianism that was advocated developed into Arianism and ultimately into Unitarianism.

John Wesley, who made no particular attempt to nurture in

Wales followers who accepted his Arminian beliefs, nevertheless exercised an influence in Flint and Denbighshire in the North
and Glamorgan and Monmouth in the South. By 1770,
because of his frequent visits to the Principality — he made
forty-six trips in all — there were about half a dozen Wesleyan
societies in the Anglicized parts of the country. Welsh Wales,
though, because of the language barrier, was almost exclusively
Calvinistic and by the time of Wesley's death in 1791, Arminian
Methodists in Wales numbered only 600. At the close of the
century, the various denominations in Wales lived together in
relative harmony. There were differences, of course, but these
differences did not at this time affect the preaching of the
essential doctrines of the Christian faith, to which, generally,
the main bodies of the non-conformist churches adhered.

During the opening decade of the nineteenth century some
itinerant Wesleyan preachers, including Edward Jones, an
enthusiastic and very effective missionary from Manchester,
under the auspices of the Wesleyan Methodist conference in
London, started to propagate their doctrines in Welsh in the
North with determination and energy. By the close of 1804
most of the northern counties had been visited by them. They
met with phenomenal success: 'Having only begun their work
in the year 1800, before the end of 1810 the travelling preachers were forty in number; the societies which they had formed,
four hundred; the members between five and six thousand;
and they had built no less than eighty chapels in nine years.'[6]
The introduction of the Wesleyan preachers, whose aim was to
establish Wesleyan Methodism in Welsh-speaking areas, recognising that the native language was the most effective medium
for the spread of their doctrines, renewed the controversy over
Arminianism, especially concerning the extent of the atonement.
This controversy raged in the pulpit and the press for the next
thirty years.

The temperature of the controversy was raised because the

Wesleyans, many of whom were young and inexperienced, portrayed the doctrines of Calvinism in an unfair and biased light, and accused those who upheld their tenets of 'deceiving the masses by preaching to them the universal call of the Gospel', while at the same time believing that 'only for the salvation of the elect was any provision made'.[7] As a reaction against this, those who cherished the doctrines of Calvinism, set forth Arminianism, 'as a system which was followed by nothing but evil; as a system, wherever it had gone, that had withered and blighted all true religion, and had become the source of every corruption'.[8] The strength of their reaction was because they identified Wesleyanism with the cold Pelagianism of the previous century, with its leanings toward Arianism and Unitarianism, and which had caused such havoc among the Particular Baptists of the south-west as late as 1799.

Both parties, by an inordinate zeal for their own systems, became extreme, and pushed each other further and further apart. Christmas Evans, who was himself deeply embroiled in the controversy and fiercely attacked the Wesleyan Methodists during the first decade of their history, notes the division among the Baptist denomination, and its preoccupation with the controversy at the expense of the essential doctrines of the faith, when he says retrospectively:

> The Baptist army became now divided into two bands; some entered the territories of high Calvinism, more so, it seems, than they were before; others ... plunged headlong into the mire of Arminianism. If they were not *wholly* so, undoubtedly their sermons, their taste, and their spirits savoured strongly of the Arminian leaven. The person of Christ, the grace of God, the atonement of the cross, the power of the Holy Ghost, and the various connecting links of the scheme of salvation, were in a great measure cast into the background; also, the brethren who adopted the other side of the question went much too far, by limiting the virtue of Christ's sacrifice in itself, and not in its appointment as a covenant-atonement — and they

almost hesitated to say to the dry bones, *Hear the word of the Lord.*[9]

Even mild and reasonable men, along with their hearers, were affected; others, with strong and determined temperaments, such as John Elias, found it hard to avoid becoming extreme. Williams of Wern, who at the beginning of his ministry was a staunch hyper-Calvinist, once observed to Dr Thomas of Liverpool the enthusiasm of the populace to condemn the Wesleyans, 'No sermon was of any value at that time unless it contained a bullet against Arminianism; and I blush when I think of the colours in which I myself often painted it.'[10]

Christmas Evans was by no means guiltless in the controversy and, when the contentions were at their fiercest, his 'sword was as bloody as any in the whole of Wales'.[11] In recounting the theological movements in Wales during the nineteenth century, the Calvinistic minister Owen Thomas, an authority on the history and development of preaching in Wales, remarked, 'We have heard many say that Christmas Evans at this time, could hardly preach a sermon without showering Wesleyanism with derision.' His North Wales Associational letter of 1806 illustrates this point with jarring clarity: Wesley's system, he wrote, 'is extremely frightening. It is a black toad, scabby in the passion of its poison, affecting all the sweet flowers in the garden of the Bible. Beware of it as you would beware a snake in the grass, dear brethren, for it contains a multiplicity of error.'[12]

Christmas Evans disagreed with Wesleyan apologists such as Edward Jones, John Bryan, Owen Davies and John Hughes on three main points: free will, the nature of election and the extent of redemption:

> Mr Wesley states: 'Free will has been restored to all,' whereas the word of God clearly shows that all the lost are bereft of such a will: 'You will not come to me,' says Christ... The Bible teaches us that a free will which is bent on good is not

restored to anyone except those in whom the creative, ani-
mating, reviving power of the great Mediator, in the day of his
gracious victory, is breaking down the dominion of sin and
thus, by enlightening their understanding, is freeing their will
from the bondage of sin... I am sorry that Mr Wesley and
Christ are so contrary to one another... The lost have no will
to take of the water of life freely, but rather their minds
despise God and prefer the path of death... Since the fall,
man always wills that which is evil and this will is so strong
that a virtue and power outside of himself and possessing
divine influences are necessary before the will wills that which
is opposite to evil.

God, argued Christmas Evans, conquered man's stubborn will
in election, which is wholly of grace and therefore outside the
influence, efforts or responses of man's will. 'In the act of elect-
ing men before the foundation of the world, God had predes-
tined such to the adoption of sons and had immutably
foreordained to give them faith, repentance and holiness as
consequences of his design.' Therefore man has no power to
contribute to his own salvation. God has 'mercy on whom he
wills. He wills to show mercy to some, his anger to others.' In
other words, 'The application of the atonement made by Christ's
death is for those whom the atonement itself was made.' But
Christmas Evans went further than the moderate Calvinists, who
believed that the atonement was sufficient for all but applied
only to the elect, when he upheld the view of perfect equality
between the death of Christ and the number of elect. 'The
essential purpose of his death,' he said, 'was to bear the sins of
particular persons and to make atonement for particular
persons.'[13] Such a high-Calvinistic stance caused uneasiness
among his supporters and led him into a fierce debate with the
Methodist leader, Thomas Jones of Denbigh.

Before condemning Christmas Evans too harshly for attacking Wesleyanism and for adopting unorthodox views, it must
be understood that he lived at a time when the fundamental

beliefs of predominantly Calvinistic Wales were being challenged by a doctrinal system that many thought of as a dangerous error. It seemed to them to be literally a matter of life and death to establish the truth of the gospel and to oppose vigorously Unitarians, Deists and sceptics; thus they regarded themselves as the defenders of the true faith and the upholders of God's glory, the God-given bulwarks against error. With this in mind it is easier to understand why Christmas Evans reacted as he did. The two principal causes of his 'righteous indignation' were

> ... the gross misrepresentation by his opponents of truths he held to be fundamental. Calvinists were being unjustly charged with ideas that bordered on blasphemy and his righteous soul rebelled with the result that his indignation was often counter productive. The other thing was this, that the Wesleyan-Arminian position was also being misrepresented by those who claimed to champion its cause. Tracts like *A Blow at the Roots* by John Wesley, were translated into Welsh, and such translations contained views that misrepresented the original, and instead expressed views neither sound nor evangelical. Extreme and over-emphasised arguments now characterised the controversy and Christmas Evans, always quick to react to circumstances, inflicted more wounds on his own charitable nature than on his opponents.[14]

Christmas Evans was the first to go into print against these translated works of John Wesley. He published a small book in 1803, *The Character of Sound Doctrine ... or An Antidote for the Poison of Arminianism*, which was printed at Carmarthen, followed by several other books, including *Mene Tekel: A Review of a Booklet by Mr Wesley Entitled 'A Blow at the Roots'* (Caernarfon, 1806), in which he opposed 'Wesleyanism'. His views in these writings are extremely Calvinistic. In 1811, in response to the growing numbers of 'moderate Calvinists', he gave further expression of his Calvinistic orthodoxy in a tract *Particular Redemption*, which was intended far more to counteract moderatism than the Arminian view of redemption. It is a brief and somewhat carelessly written attempt to determine exactly what constitutes the particularity for which he argues.

In the tract he introduced 'commercial metaphors', believing in a kind of 'quantitative calculus of the atonement, which held that it was exactly, mathematically equivalent to the amount needed to save the elect'.[15] In other words, 'for Christ's redemption to have been all embracing, he would have had to have suffered quantitatively greater pain on the cross'.[16] 'Oh, the amount of infinite suffering Jesus bore when he took upon himself the curse we deserved, and that curse being equal to the number and weight of our sins in the minutest detail!' Christmas Evans exclaimed. 'There would be no reason,' he continued, 'perhaps, as far as righteousness is concerned, to suffer as much to atone for the sins of a small child as to atone for those of Saul of Tarsus... It is fitting to note that the Holy Spirit explains our redemption by using financial idioms ... showing us by such comparisons that the atonement in Christ's blood is correspondingly similar.'[17]

When he reviewed the controversy Christmas Evans admitted that 'The first intimation given in a printed form in Wales of an atonement *equal* in weight and value to the amount of crime, and not an atonement corresponding with the dignity of the divine person who gave it, was hinted in a small pamphlet of mine, published some years ago. I regret the word *equal* in the above connection.'[18]

In 1814 John Elias fell into the same error of equivalence as Christmas Evans. Elias hotly opposed the Arminian Methodists and later blamed them for breaking up the unity of doctrine in the North Wales religious bodies. In his determination to speak against a general redemption and to uphold the efficacy of Christ's blood, he stated in a sermon on the atonement 'that the propitiation of Christ was enough and no more than to make the scales of justice even, that it was a full *equivalent* for the sins of all the elect'.[19] He preached this sermon in several places, before he reached Denbigh, where he stayed with Thomas Jones. Jones resolutely opposed the commercial doctrine and maintained that the efficacy of the atonement was not measured in terms of sin but by the infinite value of the Saviour who died. In the ensuing conversation with Jones, Elias was led to see 'the infinite intrinsic sufficiency of Christ's satisfaction and merits'. He promised never to use equivalent expressions again, but, he said, 'It is as clear to me that for the church alone [atonement] was made.'[20]

Christmas Evans was also embroiled in controversy with Thomas Jones. Eight years after *Particular Redemption* was published, Jones, in an appendix to his *Discourses on Redemption* (Denbigh, 1819), commented on *Some Matters Seen in a Treatise on Particular Redemption, Written by Mr Christmas Evans of Anglesey and Published by him a Few Years Ago*. Jones was unnecessarily reproachful towards his opponent, heavily condemning his extreme and 'commercial' opinions, and calling them '*constructive* blasphemy'.[21] They should be 'refuted and refused by the church of Christ with fear and trembling arising out of true love and respect for Christ', he warned, for they have deviated from the 'true revelation of the *infinite merit* of Christ's sacrifice... And is there not here, hiding under the shadow of "number, weight and magnitude", an imagination that lacks wisdom and caution?'[22]

Thomas Jones's book was published in mid-October, 1819. At the time Christmas Evans was preaching in Denbighshire, where he saw the book advertised. He read a summary of its contents and the intended criticism of his own work on *Particular Redemption*. Thinking the book had not yet been issued, he immediately wrote to Jones from his lodging house in Llangollen on 18 October. The letter is an example of Christmas Evans's gracious spirit:

Dear Brother,

I understand that you intend to criticize in print some things I have written on Particular Redemption. I beg you to wait until you see me early next week in Denbigh. I do not uphold the way of reasoning I adopted in that booklet, i.e., that of weights and measures, which inclined to set a limit to what was limitless, limitless in itself. These days I am revising the subject and see reason to renounce completely that system of weights and measures which, perhaps, grieved you deeply. I will show you what I have written on the subject and I should be grateful for your opinion of it and for your help and advice. Perhaps, at present, we are of the same opinion and if so I shall be greatly pleased. I shall let you know when I shall be in Denbigh and anticipate much pleasure as we discuss and I listen to your opinion of what I have written. It appears like a new light to me but perhaps my lack of obser-vation and my weakness account for that. May great grace be upon you.

Dear Brother, I am yours,

Christmas Evans[23]

By the time Christmas Evans called to see Jones, he had read the criticisms in the appendix of his book and appeared quite happy with them. According to Jones, their two meetings — a second meeting took place on the following Monday, 1 November, 1819 — were extremely amicable:

To add to my joy and good hope for him regarding his sub-mission to the truth, he came to my house the following week with a friend, Mr Richard Foulks. As soon as he had sat down he said that he had submitted to the admonition I had given him, as a child would under his father's rod. This was followed by a peaceable, gentle discourse among us and, as he had mentioned in his letter, he showed me a copy or booklet of his new edition on redemption. He wished me to read it and to write a few comments by his second visit at the beginning of the following week. I ... obeyed his wish.

On neither of these two days was there a hint of a quarrel between us but I remember ... that in the whole of this

> second discourse C. E. inclined to confess and to declare
> his denial of the supposition which he had supported in the
> copy he had given me to edit. In short, concerning these two
> discourses, it is fit and right for me to state that I found C. E.
> to be not only a gentle, amiable man ... but that he appeared
> to be very submissive because of his mistake, his grave
> mistake, in publishing a booklet which contains many state-
> ments which tend to set a limit to the merits of Christ's
> sacrifice ... And as for his respectful words, too respectful
> for me, poor worm that I am, I can't remember anything said
> to me by any of my dearest friends that was as respectful as
> the words uttered by C.E.[24]

On his return, men who had an interest in prolonging any supposed disagreement, Baptist preachers in Denbigh most likely,
persuaded Christmas Evans that Jones had treated him
unfairly in his *Discourses* and that he should defend his former
high-Calvinistic position. They argued that 'Thomas Jones's
view of the extent of the atonement was nothing other than
Arminianism ... that *Particular Redemption* was not as inconsistent with the substance of the Scriptural view as he thought,
and that Jones's concept endangered the Calvinistic conviction
concerning the efficacy of Christ's sacrifice.'[25] Christmas Evans
should have been wise and strong enough to ignore their criticisms; instead, a booklet from his hand soon appeared with the
provocative title: *Redemption within the Circle of Election*
(Caernarfon, 1819), in which there are some 'mighty
flounderings'.[26] In it Christmas Evans unjustly accuses Jones of
Arminianism and of using 'angry, unchristian and immoral' language.[27] He defends his former work against Jones's objections,
though his views are not as rigid. He admits 'that he has abandoned the *commercial* theory of the atonement to a great extent ... and virtually holds that there was sufficient value and
worth in the death of Christ for all'.[28]

Thomas Jones, who was expecting the booklet on which he
had commented, regarded Christmas Evans's turn around 'as

a breaking of a pledged word'. In retaliation he 'published a very hurtful and blasphemous poem about Christmas Evans and his "heretical" views. This proved to be a very bitter cup for the old warrior to drink.'[29] Jones also defended himself in a letter dated 31 January, 1820, in which he summarises their October discussions and denies treating his opponent unfairly. On 18 February of that year Christmas Evans replied in a 'simple, clear, moderate' letter that was probably composed by the Denbighshire pastors. Soon afterwards, in a letter from his own hand, he bitterly attacked Jones:

> Do you not realise that it is you who has let in the sea to drown the 'Cantre'r Gwaelod'[30] of our peaceful communities with your book, your poem and your letter? and that you are responsible for all the evil brought about by the flood of nicknames, blasphemy, abuse and gossip spreading throughout Wales and part of England? Can you look upon these atrocities as Nero looked at Rome ablaze in flames kindled by himself? Have you not, by means of your book, poem and letter, three firebrands, kindled discord in three allegorical colonies belonging to three sects in Wales today?...
>
> What would be the result if all the preachers in Wales followed your example and slandered, misinterpreted, nicknamed, libelled and disclosed secrets? Would they not before long be as evil as the pagans of the South Sea?[31]

It is not known whether Thomas Jones would have replied to this attack, for the controversy was brought to a sad and unexpected end with his death on 16 June, 1820, at the age of sixty-four. Christmas Evans was stunned. Years later the wounds of his battle with the Denbighshire minister were still raw, as he remarks:

> Oh what trouble was occasioned me by my controversy with Mr Jones of Denbigh! How it grieved me that he should have died and gone to heaven, as I fully believe he did, while we were engaged in that controversy! Certainly, I was not treated

by him in a gentlemanly spirit; but if I could have foreseen
the consequences, I should have allowed the storm to blow
over, severe as it was, without saying one word. I now see
much of my folly in other disputes, and, although unkindly
dealt with, I ought to have borne it patiently rather than
defend myself in an offensive manner. Let us not be too
ready to rush into controversies, and when it is necessary
for us to enter into them, let us do so in 'the spirit of meekness'.[32]

Both men were, to a degree, to blame — Christmas Evans for
taking an unscriptural, narrow and one-sided view of the work
of Christ in his books, for becoming too involved in the personal side of the debate, and for being unduly influenced, to
his own detriment, by men less able than himself; and Thomas
Jones for attacking his opponent with too much vigour, and,
while Jones maintained the infinite and illimitable sufficiency
of Christ's work, for robustly attaching particularity to the atonement, and of course confining to that extent the sincere invitations of the gospel. Once Christmas Evans had understood that
it was the infinite value of Christ's person rather than the depth
of his agony or the weight of sin that decided the extent of the
atonement, he became more guarded as to his dogmatic asser-
tions and abandoned for good his mathematical concept of
redemption.

One of the men whose theological works helped Christmas
Evans come down from his high Calvinistic position was Andrew
Fuller (1754-1815), an entirely self-taught man, who had
successfully propagated an evangelical Calvinism in England.
Fuller had been raised in the deadening atmosphere of
hyper-Calvinism, where 'noninvitation and nonapplication' were
practised and where his pastor, John Eve, rarely addressed himself to the unconverted. This teaching, he says, admitted 'nothing spiritually good to be the duty of the unregenerate, and
nothing to be addressed to them in a way of exhortation,

excepting what related to external obedience. Outward services might be required, such as an attendance on the means of grace; and abstinence from gross evils might be enforced; but nothing was said to them from the pulpit in the way of warning them to flee from the wrath to come, or inviting them to apply to Christ for salvation.'[33]

Hyper-Calvinists gained ascendancy among Baptist churches in the late eighteenth century and taught that, as Christ is the Saviour *only* of the elect, it is not the duty of unconverted sinners to believe in Jesus Christ for a salvation that is not provided for them; and, as fallen human beings, incapable of any saving good, it is a vain exercise to exhort them to do what they cannot do. Fuller's biographer, speaking of the men whose theology misdirected the eighteenth century Baptists, after admitting that all the leading truths of the gospel are maintained in their works, goes on to say that 'By stretching what are usually called the doctrines of grace beyond the scriptural medium, they introduced a system of hyper-Calvinism, which extended its baleful influence over nearly all the churches, and covered them with a cloud of darkness.'[34]

In 1785 Fuller published *The Gospel Worthy of All Acceptation*, the leading design of which was to prove 'that men are under indispensable obligations to believe whatever God says, and to do whatever he commands; and a Saviour being revealed in the gospel, the law in effect requires those to whom he is made known, to believe in him, seeing it insists upon obedience to the whole revealed will of God'.[35] It exercised a profound influence over the Calvinistic views of Baptist churches, and to some extent over those of other denominations — an influence freely acknowledged by both friends and enemies; it instilled new life into numerous churches in England, convinced many that their Calvinism was too extreme, imparted to British evangelicals a world-wide vision, affected greatly men like William Carey, and laid a firm doctrinal foundation for the promotion of the modern missionary campaign. In all it confirmed the high praise paid to the author by John Angell James, who, in his lectures to theological students, described Fuller's works as containing 'the most entire union of sound Calvinistic divinity ... Christian ethics and religious experience ... in the English language'. John Ryland called Fuller 'the most judicious and able theological writer that ever belonged to the Baptist denomination';[36] and Robert Hall said of him: 'He was a man whose sagacity enabled him to penetrate to the depths of every subject he explored; whose conceptions were so powerful and luminous, that what was recondite and original appeared familiar, what was intricate, easy and perspicuous, in his hands; equally successful in enforcing the practical, in stating theoretical, and discussing the polemical branches of theology.'[37]

In 1809 Fuller's views were preached from some Welsh pulpits. Micah Thomas was one of the first in Wales to come under their influence, but it was J. P. Davies of Tredegar who was their principal exponent. John Roberts, Llanbryn-mair, a disciple of Edward Williams,[38] was also instrumental in spreading the 'new doctrine'. Throughout the ensuing controversy he steered a middle course, rejecting both higher Calvinism, which he foresaw would 'lead the people direct to the whirlpool of Antinomianism',[39] and the extremes of Arminianism; thus he invited bitter criticism upon himself from both parties. According to Rhys Stephen, Roberts was 'one of the loveliest of men, and was honoured by his Lord with a lengthened and extensive influence. Whatever he wrote, it was with dove-like sweetness and infantile simplicity; actuated only by ambition to do good, he was untiring in season and out of season, both with pen and tongue, to diffuse abroad the savour of the name of Christ.'[40] In 1814 he published a book (*Cynnygiad Gostyngedig*) of twenty-four pages in the form of two letters to a young friend, believed to be John Breese, a student from Roberts's church, in which he opposes the high Calvinistic strain of Christmas Evans, though he does not name him, and reiterates the system of Williams.

In his efforts to spread a less severe Calvinism throughout the Principality, Roberts provoked Thomas Jones of Denbigh,[41] who, in his opposition, was very lenient towards Mr Roberts. Jones published a small book (1816) that contained a dialogue between two writers on the redemption, one of whom was Roberts. The work is an effort to prove the error and danger of Roberts's views. By 1819 he felt it necessary again to 'denounce the views of John Roberts ... and included observations on *Cynnygiad Gostyngedig*' in an enlarged version of his very able work on redemption.[42] He does not oppose Roberts directly, but rather defines the true meaning of the atonement, which, he argues, is infinite in value, bringing blessing to the entire human race, but limited in scope.

During his own controversy with Thomas Jones, Christmas Evans softened the tone of his preaching and adopted Fuller's views of Calvinism — views which tempted some of his 'best and most affectionate friends in the ministry' to accuse him of Arminianism, synonymous in their eyes with Fullerism. While Christmas Evans 'could not at any time perceive the propriety, and admit the justness of all the propositions of that great and holy man', yet it is true that 'He always entertained the highest esteem for Mr Fuller's character, both as a Christian preacher, and a polemical writer,'[43] and regarded him as 'one of the principal divines since the days of the apostles — he was an apostolic man'.[44]

It was probably around 1820, not long after he had laid aside his 'extreme and commercial views of the atonement', that Christmas Evans received a letter from a person who wanted to know his opinion on 'high, low and moderate Calvinism', and of which school he himself belonged. The reply he gave is as follows:

1. I believe none will be saved but those who, in the divine purpose, were written in the Lamb's book of life.

2. That those only were given to Christ, to constitute his body and his church, as mediator.

3. That them only he represented, and for them only he gave himself a reconciling sacrifice, to bring in to them an everlasting righteousness. He is a Head and Surety unto them, and for them he intercedes.

4. And all they shall be called by the power of the Holy Ghost, according to the eternal purpose. They only will believe and shall be justified, and sanctified and glorified, and not one of them shall perish.

Moderate Calvinism I do not understand in this connection... If a moderate Calvinist is one that does not believe all the points respecting the salvation of the elect from the pre-destination to the glorification, but rejects some of them, doubts others, and half believes the remainder, — if that is a moderate Calvinist, I have not learnt his creed from the Bible.

Low Calvinist, I will tell you how low I am:

1. I believe that the fulfilment of the law by Christ was perfect, — that it was impossible that there could be ... sufferings more full to swallow up the curse, and a greater divine person to set a value upon the whole, and impart efficiency unto it to bring the elect to God, even those whom he represented; and had all mankind been represented by him, as by the first Adam, that HIS ONE perfect righteousness would have been sufficient to bring all mankind to justification of life...

2. I descend from the heights of sovereignty, with the testimony and invitations, and the great promise of the gospel to save all to eternal life who believe in Christ...

3. I believe the testimony of the Scriptures, that every soul shall be saved that believes the gospel in its true import...

4. I believe that it is the duty of every man having the use of reason, to believe and repent, and that a man's enmity does not excuse him, though it is unconquerable by any power but the power of God.

5. I believe, also, on the grounds of the same Scriptures, that no man believed and repented of himself since the fall of Adam; no, not *one*, but those who were called according to the purpose...

6. I perceive in the gospel of Christ, grace and righteousness sufficient to save all that believe, and a right in it to every believer without any distinction, upon the testimony of God.

7. That it was the builders that rejected the stone, which as a foundation was sufficiently strong to have held them up from sinking into everlasting perdition.

8. I have learned from the Scriptures, that no sinner who ever repented and believed in Christ was rejected here or in death, and that none such shall ever be rejected ... it is not a respect of persons in him to regenerate some by his sovereign power, that they may believe in the Redeemer's name, while others are left in their obduracy. This is but grace, or a free favour; and in this he glorifies himself.[45]

During the controversy that surrounded Christmas Evans's departure from Anglesey, and the debate over the right form of ecclesiastical government, his 'honest and open' character was maligned and his intentions misrepresented. Many of his former friends, without good reason, joined the accusers. Some faithful brethren did take his part, whose names are honourably noticed in his journals, but 'He thought that they had not the same power to defend him now as on previous occasions, "for they had suspected him of Arminianism" (Fullerism). Because of this the strength of their power and judgement was weakened, "to my great loss", said he, "in this gap; though they were still with me, yet they had lost their sword and their staff."'[46] He was charged with being too free in his invitations of the gospel, and of preaching a watered down Calvinism, which to the Welsh Baptists was not far removed from outright Arminianism.

I am credibly informed [writes Rhys Stephen] by persons who well knew Christmas Evans at that period of his ministry, that the general texture and complexion of his preaching was much expanded and liberalised; and so much so, I apprehend, was this the case as to give those who were already intent upon annoyance, some rather colourful pretext for their mischievous activity. Still, in the majority of instances, it was only a pretext, and gladly did those, who were either tired of his control, or determined upon provocation, avail themselves of it. Without the slightest hesitation of conscience or prudence, the *odium theologicum* was resorted to; and he who was the father of the churches found his name given out 'for evil', as a teacher of heresy and a corrupter of the faith.[47]

These accusations of liberalism are hard to reconcile with the fact that he opposed the men they chose as pastors because they *too much inclined to Arminianism*! It is apparent that, along with the works of Fuller, the writings and conversations of such men as Joseph Harris, J. P. Davies, Micah Thomas and others did modify the stern and severe rigidity of his Calvinism during this period, but at no time did he embrace Arminian doctrines.

In later years Christmas Evans looked back over this troubled time and thought that 'Some individuals were benefited by it, yet I think, upon the whole, that the injury sustained outweighs the amount of benefit realised;' and that the 'best way to oppose Arminianism is that adopted by Mr Fuller', though, he admits, Fuller's system 'contains a greater check upon Antinomianism'.[48] The controversy, says he, 'occasioned much schism and confusion, by furnishing an opportunity to many young preachers, under Mr Fuller's shade, of becoming rank Arminians in spirit and doctrine; as if they intended to oppose, rather than follow that eminent man'. Other ministers and churches were driven to the opposite extreme, 'And in order to be sufficiently distant from Fullerianism, as they called it, would not willingly acknowledge the infinite virtue of the atonement in its nature, and hesitated to invite sinners to Christ.'[49]

There is little doubt that these 'spiritual wranglings' affected the spirit and power of preaching, but thankfully not as much or for as long as Christmas Evans intimated; 'For, in the first place, fixing and defining theological views was a secondary and subordinate matter, while the preaching of Christ and the salvation of souls was of paramount importance in the sight of all; and, secondly, the men were nobler, wider, wiser and better than their creeds.'[50] If the success of the Welsh Baptist churches is taken into account, their growth was faster in the first thirty years of the nineteenth century than in the final four decades of the previous century, when Welsh Baptist numbers quadrupled. 'Controversy was obviously one of the symptoms of vitality not inertia,'[51] although to Christmas Evans, without the theological distractions, growth would have been even more rapid.

When we walk through a field of battle, slippery with blood, and strewn with the bodies of the slain — when we hear the shrieks and the groans of the wounded and the dying — when we see the country wasted, cities burned, houses pillaged, widows and orphans wailing in the track of the victorious army, we cannot help exclaiming — O, what a blessing is peace! When we are obliged to witness family turmoils and strifes — when we see parents and children, brothers and sisters, masters and servants, husbands and wives, contending with each other like tigers — we retire as from a smoking house, and exclaim as we go — O, what a blessing is peace! When duty calls us into that church, where envy and malice prevail, and the spirit of harmony is supplanted by discord and contention — when we see brethren, who ought to be bound together in love, full of pride, hatred, confusion, and every evil work — we quit the unhallowed scene with painful feelings of repulsion, repeating the exclamation — O, what a blessing is peace!

Christmas Evans preaching on John 16:33.[1]

14
Sorrows and Trials

When Christmas Evans was nearing sixty he suffered the most painful and testing afflictions of his life. Undoubtedly one of the more pressing and heartfelt was the death of his beloved and excellent wife Catherine early on the morning of Wednesday 22 October, 1823, the day before their thirty-fourth wedding anniversary; 'and to no man could such a loss be a much greater calamity'.[2] Catherine was fifty-seven years old. At the time of her death she was staying at the home of Robert Ambrose, minister of Bangor Baptist Church, awaiting medical treatment. Catherine had been a perfect soul mate for her husband, lifting him up when the burdens of his ministry were set to overwhelm him; encouraging him with words of wisdom from the rich stores of her own faith; aiding him with the more practical side of ministerial life; offering support, with tenderness and intelligence, when the enemies of the gospel encamped around him. Throughout their married life she was content to live, what must have been at times, a lonely existence, without children, while her husband travelled throughout the Principality preaching the good news, but she was never heard to complain and was always ready to welcome her pilgrim home. After her death, and while still in mourning, Christmas wrote a moving and graphic tribute to her in *Seren Gomer* under the title *A Sorrowing Widower and an Exile in the World*, a few extracts of which we give below. The translation is abridged, yet it still imparts a vivid picture of her affectionate, strong and pious character:

> Her faculties were above the common order; she was diffident, but strong-minded. If she gave her view of a passage of Scripture, she never failed entirely, at least, of the mark. She had very elevated views of the sacrifice of Christ, which was her rock and strong tower. She was sharpsighted to discern men and things, and a little observation generally sufficed to enable her to form a pretty correct opinion. She speedily detected selfishness and conceit, however they might be attempted to be concealed under the guise of humility. She watched over her fellow-members in the church, and was sharp and earnest in her opposition to levity and sin. Her honesty was transparent; and confidence in her was never abased. She was ever anxious to restore the straying, and bring back the prodigal. Her temper was excitable, but she readily forgave; to this there was but one exception during the forty years of her religious life:— in this case she had been grievously injured, and it required a long and arduous struggle to remove the agony, and to reinduce kindly feeling; but by earnest and protracted reflection and prayer, she was enabled, before she was called to eternity, to forgive the deep transgression, and to bury the very remembrance in the compassion and merits of the Redeemer...
>
> She never had robust health, but was a woman of good courage. She accompanied her husband on five of his journeys through the greater portion of Wales; and some in the depth of winter, through storms of rain and snow and hail, and over dangerous estuaries and ferries, with fortitude and cheerfulness. Her feelings were identified with the cause of Christ in her own land; its prosperity was her joy, and its reverses invariably produced anguish and bitterness of spirit. The last two years of her life were spent in much debility and pain; she had a complication of disorders, and was hastening to the grave. Great strength of spirit was given to her, and she submitted herself heartily to the divine will. The last

night of her life, she frequently repeated a beautiful Welsh hymn; and, having three times ejaculated *'Lord Jesus, have mercy on me!'* she breathed forth her hopeful spirit into His hands.[3]

Christmas Evans was helped through his grief by the kindness of one of the island's young ministers, Hugh Williams, who preached the memorial sermon in Cil-dwrn Chapel on Saturday morning, 25 October. Catherine's mortal remains were buried in the small cemetery attached to the chapel.

The arduous labours and numerous duties that Christmas Evans had to perform began to affect his health, and his strength, under the strain, waned; yet, in the same year as his wife died, ignoring his own physical condition, he undertook a journey to South Wales in order to collect money for the chapel debts in Anglesey. On his journey he 'caught a violent cold, which settled in his eye',[4] and for a time he lay on the brink of eternity. He received medical treatment at a hospital in Aberystwyth and was unable to preach for nine months. There seemed little chance of retaining the sight of his remaining eye, a constant 'thorn in the flesh' to him. Before his southward journey it had troubled him; in fact, for years it had grown steadily weaker, due to the exertions of travelling and preaching, and the lack of consideration he paid to his own physical welfare.

During this enforced sabbatical 'The friends at Aberystwyth paid him every possible attention; while, from Mr Evans, the Pastor of the Baptist Church, and from Mr Simon James of Penrhyn-coch, he received uninterruptedly such sympathetic kindness as ministers of Christ can, and love to supply, to each other.'[5] With their support and companionship his spirit retained its energy and strength, and he felt confident about returning to the pulpit, believing that God had a great work for him to undertake before he called him home, though many of his friends were convinced that his earthly course was about to finish. In due time he recovered and returned home, albeit in a much weakened state, only to become embroiled in a number of unhappy disputes with the churches under his charge. Over the next two years these contentions became more heated and personal, until he decided, with great sadness, to leave the island.

It was about this time, soon after his wife had died, that he was thrown into panic and fear by an insulting letter he received at a monthly meeting, 'at one of the contests with spiritual wickedness in high places', as he called it.[6] It was from a 'brother' in the church, threatening him with civil prosecution on account of slander or a chapel debt or some such thing, for which he was deemed responsible, but of which he was entirely innocent. In the case in question, he had only acted in his ministerial capacity and he knew there was no ground for action; nevertheless, he was deeply disturbed by the threat of legal action because the honour of Christ's name was at stake, and with no human companion to confide in, he was brought to 'agony of grief'. On his return home from the meeting he enjoyed 'fellowship with God during the whole journey of ten miles'. On arriving at his house, he thought to himself: 'This person and his relations threaten to cast me into a court of law — a place in which I have never seen. I will put him and them, first of all, into the high court of Jesus Christ, the fountain of law and authority.'[7]

He then went upstairs to his room 'and poured forth my heart before the Redeemer, who has in his hands all authority and power'.[8] The prayer he offered on this occasion is a beautiful example of the depth of communion he experienced with God, and the reverence and humble dependency with which he approached the throne of grace:

O Blessed Lord! in thy merit I confide and trust to be heard. Lord, some of my brethren have run wild; and forgetting their duty and obligations to their father in the gospel, they threaten me with the law of the land. Weaken, I beseech thee, their designs in this, as thou didst wither the arm of Jeroboam; and soften them, as thou didst soften the mind of Esau and disarmed him of his warlike temper against thy servant Jacob after the wrestling at Penuel. So disarm them, for I do not know the length of Satan's chain in this case, and in this unbrotherly attack. But thou canst shorten the chain as short as it may please thee.

Lord, I anticipate them in point of law. They think of casting thine unworthy servant into the little courts here below; but I cast my cause into the High Court, in which thou, gracious Jesus, art the High Chancellor. Receive thou the cause of thine unworthy servant, and send him a writ, or a notice, immediately — sending into their conscience and summoning them to consider what they are doing. Oh, frighten them with a summons from thy court until they come and bow in contrition at thy feet; and take from their hands every revengeful weapon, and make them deliver up every gun of scandal and every sword of bitter words and every spear of slanderous expressions, and surrender them all at thy cross. Forgive them all their faults and clothe them with white robes, and give them oil for their heads, and the organ and the harp of ten strings to sing for the trampling of Satan under our feet by the God of peace.[9]

After 'about ten minutes in prayer', he was not wholly satisfied as he felt no inward assurance of acceptance or success; so

... I went up again with a tender heart; I could not refrain from weeping with the joy of hope that the Lord was drawing near to me. After the seventh struggle I came down, fully believing that the Redeemer had taken my cause into his hands, and that he would arrange and manage for me. My countenance was cheerful as I came down the last time, like Naaman, having washed himself seven times in the Jordan; or Bunyan's Pilgrim, having cast his burden at the foot of the cross, into the grave of Jesus. I well remember the place — the little house adjoining the meeting house at Cildwrn, where

I then resided — in which this struggle took place; I can call
it Penuel. No weapon intended against me prospered and I
had peace at once to my mind and in my (temporal) condition.[10]

He prayed frequently in this way 'for those who would injure
me that they might be blessed, even as I have been blessed',
and remained thankful to God for the furnaces of affliction in
which he had been tried, 'and in which the spirit of prayer has
been excited and exercised in me'.[11] Needless to say the threat
of legal action was never executed, nor did he hear any more
about the matter.

The Baptist meeting places in Anglesey at this time
numbered about twenty, with many members attached to each
one. There were twenty-eight ordained preachers in the various
congregations which, up to this point, constituted only one
church of which Christmas Evans was the recognised head.
These preachers, many of whom subsequently entered the regular ministry in Wales, England and America, were co-pastors
with him *over all* the churches and had seen him, by the grace
and power of God, turn a 'waste and howling wilderness'[12]
into a fertile plain, where the seed of the word, planted by his
hand, grew and produced a crop. Several of them had been
'made free citizens of Mount Zion' through his instrumentality
and consequently held 'their father and leader' in such high
esteem 'that they would have him take the lead in all their
deliberations ... and paid a due respect to his opinions on every
subject'.[13] According to J. Davis, who was well acquainted with
Christmas Evans at this time, these men 'would not move a
single step, in any important undertaking, without consulting
him'[14] — a high regard that was soon to change.

In his weakened state there proved to be too many preaching places for him to cover on his own, and he could not
continue his pastoral visits as previously. He had tried to

persuade young preachers from the South, such as Daniel Davies of Merthyr, to work alongside him, but without success. He saw the wisdom of churches having their own ministers, so in a letter to the monthly meeting at Llanfair Mathafarn Eithaf in the summer of 1823, he 'encouraged and advised them to form themselves into [four] separate churches, or that every two or three stations should unite and call a minister';[15] and, as he wanted to retain a measure of control over these new bodies, he recommended ministers to them, although he regarded complete independency as the ultimate aim.

However, it appears there was a shortage of suitable men to meet the needs of the various branches, with many of the preachers bickering among themselves: 'We need men,' urged Christmas Evans in his letter, 'with more of the spirit of the ministry in them; men with no goal except to extend the kingdom of Christ... If you ask, "What disagreeable spirit reigns among us?" (1) It is the spirit of self-seeking and not of desiring the good of the cause. (2) An unbelieving, unsubmissive spirit towards one another — from Wil Philip to Christmas Evans. Everyone wants to be king — to be chief; and this never failed to lead to destruction.' Then in a postscript he advised them to 'Change the Methodist plan or system, if you want to keep up with matters. It has been of benefit to us but it has served its purpose. We, by trying to work the whole farm, have failed to do justice to any part of it.'[16]

According to Rhys Stephen, his intentions to 'divide the church' and his somewhat muddled and hesitant approach to the proposed changes did not meet with universal approval:

The younger men among the preachers could scarcely sympathise with him at all, in his attachment to the system, or rather no-system, which had obtained amongst the Anglesey Baptists; the middle-aged men would be much divided between their approval of the Congregational system and their deference to the sense of duty and propriety, which,

under the then present circumstances of the interest there,
Mr Evans keenly felt and sturdily avowed. He maintained
that with numerous but feeble churches, it was better to proceed with the modified Congregationalism he had been
obliged to adopt, than to carry out fully, and without qualifi-
cation, the entire Independent platform. This he would seek
to prove by reference to the success of the Methodist
economy in England and Wales; admitting, the while, that
the New Testament economy unequivocally favoured the
separate existence and separate government of each Christian church. The first result was a kind of compromise — not
avowed on either side to be one — which resulted in the
settlement of a pastor over the church at HOLYHEAD.[17]

On 19 April, 1825, William Morgan, from the Baptist Academy,
Abergavenny, was ordained as the pastor of the church at
Holyhead — the first on the island to appoint a permanent
minister, in line with the larger Baptist churches of the main-
land. Morgan was a fine preacher and unequalled on the island
except by Christmas Evans, though he had a tendency to work
too hard on his hearers' emotions. Robert Jones of Llanllyfni
thought him to be as able as John Elias, though not as lucid. In
1839 he published a *Memoir* of Christmas Evans and gave the
profits from the sales to Mary Evans, Christmas's second wife.
At his ordination Christmas Evans offered the prayer and laid
hands on him. He afterwards gave the 'charge' to the minister
and to the church from 1 Thessalonians 5:12-13, a synopsis of
which is here given:

Duties of the Pastor
1. To visit the people, but make no long stay with them.
2. To maintain godly intercourse on the Lord's Day.
3. Not to spare any in their sins, because they will not
spare him hereafter.
4. To make a difference between old transgressors and
occasional ones. The former are (by kindness) hardened in
their sins; the latter receive leniency with gratitude.

5. To take notice of the spirit of the church.

6. To read much, but not to appropriate and use the sermons of others; but to study for himself.

7. Not to interfere in the affairs of the people, as for instance, in references to marriages, &c.

8. Not to receive calumny and backbiting.

Duties of the Church

1. To pray for the pastor.

2. That he might be without fear amongst them.

3. To attend to him as to a messenger from God.

4. Not to neglect the assembling of themselves together.

5. To adhere to him in his tribulations, as did Onesiphorus to Paul.

6. To respect him for his work's sake: not receiving an accusation against him but with two or three witnesses.

7. To submit to him according to God's word.

8. To attend duly to his temporal affairs.[18]

Some of the other branches, after witnessing the success of the church at Holyhead, also wanted to be independent and to step out from under Christmas Evans's 'absolute' authority, so they refused the ministers he recommended and accepted others, who he thought were too Arminian for Calvinistic churches. This defiance of his authority cast a black cloud of sorrow and distress over his mind. He thought their actions were deliberately provocative, and neither grateful to him nor beneficial to themselves, and with little hesitation or tact told them what he thought of their behaviour. Their reaction to his rebuke was one of indifference and even contempt, 'and he found himself, in certain parts of the island, superseded by his own children, or, what was more galling, by strangers'.[19] As a result, a bitter party spirit arose and a general contention was felt among the congregations. One party supported Christmas Evans, while the other grew restive and self-willed, resenting his advice.

One of the problems was that the church at Amlwch wanted to appoint the Fullerite, Hugh Williams, as their minister. This displeased a faction of the island's leaders, who feared that the cause would be ruined by Arminianism. Their views appear to have influenced Christmas Evans, who not only distanced himself from the lower Calvinism he had formerly embraced, but supported his old friend John Roberts, Pen-sarn, and not Hugh Williams, for the Amlwch pastorate. Inevitably he was accused of favouritism by many who were outraged, and by June, 1825, the situation was critical. In the letter of the Anglesey Association of that year, Christmas Evans warned that 'church independence was threatening to get out of hand' and that 'God's judgement was about to fall on the rebellious'. In order to regain control, he 'advised the congregations to give precedence to the mother-church and its minister in all things, to refrain from seeking independence unless they had a lawful agreement with the mother-church before doing so, to choose only approved men to be ministers of these independent branches, and to ensure that no branch incorporates itself irregularly for personal ends rather than holy ones'.[20] Furthermore, he adds:

> The spiritual incapability of the churches to choose ministers is something that has amazed me more than anything else I have seen among saints for forty years. I have noticed, with some dismay, that there is a strange inability among congregations to recognize men and matters. They cannot differentiate between one gift and another...
>
> I have noticed in particular that churches in general, when it comes to a matter of choosing, are more attracted by those gifts which have the least spiritual value and which are short-lived...
>
> What is the reason for this in the churches? Nothing other than a wavering childishness against which Paul warned us, a wavering which causes one to follow every wind of doctrine; and it also shows how very little of the Spirit of Christ the churches possess, but rather much of the flesh and the world.[21]

The members of Amlwch were not prepared to submit to Christmas Evans's demands and some, angered by his rejection of Hugh Williams and his favouritism towards John Roberts, were 'guilty of blaspheming and disparaging the minister of the mother-church and by doing so belittled and weakened the discipline of the church throughout the country'.[22] Others threatened to break away from his authority altogether, claim absolute independence, and to ordain Hugh Williams as their minister regardless of what the one-eyed preacher thought. Such an attitude infuriated Christmas Evans, who, after the monthly meeting at Capel Gwyn, 6 September, 1825, excommunicated Hugh Williams, his father and four other members of the Amlwch connection 'for causing strife among the brethren'. Not surprisingly Christmas Evans was charged with dictatorship. Hugh Williams reports what happened next:

In that meeting, after the excommunication procedure, J. Roberts, Pen-sarn, announced that Christmas Evans would be preaching in Amlwch the following Sabbath. That night, the night of the service at Capel Newydd, quite a large number of Amlwch brethren gathered together. I yielded to their judgement; if they believed that my excommunication was according to rule, then I would submit and would be perfectly calm in my mind concerning the issue. They voted, as one, against my excommunication. Because there was great commotion in the town, it was decided that the wisest thing to do was to send word to Christmas Evans advising him that it would be better if he did not come to Amlwch that Sabbath in case he should bring more people with him and cause a riot to break out. The church decided to meet in a private house that Sabbath day, so we held our morning service at 2 o'clock in a house called Battws and the evening service in Palmer's house. Some time later many brethren from Denbighshire were called. A meeting was held at Pen-y-sarn and the unanimous decision was that Amlwch had been unfairly treated. This helped to soothe matters somewhat. But Christmas Evans and others expressed great dissatisfaction regarding the decision.[23]

From this time the Amlwch branch became an independent church, and, as its members had deliberately and publicly rebelled against Christmas Evans's authority, it signalled the beginning of the end of his reign on the island.

Meanwhile a problem had arisen at Holyhead, where the old church leaders clashed with William Morgan, accusing him, among other things, of 'Sandemanianism, spiritual pride and tyranny'. Morgan was furious at such outrageous charges, but instead of resorting to the monthly meeting to resolve the dispute, 'He was presumptuous enough to excommunicate them on the spot.'[24] William Jones, one of the men expelled, held the keys to the chapel, and he decided, as an act of retribution, to lock the minister out of the building. At the monthly meeting at Brynsiencyn, 8 November, 1825, it was decided not to blame Morgan, who admitted wrongdoing and promised not to act in such a way again, but to urge the excommunicated members to join another branch and to reopen the Holyhead church to the minister.

By early 1826 the dispute was so acrimonious that a delegation of four ministers from Denbighshire, at least one of whom was a Fullerite, were called upon to try and bring about a reconciliation between the factions. They met at Bodedern, but failed to bring the parties together. In fact, Christmas Evans's position was 'more precarious after this meeting than anyone could have imagined previously',[25] which made him particularly sensitive to the arbiters. He regarded them as 'a real threat, not only to his own personal rule but to the good of the cause in general. That is how he interpreted a dream of his after the difficult meeting mentioned above. He saw four black bloodhounds attacking his mother and he had to defend her... The mother, of course, was the church in Anglesey, the dogs were the four ministers from Denbighshire.'[26] As far as he was concerned the two reasons for the dissension were: 'the desire to enforce congregationalism in Anglesey and by so doing

forfeiting church unity; and secondly, the supposedly unorthodox views of the younger preachers', which, he thought, would
lead the churches 'headlong into Arminianism'.[27]

Although his position as leader of the Anglesey church was
threatened and the 'Arminian faction' growing in strength, Christmas Evans agreed to ordain Hugh Williams at Amlwch on the
understanding that he would adhere to the 'old doctrines'. The
service took place on 7 April, 1826. But instead of using the
ordination service as an opportunity to restore unity, Christmas
Evans wrote a letter to those who had been excommunicated
at Holyhead, 'because I consider Wm. Morgan's behaviour
towards you ungracious, rash, wrathful and irregular'.[28] He was
also angry with the men from Denbighshire for not standing
against the 'young pretenders' in a more determined fashion,
and, in a letter to John Roberts on 28 July, 1826, accused them
of undermining his authority and of being 'a great blessing to
the inexperienced hotheads ... by their work in affirming the
right of every church to call a minister, not to mention the danger of breaking the law of love with the sword of Independence. No one has the right to forbid anyone from consulting
and seeking the advice and guidance of those who were
fathers of the church in Anglesey.'[29]

In many ways Christmas Evans, in his desire to oversee all
the Baptist churches on the island, was acting similarly to William
Carey, who opposed the home committee of the Baptist
Missionary Society and their desire to control affairs in India.
'Carey claimed the right to appoint missionaries and professors, assistants and co-workers where and when he thought
best ... without consulting the home committee, who were
determined to retain control.'[30] In the same letter to Roberts,
Christmas Evans compared himself to Carey:

It would be interesting if the Independents of Anglesey were
to go to India and inform the established churches or the

small congregations that they had the right to appoint ministers without consulting the old missionaries at Serampore — that would be papacy. It would bring chaos into India as there is in Anglesey. When the Indian churches refuse to accept the advice and leadership of Carey, Marshman and Ward, it will be a dark day. Christmas Evans is Anglesey's Carey, and John Roberts and Richard Rowland and John Michael are Marshman and Ward. The Prince of the power of the air rides in other coaches besides the Episcopalian and Presbyterian. He does his big mischief in Wales by riding in his coach of Independency. That is the fashionable coach at present, and every demon desires to enter it. I am an Independent — second to none — but not an Independent to split churches, and undermine the men of Serampore, and infuriate the Indians and drive them beyond advice. God forbid that I should ever do that.[31]

Christmas Evans was not deliberately contentious, nor disposed to maintain debates as to his rights, though he could be touchy and act rashly, and was often unwilling to yield to caprice and faction. Sometimes he was inconsistent and too severe in his judgements; on other occasions, when patience and tact were all that were necessary, he moved with undue haste and thereby aggravated a delicate situation. With his sensitive nature and powerful imagination, he tended to magnify the 'wounds of battle' so that 'The bite of a gnat became the cut of a sabre,' and to react in a way that further rankled his opposers.

During the troubles in Anglesey there were occasions when he held onto his authority with an iron-like grip. Instead of allowing the individual congregations the freedom they desired, he insisted on their allegiance and submission, overreacted to their demands, and suffered personal rejection when they disagreed with him. He had served them faithfully with integrity for nearly forty years, and in return he thought he was entitled to their unwavering support. But with the wind of change on the island, he should have been more prepared to bend his will and compromise his ideals, keeping a clear conscience, rather than to resist the inevitable in a provocative manner. In an address delivered by him at this time 'His antipathies were freely expressed, the leaders of the opposition were brought in by name, and his authority was asserted in unmistakable terms,'[32] which neither pacified his opponents, nor improved his own standing among the congregations.

On the other side, the Anglesey Baptists should have shown their father in Christ much greater respect and patience, treating his opinion, not with scorn, but with the deference it deserved. For them simply to 'throw out' his years of experience and to ignore the treasures of his wisdom as if they mattered little was an insult that weighed heavily on the aged warrior, who had fought so successfully on their behalf. But not satisfied with this insolence, 'Some persons were unkind enough to attempt injuring my character by fabricating a falsehood upon me, which, though it was not criminal, yet it was a falsehood, and, as they say, had occurred (though it never in fact occurred) thirty-four years before.'[33]

However, before proceeding with the Anglesey contentions and in order to give a balanced and accurate view of Christmas Evans's character during these troubled years, it is as well to consider the opinion of Maurice Jones, whose principal intimacy with Christmas Evans was when 'the great man' was approaching sixty years of age. Jones was 'honoured with as free and easy an access to him as the conditions of such friendship could yield', living with him for weeks at his own house and being his 'frequent companion in his itinerancies in Anglesey during one summer'. This intimacy afforded him opportunities of observing Christmas Evans when he was 'withdrawn from the influence of public excitement' and public scrutiny. In a letter dated 'June 5, 1846', he comments on 'the confiding simplicity' of his host's nature, which was easily observable even to casual acquaintances.

A mind with less distrust and suspicion, with less reserve and concealment, with less artifice and ceremony, could hardly be found. Whatever blemishes belonged to him, whatever faults in spirit or in action, would present themselves glaringly to the attention of all observers. From this very openness of his character all would come forth in simple and crude deformity, with no attempt at covering or restraining on his part. This often made his conduct liable to misconstruction; but when rightly understood and appreciated, it gave an irresistible charm to his varied excellencies, and made his society exceedingly fascinating.[34]

Jones then mentions the ardency and warmth of his nature, its intense passion and glowing emotions — 'What fire would kindle in that brilliant eye, what vivacity would beam from that expressive face!'— all complimented by an 'easy and natural' expression of piety in his everyday life.[35]

At times the censuring and strife among the Anglesey churches were severe and the wounds Christmas Evans bore so deep that he contemplated 'retiring, old as he was, from the field, the fragrance of which had proclaimed that the Lord had blessed him there'.[36] Several older ministers, who were convinced that his usefulness on the island was over, were not slow in coming forward to voice their opinions, thus adding to his distress. After he had left Anglesey he thought of himself when he remembered the fable about the old lion that had been king of the forest. 'Once every creature feared him and paid him homage. When he grew old and was unable to leave his den, all changed. The creatures gathered to despise him. Among the animals was Jack the Ass who turned his back to the lion and kicked him. That upset him more than all else.'[37]

In his diary he expressed great wonder that 'I did not sink into the grave under the weight of sorrows that came upon me in my old age, together with an accumulation of trials of all kinds; but the Lord sustained me. There was in the midst of all a strong persuasion in my mind that there was yet much work for me to do for God in the world, as well as much to suffer, ere I died.'[38] He felt sure that his ministry would be 'instrumental in bringing many sinners to God', a confidence that arose from 'my trust in God, and in the spirit of prayer that possessed me. I frequently arose above all my sorrows.' 'Nothing could preserve me,' he said, 'in cheerfulness and confidence under these afflictions but the faithfulness of Christ.'[39]

With an assurance of future success, he continued to preach with great unction and was burdened, as ever, for the salvation of souls. 'If I only entered the pulpit,' he comments, 'I felt raised as it were to Paradise — above my afflictions — until I forgot my adversity; yea, I felt my mountain strong, my mind was in such a heavenly frame, and as anxious as ever for the conversion of sinners. The truth appeared to me in its power like a hammer in its strength. The doctrine dropped as sweet as honey, yea, sweeter than the honeycomb, and as comfortable as the best wine.'[40] He longed for unity among the ministers of the island and wished they would join him, according to the promise, 'If two of you agree to ask the *same thing*, it shall be given unto you of my Father which is in heaven;' for, he says, 'I had such confidence that then I should see prosperity attending the ministry, and that I should not die until I had finished my work.'[41] He said to Richard Rowland, 'Brother, the doctrine, the confidence and strength which I feel, will make some persons dance with joy yet in some parts of Wales.' 'Yes, brother,' said he, with tears streaming down his face.[42]

However, his desire for unity was not realised and it became increasingly difficult for him to exercise any meaningful influence in the monthly meetings and elsewhere. He could express his opinion and protest against the 'authoritarianism and independence of the young preachers', but he was in the minority and increasingly sidelined. On 2 August, 1826, the day of the monthly meeting in Capel Gwyn, the decisive 'battle' took place.

Christmas Evans and 'His friends Richard Rowland, John Michael and William Roberts expressed their dissatisfaction with the events of the previous autumn, not only that "the old pillars of the church, who had borne the burden and heat of the day with us for many years", had been expelled, but also that it had happened without William Morgan consulting the monthly meeting.' Then, rankled by the spirit of independence that was abroad, Christmas Evans said, 'We are not afraid of Amlwch, Llanrhuddlad or Holyhead because it is impossible to live with them; therefore we are going to set up our own house with no fear of the future. They have *broken the tie of church unity in Anglesey.*'[43]

The following day, disillusioned and downcast, he wrote to William Jones and the others who had been expelled by William Morgan, and communicated his intention to leave the island, maybe for ever: 'I do not know for certain whether I shall ever see you again... Morgan's imperiousness,' he said, 'is one reason why I, C. Evans, am leaving the country.'[44] For about a year he had wrestled with God in prayer, seeking guidance, and on the day before his letter to Jones (presumably after the conclusion of the monthly meeting in Capel Gwyn and his decision to leave Anglesey) he wrote out seven supplications to the Lord, imploring divine aid for his future ministry:

> **1.** That the Lord would pour unction on the first services so that many would be converted.
> **2.** That by his immortal hand he would order everything, so that I might be able to open my mouth boldly.
> **3.** That he would use me in the conversion of some particular people who would support the cause, and in discovering gifts.
> **4.** That he would prepare for me a peaceful home in which to end my days.
> **5.** That he would safeguard me all the way and lead me to do God's will and not my own.

6. That he would help me to subdue the spirit of unnecessary, divisive debate in those areas. Amen, and Amen.

7. That he would allow me to plant trees in the vineyard,
enough for me to eat of their fruit; and to feed a flock large
enough for me to drink its milk.

C. Evans, Tanybryn, Sir Fôn.[45]

During those twelve prayerful months 'the visions of my head
in the night seasons', as he called his dreams, appeared to confirm the leading of Divine Providence. Finally, after wavering
between two opinions for quite some time, and believing he
had found the Lord's will, he determined to leave Anglesey, a
decision the islanders were soon to regret. In his own words, he
says:

> Everything now contributed to remove me from Anglesey.
> The unbending disposition of those who were offended at
> me, and the ardour of my spirit, believing that there was
> work for me to do in some other field of the harvest of the
> Son of Man... I was much like Jacob, leaving his father and
> his mother, going with his staff only over Jordan; so was I,
> leaving the church. I had prayed, yea, I had strove with God
> for its prosperity and had laboured nearly forty years with it
> — now leaving it — possessing nothing of this world's goods,
> save the horse upon which I rode and a small amount of
> silver in my pocket; and scarcely could I say that these were
> mine.[46]

William Morgan, taking a retrospective view of the conflict, firmly
believed that, whatever disagreements there were between the
two parties, Christmas Evans's 'counsels ought to have been
received with due acknowledgement of his age and experience,
and that his reputation should have been energetically vindi-
cated'. 'I am at this moment quite convinced,' he says, 'that
more strenuous exertions should have been made to defend
the character of the innocent; and I am also of opinion, and I

say it with gratification, that had I seen things then as I do now, and possessed the same spirit, I should have endeavoured to bring the unoffending safely in my arms through the archers to a safe place, and would not have permitted Mr Evans's name to fall in the street without an advocate.'[47] He then paints a very sad picture of the great preacher, who had worked so hard for the people of Anglesey, leaving his home, ostracized and rejected by his own spiritual children:

> It was an affecting sight to see the aged man, who had laboured so long and with such happy effects, leaving the sphere of his exertions under these circumstances; having laboured so much to pay for their meeting houses, having performed so many journeys to South Wales for their bene-fit, having served them so diligently in the island, and passed through so many dangers; now (some of the people) with-held their contributions, to avenge themselves on their own father in the gospel; others, professing to be friends, did little more; while he, like David, was obliged to leave his 'city', not knowing whether he should ever return to see 'the ark of God and his tabernacle' in Anglesey again. A dark cloud hung henceforth on the Baptists in the island. But God is good to his cause, and permits nothing to befall his peo-ple that is not for their good. He was merciful to Mr Evans, and protected him in his troubles; and we find room to hope in his mercy, that for the sake of Christ, and his name in the world, he will not permit the cloud to pour forth judgements on those who were misled, and whose arrows were bitter against his aged servant.[48]

There is no hiding the fact that Christmas Evans was deeply hurt by the trials he suffered in Anglesey and the unjust treat-ment meted out to him, but he was not a man to 'hold a grudge' or to look back more than occasionally with regret. Hence, as he meditated 'on the goodness of God towards me in Angle-sey, both before going there and since I left', he could say with gratitude:

Now in my old age, I see the work prospering wonderfully in my hand, so that there is room to think that I am a blessing to the church, and the church is such to me; whilst I might have been a burden to it, or rather a curse, by which she might have been induced to wish me laid in the earth, that I might no longer prevent the progress of the work. Thanks be to God, that it is not so! though I deserve no better; yet I am in the land of mercy. This is unto me according to the manner of God unto his people.[49]

And still the gospel retains its convincing and quickening virtue. Wherever it is proclaimed in its purity and accompanied with the power of the Holy Ghost, proud and hardened sinners are pricked in their hearts and forced to cry out, 'Men and brethren, what must we do?' It answers the question. It points to the crucified and saith, 'Believe and be saved!' It reconciles the enemy unto God. It makes the blasphemer a man of prayer, the sensualist a man of purity, the inebriate a man of sobriety; and where sin abounded, grace much more abounds.

The dead whom Jesus quickened had no time to inquire into the mysterious process by which the work was wrought. They sprang instantly into life by the power of God. Yet the evidence of the change was clear and incontestable. So it is with the transforming effects of the gospel.

Christmas Evans preaching from 1 Timothy 1:11.[1]

15
Caerphilly: The Best Years

After thirty-five industrious and productive years, during which the light of the gospel had spread its lustrous rays throughout 'the dark isle', Christmas Evans left the scene of his labours under a cloud of despondency. His health, exasperated by the troubles, had deteriorated rapidly and he was nearly blind; his robust constitution, usually vigorous and determined, was much enfeebled and reaping the effects of years of selfless exertion; and his legs, formerly so dependable and strong, were swelling painfully — physical ailments that were to prevent him from baptising the Caerphilly converts. In spirit he was downcast and, as many of his former friends had forsaken him, he felt lonely and insecure.

He had also been under considerable financial strain during the final years of his Anglesey ministry, which had influenced his decision to leave the island. In 1825 things were so tight that he had appealed to the Baptist Fund in London for extra assistance. Thomas Thomas (Cardiff), in a letter to John Pritchard dated 20 January, 1826, mentions his 'pain' at hearing the indignation of English Baptists towards the frugality of the Welsh:

I assure you that this has brought great disgrace to our
nation in the sight of the ministers in London. It was painful
for me to hear these men, rather sparing with their words,
especially when suggesting something unfavourable about
others, saying, 'What! Is this the generosity of your fellow
countrymen? Is there no ability or tendency in the whole of
Wales to support, in old age and weakness, a man who is
regarded in your country as Robert Hall is in England — he
who has worked so untiringly for so many years in the ministry, who has built so many chapels and collected towards
them, and travelled so many times through Wales to preach
the word?'[2]

When John Michael, one of Christmas Evans's faithful friends
on the island, urged him after his exile to return north, the latter
replied, 'I am sad to think and say this, but I found the men of
Anglesey good at making promises but poor at paying.' He
was owed £30 in all, £20 in wages and £10 for clearing chapel
debts out of his own pocket. After repeatedly asking the church
for the money, he said in earnest to Michael, 'Not as a beggar
or a poor man do I ask you to pay the £10, but as a servant of
the Lord, as a worker who is worthy of his wage. Pay, or give
up all profession of godliness... In shame, pay. In case of the
punishment of God, pay. In case of pain in death, pay.'[3]

As always his habit at such times was to seek consolation
from above and to meditate on the living word, wherein is life.
In a sermon on Colossians 1:26, probably preached by him
during his Caerphilly pastorate, he included a number of personal reflections that may allude to the distresses he experienced in the latter part of his Anglesey ministry and the strength
he found in God and his 'book'. 'I am very thankful for books
written by man,' he said, 'but it is God's book that sheds the
light of the life everlasting on all other books.' This book placed
him in the presence of the Almighty, 'who has in him something
that would destroy me for ever, and yet something that spares
and animates me; pressing me down and, at the same time,

saying, "Fear not"; something that melts me into penitence and at once causes me to rejoice in the faith; inspiring me with the fear of joy; something that creates a wish in me to conceal myself from him and then a stronger wish to stay for ever in the light of his countenance'.[4]

The word of God obliged him 'to confess, against myself, my sins unto the Lord; and to cry out for a new heart and a right spirit; for the author of the book knows all'. When he yielded to 'pensive reflections, under a sense of sin', and saw 'the tops of dark mountains of disease, and trouble at the terrors of the grave', he only had to search the Scriptures to find 'infinite goodness, fairer than the Shekinah of old, looking at me, out of eternity; it is like the smile of the eternal king from his throne of mercy, lifting me up out of despair'. When he was 'weak and distressed and alone and none to receive my tale of sorrows, none to express a word of fellow-feeling or of care for me, in the living oracles of the gospel I see divine wisdom and loving kindness looking at me tenderly, compassionately, through the openings of my prison, and I feel that he who dresses the lily of the field, and numbers the sparrows, is near me, numbering the hairs of my head, listening to my cries'.[5]

In July, 1826, towards the end of the conflict in Anglesey, Christmas Evans was invited, on the recommendation of several respected ministers, to take charge of the Baptist Church at Caerphilly, Glamorganshire, which had been formed in 1784. From 1821 the small Caerphilly congregation of 65 or so members had worshipped in a new chapel, Tonyfelin, in the centre of the village. The previous pastor Griffith Davies, a noted evangelist and planter of churches, had resigned some time before Christmas Evans was invited. In 1827 he died of cancer. Christmas Evans's proposed move south was confirmed by various assurances of divine guidance, which strengthened his resolve to leave the island of his trials. One of these assurances was occasioned by the visit to North Wales of Benjamin Price, who

The old Tonyfelin Chapel (right) and manse, Caerphilly.

Plaque on Tonyfelin Chapel.

in 1844 retired from the ministry to become a superintendent for Wales of the Baptist Missionary Society, with the task of arranging the visits of missionaries and receiving collections,[6] 'and in this post performed his most important life's work'.[7] In an interview with Christmas Evans before his call, the following conversation took place:

> 'Well, Mr Evans, if you have really made up your mind to leave, I know of a place for you.'
> 'Do you indeed? Well done, Ben; and what place is it?'
> 'Caerphilly.'
> 'Well done, Ben. Caerphilly; that's the place. Caerphilly; well done, Ben. Now, dear brother, write instantly to Caerphilly, and tell them I'll come to Caerphilly.'
> 'No, Mr Evans, that will never do, it would appear as if you were far too ready to go; it would make you too cheap. I'll put it in this way, that if they were to give you a call, you would perhaps accept it.'
> 'Better still; well done, Ben. Make myself too cheap; yes, it certainly would; well done, Ben. I thank thee, Ben.'[8]

Price wrote to the deacons at Caerphilly and their response was very favourable. On 28 July, 1826, Christmas Evans wrote to his friend John Roberts:

> I have received a call from the church at Caerphilly and I am, after two Sundays, going there... It is time for Daniel to pray earnestly about the move to Babylon. If he can carry the old harps with him from Anglesey and sing the songs of Zion in Caerphilly to his satisfaction, then it is certain that the Daniel of Anglesey will go there to live and to die, according to his present thoughts. I am as popular in these communities as in any part of Wales; and the Lord has approved my ministry in these areas as much as anywhere in Wales... I do not know, brother, how things will turn out, but I am confident that God is in a covenant with me, and that he will look after me in old age.[9]

So, in the sixtieth year of his life, August, 1826, and in failing health, he set out alone on a difficult and tedious journey of some two hundred miles to his new field of labour in the South. He left 'behind him the most affecting associations, bearing in his very spirit the most vivid reminiscences of past trials and triumphs; while the experience of a forty years' ministry ena- bled him to look forward with complacent hope to that which awaited him in the place whither the Lord his God was leading him'.[10] On his way from Llangefni to Brynsiencyn, and as he meditated on the affliction that had caused him so much grief, he 'felt such tenderness of heart, and that Christ's presence was so near me, that as the coldness of my nature dissolved, I could not refrain from breaking out in supplications and tears. The wrestling lasted for some hours.' His fears dissolved and faith triumphed, and, as he says, 'I had strength given me to entrust myself and my ministry to Jesus Christ with a confidence that raised me above all my troubles. I again entered into a covenant with God, which, however, I did not write.'[11]

The covenant he entered into with God, but 'did not write', may have been a new covenant or a recommitment to the old covenant he had made soon after his deliverance from Sandemanianism. Either way, it is another example of the stead- fast devotion that pervaded his life and his willingness to commit himself wholeheartedly to God and his purposes.

By the time he reached Caerphilly, a small village in a moun- tain valley, on 1 September, he was in a happy mood and thank- ful to God for his mercies. Before his arrival some of the residents of Caerphilly, who had heard the rumour of his decision to minister among them, dared not believe he would come, think- ing that at the last moment his heart would fail him and move him to stay in his beloved Anglesey. His settlement in the area was a historical event in the region round about, and all de- nominations and conditions of people were caught up in the excitement, and with wonderment and gladness the report of his presence was propagated and received, 'CHRISTMAS EVANS IS COME!' 'Are you sure of it?' was the incredulous reply. 'Yes, quite sure of it; he preached at Caerphilly last Sunday. That I know from a friend who was there.'[12]

He began his ministry at the Baptist Church in Caerphilly, without taking upon himself the pastoral care completely, in the same way as he had started in Anglesey, by calling the church together to pray that God would pour out his Spirit on them and prosper the preaching of the gospel. His aim was to secure through prayer the presence and blessing of God, and subsequently the salvation of men, as is evident from his own remarks:

> I had heard that ministers and churches in America are favoured with great prosperity and powerful revivals, by continuing to seek them by prayer. I considered that the same spirit was with us; we agreed, therefore, under divine influence, to seek in the name of Jesus the outpouring of the Holy Ghost, with the word and ordinances, to render them efficient for the salvation of men and the glory of God. We succeeded, and received blessings in answer to prayer like that of which I had read as enjoyed by our brethren in America.[13]

On 20 November, 1826, in a letter to David Richards, the first settled minister of the church at Caerphilly, he wrote enthusiastically, 'I have never been as comfortable as I am since I have been here. There is a great movement in this forest. We have received seven backsliders and thirty-six new converts... We have sixteen in the fellowship who are ready to be baptized and signs of many more. In the village of Caerphilly and the district of Bedwas, the breeze is blowing.' A few days later he wrote to John Roberts and contrasted the 'happiness' of the Caerphilly church to have him as their pastor, with the 'indifference' of the people of Anglesey to lose him.[14] 'Praise the Lord, brother,' he said to Richards, on 15 April, 1827, 'this final part of my difficult journey through the empty wilderness ... has been ... the most comfortable, entertaining and successful since the beginning at Lleyn.'[15] Within two months of his arrival the regular congregation had risen to about a hundred and by the autumn of 1827 the membership numbered 160.

Unlike in Anglesey, where he had preached to different congregations, often using the same sermon several times, in Caerphilly he preached to only one congregation every Sunday and so needed a steady supply of new sermon material. He rose to this challenge, surprising many with the abundance of his resources, and making it clear, 'contrary to a pretty prevalent opinion, that his good preaching was not confined to a few good sermons, slowly prepared and often repeated; but that he was quite capable, from week to week, to get up discourses quite equal to his greatest and most celebrated single efforts'.[16] Many of these sermons spread into other parts of South Wales. After the morning service it was common for members of the congregation to return home and discuss the sermon with their neighbours, so that by the end of the day throughout large areas of Glamorgan and Monmouth, Christmas Evans's morning sermon had been 'preached again' to many who had stayed at home. They were also long remembered. Paxton Hood relates a conversation he had with an old lady, who, forty years after hearing Christmas Evans's sermons, said with tears, 'We used to reckon things as they happened by Christmas Evans's sermons. People used to say, "It must have happened then because that was the time when Christmas Evans preached *The Wedding Ring* or *The Seven Eyes*, or some other sermon" which had been quite a bookmark in the memory.'[17]

He preached one of these memorable sermons at the opening of the Baptist chapel in Merthyr Tudful. Micah Thomas, a friend of Andrew Fuller and the president of the Baptist Academy at Abergavenny since its opening in January, 1807, had already preached a fine sermon from Zechariah 13:7, when Christmas Evans stood up. He had only recently become a resident of the county and the congregation was breathless with expectation and excitement at the prospect of hearing him. He looked remarkably well, though somewhat aged, and had a large handkerchief tied about his head which he did not immediately remove. His text was 1 Timothy 3:16 and in a low husky voice, he introduced his subject before proceeding, in clearer tones and with deeper emphasis, to speak on 'God manifest in the flesh', and, in his own inimitable way, on the resurrection of Christ, turning the morning of the third day into 'the day and hour of appeal':

> The soldiers came back to the city, probably about nine o'clock in the morning, and they went to the leaders of the people, who had employed them. The leaders seeing and knowing them, exclaimed, 'Here is the watch! What is the matter? What is that dread that overcasts their faces? Come in here! We charge you to say the truth.'
>
> 'You have no need to charge us. The fright and horror are still in our hearts.'
>
> 'How? What has happened at the grave? Did his disciples come and take him away?'
>
> 'They! No, and if they had, our spears would have sufficed for them.'
>
> 'Well, but how was it? What *has* taken place?'
>
> 'Behold, while we were on the watch, and about the dawn of the day, a great earthquake, like unto the one that took place on Friday afternoon, *when he died*! and we all fell powerless to the ground. Looking up we saw an angel in a white robe, his eyes like the lightning, so vivid and piercing, that the mightiest armies of Caesar would fain have escaped from them in a moment. We, not able to bear this sight, were obliged to look down at once. We endeavoured again to raise our eyes, and we beheld one coming out of the grave, passing by the angel, who now sat upon the removed stone, arrayed in such triumphant majesty that the earth never

witnessed such a sight before. Yes, HE WAS LIKE UNTO THE
SON OF GOD.'

'What became of the angel?'

'Oh, a legion of them came down, and one of them, very
fair, like a young man, entered the grave and sat where the
head of Jesus had lain; and immediately another also, looking fair and beautiful, sat where his feet had rested.'

'And did the angels say anything to you?'

'No, but they looked with eyes of lightning.'

'Saw you not (his friends) the women?'

'O yes, they came there, but he had left the tomb before
their arrival.'

'Talked the angels to them?'

'Yes, they seemed to be of one family, and most intim-
ately acquainted with each other.'

'Do you remember anything of the conversation?'

'Yes. "Fear you not! Let the Pharisees and Darkness fear
today! You seek Jesus! He is not here; for he has risen
indeed. He is alive and lives for ever. He is gone before you
to Galilee." We heard one angel say, "Come, see the place
where the Lord lay." Another angel addressed a woman called
Mary and said, "Woman, why weepest *thou*, while thy Lord
has risen indeed, and is alive so near unto thee? *Let his
enemies weep today!*"'

'What! How say you — *close that door!* You, *tall* soldier,
approach. *Was it not you that pierced his side?*'

'Yes, it was I; and this relation is all true. I pray I may
never witness such a scene again. Oh alas! It is all true. He
must have been the Son of God.'

The Pharisees lost their case on *the day of appeal.*[18]

Later Christmas Evans wrote a synopsis of this sermon at the
request of the editor of the *Welsh Baptist Magazine*, and it
appeared in the first edition in January, 1829. Some who had
heard the sermon at Merthyr were unhappy with the outline as
it failed to do justice to the original, so when he subsequently
occupied Mr Davies's pulpit for a Sabbath, he was asked by
Thomas Griffiths to preach it again during the evening service.
'Having made a humorous remark on the strangeness of a man

preaching his own printed sermon, he cheerfully consented.'
Rhys Stephen, who admits to having 'the faintest trace of
memory as to sermons I may have heard', found it quite unforgettable. 'In its oratorical excellence,' he says, 'it stands alone,
even among his great achievements, especially in the report of
the soldiers. *We heard them talk, had a clear perception of the
difference of tone and variations of countenance; and more
especially still, when one of the chief priests, in an agonising,
anxious whisper*, said, "Shut the door", and singled out "the
tall soldier". Such a combined triumph of sanctified fancy and
perfect oratory I never expect to witness again.'[19]

Throughout the two years he remained at Caerphilly his
preaching 'attained a power and an eminence it had never
before reached, and it was crowned with lasting success'.[20]
Multitudes came to hear him, many travelling across the
surrounding hills from all directions, and there were conversions and baptisms, not only in Caerphilly, where he had the
pleasure and honour 'to examine about one hundred and forty
candidates for baptism, and receive them by the right hand of
Christian fellowship into the communion of the church',[21] but
in Bedwas and in churches as far away as Newport and
Bridgend. The young were especially affected by what they
heard, and many notorious sinners submitted to Christ. Older
people too, some of whom had lived a life of drunkenness,
were so thoroughly transformed that publicans, angry at losing
their most faithful customers, complained that since Christmas
Evans's arrival in the area their 'intemperate profits' had been
markedly reduced.

One young man, Caleb Harris Edmunds, through the ministry of Christmas Evans, 'became a decided convert to the faith
of Christ, and to the obedience of that faith. He became a
member of the church at Tonyfelin, and was found walking in
the commandments of the Lord blamelessly.' It was soon
discovered that he had a wonderful gift in the ministry of the

word and, with the backing of a godly family and the influences of a good education, he was 'at once almost a complete preacher'.[22] To prepare for the ministry he went to Bristol College, where, sadly, after only a few months training, he died. Another young man whose life was changed for the good was Morgan Evans, 'who became an earnest hearer of the new pastor, and speedily a thorough disciple of the Lord Christ'. He was a close friend of Caleb Edmunds and was initially hindered from entering the ministry 'by the cares of a family and engagements in business'.[23] In the course of time, however, he became the pastor of the church at Tongwynlais, only five miles from Caerphilly, but he too died prematurely, suffering a brain-fever and passing into glory in December, 1841.

The people of Caerphilly had not experienced such a move of God for twenty-five years, and in response were filled with confidence and joy. Perhaps they were reminded of the year 1772, when there had been a profusion of religious blessing in the Caerphilly area which was reckoned by Edmund Jones to be an 'uncommon work' that transformed the beautiful country into 'a Beulah'.[24] Christmas Evans, in spite of years of prosperous preaching, had never seen such 'life in things'. 'There is no jumping or rejoicing,' he wrote in the letter to David Richards at the close of 1826, 'but much crying and singing. The chapel has become much too small during the last two months. Brethren from other churches — especially from Basaleg, Pontypridd, Castleton, Llys-faen, Hengoed, Cardiff and Whitchurch — gather in crowds on Sundays, particularly at the monthly services... The Sunday School is crowded out. I preach twice on Sundays and twice on weekdays, and in special services in the neighbourhood.'[25] In a letter to the 'Gentlemen Managers of the Particular Baptist Fund in London', dated 'Jan.4, 1829', after his removal to Cardiff, he remarks, 'I had never enjoyed such freedom and energy and success in any two years of forty-four of my ministry, as I have got at Caerphilly.'[26]

Before the outpouring of God's Spirit and the influx of new converts described above, Christmas Evans had a remarkable dream which he noted in his diary. This dream he believed to be of divine origin because of the blessing of God that attended his ministry at Caerphilly and because of the success of the gospel there:

> He thought he saw himself in a meeting-house very much like the one at Caerphilly, and hanging over and above the house there were many harps, wrapped in coverings of green. Then he said, 'I will take down the harps of heaven here.' In taking away the covering, what appeared, but the Ark of the Covenant of the God of Israel standing opposite the table, and upon it was inscribed with golden letters in Hebrew, — JEHOVAH CABOD. Then he cried, 'Brethren, thanks be to the Lord! Here he is come to us according to his promises, and to our prayers and expectations.'[27]

It was under the place where he saw the harps that he welcomed the one hundred and forty new members, who, he says, had been tuned to the song of redemption.

As has been mentioned, he was not confined to Caerphilly during his pastorate there, but frequently preached away from home, and 'On all public occasions which he could be persuaded to attend, he preached at ten o'clock in the morning.'[28] A brother usually delivered a short sermon before him in order to prepare the way for the greater man. The first Association he attended, as resident pastor in the South, was at Pontypool in June, 1827, 'where he preached ... to the immense delight and gratification of, at least, five thousand persons, from Philippians 2:6-8'.[29] He also attended the conferences of his brethren in South Wales, but, desiring not to interfere with the conduct of affairs, kept a very low profile. At the business conference following his first Association, to the great disappointment of many who were eager to hear his views on the matters discussed, he uttered only one word! During the meeting an attack was made 'by a good brother, whose spirit has always been *a little Ishmaelitish*', on the Abergavenny Academy, which, according to the 'vindicator of the Academy', amounted to *libel*, a charge he uttered in English. This incensed the alleged libeller, who repeatedly appealed to the moderator to see if what he had said amounted to libel. The presiding brother 'pleaded ignorance of the jurisprudence' necessary to give a formal reply, but was pressed for an answer. Eventually he admitted that he could not recall 'an apt Welsh word for libel, when he suddenly heard the slow and solemn voice of Christmas Evans supplying the term *cabldraeth*'.[30]

A few years later, at the conference of the Association at Cowbridge, he was almost as reserved, and only spoke up when he felt the occasion demanded it. During the previous year David Evans, 'a man of great and well-deserved influence' and a long-standing secretary of the Association, had died.

> All the Baptist churches of Montgomery, Radnor, Brecon, Monmouth and Glamorgan, excepting those beyond the Tawy, were included in this organisation; and the secretary had to attend to all their statistics, and to attend all the Association meetings, at whatever distance from his own home. For these labours he had, as compensation, the profits of the Annual Circular Letter, which was only a penny pamphlet, and could, of course, produce but little, in clear gain, above the cost of printing and circulating.[31]

After an affectionate tribute had been paid to the memory of the deceased brother, John Jones of Newtown, David Evans's close friend, was elected his successor. At this stage in the proceedings, a brother stood up and suggested that 'A proportion of the profits of the Circular Letter should henceforth be given to the writer of the Circular, instead of being given in their entireness to the secretary, intimating at the same time that he had, some years before, mentioned it, and had abandoned his purpose out of deference to Mr Evans, who evinced some feeling on the occasion.' Christmas Evans, whose opposition was aroused by such a miserly opinion, said with emphasis and with a large tear trickling down his cheek, 'I consider the entertaining of the question a degradation to the Conference.'[32]

John Philip Davies of Tredegar (1786-1832) was one of the most fluent preachers of the day. He exercised a profound influence on the theology of his countrymen, and was not only regarded as a mighty theologian and a clear and ready expositor, but universally acknowledged as one of the best informed and most judicious ministers in the Principality. When terminally ill, he spent four or five months undergoing medical treatment at Caerphilly soon after Christmas Evans's settlement there, and both men greatly enjoyed each other's company. They conversed almost every day and Davies was particularly impressed by his friend's 'insatiable thirst for knowledge' and his 'really extensive and varied stores of information', gathered during his busy life. Both men delighted to compare notes and Christmas Evans welcomed 'every hint and intimation of improved construction of a text, or a new definition of a principle' that his companion could suggest.[33]

Davies also thoroughly enjoyed Christmas Evans's preaching, which he usually managed to hear on Sunday mornings. Rhys Stephen observes:

It was not the vivid flashes of his eloquence — with these he was of old acquainted — but it was the fulness and variety of his matter, from Sabbath to Sabbath, that astonished this most amiable and able critic, giving him quite a new impression as to the order of Mr Evans's mind. On his return home, somewhat recovered, I have as clear a recollection of his communicating this discovery, in my hearing, to one of the deacons of his church at Tredegar, Mr Thomas Griffiths, as I have also of the delight which it gave us to know that Mr

Evans's company and ministry had been productive of so much comfort to our most affectionate but dying pastor.[34]

It appears from the Tonyfelin account book that his salary was £48 a year, which included a house, free from the usual rent and rates, and situated under the same roof as the chapel, and adjacent to the chapel a small field (about half an acre) in which he kept his pony at a cost of £12 a year. He was also obliged to keep a maid, who was paid £10. In 1827 the total amount paid to him was £53. 18s. 3d. This included £1. 18s. 3d. for a great coat; £4. 5s. 0d. for a horse and beer, one shilling for a spur and 14s. 10d. to Martha Williams. The following year he was paid £12 every quarter.

He found it very difficult to make ends meet and would have run into debt had his salary not been supplemented by a small allowance of £10 from the Baptist Fund and the generosity of friends. 'Mr Jones of Pontypridd has given me sufficient hay to feed my pony for this year of scarcity,'[35] is one example of the help he received. His health was generally good, although he broke a leg during his stay, but it mended well with little discomfort. Every month he preached around the neighbourhood in the houses of 'Mr Llewellyn, Bedwas; Mr Jenkins, Rhydri, a rich man converted from drink since I came here and a constant listener but not yet a member — but he has asked for a monthly preaching service in his home. I preach in another house near Taff's Well and in the chapel there every Thursday. One great advantage of this house preaching,' he says, 'is that I do not go out to the cold air in perspiration, a great comfort to an old man.' In the same letter he makes the comment: 'I have no desire to return to Anglesey.'[36]

Although Christmas Evans had 'no desire to return to Anglesey', it seems that his opponents on the island were sorry for the way they had treated him, and longed for him to return for the sake of the church. John Michael wrote to him in January,

1828, saying, 'I went to Llangefni last Sunday. I was pleased to
see their attitude. They have decided to hold a prayer meeting
to implore the Lord to move your heart to come back to us...
Oh that your mind could be inclined to come and visit your old
comrades! I cannot imagine the joy that would be felt.'[37] However, the memory of his departure was fresh in his mind and
the wound still open. He wrote back on 20 January, 1828, and
accused the men of the island of breaking their promise to
reimburse him: 'It is a strange thing that Anglesey has become
so inhuman and unrighteous, and unfaithful to its promises
regarding religion.' He then poured contempt on the younger
generation of preachers, who had caused him so much trouble,
before expressing contentment with his ministry in Caerphilly:

> What a poor thing I would be if I went back to Anglesey in
> my old age to fight and battle with a lot of vain ministers! I
> do not like their doctrine, their noise, their talents, their spirit,
> their taste... Indeed, brother, the misery of the churches lies
> in their spirit and the taste corresponds entirely to self-made
> preachers, without heaven having placed a golden seal on
> their ministry to call the lost, or awaken the community, or
> increase the congregation of the Lord; but Satan — the god
> of this world — has placed his seal on their labours to tear
> apart the churches, disturb communities, and bring plagues
> out of slander and gossip...
>
> I cannot imagine that I would leave this peaceful place in
> which the Lord has placed so many seals of my ministry,
> and turn out into the Bay of Biscay. I love my children in
> Anglesey. I love my children here, too, and they are younger
> and need to be nurtured more... There is here a church of
> around 200, with many of them going about the community
> to pray — not a dry doctrinal people, but a happy people of
> heaven. It is so pleasing to see them in fiery meetings and,
> through the goodness of the Lord, I am experiencing more
> of these than ever. They weep and shout 'amen' and give
> thanks more than I ever saw in Anglesey.[38]

Although he was settled in his accommodation, with a housekeeper, he mentioned to a friend that he would prefer a servant
from the North as it seems his present housekeeper knew nothing
about the mode of living to which he was accustomed. Upon
discussing this change of personnel, it was suggested to him by
his friends that he might marry again, and the name of a rich,
noble woman was put forward along with the temptation of
bettering 'his entire worldly circumstances by the alliance', and,
because of her wealth, making himself 'pleasantly independent
of churches and deacons and county associations'. When it
was first suggested to him 'He seemed to think earnestly for a
moment, then broke out, "Oh, oh! I tell you, brother, it is my
firm opinion that I am never to have any property in the soil of
this world until I have a grave. I shall then have my full share of
it;" and he would talk no more on the subject.'39

Some time later a friend visited him and found him in grave
meditation, which he at length broke by saying, 'I want a wife,
you see; I want a wife.'

'A wise thought, Mr Evans, if you can be well suited; but
who is she to be?'

'They talk to me about Miss —, and tell me she has money;
but it isn't money I want, but a wife.'

'Well, there is Mary, your old housekeeper; she knows more
about your feelings and habits than any other person can do,
and you know her. Will she suit you?'

'Aye, Mary — Mary, my old servant — aye, Mary is a good
and faithful woman.'40

He started to write to his former housekeeper Mary Jones,
and in one of his letters proposed marriage. There is no record
of her reply but letters passed between the couple for several
weeks before he persuaded a neighbouring minister, Thomas
Davies of Argoed, to travel to Anglesey — a round trip of nearly
400 miles! — in order to bring his faithful housekeeper to the
South. Davies 'set out with two saddled horses, telling all and

sundry on the way that he was to return with a wife for Christmas Evans'.[41] On the journey north he preached at several chapels along the route, appearing in no hurry to reach his destination. Evidently Mary Jones took some persuading to leave Anglesey, but on Monday 21 April, 1828, she left Llangefni with her chaperon. At each stage of their journey they received welcome hospitality, and finally arrived at the chapel in Caerphilly on the following Thursday evening, just as Christmas Evans and his congregation were filing out of the prayer meeting.

On Monday 28 April, they were married by Rev H. Williams in the presence of Richard Evans and John Williams in the parish of Eglwysilan, Glamorganshire, which is the same parish in which George Whitefield had married Elizabeth James of Abergavenny on 14 November, 1741. The names of these great men are found in the parish register. Christmas Evans was sixty-one and Mary Jones, who signed her name with an 'X', was about thirty-five. The marriage was a very happy one and his new wife 'paid him the most untiring and affectionate attentions to the last moment of his life'.[42] 'Mrs Evans,' he remarked, 'has renewed her youth and is full of her first love — she sings as in the days of old. She talks of spiritual things all day long and never tires.'[43] She survived her husband and, apparently, in her old age and out of regard for the memory of Christmas Evans, C. H. Spurgeon secured for her a small allowance from an English Baptist fund.[44]

Although his one eye was very weak and his body afflicted with various infirmities of old age, he still loved to read and, as J. P. Davies had noticed, his desire for knowledge remained as keen as ever. One of the books he read for the first time at Caerphilly was Dr Pye Smith's *Scripture Testimony to the Messiah*, thanks to a gentleman of the congregation who had bought it for his use. He thoroughly enjoyed Smith's arguments, incorporating many of his ideas into his own sermons and making them a regular topic of discussion. Rhys Stephen remembers

listening with wonder to his conversation with Saunders of
Merthyr, in which he gave the substance of Smith's comments
on John 17:3:

> I distinctly remember that when Mr Evans said, 'Mr Saunders,
> you will observe that, on these grounds, the knowledge of
> Jesus Christ, here mentioned, is the same knowledge as
> that of the only true God, and that the knowledge of the
> former is as necessary to salvation as the knowledge of the
> latter; indeed, they are one and the same thing.' 'Yes, yes,'
> was the reply. 'Capital, very excellent! I never heard that
> interpretation before.' I was then a youth and was not aston-
> ished by the interpretation, which, of course, was new to
> me, so much as by the admission of the aged men *that this
> was new to them!*[45]

He was very much comforted by some of the neighbouring
ministers, who showed him great respect and with whom he
loved to converse. Among his friends at this time were Evan
Jones of Castleton, a Baptist minister from the North, who was
well-acquainted with the affairs of his denomination there, and
who was always willing to meet him at any expense of time and
trouble; David Edwards of Beaupré; his son Evan Edwards of
Caerphilly; and Griffith Hughes, the pastor of the Independent
Church of Groes-wen, who had been in that charge for many
years. The latter was a native of Cwm-du in Carmarthenshire
and one who possessed all the attributes of a fine preacher —
'a cheerful temper, a clear voice, ease of speech, fire, thunder,
and a popular style'.[46] He was a self-taught man, whose theology was well-informed. 'His Calvinism was of a more expan-
sive circle than Christmas Evans's, but this was no bar to their
friendly intercourse. They were mutually fond of meeting each
other, and the vivacious sprightliness of Mr Hughes never failed
to have a complacent influence on Mr Evans.'[47] During his time
Groes-wen became the mother church of many new causes
and a spiritual centre.

Throughout his settlement at Caerphilly he was a caring and diligent pastor, who attended all the private meetings of the church, and endeavoured, by word and deed, to encourage the members of his congregation to walk in the ways of the Lord. He published a sermon, a biographical article and three essays with that aim in view. It is evident from his diary that the two years he stayed in Caerphilly were among the happiest of his life: 'I never spent a short time — about two years — in greater comfort; for the ark of God had appeared there.'[48] He had hoped to finish his course in that place, if it had been the will of Providence, but sadly problems arose. 'I had not my desire in that respect,' he says, 'owing to some things which brought no guilt upon my conscience, but certainly must have done so upon other persons. It is not prudent to notice them.'[49]

The problems that he thought were 'not prudent to notice' centred around various disagreements between himself and some of his congregation. The deacons and members had for some years managed the affairs of the church, without the oversight of the pastor, Griffith Davies, who since his ordination in 1821 had lived in a neighbouring parish and at Cardiff. Davies was content to act as pastor, fulfilling his ministerial duties, without exercising the rights of a pastor to 'rule over' the church under his care. It was therefore the deacons who held authority in the church — an authority they were reluctant to hand over to their new pastor. Such a substitution of roles Christmas Evans could not tolerate. A conflict of interests ensued which culminated in his departure from Caerphilly. Rhys Stephen observes that Christmas Evans

> ... was not, at his time of life, with his previous experience as the pastor of the pastors and churches of a whole county, the best adapted to be the successful and happy pastor of a single church of long standing, and addicted from habit to much self-government without the pastor. Nor should it be forgotten, that the confinement of his pastoral solicitudes to

one place aggravated these difficulties. In Anglesey, when his visit to one church produced painful anxiety, on the morrow's morn he visited another; and its affairs came to his relief — dividing the attention, and relieving him of the sadness. While in one place, he felt and retained the undivided influence of everything that annoyed him, and brooded over his sorrows, until the molehill enlarged itself into a mountain in his eye, and small hindrances were augmented into stupendous calamities. Thus it turned out, that, as soon as the excitement of the revival was over, and the church turned its attention to its ordinary affairs, Mr Evans, claiming, probably, the full amount of his power, met an unwillingness, at least an unpreparedness, to fall in with his way; and a somewhat cool determination was evinced that, in these matters, they would pursue their former course.[50]

With little or no direct controversy, he decided to leave. It was too late in life, so he thought, to change the habit of his mind to make it acceptable to the church, and there seemed little prospect of the leading members of the congregation compromising their position. He still loved many of them and desired their prosperity. 'May not our mistakes,' he said, 'be charged upon any of us in the day of judgement, but may we be graciously made to confess our faults on earth, where the fountain of grace and of pardon is opened.'[51] No doubt the contentions that had caused him so much grief in Anglesey were resurrected in his mind, and rather than suffer the 'wounds of battle' again, he accepted a call, against the advice of some of his friends, from the Welsh Baptist Church in Cardiff.

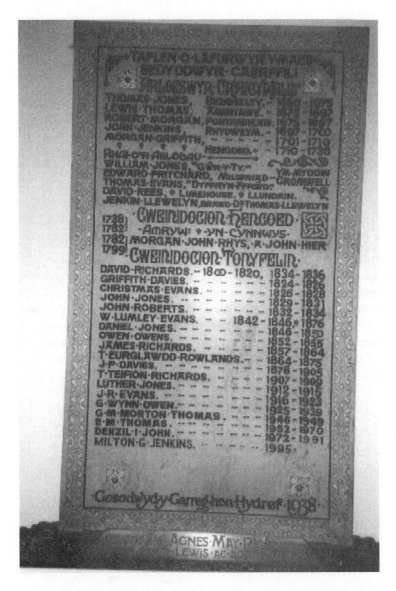

A plaque in the present church, Tonyfelin, Caerphilly.

The Christian is engaged in a warfare, 'not against flesh and blood, but against principalities and powers, against the rulers of the darkness of this world, against spiritual wickedness' — or wicked spirits — 'in high places', who go about like roaring lions, seeking whom they may devour; assailing the servants of Christ ... swarming up from the sea of corruption within and around us, like the frogs of Egypt, and entering into our very bed-chambers and closets of devotion.

Christmas Evans preaching on Ephesians 6:16.[1]

16
Cardiff: Vale of Contention

Christmas Evans had resided at Caerphilly for about two years, when he was invited by the deacons of the Tabernacle Church, Cardiff, which was without a pastor, 'to come to them to try and raise the cause as it pleased God to be the case at Caerphilly'.[2] After careful consideration and prayer for divine direction, and with no little anxiety pressing on his mind and exciting his feelings, he accepted the invitation, believing that it was God's will for him to labour, for some time at least, in that town. Before removing to his new charge, which was only about eight miles from Caerphilly and in the same county, he entered into a new covenant with God, which he wrote out, dated and formally signed after his settlement in Cardiff. This covenant was the third he had made before God in the capacity of a Christian and a minister of the gospel, and it was found among some of his papers after his death. It was enacted on his return from the village of Tongwynlais in the vale of Taf, late one evening as he travelled over Caerphilly mountain, and while he was still uncertain as to the future. The spirit of prayer descended 'very copiously' on him. He wept for some hours and cried wholeheartedly to Jesus Christ for his blessings. 'I found at this time,' he comments, 'a particular nearness to Christ, as if he

Tabernacle, the Welsh Baptist Church, Cardiff.

A plaque in the Tabernacle Church, Cardiff. The
translation reads: 'In memory of Christmas Evans, one of the
nation's greatest preachers. He endured as seeing
him who is invisible.'

were close by me, and my mind was filled with strong confidence that he attended to my requests, for the sake of the merits of his own name.'[3] The covenant is a heart-warming and challenging document:

I. Grant me the great favour of being led by thee, according to thy will — by the directions of thy providence and word, and the disposing of my own mind by thy Spirit, for the sake of thine infinitely precious blood. Amen. — C. E.

II. Grant, if I am to leave Caerphilly, that the gale (of the Spirit's influence) and religious revival I had there may follow me to Cardiff, for the sake of thy great name. Amen. — C. E.

III. Grant thy blessing upon bitter things, to brighten and quicken me more and more, and not to depress and render me more lifeless. Amen. — C. E.

IV. Suffer me not to be trodden under the proud feet of members or deacons for the sake of thy goodness. Amen. — C. E.

V. Grant me the invaluable favour of being in thine hand, the means of calling sinners unto thyself, and of edifying thy saints wherever thou wilt send me, for the sake of thy name. Amen. — C. E.

VI. If I am to stay at Caerphilly, give me some tokens as to Gideon of old, by removing the things that discourage me and are in the way of the prosperity of religion in that church. Amen. — C. E.

VII. Grant, Lord of glory, and Head of thy church, that the Ark of the cause which is thine in Anglesey and Caerphilly, may be sustained from falling into the hands of the Philistines. Do not reject it; spare it speedily, and lift up the light of thy countenance upon it; and by thy Spirit, word, and providence, so operate as to carry things forward in the churches, and neighbourhoods in such a manner as will produce changes in officers, and measures that will accomplish a thorough improvement in the great cause, for the establishment of which in the world, thou hast died; — and by scattering those that delight in war, and closing the mouths of those that occasion confusion. Amen. — C. E.

VIII. Grant me waytokens by the time I begin my journey to Liverpool, and from thence to Anglesey, if it is thy will that I should go thither this year. Amen. — C. E.

IX. O grant me succour beneath the shadow of the sympathy that is in thee towards them who are tempted, and the unbounded power there is in thee to be the relief of such. Amen. — C. E.

X. Accept of my thanksgiving a hundred millions of times, that thou hast not hitherto cast me from thine hand, as a darkened star, or a vessel in which there is no pleasure; and suffer not my life to be extended beyond my usefulness. Thanks, that thou hast not given me a prey to the teeth of any. Blessed be thy name. Amen. — C. E.

XI. For the sake of thine infinite merit, do not cast me, thy servant, under the feet of pride and injustice, of worldly greatness, riches, and selfish oppression of any men, but hide me in the secret of thy tabernacle from the strife of tongues. Amen. — C. E.

XII. Help me to wait silently and patiently upon thee, for the fulfilment of these things, and not become enraged, angry, and speak unadvisedly with my lips, like Moses, the servant of the Lord. Sustain my heart from sinking, to wait for fresh strength from Zion. Amen. — C. E.

XIII. Help me to wait upon thee for the necessaries of life; let thy mercy and goodness follow me while I live; and, as it hast pleased thee to honour me greatly, by the blessing thou hast vouchsafed upon the ministry through me, as an humble instrument, at Caerphilly, after the great storm had beaten upon me in Anglesey, like Job, grant that this honour may continue to follow me the remainder of my days, as thou didst unto thy servant Job. Amen. — C. E.

XIV. Let this covenant abide like the covenant of salt, until I come to thee in the world of eternal light. I entreat aid to resign myself to thee, and to thy will. I beseech thee take my heart, and inscribe upon it a deep reverence of thy self, with an inscription that time and eternity cannot efface. O let the remainder of my sermons be taken by thee from my lips; and those which I write, let them be unto thee for a praise. Unto thee I dedicate them. If there should be anything in them conducive to thy glory and to the service of thy kingdom, do thou preserve it, and reveal it unto men; else, let it die like the drop of a bucket in the midst of the scorching heat of Africa. O grant, that there may be a drop of that water which thou alone canst impart, and which springs up to eternal life, running through all my sermons. In this covenant, which probably is the last that will be written between me and thee on the earth, I commit myself, my wife, and the churches amongst whom I have preached, to the protection of thy grace, and the care of thy covenant. Amen. — C. E.

XV. Let this covenant continue when I am in sickness or in health, or in any other circumstance; for thou hast overcome the world, fulfilled the law, finished justifying righteousness, and hast swallowed up death in victory, and all power in heaven and earth is in thine hands. For the sake of thy most precious blood and perfect righteousness, note this covenant with thine own blood in the court of the memorials of forgiving mercy: attach unto it thy name in which I believe; and here I, this day, set my unworthy name unto it, with my mortal hand. Amen. —

Christmas Evans. Dated, Cardiff, April 24, 1829.[4]

After having entered into this covenant he went to Cardiff, 'heartily and unhesitatingly, like a merchant that should send his vessel to sea after it had been registered in the insurance office. I had nothing now to lose,' he comments, 'for I had given myself up to the possession of Jesus, the Mediator of the New Testament, for time and for eternity; and so I have had to abide here in the secret of his tabernacle for these nine months.'[5]

He moved to Cardiff in September, 1828, about 'nine months' after he had formulated the above covenant, and lived at 44 Caroline Street, just around the corner from the church. Many of his friends, who knew about the low spiritual state of the church there, caused partly by the conduct of his predecessor, who 'fell most horribly into immorality and the interest was shaken to the very foundation',[6] did not regard it as likely to be a happy settlement. In a letter written on 7 November, 1828, to John T. Rowlands, an Anglesey man originally and at the time a Welsh Baptist minister in London, Christmas Evans first admits that 'eye-trouble and dissension within the church' at Caerphilly had made it 'almost impossible' for him to remain there, though he had been instrumental in increasing the membership from 65 to 200. He then turns his attention to Cardiff, remarking that the behaviour of the pastor Robert Pritchard had dealt a serious blow to the cause in the town. He expresses confidence that he will reap a 'rich harvest' of new members in the near future, but finds that his meagre salary does not permit him to make both ends meet. However, he describes this period of his life as 'like the best time ever for me' in regard to zeal, mood, heavenly taste, meditation and public speaking. 'I am a wonder to myself.'[7]

Matters in the church were made worse by the fact that the disgraced pastor, who had been separated from the church because of his behaviour, remained in the town and attended the chapel, apparently without the slightest sense of shame for his conduct. Christmas Evans soon formed the opinion that he could find no marks of salvation in this man's life. In his letter to John Rowlands he says that 'Without doubt [Pritchard] lived in sins such as adultery and drunkenness all the days of his ministry and was able to hide them by flattery, lies and craftiness.'[8] He was deemed very harsh in his attitude by some of his congregation who remained loyal to their former leader. He stood firm, though, always stating his reasons, and in the following years was proved right; 'for, since, more than one opportunity has been furnished the unhappy man to retrieve his character, and he has just as often "wallowed in the (same) mire"'.[9]

On 3 January, 1829, he wrote to William Paxon thanking him for a gift of £10 from the Baptist Fund. In the letter he gives details about the first three months of his Cardiff ministry and enthuses that the hearers are restored 'as numerous as ever'.

During that time about twelve were baptised and five restored. As he was in the decline of life and suffering 'various debilities', he did not take upon himself the ministerial or pastoral care. Another minister was called to baptise, although he did administer the Lord's Supper himself. He then relates to Paxon the financial straits he was experiencing:

> What I have received these three months from the congregation is ten pounds. [He had been promised £60 per annum.] I hope when the party of the fallen minister be restored to a sense of duty they will be able to give me more. The rent of the house I live in is £12 and taxes, thirty shillings. For keeping a horse to go to villages costs £12. My family consists of myself and my wife, a religious woman from thirty to forty I have lately married; she had no riches. In getting furniture to our new house, we have run into small debts here, and about five pounds in Anglesey still remains. I am not engaged in any secular business.
>
> I have no other sources whatever to depend upon or to receive a shilling from them. By considering the above you may easily guess, sir, how glad and thankful I was to receive the ten pounds from your fund, not to bank them, but to send them out to answer demands upon me. This truly is my situation in this world, and with a grateful heart I receive your liberality,
>
> *With respect, yours, Christmas Evans.*[10]

On the same sheet of paper as the above was another letter, dated 'January 4, 1829', and addressed to the 'gentleman managers of the particular Baptist fund in London'. He thanks them for their generosity and summarises the doctrinal statement of the Cardiff church, 'which believes that there are three divine persons in the Godhead; that Jesus is God and man; in personal and eternal election, particular redemption, the necessity of divine influence to quicken the dead soul and in the perseverance to the end of all true believers'.[11]

He laboured with his usual energy and zeal for his master's

sake, 'enjoying much and near communion with him, and daily walking in the light of his countenance',[12] and longing for the 'Caerphilly experience'. He was greatly influenced by the revivals in America and Wales that occurred in 1828,[13] and the Baptists and Congregationalists throughout England set aside Good Friday of that year as a day of prayer and fasting in all the churches to implore God to pour out his Spirit in like manner on them and on all parts of the world; and the following year the churches in England and Wales, including the Baptists at Cardiff, observed 17 April for a similar purpose. On that day Christmas Evans wrote about the religious revivals of Wales and the reaction of the English to them:

> The powerful awakenings, and extensive revivals with which God has blessed Wales, were like a mighty rushing wind, carrying all before it, and thus did more in one Sabbath to promote the interest of the kingdom of heaven, than can be effected in an age by a dead and lifeless preaching. 'The earth as it were grew in one day, and a nation was born at once.' There is no country that has been so extensively blessed with these reviving visitations as Wales, except America.
>
> Thirty-five years ago, the English brethren regarded these revivals very contemptuously, and called them enthusiasm; and, marvellous as it may appear, those revivals seemed as much to scorn our brethren in England as our brethren there scorned them; so that they did not honour England with their awakening presence. But O, how clear it is, notwithstanding all the learning and order of our brethren (the English) in religious matters, that there is yet need of these showers of blessing on the sides of the hill, seeing there are such extensive districts of England destitute of the preaching of the gospel. But the Baptist Missions to India, and other parts, have contributed much to effect a considerable change in our English brethren, as it regards warmth and fervency in religion...
>
> If God should bless our brethren in England with these revivals, they shall know that they are as high as themselves, and must, like the lightning from the throne, have their own

way, or they will take an affront, and flee from them, as the cloud of glory did from Israel of old.[14]

Ten days later, from the prayer in his diary, it is obvious that he was experiencing various 'impediments and discouragements' in the church at Cardiff that were obstacles to religious progress, and harmful to his own walk with God, causing him more than a little distress. As with all things, he laid it before the Lord:

April 27, 1829. I earnestly entreat thee, blessed Jesus, for the sake of thine own name, to regard me in this request * * * *. Let things be ordered, O Lord, that they may not be impediments and discouragements unto me, and a hindrance to the progress of religion. O interpose between me and these obstacles, O Lord, that I may have no occasion to dispute with any, and so embitter my spirit! Thy power is infinite and thy wisdom is infallible. Stand thou between me and all contention, that no ill effects come upon me. I flee to hide myself under the shadow of thy wings. Permit nothing to blunt the edge of my talents, my zeal or my success — nor corrupt the church. Grant me this for the sake of thine infinitely precious blood. Set thy name to this request in the court of heaven, and let Satan's party grow weaker and weaker, and the cause of truth and righteousness become like the house of David, and the house of David like the angel of the Lord. Deliver me, that my spirit be not irritated, and I speak unadvisedly with my lips, as Moses did. Hide me in thy pavilion from the strife of tongues * * * *. I am as it were on the verge of eternity; O save and preserve me by thy boundless power. Amen, amen, amen. Lord, regard, behold, hear and spare. — Christmas Evans. Write this in thy book, O my Lord, and my God. Let none be disappointed that wait upon thee, gracious Lord. — Remember me.[15]

The causes of offence within the church troubled him and it was not long before he felt uneasy. It seems that the church, as at Caerphilly, did not want to be ruled by any one individual, who would have the right to exercise the authority entrusted to him. So when Christmas Evans, a man used to taking the leading role, intervened to stop various old customs, great opposition arose.

One of the customs that annoyed him was that of praying publicly in the house of God on the Sabbath for the relations of the dead. In response he prayed, 'Lord, take into thy gracious notice that which distressed my mind, in reference to relinquishing the empty custom of praying for the relations of the dead. Lord, regard this request for the sake of thy meritorious name. — May 8, 1829.'[16] This practice, he feared, was a form of flattery that proceeded more from a desire to please men than from a heart on fire for God. 'Such prayers,' he observes, 'are become a practice with many preachers in Wales, who *spin* out many petitions on such occasions, with little or none of the heart in them, but being caught by the evil genius of some flattering practice, have succeeded too much in some neighbourhoods; the custom having been begun by preachers, who expected to gain people to their standard by something beside the preaching of the commission.'[17]

To add fuel to the smouldering fire of discontent and misunderstanding Christmas Evans's view of church government was at odds with some members of his congregation. He was decidedly in favour of Independency, but was aware, particularly after his Anglesey experience, that it could 'be carried to too great a length, and become an unscriptural inundation, sweeping all away by the force of its current, and so prove extremely dangerous among Baptists and Independents'.[18] He endeavoured to take a moderate view, with the authority of the elder or pastor kept in check, in the hope of avoiding the extremes that could arise. He was alert to the dangers of allowing too much power to the deacons, who were often ready to usurp authority, as in the example he cites below, where he alludes to a certain church or churches in which he had witnessed 'unscriptural deaconship'. He observes that it was not the extremes of Presbyterianism that 'were properly descriptive of the evil at — or — ', for the minister, the elder, 'did not hold the helm of government — but the deacons'. Nor was it 'from Independency usurping the powers of Presbyterianism which are marked for it in the New Testament, that the evil proceeded. Independency,' he says,

> ... is the voice of the majority of the congregation, and when this is under the direction of the elder, or moves in a respectful consultation with him or them, matters are conducted in a brotherly manner: for the elder is set to govern in the Christian congregation, not according to his own notions, but according to the word of God; not to domineer over God's heritage according to his own rules, but to govern in the fear of God, after the rule of Christ. But this was not the case at — ; it was not the voice of the majority of the most pious members of the congregation that prevailed in that instance. Therefore, both Presbyterianism and Independency must be vindicated from the imputation of disturbing congregations; and the whole blame be cast upon unscriptural deaconship, which like a mighty flood carried away the two sea-walls of protection which Christ had set up — even the rule of eldership and the vote of Independency.[19]

The unpleasant differences of opinion and contentions that existed for some time in the church caused him much grief and sorrow, and drove him to cry out earnestly to God. Eventually, after further wranglings, he separated from the church with feelings of animosity, and several of the best and most faithful hearers, some of whom were leading men in the town, left with him and never returned. When his successor David Jones became pastor of the Tabernacle, he complained that the problems surrounding Christmas Evans's departure 'had left a coolness behind' and that 'the spirit of prayer was almost gone'. According to Jones, the fault lay 'in the one-man ruling'.[20] In spite of these troubles and disagreements, Christmas Evans could still say that 'There were many persons in the church at Cardiff, the most excellent I ever knew in any church that I had been.'[21]

Before his removal he was on very friendly terms with many of the ministers in the neighbourhood of Cardiff, whom he regarded with the highest esteem, not least for the personal and family comforts they afforded him. 'I have,' he remarks, 'a great regard for brother Evan Jones, Castleton,[22] and brother J. Williams, Waun Treoda, for their attention to me.'[23] He speaks respectfully of William Jones,[24] pastor of the English Baptist Church at Cardiff, 'who generally made it a point of seeing him every day, and who did everything in his power to assure his mind when he was given to despondency, and generally to administer to the sustentation and solace of his spirits'.[25] He concludes his remarks on him by adding 'Bless him.'[26] In the letter to J. T. Rowlands, already referred to, he expresses his appreciation of John Philip Davies, 'who excels as a divine', while he deprecates 'the overweening conceit' of Hiley[27] and John Jenkins of Hengoed,[28] and the spirit of self-importance exuded by many of his fellow ministers. He also extols the 'devoted attentions' of his wife Mary, whose support and companionship were a great source of strength.

A man whom he had admired for some time and one of the most remarkable ministers for popular talents and extensive usefulness throughout the Principality was 'David Jones of Pontypool', as he is generally known, and of whom Christmas Evans makes honourable mention. Jones was converted through Howel Harris and, although a Calvinistic Methodist in temperament all his life, he joined the Baptists at Pen-y-garn, where he began to preach. Christmas Evans had some intercourse with him in the early part of his ministry and wrote a brief memoir of him, which was published in a Welsh periodical in 1830. He praises his gifts as a preacher, representing him as equal to Daniel Rowland in power and eloquence, and as one 'who neither thought nor said anything like ordinary men'. He goes on: 'His sayings were curt and ingenious, reminding one of nails, sharp-pointed and dipped in oil. He was one of the most witty men of his time... His ministry was exceedingly evangelical, and was the means of rousing multitudes from the sleep of sin in various parts of Wales.'[29]

Throughout his stay in Cardiff his love of reading and 'unfaltering curiosity to know what was passing in the literary as well as religious world' remained undiminished. Whenever the opportunity to increase his knowledge presented itself, he grasped it with unbounded joy, as the following instance related by Rhys Stephen shows:

> We met at a Quarterly Meeting at Llantrisaint, and after the morning service, being alone together, he asked the young minister *what he was then reading*? The reply was, that he was going slowly through *BEATTIE ON TRUTH* a second time. Christmas Evans immediately, and with great vivacity, rejoined, 'You must come to Cardiff before you return to Swansea, and give me the substance of Beattie; was he not the man that replied to David Hume, eh?' Being told that I had the book in my pocket, and would cheerfully give it him, but that the print was very small; he, with still greater eagerness, said, 'I can manage that; I will take it, with many thanks.' It was a pleasure to give it him, and he pocketed it with as much glee as ever school boy did the first prize at the end of the session. In three days afterwards I called upon him at his own house, and spent a couple of hours with him, and I could get no conversation but upon BEATTIE. He was thoroughly absorbed in the old arguments against Hume and his school of scepticism and unbelief.[30]

There is little doubt that there was a considerable abatement of power in his preaching at Cardiff, especially in comparison with his Caerphilly triumphs, which was partly due to his age and partly because of the constant wranglings in his church. There were notable exceptions, however, especially on his travels. In

1829 a new English Chapel was opened in Charles Street, Newport, and Christmas Evans, along with Robert Hall, was invited to preach. Hall preached in English in the morning and evening, and Christmas Evans in Welsh in the afternoon. The former was 'overwhelming in the morning. The atmosphere was electrical, and the silence so intense it was as if no one breathed.' In the afternoon Christmas Evans, who only had the text and main headings of his sermon in English before him, was 'at his mightiest'. Many shouted, 'Amen! Amen!' and Robert Hall, who sat in front of the preacher, with a burst of emotion cried, 'Glory be to God!' as the tears trickled down his cheeks. After the service Hall followed Christmas Evans into the vestry, thanked him and, placing his hand on his head, exclaimed, 'May Jehovah bless you.' He then took Christmas Evans's 'hand in both of his and, looking straight into his eagle eye and bidding farewell, he left'. 'That service was spoken of for half a century afterwards as one of the greatest ever held in Monmouthshire and as one when Christmas Evans was par excellence the greatest preacher of his day.'[31]

Every minister of the gospel is a 'drawer of water' to his congregation, from the 'Spiritual Rock' which follows the church. He must be clothed with meekness from heaven, or the provocations of the people will be apt to embitter his spirit. God would have us minister mercy in the spirit of his own mercy.

Christmas Evans preaching on 1 Corinthians 10:4.[1]

17
'The Old Field Marshal'

For some time Christmas Evans had been urged by his ministerial brethren to prepare for the press a series of sermons, that
had been in the course of his ministry 'the most useful ... for the
conversion of sinners'.[2] He had given it much thought in the
past, but in Anglesey he had had no time to engage in the work
because his circumstances required so much travelling every
week, and for the two years he was at Caerphilly he 'left the
work to lie by'. It was not until his settlement at Cardiff that he
began to work seriously on the project, more out of a sense of
duty than anything, writing out about two hundred sermons,
many of which have since been published. He was about
sixty-four, much debilitated in bodily strength and almost blind,
though he could just about see without a glass at a short distance; all the same, he worked on them with the enthusiasm
and vigour of a much younger man. Most of them were preached
on the Sabbath and written out in full during the following week,
with the intention of presenting them to the public 'in sixpenny
numbers'.

Inevitably the sermons lose their dramatic representation and
vital force when put on paper, but they are still fresh and alive.
The introductions are brief and there are usually two or three
main divisions. Throughout they are full of Scripture verses —

often long paragraphs are made up of proof texts and at other times each sentence is supported by a verse from the Bible — and they include many quaint, apt and concise sayings. The language is forceful and beautiful, and the manner methodical, impressive and frequently conversational. Their arrangement and order are natural, with each part of the discourse relating to and dependent on the others. The thoughts are rarely confused or loose or hard to follow, but selected with care, with only the most appropriate employed and those that are best suited to illustrate the theme. In preparing his sermons with such assiduity, Christmas Evans saved himself from the 'extravagance of fancy' that frequently overtook him in the pulpit; 'In the coolness of his study he repressed the ardour of his mind till the right time; and ... excepting an occasional confounding of figures, there is little of this wild exuberance.'[3]

He wrote dozens of letters to ministers and others, asking them to summon up support to make the venture a financial success. His efforts were not helped by the publishers, who were slow in delivering the printed sermons to the subscribers, many of whom had not paid their subscriptions. However, some of his most heart-stirring and striking sermons were never prepared for the press by him, which meant that only small extracts were made available to the general public by others from memory. He also wrote and published a few hymns at this time, and many of them exhibit, not only a deep knowledge of Christ, but the precious intimacy he enjoyed with God.

Before he embarked on what would be a time-consuming task he wrote in his diary for 2 February, 1829, the following prayer for guidance, wisdom and strength that again exemplifies the spirit of dependency upon God in which he lived. He attempted nothing without an assurance of divine approval and blessing:

I come unto thee, my great Lord, to consult thee, who art the Head of the church and the Head-Prophet and Teacher of thy people. Shall I proceed with the work or not? Is it a part of my duty, or is it a foolish notion of my own? I entreat thy gracious direction in this matter, for the sake of thy great name.

Suffer me not to afflict myself, when my eyesight is so weak, with a work that thou wilt not bless, but which shall be buried in the land of forgetfulness. If thou wilt not open a door — with thee are the keys of the house of David — in thy providence, that I may obtain subscribers, and bring the work through the press, without hazarding myself in such a way as will involve me in debt and disgrace; and also if thou, the great feeder of the flock, wilt not direct me to give the true gospel, not only without error, but with the savour and unction which accompanies the works of Bunyan and others, which thy Spirit is likely to make use of whilst thou hast churches in Wales; if they should not be for thy glory in the building up of thy church and the calling of sinners — if these objects should not be accomplished by the publication of the sermons, dispose my mind to relinquish the undertaking.

But if thou wilt patronise the work, strengthen me to accomplish the design. Lord, thou knowest I feel my own insufficiency for such an important enterprise, and my own unworthiness to solicit of thee such a favour; but I cannot refrain from making these requests; therefore, for the sake of thine infinite merits, according to thy manner unto thy people, grant unto me my request. Amen.[4]

The extracts below are taken from the *Wrexham Edition* (1880) of the Welsh sermons prepared for the press by Christmas Evans himself, edited by J. Hughes and translated, somewhat freely, by Owen Jones. The first describes, with typical imaginative detail, the kind of hearer Satan would be if he came one day in human form into a congregation and listened to the word of God:

We may fancy that, in order to hinder and annoy as much as possible, he would take his seat in a conspicuous place, either under the pulpit or in front of the gallery, before the eyes of all. Then he would pull ugly faces and close his eyes, and appear as if asleep. He would most anxiously guard against giving the slightest indication of being touched by what was said. Not a trace of conviction, submission, peace and joy should on any account ever appear. He would scowl and knit his brows, and shake his head, and show every disapproval of the gospel he hears, as if he would change every man in the place into the same devilish disposition. Such, I say, would be the deportment of the arch enemy as a hearer of the word of God. But have we not seen many that have the name of Christ upon them an exact picture of this?[5]

There has never been, nor will there ever be, a mightier or more memorable conquest than the ever-increasing triumph of Christ that was established by his death on the cross and his resurrection from the grave — a triumph that will reach its 'climax of glory' when he returns. This is the theme of the second extract:

The Virgin's Son has won his victory by his death, and has started his triumphal march from the grave. And the glory of his triumph increases more and more; it is mightier after three days in the grave of Joseph of Arimathea than upon the cross; and forty days after, his chariot passes from the gates of Jerusalem through the gates of the heavenly city into eternity, and thousands of angels minister unto him and escort him home, with the noise of trumpets and jubilant song. This victory is ever memorable. The triumphs of the mighty wax dim before its glory, and they exist no more, except on the pages of history. But the triumph of Christ is a present fact of all ages, as grand and glorious as ever, and he rides forth now conquering the hearts of men...

And when the last trump shall sound, when Jesus shall appear on the clouds, when the earth and the works that are therein shall be burned up, when the heaven shall depart as a scroll that is rolled together; when the dead shall rise and the books shall be opened, the conquest of Christ will reach its climax of glory.[6]

One further extract compares the misery of a soul that has been 'cast down into the unquenchable fire', with the matchless jubilation of the redeemed:

The loss of a soul is the greatest loss that ever happened. If you were to gather together all the losses caused by the deluge, by the fire upon Sodom, and by the bloody wars of many ages; if you were to measure, I say, the magnitude of these losses in wealth, in kingdoms, in the blood of men and dear relations, what grief, what woe, what pangs, what sighs, what deep and heavy groans, what dire wailing would they involve, from Abel to the present day! If all the misery of past times was gathered together into one terrible groan, it would be a trifle compared with the woeful groan of a soul that has been cast down into the unquenchable fire, not for a thousand or ten thousand years, nor for years innumerable as the sand on the sea shore, but for ever and ever. Blessed be God that we have not met with this irretrievable calamity.

There has been, on the other hand, great gain in the world, and great joy for the acquisition of wealth and glory, and for the victories obtained on land and sea, and for the possession of dear relations. But if you could gather together into one all the joys that have flowed in the river of time, yielding pleasure on its way to the millions of the human race; what is this after all compared with the salvation of a single soul? It is but like the chirping of a robin in the woods of Windsor compared with the jubilant song of millions of the redeemed.[7]

As he demonstrated in his attitude before he wrote out his sermons, he was eminently a man of deep devotion, who never undertook a new enterprise without earnestly seeking God's counsel. The slander he had endured during his long life, the troubles in the churches he had pastored, personal afflictions, coupled with extreme poverty, all tended to move him to approach the throne of grace on bended knees. He considered himself entitled, through Christ, to all the blessings of the gospel and to the immediate presence of God. During his ministry at Cardiff he withdrew more and more from public gaze to fellowship with God, sometimes enjoying whole days and part of the night in secret and fervent prayer. His usual practice was to retire to his room for devotion several times a day — up to twelve times a day occasionally — and he frequently rose at midnight to converse with God. This prayer life was the foundation of all his work and the reason behind his success — a success that is amply borne out by the fact that, although his preaching powers declined during his troubled Cardiff pastorate, eighty members were added to the church under his ministry in the space of two and a half years.

However, in spite of his most vigorous and prayer-filled efforts, he failed to introduce better order into the church at Cardiff, which caused him increasing sorrow. Many in the congregation were dear to him and he had hoped to stay, but he did not want to distress himself further with the various difficulties and offences that were predominant, or prolong the contest with his opponents. So at sixty-five years of age and in poor state of health, he felt obliged, 'through the intrigue of a faction, to retire from the two stations he occupied in South Wales, where his labours had been so signally blessed for the conversion of sinners'.[8] God, he believed, had another field of labour in which he could sow the seed of the word. With that conviction, he gave himself entirely to the Lord, along with his wife, family, friends and assistants in the work of the gospel; and committed into his Father's wise and just care the troublemakers in the church:

I have given my soul anew to Christ: my body, my talents, my influence in preaching; my name, my character as a man, as a Christian and as a preacher of the gospel; my time and the remnant of my opportunities; my success, my peace and comfort as a Christian and a minister. I have resigned all afresh into the hands of Christ. I have commended to his care also my wife and all the circumstances of my family and my friends and assistants in the work of the Lord, for whom I pray earnestly that they may be blessed throughout Anglesey, Caernarfon, Caerphilly, Cardiff and indeed in all the counties of Wales — there are many of them who were helpers to me in my day. I will say, in the language of Paul, and I hope with affectionate emotions of love to Jesus Christ, 'The Lord grant unto them that they may find mercy of the Lord in that day.' It is a great privilege to a minister to retain beloved friends, who have helped him with their prayers and sympathy. O bless those whom I have and preserve the new race, the new generation of them that I have found in these parts.

I committed to God also those who obstruct the progress of the cause here, and disturb the unity and brotherly love of the church. Let Christ, whose the church is, and let not me, remove every obstacle, either by changing and melting in the love of the gospel, or taking them somewhere else, where they shall not be a curse and an impediment to the cause — and by the means that shall seem fit in his sight. A word or a nod of thine shuts and opens heaven and earth, and all the locks of the land of *Hades*, or the invisible state. For the sake of the blood of thy covenant, grant the above things unto me, thine unworthy servant.[9]

Towards the end of his stay at Cardiff, when he was assailed with conflicts from within and without, he wrote a letter to the editor of the *Welsh Baptist Magazine* (*Y Greal*), in which he views himself as an old general still on the field of battle. He looks back, with a touch of bitterness, over his long and eventful life, as well as forward to further usefulness, perhaps in another part of Wales. It is interesting to note that at this time he had received 'an earnest invitation to return to Llangefni in Anglesey':

I am getting old and fast hastening to the side of the river. It is not easy for you as a young man to enter into the feelings of one who will soon bid farewell to all the tedious ways of the valley of life. What feelings do you suppose an old general would have when he looked back upon the battles which he had fought in Egypt, Moscow, Leipsic [Leipzig], Spain and at great Waterloo, and when he found himself in the company of men who had never fired a shot, yet fancied themselves competent to discuss with him the campaigns of Emmanuel's wars? They prefer their plans to his after all, and he is pained to witness their ignorance, perversity and presumption, especially as with their plans they have never achieved a single exploit. I have lived to see all this coming, without fail, to pass.

It appears to me only as yesterday when I first went into Anglesey, my wife with me, on a day of unusual frost and snow... I remember the battles which I fought there; the powder and the fiery bolts of prayers and sermons; the sword, the bow and the arrow, the shield and the buckler, on the fields of Brynsiencyn, Llangefni, etc; the prisoners of war that were taken, and the arms and ammunition of the enemy that fell into the hands of the army of Emmanuel. I remember the march-tunes which we used to sing on our way to and from the field of battle.

I cannot but remember, with mingled feelings, those eminent officers who led the unconquerable hosts of the Methodists of those days, in Anglesey and Caernarfonshire, not less men than the seraphic Robert Roberts of Llanllyfni, Evan Richardson, the sweet singer of Caernarfon, and the gifted John Jones of Edern; but they have all retired, and I am still on the field, having fought the battles of Copenhagen and Waterloo in Glamorganshire. The distant echoes of our march tunes, in Lleyn and Anglesey, still sound in my ears, and I have a black book in which are graved the names of the betrayers with a 'pen of iron and lead'; and the names of those who turned not back in the day of battle are written in the book of 'the white stone and the new name' with the red ink that flows from the rock of Calvary.

Since I resigned the command in Anglesey, I have been looking out for fields which most required an old field marshal, who knows how, through God, to handle as of old the sword and the bow. I took some part in the wars at Caerphilly, and by the mighty arm of the God of Jacob, some hundred and forty prisoners of war were led captive under the banner of Emmanuel, and they were enlisted in his army in the course of a two years' campaign, as vigorous as any I ever saw.

After that, the old field marshal went to Cardiff, where the army was in the greatest danger, its leader having been shot down by great Diabolus. The divine power upon which the old field marshal relies, took here again some scores of prisoners of war, and I trust they will be sustained in the new army to the end. My plan, since leaving Anglesey, where I was for nearly forty years, is to go to those places where there is required an old reaper, an old mower, as well as an old warrior; and to go on cheerfully as long as the army and the sub-officers submit to the king's laws, and do not frown upon me and 'turn into their own ways' instead of listening to their superior who, like a shepherd, shows them the way, as Evangelist did to the pilgrim. He is now too old to have any squabbles with deacons or anybody else; rather than that, he would act upon John Wesley's plan, which removes the minister every two years.

Since this is my plan, it need not surprise you to learn that I have taken the command in some other part of the land of Emmanuel... I don't know where I may end my days, but my prayer is that the Lord may give me some work to do while I am here, strength and peace to do it, and the help of Aaron and Hur to hold up my hands, by defending my person and my doctrine; and I pray that Aaron and Hur may not allow any curs to snap at the old 'ox that treadeth out the corn', to lay hold of his innocent snout, and even hang by it, as some of these creatures are apt to do when they are permitted, if they manage to get inside the King's barn.

I have received an earnest invitation to return to Llangefni in Anglesey, but I don't feel inclined as yet to go. May God care for them! Aaron and Hur could keep me here as long as they liked, if they would and my prayer is, that things might take that turn in Cardiff. I have preached a great deal in all the churches of Wales.[10]

He was invited by his faithful friend, Daniel Jones, to attend the Welsh Baptist Association in Liverpool, held during Easter, 1832, and where he had been many times before. With the opportunity of consulting his ministerial brethren about his future, he gladly accepted. His appearance there delighted the members of the Association, who offered him every honour and comfort, and received him as one brought back from the dead. It is observed by his Welsh biographer, William Morgan, who attended the Association that, 'The energy which accompanied Mr E's preaching ... was astonishing; scores were stirred up to a concern for their souls, and life and animation appeared in the whole congregation.'[11] Hundreds of others wept for joy to see him again in their pulpits.

During his stay a special meeting was convened by the brethren in order to discuss with him a destination and to advise him upon his future course. He had received an invitation to Bodedern in Anglesey, and from a church in Carmarthenshire, but was not inclined to accept either. Pastors were also needed at Llanidloes and Llanfair Caereinion, Montgomeryshire. He visited both places on his way to Liverpool and was warmly welcomed, noting how he 'experienced melting seasons in them, but we could not knit together'.[12] He told the conference the various invitations he had received and his reluctance to accept them. A group of ministers urged him to resettle in Anglesey, but they were outnumbered by those who pointed to Caernarfon, where the cause of Christ was low and the members of the church financially poor. The minister David Rees had departed for Dowlais two years previously. Christmas Evans was eager to return to the North, the home of his wife and the place where he had been so mightily used of God. By this time the enmity that had existed between him and the men of Anglesey had all but disappeared and in an article he wrote in 1832 he referred to himself as 'brother C. Evans, formerly of Anglesey', as if to announce to the readers that a reconciliation had taken place.[13]

Daniel Jones, Simon James and several other ministers had thought of trying to establish the Baptist cause in Caernarfon, one of the most beautiful and populous towns in North Wales. There had been preaching there by the Baptists for forty years, during which time the members of the church had met in dwelling-houses and hired rooms, for they owned no regular place of worship. About seven years before Christmas Evans's settlement in the town 'A chapel [Caersalem] had been built in faith, several trustees becoming personally answerable, by prom-issory notes, for the debt. These trustees were now deceased, excepting the brethren Evan Evans of Garn, in extreme old age, and Daniel Jones'[14] upon whom the principal care devolved. The debt, notwithstanding the collections that were made, con-tinued to increase, owing to monies taken up to pay the interest upon about £750, until the whole amounted to £800 by the time Christmas Evans moved north. It is almost certain that he received his call to Caernarfon so that he could help collect towards this debt.

His desire to return to the North delighted the members as they were deeply concerned about the Baptist cause in that part of the Principality. 'The spirit of prayer fell upon all present, and many a hearty petition was offered up to God that he might bless him there, and make him a blessing.'[15] One minis-ter, however, expressed his opinion in an impudent manner. The meeting room was crowded with ministers and others all making suggestions, with many urging him to go to Caernarfon, when one present stepped forward and said, in a somewhat determined fashion, 'Oh no, you had better not go to — , but to Caernarfon; for it is not likely your talents will suit — , but they may suit Caernarfon well.' This unexpected and imperti-nent interjection excited a momentary smile from Christmas Evans, whose talents as a preacher attracted crowded congre-gations at that church, as well as at many others in the Princi-pality. The only notice he took of this abrupt remark was to open his large eye upon the speaker and ask in good humour, 'Whence art thou come? When didst thou come out of the shell?'[16]

This interruption did not divert the conference from their discussion, much to the relief of those brethren who were anxious for him to finish his course among them. His mind was finally settled when John Kelly, a pious minister in Denbighshire, shared with him a vision he had received respecting his transfer to Caernarfon, and that he had made it a matter of prayer for more than six months. His own preference for Caernarfon over Anglesey is expressed in his diary:

> There was an earnest desire on the part of many that I should return to Anglesey; but though I had a number of friends there and some, who had acted a cruel part towards me on the occasion of my leaving in the first instance, had, in the course of the seven years that had intervened since that time, been much changed through the gracious and chastising providence of God; — some lamenting deeply their conduct towards me — some, under the frowns of the world, had fallen into disgrace; and others had been removed by death; yet notwithstanding these things, I felt no inclination to go thither. But I perceived that the Lord, even in our days, manifests his displeasure in the dispensations of his providence, for the wrong that is done to his servants who seek his glory. I wish that nothing unseemly that may have been done to me by any in Anglesey, Caerphilly and Cardiff, be charged to their account in the Judgement: but that they may have repentance here, and mercy of the Lord in that day — even Alexander, the coppersmith himself. I felt my mind, however, disposed to attempt Caernarfon.[17]

The members of the Association were pleased with his desire 'to attempt Caernarfon', and his brethren, both Welsh and English, assured him that every effort would be made to secure a comfortable settlement in the North, with all the necessities of life provided for him. Two of his friends in Liverpool, William Rushton, who had written *A Defence of Particular Redemption* in reply to Andrew Fuller, and his son, both members of the church under the care of James Lister, supplied him with a small gig in which he journeyed north with his wife. The gig was drawn by his old horse Jack, who was over twenty years old and had been his travelling companion when he had left Anglesey six years before. It is said that he could recognise his master's voice from a distance, responding to its distinctive tones; 'That is to say, the horse opened his ears the moment his master began to speak, made a kind of neighing reply when the rider said, as he often did, "Jack, bach, we have only to cross one low mountain again, and there will be capital oats, excellent water, and a warm stable."'[18]

He returned south in order to dispose of his furniture and make final arrangements for the move. After his last Sunday in Cardiff, which in a letter to a friend he called 'the ides of March' and his farewell sermon *The Death of Old Caesar in the Capitol*,[19] he set out with his wife in the gig to Caernarfon, arriving there, with much trepidation, on a Friday evening in midsummer, 1832.

Fear and dread seized me when I saw the town, upon thinking that there were none there to receive us, or to support us. I dreaded to see the Sabbath coming, but come it did, and a very great crowd of hearers assembled, many more than the meeting-house could contain.

Christmas Evans.[1]

18
Caernarfon: An All Round Ministry

Christmas Evans's arrival at Caernarfon was greeted with delight across the north of Wales and produced quite a sensation in the town. He was well known to most of the religious people there, having preached to them on many occasions during his ministry in Anglesey, and had proved to be very popular. On the first Sunday after his arrival he preached at half past four in the afternoon in order to accommodate members from other places of worship. The chapel was crowded with expectant hearers, and many more gathered outside, so he positioned himself by the window and preached his sermon from that vantage point. For some time large congregations followed his ministry, on Sundays and during the week, but 'owing to the Baptists being few in number, and the effects of their former disordered state still remaining',[2] and because in the main his hearers were members of other churches, when curiosity had been satisfied, they returned to their own spiritual homes.

Although there was great readiness to hear the gospel when Christmas Evans arrived, the Baptist cause in Caernarfon, as has been intimated, was in a pitiful condition. The Baptist church had been established in 1799 and there were about forty-five

members, but they were constantly wrangling among themselves. Edmund Francis, the first stated Baptist minister in the
town, had 'embraced Sandemanianism many years since, and
the spirit of that system had been imbibed by many individuals
who did not join Francis's party'. Several other persons, who
were immoral in their lives, 'wandered about under the name
of preachers', and attempted to take advantage of the destitute
condition of the church. They forced their services upon the
people, and thereby damaged the cause in the town.

> And it is observed further, that most, though not all, who joined
> the Baptists in the town, were of the lower class, as to circum-
> stances as well as morals; and Mr Evans laments 'the want of
> a few judicious, prudent, faithful and pious persons, who
> should be like facing stones, to keep the filling stones in their
> proper places, and out of sight in the building; for there is no
> doubt there were some there who injured the cause of reli-
> gion to a lamentable degree, by acting out of their proper
> sphere, who might be useful men if kept in their right place'.
> The fault was not in their principles (except some of them,
> who were influenced by a Sandemanian spirit), but their
> order was deplorably defective.[3]

A dissolution of the church had been suggested by some at the
Liverpool Association, which would have enabled Christmas
Evans to 'begin the cause anew', but he decided to reform
things, if practicable, rather than exclude all the members at
once.

The debt on the meeting house was a constant worry, which
was compounded by the poverty of the people, who could not
even repay the interest. Collections had been made in the Welsh
churches to liquidate the debt, but the huge sum still proved a
very heavy burden. Daniel Jones prevailed upon John Edwards,
formerly of Llangollen, to visit some parts of England, Ireland
and Scotland in order to raise money. There was already 'some
knowledge' of Christmas Evans among the ministers in those

countries, especially as the author of the celebrated *Specimen of Welsh Preaching*, which had been translated into English and published in several periodicals, and had earned genuine admiration from the most eloquent men of the day.[4] Edwards had the *Specimen* reprinted and distributed copies of it wherever he went, thus making known to a wide audience the pastor of the church for whom he was collecting money. By his ceaseless efforts £400 was collected, which enabled the trustees to pay off a mortgage of £300 and secure the deeds.

Throughout the time that Edwards was engaged in collecting, Christmas Evans 'did not fail to pray to God earnestly, twice every day, and some days much more often, to bless, prosper, preserve and protect him in his laborious undertaking. "Everything," said he, "that is lawful and especially everything belonging to the cause of Christ, must be made a matter of unceasing prayer, or it can never succeed."'[5] In his diary he made the following entry: 'It may be that there are several things which show faintly that the Lord sent me to this place; for he made me the instrument of saving the meeting house from being sold; and thereby was the means of preventing the creditors from annoying brother Jones for the money for which he had become responsible.'[6]

Christmas Evans maintained a very good reputation for his faith and piety with all classes in Caernarfon, and was treated with the utmost respect by ministers of all denominations. 'The brethren joyfully welcomed him to every place; at once consulted him as to when he would preach, and how all the arrangements would best suit his convenience. In all these respects the closing years of his life were singularly happy, free from the troubles and sorenesses which had annoyed him during a great portion of his days.'[7] The local Independent minister William Williams became his daily visitor and companion. If for some reason Williams did not arrive at his usual hour, Christmas Evans would address his wife with the words, 'Mary,

fach, where is Williams today?'[8] The Methodists of both connections, together with the Congregationalists, whom, out of
gratitude for sustaining his hands in Caernarfon, he called the
'Aarons and Hurs', were similarly kind and hospitable to him.
These denominations had a considerable number of members
attached to them, with large and elegant places of worship,
especially the two denominations of the Methodists. They had
watched with interest and for many years his course in Anglesey, and the development of his ministry afterwards, so when
he returned to the North they were ready to do all in their power
to make his position as congenial as possible.

Christmas Evans was also respected for the devotional way
he conducted the *cyfeillach* (fellowship), a meeting in which
religious experiences were discussed, 'with members contributing
either as they were asked by a minister or deacon, or spontaneously as they were moved by the Spirit'. He generally opened
these weekly meetings himself with a short psalm or a para-
graph from another part of the Bible, followed by a few original
and relevant comments, and a fervent prayer. 'Then he would
give a short lively address which would warm everyone's heart
and invite someone to talk of his experience. He never called
anyone by name but left the invitation open to all. If no one
responded, he ended the *cyfeillach* with no more ado.'[9]

At the end of his first year at Caernarfon the prospects of the
church appeared more favourable, and he thanked God for the
progress that had been achieved and the grace given to him.
'Many things are better than they were a year ago,' he
observed. 'All things here were like a waste howling wilderness,
yea, the dwellings of dragons, where they made their nest night
and day. I do not know what the Lord may be pleased to
accomplish here yet, "to the praise and glory of his grace". The
sin of drunkenness, and the spirit of contention, were the two
most dangerous monsters I met with in this town.' Then, after
lamenting the death of Simon James, who died without seeing

'much order secured amongst the people', he commented on
the 'great disadvantage in attempting to raise the cause a second time, where it has been once impeded in its progress; for
thereby Satan gets a double advantage against it; one by the
scandal given in the disgrace and fall of an immoral professor,
and another by urging constant objections to religion afterwards
on that account, so that the cause is in danger of being crushed
in its weakness'.[10]

There is little doubt, for all his labours and zeal, that he found
it difficult to smooth out matters in a small church that was
tossed to and fro by a spirit of disunity and still infected by the
withering blight of Sandemanianism. As late as 12 August, 1836,
he complained to Robert Jones (Llanllyfni) that 'The difference
[with Sandemanianism] was not in the substance of the doctrine, but in the spirit. John Jones,' whom Christmas Evans
blamed for the troubles, 'took delight in forming a difference
where there was no difference. Nobody in his age has been so
destructive to the Baptists in North Wales as the eloquent John
Jones of Ramoth. His spirit was impious.'[11] The contentions
and spiritual barrenness were a constant source of discourage-
ment to him. However, by enforcing a strict code of discipline
he slowly managed to move the church away from the ill feeling of the past to a more harmonious and unified position, and
to engender a holy, controlled and spiritual attitude in many of
its members. He received another invitation from his former
church at Llangefni at about this time, but he decided, in spite
of the many disadvantages, to stay at Caernarfon.

Christmas Evans's popularity was never greater than during
the last few years of his life, when he experienced renewed
liberty and power in the pulpit, both in public prayer on behalf
of small churches and other ministers, and in preaching. In a
letter to a friend, after commenting on a passage from the *Song
of Solomon*, a book from which he delighted to preach at this
time, he said: 'I thought of the small churches in the county of

Caernarfon, from Rhoshirwaun to Llanrwst; I besought Christ, with all earnestness I hope, to come and lodge in them. I have also given all the churches of our denomination in Anglesey and Denbighshire to the peculiar care of Christ; beseeching him to come and plant in all of them the scions of his grace, and water them with the showers of [his] Spirit.'[12] It is said, in answer to his petitions, 'that the spirit of prayer was never experienced so largely in all the churches and by all the ministers, excepting once, which was before the great revival in Anglesey'.[13]

Some of the fruit of his preaching labours he never realised, as it was not until after his death that several people declared him, under God, to have been the means of their conversion. His descriptive powers, which had always been forceful and impressive, continued to improve with age and his friends noticed how animated his talents remained — the cause of which he attributed to 'the peculiar goodness of God to him, who appoints one thing over against the other; the sweet against the bitter, and the cheerful against the sorrowful, that a balance counterpoise might be preserved'.[14]

During his settlement at Caernarfon he visited the South Wales Associations on a few occasions. He also had opportunities to visit some of the North Wales Associations that were held at Llangefni, Llanerchymedd, Holyhead, Amlwch, Rhuthun and Pwllheli. In July, 1832, he attended the Anglesey Association that was held at Llangefni in a field very near to his old home, Cil-dwrn cottage. The announcement of his visit, after an absence of six years, created unprecedented rejoicing and anticipation, 'and it was thought that there were present on that occasion about two thousand persons more than usual, who had come expressly to hear him'.[15] The people, who received him as one back from the dead, expected him to be frail in body and less animated than they remembered, but to their surprise and delight his appearance and preaching were full of vitality and vigour. As soon as he stepped onto the platform they were heard to remark: 'He does not seem at all older' and 'He looks more like a man of forty-five than of sixty-five.'[16] He preached at ten o'clock in the morning with great fervour and effect from the text: 'And so will I go in unto the King, which is not according to the law; and if I perish, I perish.'

> His introduction was brief, as usual, and there was, it is thought, a visible effort to restrain and husband his emotions and energies through the less congenial task of statement and elucidation, which he was glad to get over as soon as possible, until his subject admitted of the full play and revel of his fancy, when he poured forth a stream of inspired imagery worthy of his mightiest days. The whole assembly yielded to the sway of his eloquence; and when, towards the close, he referred to his own past in Anglesey, to well-known preachers who had 'entered into rest', and to the probability that 'they should see his face no more', mingling with these allusions the most solemn appeals, in cases where the loud response did not relieve the burden of the pathos within,

> > 'Woman's tears fell fast as rain,
> > And rough men shook with inward pain,
> > For him they ne'er should see again.'[17]

The whole congregation, consisting of somewhere between ten and twelve thousand people, were 'charmed and enlivened by his evangelical eloquence, as if fresh gales from Mount Zion blew upon them'. His Welsh biographer, who was among the hearers, says that 'There was sumptuous feasting there on the dainties of the board of grace, and sweet drinking of that river from which the saints are watered. "They shall be abundantly satisfied with the fatness of thy house; and thou shalt make them drink of the river of thy pleasure."'[18]

The older members of the churches in Anglesey, who could remember the religious state of the island before Christmas

Evans's arrival, the changes for good he had instituted, and the resurrection of their own Association to great prominence, were overcome with feelings of joy to see the old preacher again and their love for him was renewed. This acceptance in the place of past trials was to Christmas Evans an answer to prayer, for 'He had earnestly besought his Lord that he might not be humbled in the presence of his former charge, and that the field of former achievement might not be the scene of weakness and confusion.'[19]

He preached at two Associations at Holyhead, the first in 1834, when his text was Hebrews 6:19. There were many seamen present and, with force and beauty, he described the believer's hope as the 'anchor of the soul'. He set forth the 'necessity of its having, not a bare rock, but a rock covered with clay; not abstract divinity, but "God manifest in the flesh", in order that its hold may be "sure and steadfast", securing the Christian against spiritual shipwreck amid the many storms of the world!'[20] The last Association he attended in Anglesey was also held at Holyhead in 1837. On that occasion he preached from Colossians 2:14-15 one of the most effective sermons he had ever delivered. 'We are entirely at a loss,' says one, 'for words to express its most astonishing effects. Everything was, as it were, cut down before it.'[21] 'The powerful manner,' writes another, 'in which he described ... the great roaring lion, together with all the hosts and principalities and powers of hell, death and the grave, giving way when Christ cried "It is finished!" was indescribably grand and majestic; one might have thought that the scene was actually before the eye and that Jesus could be then seen laying hold of the powers of darkness, casting them forth and making a show of them openly.'[22]

On other occasions the effect of his preaching was equally overwhelming. It was a dangerous coast near to Caernarfon and the 'horrors of shipwreck' were sometimes described by him 'with a force and graphicness' that his hearers could not forget. He once painted the scene 'so powerfully — the raging hurricane and the helplessness of the foundering barque — that, said the auditors, it was fancied the place beneath them was giving way, and they were sinking into the deep; then the life-boat and the rescue, applying it all to the lost sinner saved by Christ, until there was a tumult of happiness and joy'.[23] All the scenery around him was used to good effect in his sermons, especially the recent introduction of gaslight into the town, which took such a hold of his imagination that for awhile nearly every sermon included some allusion to it. The lighthouse at Skerries was also employed by him to illustrate the gospel:

> Birds on dark and stormy nights, having neglected to nest before the approach of night, lost their way in the dark, and scores of them flew towards the lighthouse light, knocking themselves against its glass, and were found dead, strewn about the place on the following morning.
> It is similar with thousands of souls that know not Jesus, and that have not nestled in the tree before night, and that are overtaken by the storm of death, and knock themselves against the great lighthouse of the law of Sinai, expecting to find refuge there; but it is too weak through the flesh to impart life to a single sinner. Is there a place to nestle before the night of death approaches? Yes. 'The kingdom of heaven is like unto a mustard tree, which one planted in his garden.' God be praised that it was planted in this world of ours; 'and it grew into a great tree, and the birds of heaven came and made their nests in its branches'.[24]

Christmas Evans preached at the anniversaries of the Bible and Missionary Societies in Caernarfon, where his addresses met with great approval. He had always been a keen supporter of the Bible Society and willing to promote the cause of missions, often travelling to Bristol and London to enthuse support and declaring to all and sundry his vision of the ever-widening triumph of the gospel. 'The mighty angel,' he said in one sermon, 'having found an old copy of the everlasting gospel, which the Pope had kept locked up in his bureau for many centuries, is flying in the midst of heaven, in sight of all the world. His progress is rapid as the wings of the wind, and his sweet strong voice is publishing the glad tidings to all people.'[25] He was ever ready to urge his brethren to give generously to the 'great missionary enterprise'. While you are casting your money into the treasury, he would say, 'Let me remind you that your gold and your silver are beautiful birds plumed for flight, that Christian liberality is the scissors with which you may clip their wings, and a short winged bird is better than none.'[26]

It is said that Christmas Evans did more for the renaissance of missionary work and the birth of modern missions than anyone else in Wales, pleading with the churches and his fellow ministers to support the proclamation of the gospel in the newly discovered countries in East and West and 'for bigger visions and wider horizons'. 'In the dispute between Seniors and Juniors at Serampore and Calcutta, Evans was the only representative from Wales on the celebrated Corresponding Committee. During the last thirty years of his life he never once forgot foreign missions in his prayers.'[27] He was also instrumental in reviving the monthly meetings in Caernarfonshire and adjacent parts of Anglesey: 'To see him coming to those meetings,' says one of the ministers, 'was a feast to our souls.'[28]

During his busy schedule of preaching Christmas Evans prepared for the press a work entitled *Lectures on the Apocalypse*. Before its publication he said to Daniel Jones (Liverpool) on 20 May, 1834, with his own interpretation of *Revelation* in mind: 'Couldn't we think that four of the angels [by the throne of God] are working particularly in our days? The first is the angel of the Bible, taking care to translate it, print it and distribute it. The second is the angel of preaching, or revealing the secrets of the kingdom of heaven, to destroy idolatry. The third is the angel of the Sunday School, the symbol of which is an open book. The fourth angel is our meeting houses, and his cry is "Worship the Blessed"'[29]

The *Lectures* were published in 1835, with the expectation 'that this work will be more popular than any other ever published by him, because there is more originality in it, and more of the peculiarity of his own transcendent gifts in it than in any other'.[30] At the time of trying to understand the *Book of Revelation* he was in a 'feeble state' physically, yet he managed, with fervour and diligence, to deliver and print the *Lectures*. They are not very important as far as the science of interpretation goes, but they do 'exhibit a comprehensive summary, with many striking comments in passing, of the generally received scheme of that wonderful portion of the New Testament' and 'remain a monument to the sacred and indomitable industry which characterised him to the close of his life'.[31] In the preface to the book he gives his reasons for writing on such a difficult subject and for completing the work in 'less than three months':

First, because I spent half a century in attempting to preach without ever trying to understand the Revelation according to the expositions of the best interpreters...

Secondly, because he who considers the Book is pronounced 'blessed'.

Thirdly, it is in compliance with the wishes of several preachers.

Fourthly, I desired to make the Book more useful to the preachers and the churches, by means of a brief and plain exposition of it.

Reader ... the subject took such a hold upon me, that I could not sleep at night. I feared it would have injured the little health I had. My mind was filled with such intense and prayerful zeal, together with heavenly pleasure, that I was compelled to travel in four-and-twenty hours over a space that would have required a week but for my enthusiastic excitement. I was obliged, in less than three months, to run through all the observations which are placed before thee in this volume. For the strength given me, I thank the Lord. It became me to finish the work with all my might, for I wrote it on the verge of the grave.[32]

As has been mentioned the 'sin of drunkenness' was rife in Caernarfon. Christmas Evans, for most of his life, was far from being a teetotaller. In fact, 'Word had spread abroad that he drank enough beer and spirits at a go to intoxicate six men,'[33] yet no one found any cause to accuse him of being drunk and disorderly. He himself admitted: 'I've been drinking a little ... for over half a century, without harming my body, my mind or my circumstances; nor have I disgraced the excellent name, through the great grace of heaven.'[34] However, the time had come, he thought, as an example to others and in regard for the weaker brother, to put away completely rum, gin, brandy and whisky, as well as beer and wine, and to throw himself, with his usual enthusiasm, into the temperance movement. He travelled to Liverpool, Manchester and Birmingham in support of its cause and his motto became: 'Touch not the liquid fire!'[35]

In one crowded meeting he shared for the first time a dramatic dream, at the close of which, says a young observer, he looked up to the gallery and 'His one eye flashed as I have never seen any other eye flash in my life.' A fellow minister, Mr W — of A — , at the time could not lend his support to the temperance movement, and said initially that he would not be present to hear Christmas Evans, for he feared a personal reference to himself; 'Yet such was the fascination that he could not stay away. He came to the meeting late and crept into the gallery, where the preacher's eye, which had long been searching for him, at length discovered him.' Christmas Evans at once proceeded to say:

> I had a strange dream last night. I dreamt that I was in Pandemonium, the council chamber of hell. How I *got there* I *know* not, but *there* I was. I had not been there long before I heard a thundering rap at the gates. 'Beelzebub! Beelzebub! You must come to earth directly.'
> 'Why, what's the matter now?'
> 'Oh! they are sending out missionaries to the heathen.'

'Are they? Bad news that. I'll be there presently.' Beelzebub rose and hastened to the place of embarkation, where he saw the missionaries and their wives, and a few boxes of Bibles and tracts, but, on turning round, he saw rows of casks piled up and labelled gin, rum, brandy, etc. 'That will do,' said he, 'there's no fear yet. The casks will do more harm than the boxes can do good.' So saying, he stretched his wings and returned to his own place.

After a time came another loud call, 'Beelzebub!'

'Yes,' replied he.

'They are forming Bible societies now.'

'Are they? Then I must go.' He went and found two ladies going from house to house distributing the Word of God. 'This will never do,' said he, 'but I will watch the result.' The ladies visited an aged woman, who received a Bible with much reverence and many thanks. Beelzebub loitered about and when the ladies were gone, saw the old woman come to her door and look around to assure herself that she was unobserved. She then put on her bonnet, and with a small parcel under her apron hastened to a public house near, where she exchanged her Bible for a bottle of gin. 'That will do,' said Beelzebub with a grin, 'no fear yet,' and back he flew to his own place.

Again a loud rap came and a more urgent call. 'Beelzebub! You must come now or all is lost! They are forming teetotal societies.'

'Teetotal! What is that?'

'To drink no intoxicating liquors.'

'Indeed! That is bad news. I must see to that.' He did, but soon went back again to satisfy the anxious inquiries of his legions, who were all on the *qui vive* about the matter. 'Don't be alarmed,' said he. 'It is an awkward affair, I know, but it won't spread much yet, for *all the parsons* are with us, and Mr W — of A — ' (here the preacher's eye glanced like lightning at him) 'is at the head of them.'

'But I won't be at the head of them any longer,' cried Mr W — ; and immediately walking down out of the gallery, he entered the table pew and signed the pledge.[36]

Christmas Evans

On another occasion, after a rousing speech, the mayor of Caernarfon presented him with a generous gift as a token of his appreciation. Having taken the teetotal pledge at seventy years of age, Christmas Evans contributed to the press at Caernarfon an essay on *Total Abstinence*. He was afraid that teetotalism and Christianity would become synonymous and that total abstinence would be regarded as sufficient for salvation. 'It is necessary,' he warned, 'to wash the drunkards, and to justify and sanctify them.'[37] Rhys Stephen regards the essay as

> ... a composition of great vivacity; but though in the body of the little work he pleads the cause of total abstinence with his usual earnestness, in a somewhat lengthened preface, he as earnestly insists upon divesting the movement of the religious character with which it was then, and in his neighbourhood, the fashion to invest it; and hereby the innocent author gave deep offence to many of the *intemperate* advocates of temperance. Though he manfully kept his own pledge, he became soon sickened by the spirit of the teetotal apostles of the day; felt especially disgusted at the exhibitions of *former* drunkards, and at the abuse they were encouraged to pour upon men who had never been addicted to the vice; and, in his very last journey, he told a friend of mine that, through the rampant folly of some of the principal leaders in the cause, 'the devil had taken fourteen ounces out of the pound'.[38]

During his Caernarfon pastorate he liked to review the dramatic change that had taken place in Wales since his youth, although, as he remembered the past, there were times when he thought he was ungrateful to God for the prosperity he had previously enjoyed, and these fears moved him to seek 'a renewed manifestation of the divine presence, and [he] often cried earnestly for a strong faith to lay hold of the promises'.[39] He determined to look back over fifty years of ministering the gospel with thankfulness to God for his mercies and providential care. 'I had in the midst of all, great cause for thankfulness that the Lord had replenished my spiritual store and stock of thought to some considerable degree... I observe, with wonder, how my poverty contributed to my more general usefulness; for on that account I was obliged to travel very considerably, when otherwise there would have been no necessity.'[40] He also penned in his diary the following reflections:

> I have been thinking of the great goodness of the Lord unto me throughout my unworthy ministry, and now, in my old age, I see the work prospering wonderfully in my hand, so that there is reason to think that I am in some degree a blessing to the church, when I might have been a burden to it, or rather a curse, by which she might have been induced to wish me laid in the earth, that I might no longer prevent the progress of the work. Thanks be to God, that it is not so! though I deserve no better; yet I am in the land of mercy. This is unto me according to the manner of God unto his people.[41]

Although Christmas Evans was still very much a 'blessing to the church', his earthly course was quickly drawing to a close.

The church in every age has suffered great loss in the death of her most able and efficient ministers. The strongest pillars in the house have fallen; the tallest trees in the forest have been cut down. 'The fathers, where are they? And the prophets, do they live for ever?' Where are the apostles and evangelists? What has become of the great reformers of every age? They have gone the way whence they shall not return. They have ascended in their chariots of fire. Though safe in heaven, they are lost to earth. But the Holy Spirit is a 'Comforter' who shall 'abide with you for ever'. The hands have all departed, one after another, and new crews have been shipped from age to age; but the Captain is still alive; and has remained on board, ever since he first took the register and the compass on the day of Pentecost; and will never leave the ship, till he brings her in from her last voyage, and lays her up for ever!

Christmas Evans preaching on John 14:16-17.[1]

He, who himself passed through death, who is the Lord of the sea, stands firm as a high priest in the midst of Jordan, until the weakest of the tribes reaches the other side of the river safe and sound.

The testimony of conscience imparts agreeable feelings, coupled with the testimony of the Spirit, that the passage fare has been paid by Jesus, and that the Christian has in his hand the white stone and the new name for presentation on the pier head beyond, nigh unto our Father's house. Here is a richly supplied entrance, a long afternoon, the sea calm, and the wind prosperously filling every sail. 'Now lettest thou thy servant depart, O Lord, according to thy word of peace. For mine eyes have seen thy salvation.'

Christmas Evans.[2]

19

'Wheel about, Coachman, and Drive on'

It appears from a letter that Christmas Evans wrote to the 'ministers and members of the Baptist churches in Wales', probably sometime in 1836, that he had determined, much to his disappointment, never to 'attempt visiting my dear brethren in South Wales any more'. He had left home the previous year with the intention of touring the South, but his strength had failed him and he was obliged to return home. The following year (1836) he tried again, but was 'afflicted with a severe disorder that affected my intellectual powers for a season'. With no prospects of future travel he sold his little gig and so lived, in his own words, 'like a bird shut up in the cage of old age, to labour almost if not altogether in one place'. The faculties of his soul were still 'quite young', and his zeal and anxiety to do good as flaming as ever, but his body was weak. Although he longed for the wings of heaven to carry him among his brethren and sisters in the South, he considered that 'I shall never see them on earth any more.' In closing his letter he comments, 'The news that will sound through the Principality soon will be that I am gone the way of all the earth, and have left a poor widow behind me in a destitute condition. Have compassion upon me in the short time you have to manifest your kindness to me.'[3]

Plaque of Christmas Evans on Caersalem's modern pulpit.

Christmas Evans's actual pulpit at Caersalem.

However, after he had resided in Caernarfon for nearly five years, Caersalem Baptist Church, which was under his charge, received notice to pay the outstanding debt of £300 on its meeting house. In order to meet this debt, he was entreated by the ministers at the Liverpool Association, Easter 1837, to embark, if he could, on a preaching tour through North and South Wales. The following year, on 28 April, in compliance with their wishes, and in spite of his own feeble state and 'nearness to eternity', he set off, presumably in a borrowed gig, with characteristic ardour, on what would be his final journey through the Principality. His wife and a young preacher friend, John Hughes of Ruthin, one of his converts, who would serve as an assistant, accompanied him. Before he set out he penned in his book of last appointments the following prayer: 'O Lord, grant me my desire on this journey, for thy name's sake. My first petition: comfort in Christ, the comfort of love, the *bowels* of love and mercy in the denomination, the fellowship of the Spirit. Amen. The second petition: that the sermons I have prepared may increase in their ministration, like the five loaves and the two fishes. Amen. C.E.'[4] He also wrote in the same month (April, 1838) a moving circular, stating the object and importance of his journey, and addressed by him to several ministers and through them to their congregations. The substance of this circular was published in a Welsh Magazine, which then circulated among the Baptist Churches of the Principality, under the title *Ystorfa Weinidogaethol (Ministerial Magazine)*:

The term of the lease of life has expired in my case, even threescore and ten years, and I am very much afflicted. I have purposed to sacrifice myself to this object, though I am afraid I shall die on the journey; and I fear I shall not succeed in my errand for Christ. We have no source to which we can now repair, but our own denomination in Wales, and brethren and friends from other communities that may sympathise with us.

Oh, brethren, pray with me for protection on the journey
— for strength and health this once, on occasion of my bidding farewell to you all — pray for the light of the Lord's
countenance upon me in preaching; pray for his own glory
and that his key may open the hearts of the people to contribute towards his cause in its present exigency.

Oh help us, brethren — when you see the old brother,
after having been fifty-three years in the ministry, now,
instead of being in the grave with his colleagues, or resting
at home with three of them who are yet alive[5] — when you
see him coming, with the furrows of death in his countenance, the flowers of the grave on his head, and his whole
constitution gradually dissolving; having laboured fifty years
in the ministry in the Baptist denomination. He comes to you
with hundreds of prayers, bubbling, as it were, from the fountain of his heart, and with a mixture of fear and confidence.

Oh, do not frown upon him! — he is afraid of your frowns.
Smile upon him by contributing to his case this once for all.
If you frown upon me, ministers and deacons, by intimating
an irregular case, I am afraid I shall sink into the grave
before returning home. This is my last sacrifice for the
Redeemer's cause.[6]

His request was granted and everywhere he went he was
cordially and joyfully welcomed, receiving generous donations
of money towards the debt. He was very popular at this time,
perhaps more so than at any other time, and wherever he
preached large crowds assembled from an early hour to hear
him; so much so that on many occasions multitudes remained
outside the chapels, unable to gain admittance because of the
throng. His itinerary is remarkable, considering his age and
bodily infirmity, and again highlights the sacrifice he was prepared to make for the Baptist denomination:

May

1 & 2	Dolgellau
3	Machynlleth
4	Tal-y-wern
6	Trefnewydd
8	Caersŵs
9	Llanidloes
10	Capel Newydd
13	Nant Gwyn and Dolau
15	Pontnewydd
16	Llanfair
17	Brecon
20	Maes-y-berllan and Brecon
21	Llangynidr
22	John Edwards' chapel
23	Nant-y-glo
24	Horeb, Blaenafon
25	Ebenezer, Blaenafon
27	Llanwenarth and Llanelli
28	Pontypool
29	Trosnant
30	Abersychan
31	Pont-rhyd-yr-ynn

June

1	Gwaith Newydd
3	Newport
5	Beulah
6	Argoed
7	Pen-y-cae
8	Tredegar

10	Sirhywi and Tredegar
11	Rhymni
12	Dowlais
13	Seion, Merthyr 6
14	Ebenezer, Merthyr
15	Hirwaun
17	Seion and Ebenezer, Merthyr
18	Aberdâre
19	Pontypridd
20	Hengoed
21	Caerphilly
22 & 24	Groes-wen, Y
25	Ffwrwm Eistedd
26	Risca
27	Castleton
28	Caerllion
29	Bethel

July

1	Basaleg and Castleton
2	Llaneurwg
3	Cardiff
4	Whitchurch
8	Cardiff
9	Cowbridge
10	Bridgend
11	Aberavon
12	Neath
14&15	Swansea[7]

As he travelled through Llanllyfni, a few miles south of Caernarfon, he met Robert Jones, a colourful character and the minister of the Baptist church there. Jones was somewhat prejudiced against other denominations and was not slow in making his views known. After talking with him for awhile Christmas Evans continued on his journey. 'What kind of boy is he?'

inquired John Hughes, as the gig rumbled away. 'He's a splendid boy,' replied Christmas Evans. 'He has one big fault, though — he holds the noses of the Methodists to the grindstone.'[8]

He had arranged to travel until the end of September, going through Llanelli, Felin-foel, Carmarthen, through Pembrokeshire to Cardigan, and then back via Machynlleth, aiming to arrive home before the winter, but the Lord had determined otherwise.

On June 6 he reached Argoed in Monmouthshire in time for the Association and preached at ten o'clock on the second day with great energy and powerful effect. This was his final associational sermon and he took as his text: 'For by grace are ye saved through faith.' In his introduction, he compared an ungodly person, who is enticed by Satan to follow a life of sin, to a man he had observed at Caernarfon, who threw a few beans to a herd of swine, in order to draw them 'to the door of the slaughter-house into which they were driven to be slain'. In a similar way 'The devil by his temptations, with a bean of this sin, and a bean of the other sin, leads sinners to the gate of hell, into which they are driven to be tormented for ever and ever.'[9] He went on to portray the grace of God in man's salvation through Jesus Christ, and the peculiar work of faith to achieve that objective. When representing the powers of the gospel by the influence of the Holy Spirit, he described the gospel as 'a great *electrical machine*, as on the day of Pentecost, — he said that Christ was there turning the handle, and had commanded Peter to place the chain so as to touch *three thousand* of the hearers; — he described the Holy Ghost descending like fiery sparks on the chain, and striking them until they bounded from the first to the second Adam in the twinkling of an *eye*'.[10] 'Perhaps no sermon that Mr Evans ever preached,' says another, 'evinced more vigour of intellect, more power and splendour of genius than this; and seldom, if ever, had he more perfect command over the feelings of an audience.'[11]

Having enjoyed the blessing of God at this meeting Christmas Evans purposed to attend the Glamorganshire Association which was to be held at Pontypridd, but his frail constitution would not allow it, and a few days later he was laid up for a week at Tredegar in the house of Thomas Griffiths, a faithful Baptist. Griffiths, along with his son-in-law William James and John Roberts, showed him extraordinary kindness and did all in their power to relieve his suffering. He was in good spirits, delighting to converse on spiritual things, and his humour was as sharp as ever. On one of the days, feeling somewhat stronger, he had gone downstairs and James was helping him back up. He had only managed a few steps when he turned to his assistant and said, 'Mr James, I daresay if I believed the French were behind me with their bayonets, I should find myself able to get upstairs without your aid.' At this he removed his arm from James's shoulder and ran up the stairs, laughing heartily at the feat![12] On another occasion, in the course of a conversation, he remarked:

> 'This *is* the Gospel, this *is* the Gospel: he that believeth shall be saved. Now, in order to the truth of this declaration, every believer must be saved. If, in the last day, the great enemy found one single soul not saved whoever believed the Gospel, he would take that individual up, present him to the Judge and to the immense assembly, and say, "The Gospel is not true"; *he would then take the LOST believer all through the regions of Pandemonium and exhibit him in triumph to the devils and the damned!'*
> 'But,' said Mr Griffiths, 'that shall never be, Mr Evans.'
> 'No,' said he, planting the forefinger of his right hand on his knee, as he was wont, and in a shrill tone of triumphant congratulation, 'no, — *never*! NEVER! **NEVER!**'[13]

After recovering his strength he continued on his journey to Caerphilly, where the main street was lined with people enthusiastically welcoming him back. He preached in his old church, and those who had formerly resisted his ministrations were pleased at his return, much to his surprise. On the way across Caerphilly mountain the carriage stopped at the place where he had made his covenant with God. He then moved on to Cardiff, where he was warmly received by his old friends. In both Caerphilly and Cardiff 'He saw that many of the old obstacles in the way of his former usefulness were now removed, and the evils which then existed less perceptible had appeared more generally visible, so that the good had become more commendable by the contrast.'[14]

He proceeded to Cowbridge, Bridgend and Neath before arriving, with his wife and companion John Hughes, at Swansea on Saturday afternoon, 14 July. He was the guest of the celebrated blind preacher, Daniel Davies, who, in 1804, when only six years old, had lost his eyesight as the result of smallpox; yet he was able to fulfil all the duties of the pastorate without any peculiar difficulty. He possessed an excellent memory and was able to repeat almost any portion of Scripture as easily as if he was reading it.[15] He was a prominent man in the Baptist denomination and a fine preacher, who 'ventured deeply into the sea, high into the light and far into the palaces of God and the dwelling places of the Universal one'.[16] Towards the end of 1826 he was appointed to succeed Joseph Harris at the Welsh Baptist chapel in Swansea, where he remained until 1855. When Christmas Evans arrived at his house in Oxford Street in the carriage driven by John Hughes, with his wife sitting beside him, he looked up at Davies's large house and said, 'What's the use of building large houses when Henry VIII pulled hundreds down?'[17]

Christmas Evans preached at Bethesda, the Welsh Baptist church, at ten o'clock on the Lord's Day from 'For I am not ashamed of the Gospel of Jesus Christ', and again in the same place at six in the evening on *The Prodigal Son*.[18] Both sermons were delivered with 'as much power and vigour as ever; his ideas and illustrations rising to the highest point, while he was exhibiting and commending the salvation of Christ to his numerous audience'.[19] Daniel Davies comments that during his sermon on *The Prodigal Son* 'The large congregation was so completely in his hand that he could discuss the subject in any way he chose, and he returned to his lodging humming away, the usual sign that he was pleased.'[20]

On Monday he appeared cheerful and conversed freely with all the friends who visited him, and in the afternoon he went out to tea with David Walters, 'a gentleman whom he had long known, and who was always proud to see and entertain him'.[21] That evening he preached in English at Mount Pleasant Chapel from Luke 24:47: 'And that repentance and remission of sins should be preached in his name among all nations, beginning at Jerusalem.' He was very feeble and tired, which worried both Daniel Davies and Rhys Stephen, the minister of Mount Pleasant, and somewhat awkward, as he was never truly comfortable speaking in English; nevertheless there were a few gleams of his usual brilliance that shone through to the congregation:

Beginning at Jerusalem — why at Jerusalem? The apostles were to begin there because its inhabitants had been witness to the life and death of Christ. There he had preached, wrought miracles, been crucified and rose again. Here, on the very spot of his deepest degradation, he was also to be exalted. He had been crucified as a malefactor, he was now to be exalted in the same place as a king. Here were accorded to him the first-fruits of his resurrection. On the day of Pentecost all Jerusalem was against him. The fleet of the enemy was strong and well manned; he had but some twelve steamboats. 'What! Wilt thou, O Jesus, attack the enemy with those few boats of thine?' 'YES, I WILL.' The action commences: the boats take their place alongside of the men-of-war; actually throw their grappling irons on board — desperately attaching themselves to the mighty

four-deckers. Fearful cannonading ensues; all is smoke, darkness and confusion. Hark! You only hear some agonising
groans; the firing has ceased. Behold, the clouds
disperse, and the light of heaven breaks in fully on the amazing scene; and — infinite amazement! miracle of wonders!
— the small boats have taken three thousand prisoners in
this one engagement...

   'At Jerusalem, Lord?'

   'Yes.'

   'Why, Lord, there are the men who crucified thee: we are
not to preach to *them*?'

   'Yes, preach it to all.'

   'To the man who plaited the crown of thorns, and placed
it on thy head?'

   'Yes, tell him that from my degradation he may attain a
crown of glory.'

   'Suppose we meet the very man who nailed thy sacred
hands and feet to the cross — the very man who pierced thy
side — that spat in thy face?'

   'Preach the Gospel to them all; tell them all that I am the
Saviour; that all are welcome to participate in the blessings
of my salvation; that I am the same Lord over all, and rich
unto all who call upon me.'[22]

As he descended the pulpit steps very fatigued and sick in body
he said in English quite distinctly so that a number present heard
him, 'This is my last sermon', probably meaning it was his last
in the town, but it proved to be the last of all. His wife Mary was
very upset that he had been persuaded to preach as she knew
it would be too much for him.

   That night he was taken ill, with an attack of what was then
thought to be erysipelas, but the doctor was not called as Mrs
Evans thought it was one of his usual turns. Through the greater
part of that night and the following day he was in a partial
stupor and taking little notice of the many friends who called
upon him. 'He was in the afternoon as a piece of wood, without the inclination or ability to stir, as his wife struggled to turn

and treat him, for she would not allow anyone else to touch him.' She was adamant that a doctor should not be called, although she did promise Daniel Davies that if he was not better in a day, he could call for medical help. Christmas Evans was convinced he would recover, remarking in one of his more lucid moments: 'Don't think, dear Davies, that I'm going to die. I know that I am not going to die now, because there's an old pact between me and the Almighty that I will receive a sign from him at least a fortnight before I die, and I haven't received that sign yet.'[23]

On Wednesday 'the powers of his mind seemed to be quite restored, and his body tolerably free from pain, but he complained of some difficulty of respiration, which gradually increased'.[24] He rose about midday and walked for some time in the garden to try his strength, with a view of going to preach at Llanelli on Sunday. Many called to see how he was and he conversed with them cheerfully, feeling refreshed by their visits, but he still found it difficult to breathe, remarking to his friends that he had never experienced such symptoms before. Towards evening he relapsed and it was suggested, because of his respiratory problems and a noise in his throat, that a doctor should be called. When the doctor arrived he asked him earnestly when he thought he might be able to resume his work, although 'He appeared,' said his friend and companion Mr Hughes, 'as if something whispered to him that his earthly career was about to terminate, and that he was to expect in a very short time, the summons of his Lord and Judge.'[25]

As if to confirm Hughes's opinion, Christmas Evans said to the doctor, 'If you are going to give me any medicine, sir, pray, whatever you give me, don't give me any opium; for if I am going to die, I wish to die with my senses about me, so as to have full control of my thoughts and expressions.'[26] By this time the doctor, who had diagnosed a heart disease, knew there was nothing else he could do. He called Daniel Davies to one side and said, 'I am afraid it is quite useless to give him any-thing with a view of saving his life.'[27]

Between one and two o'clock on Thursday morning Christ-mas Evans called his friends John Hughes and Daniel Davies, whom he thanked for the hospitality and kindness he and his wife had been shown. Davies replied 'that he wished the accommodation had been better, but that he hoped he would recover again'.[28] In response Christmas Evans said, 'God has been faithful to the pact, but I failed to understand the sign.' He talked about one of his dreams, in which he had seen himself approaching a great river which he thought he did not have to cross, so he turned back, believing it to be a sign that his work was not yet complete, although he admitted, 'I had not received a command to turn back from the bank of the river; so it has now become *wheel about*, and it is necessary to go through it, but thankfully, there is no danger. The High Priest is in sight, the land too is in sight for my eyes are focused on the shore yonder, and the sound of music reaches my ears from the house of my Father.'[29]

Then, with a holy triumph that seemed to pervade his soul in the prospect of an eternity of glory, he said in Welsh, 'I am leaving you; for fifty-three years I have laboured in the sanctu-ary and my comfort and confidence on this solemn occasion are this, that I never laboured without blood in the vessel. Preach Christ to the people, my dear brethren. If you look upon me as I appear in my preaching, I am lost for ever; but look at me in Christ, I am in perfect bliss and am saved.'[30] He then repeated in a clear voice a stanza from one of his favourite Welsh hymns, about the completeness of the righteousness of Christ to clothe the naked sinner and render him acceptable to God, and expressive of his firm trust in his redeemer:

Dyma'r wisg ddisglaerwen olau	(This robe so bright and glorious
Guddia'm noethni hyd y llawr,	O'er my naked spirit thrown,
Fel nad ofnaf mwy ymddangos	So I no longer tremble
Byth o flaen yr orsedd fawr.	To appear before thy throne.)

About an hour later, he waved his hand and exclaimed in English, 'Wheel about, coachman, and drive on,' as if spying the chariot of fire from heaven. He turned over and without a struggle or a groan slipped into a state of unconsciousness. Mary thought he was sleeping as his breathing was so heavy, and she persuaded everyone to leave the room for a time so she could quietly care for him. 'After we'd listened carefully for two hours to the loud noise that came from his mouth, going now and again into the room,' Davies recalls, 'everything suddenly went silent, and though we hurried, we only just reached the side of his bed by his last breath. He gave only one sigh after we'd entered the room.'[31] Mary was asleep in the chair by his bed. His friends tried to rouse him, but it was too late. The chariot had come and taken him through the river to his eternal home. Thus, amidst the songs of angels, Christmas Evans died in the home of his friend Daniel Davies in Swansea at about four o'clock in the morning on 19 July, 1838, in the seventy-second year of his age and after more than fifty years in the ministry. The Lord had hurried to his rescue, remembering the words of his servant's covenant: 'Leave me not long in affliction, nor to die suddenly, without bidding adieu to my brethren, and let me die in their sight, after a short illness. Let all things be ordered against the day of removing from one world to another, that there be no confusion nor disorder, but a quiet discharge in peace.'

A deep sense of grief and loss gripped the hearts of thousands throughout the Principality, especially those in Anglesey who had known him so well and profited from his years of service. The funeral service, in which several ministers took part, was held on Monday 23 July, in Bethesda, the Welsh Baptist chapel in Swansea. The news of his death had spread rapidly and a huge concourse of mourners, more than ever before for a funeral in Swansea, all anxious to pay their last respects to a man they revered and loved, and to whom hundreds had listened with joy only a few days before, gathered from near and far. It was remarked that 'so much sorrow was never before witnessed on an assemblage of people as at this funeral'.[32] He was buried in the grounds attached to the chapel, with great honour and mourning, and according to Welsh custom.

> Having reached Bethesda meeting house, the Rev John Saunders of Aberystwyth (Congregationalist) read a portion of the Bible and prayed; Rev D. Rhys Stephen, of Mount Pleasant church, preached in English from 2 Samuel iii.38, and the Rev Daniel Davies of Bethesda, in Welsh from 2 Kings iv.23, and the Rev David Roberts (Calvinistic Methodist) closed in prayer. At the grave the Rev Joshua Watkins of Carmarthen, delivered an impressive oration; then the body of the great Christmas Evans was laid low, under the lock of the dark tomb, where his cheerful smile can no more be seen, and from whence his eloquent tongue can no more be heard, until the morning when the 'Resurrection and the Life' shall call his ransomed home... It is impossible for persons at a distance to conceive of the grief which prevailed in those places where he had laboured for so many years. The pulpits were soon clad in sable mourning, and so generally did this prevail, that there was scarcely a Baptist meeting house in all Anglesey that did not exhibit the emblems of mourning on the sad occasion.
>
> On the first Sabbath evening after the funeral the Rev D. Rhys Stephen preached a funeral sermon at Mount Pleasant, Swansea, from Hebrews xi.4. Sermons on the occasion were also preached at Caernarfon by the Rev D. Jones of Liverpool; at Holyhead by the pastor, the Rev William Morgan; and by most ministers of the denomination in their respective places of worship in North and South Wales.[33]

During William Morgan's memorial sermon, delivered three
weeks after Christmas Evans's funeral, many in the congregation were crying. Two stayed behind at the end, one a back-
slider, and one who had never before been in the church, so
moved were they by the tribute paid to the one-eyed preacher.
From the sorrow expressed in this service and by many in Wales
and beyond, all knew that 'A prince and a great man had fallen
in Israel.'

****

At the end of his life Christmas Evans reviewed his ministerial
career and exclaimed:

> I can now look back on my course with feelings of wonder
> and praise that God has made me what I am, notwithstand-
> ing all my defects and my sins. My pleasure today in reflect-
> ing upon what I have done is far greater and deeper than
> that of Alexander or Bonaparte in reviewing their victories
> and battles. I can travel to preach the gospel no more. Still,
> the memory of my preaching journeys through Wales is sweet
> to me. Oh thou land of Lleyn in Caernarfonshire! I remem-
> ber the pathetic meetings I enjoyed in thee; and the many
> convictions and conversions that followed. I call to my mind
> our society meetings, the weeping, the trembling, the prais-
> ing, which I witnessed in thee, Oh Salem!...
>
> Oh thou Anglesey, where I lived for nearly forty years!
> My prayers on thy roads for the blessing of God to come
> down upon thee are now gone! The powerful sermons, the
> breath of heaven, the weeping, the praising, the return of
> sinners to God at Amlwch, Llanrhuddlad, Holyhead, &c., are
> now over. I bid you all adieu. Adieu for evermore until the
> Judgement Day...
>
> With thanksgiving and wonder do I remember the fire
> and the pathos of those meetings I enjoyed in thee, Oh
> Dolgellau! I shall never struggle any more at thy foot, Oh

Cadair Idris, as I did on that ever memorable day. It is refreshing to me today to remember the services I held in thee, Oh Llanbryn-mair, &c. How powerful did the gospel appear in these places! How I felt that preaching was a pleasure, though the buildings were only crumbling barns!...

Oh Abergwaun, Newport, Pantycelyn, Llanerchymedd, &c., I bid you all adieu. And you, Liverpool, Holywell, Ruthin, Denbigh, Llanrwst, &c., where I preached in your associations; my preaching in your congregations is at an end; may Jesus be with you all, and bring you at last into the better land. I am going with Aaron into Mount Hor to die. Fare you well, Pwllheli, Nefyn and Llangïan; the ordinary meetings and the great assemblies, fare you well. The last sermon in thee, Oh Garndolbenmaen, is over for ever for me. Jesus will abide with you though I be gone. 'Amen and Amen'.[34]

So this great man and preacher, whom God equipped and used in such an extraordinary way, passed from the shores of this world to the eternal haven of rest. He is silent now and his voice, with its majestic tones, will never again thrill vast congregations or echo round the surrounding hills, but he must never be forgotten; for it is through men of his mould, who are wholly devoted to the service of Christ, that our Saviour ushers the lost into his kingdom of grace and light. As a soldier in the army of God he fought the good fight. He finished the course marked out for him and he kept the faith. Henceforth there is laid up for him a crown of righteousness, which the Lord, the righteous Judge, shall award him on that day; and not only to him, but to all who have longed for the appearance of Christ.

Christmas Evans's grave and memorial, which is in
the grounds attached to Bethesda.

Perusing the history of his long and useful life, we are most forcibly convinced that obedience to conscience, loyalty to the Saviour, love to the souls of men, and the approbation of God, were the great governing elements of his career...

He was no ordinary person, and he lived for no everyday purpose. He was one of the most remarkable men Wales ever produced. This is the man to whom Wales owes much!... The very mention of his name is electrifying... So long as there is history, and so long as there are hearts which kindle at the names of the great and the good, so long the name of Christmas Evans will live, the pride and the possession of Wales, and unborn generations will rise and call him blessed.

Thomas Phillips. [1]

With all of his reputation for pulpit eloquence and evangelistic zeal, Evans should perhaps be remembered most as a man of prayer. He never worried about the theology or philosophy of prayer; he simply prayed, and God answered... The passion in his preaching arose from the burning in his heart.

Warren Wiersbe. [2]

20

'No Ordinary Person'

Christmas Evans's appearance at Lleyn has been tactlessly described by Ebrard Rees, writing in the first half of the twentieth century, as 'so beastly and ugly ... that some were really afraid of him and were driven into the Methodist Societies because they could not bear his face when he preached hell and death. To look at him one would suspect him of being a sufferer from many diseases.'[3] D. M. Evans, whose opinion is less derogatory, says that he possessed a 'robust and athletic frame, surmounted with a head of prodigious dimensions ... with thick, coarse, black hair, not artistically arranged' partially covering his brow. His ears were large and his neck short. 'Underneath the dark, arched, but somewhat heavy eyebrows,' a large dreamy eye that was capable of a great variety of expressions: 'when pleased, most radiant; in wrath, terrible'. His 'ponderous and awkward carriage' was favoured with none of the graces common to man, and it was 'combined with an air and manner entirely his own'. He was, says Evans, cast in no ordinary mould, 'an extra-ordinary personage, perhaps the most so, on the whole, it was in the power of the country to produce'.[4]

David Owen (Brutus), who knew him well, because of the

disproportion of his limbs, sketched him as having the appearance of a man 'composed the day after a great battle of the
scattered members of the slain'.[5] While it is apparent he was
not as physically attractive as some of his contemporaries, it
would be a disservice to this great man to paint a picture of him
that is exaggerated and not compatible with reality, as some
have been tempted to do for the sake of effect. When he started
preaching he was bony and thin in the face and somewhat
clumsy in his movements, but as he matured his face filled out,
the traces of consumption that had at one time afflicted him
disappeared, and his bearing became more refined. He was
well-built and of a strong constitution, with 'a majestic appearance'.[6] David Phillips, who was acquainted with him for some
thirty years, describes him as nearly six feet tall. He continues:

> In his best days he was rather corpulent, but sometime
> before his death he grew much thinner, and was rather
> inclined to stoop in his shoulders. His countenance was broad
> and open, and his forehead large, calculated to strike the
> beholder with the idea of power and authority [his head was
> so large that his hats were either split to make them fit or
> made to measure]... His one eye was somewhat larger than
> common, and rather prominent. His searching, piercing look
> was calculated to startle the beholder, and make him look
> upon himself with shame and confusion in the presence of
> one of so dignified an appearance... If the countenance is to
> be taken as an index to the mind, there was everything in his
> countenance denoting a person of note and of unusual pow-
> ers and eloquence.[7]

One more comment about his eye from his friend and one-time
travelling companion, Jonathan Davis, will suffice: 'His eye,
while in the pulpit, was exceedingly large, round like a ball, and
projecting out with flaming brilliancy. In familiar conversation it
did not seem to be the same eye; it was now a penetrating,
scrutinizing eye, that would involuntarily create a sensation of

inferiority in the greatest man, and a consciousness that he was in the presence of his superior.'[8] When his eye became inflamed, as it frequently did, causing him great pain and keeping him awake at night, he took a little snuff, which he carried loose in his waistcoat, or rubbed laudanum on the swelling.

In addition to his rather striking physical appearance, he was known to be 'utterly regardless of his own health, ridiculously inattentive to his dress and to all his travelling arrangements'.[9] Commenting on the medicines he tried, Brutus says:

> He took, no one knows how much, opium, bark, pellets, drops, patents and every concoction, and if he saw anyone taking medicinal drugs, he had to try them out himself... I never knew anyone with such a strong constitution, and if it were not for the fact that he was strong, he would doubtlessly have killed himself. He took enough opium once, at a go, to send three or more men into an eternal slumber; and he would take Peruvian Bark, Pills, Drops, etc. in such doses that you would not have given a halfpenny for his life; but they had no more effect on him than if they had been dropped into an elephant's bowels.[10]

When he took snuff, he often spilt it on his clothes and was unconcerned about brushing it off. 'No one had ever seen,' continues Brutus, 'either before or after, such a mess on any man's front ... as on Christmas Evans's front during his *snuffing fit*.'[11] His clothes, it is said, were worn 'as if they had been thrown on by a pitchfork', and no matter how hard his wife and friends tried to rearrange them, within minutes they were untidy again. Once, when he was about to embark on a preaching tour, Catherine bought him a new hat. During the journey he stopped by a stream in order to refresh himself and his horse. As there was no bucket at hand he took off his new hat, filled it with water and lifted it up to the mouth of the grateful beast. Upon returning home his wife noted with surprise the shabby condition of the hat, so he told her the story, no doubt with a wry smile on his face. Robert Hall, who was well-acquainted with his contemporary's eccentricities, called him 'a gentleman in rags!'[12] However, towards the end of his life, there were occasions, it is said, when he looked almost regal or 'like a bishop'.

He disliked excessive personal adornment in others as well, and sometimes, in his own unique way and without any respect for decorum, he would vent his feelings. On one occasion, when in the company of others, a young minister entered the room where he was relaxing decorated with a 'showy breast-pin and who assumed some other airs of greatness'. Some of the men present addressed the young pretender, not by his simple name, as was customary, but with his full title. Christmas Evans, with the intention of deflating the new guest, went into the kitchen and found a small poker with a brass knob on one end, which he thought resembled, in an exaggerated way, the breast-pin. He immediately grabbed the poker, inserted it inside his waistcoat and 'walked with becoming air into the midst of the company. Sundry exclamations broke forth. "Christmas Evans *bach*, whatever is the matter?" Whereupon, pointing to his title to higher honours, the extemporized dandy asked with surprise, "Do you presume to call me Christmas still?" By this farcical logic the culprit was of course *reduced to absurdity*.'[13]

His concern about the future was as carefree as his sense of dress. He viewed such anxieties as not only useless in themselves, but likely to render a man 'miserable, even in paradise, if that were possible'. He preferred to make the constant inquiry, 'Lord, what shall I do *now*?', fully resigning himself to the will of God and depending on his good providence for the daily necessities of life. His time and energy were devoted to the glory of God and to the extension of his kingdom, far more than to the daily worries of this life or to fretting about the hour of death.

It was not simply his outward peculiarities that made him an unforgettable character — it was the strength of his inner walk with God. Christmas Evans was a man who possessed the spirit of prayer to a remarkable degree. Once he said, without the slightest exaggeration or Pharisaical boastfulness, 'A thousand prayers bubble up from the fountain of my soul.'[14] 'I never succeeded in anything for the good of others,' he remarked on another occasion, 'without making it a matter of prayer.'[15] He had a devotional frame of mind that entered frequently and fervently into fellowship with God, which he considered to be the soul of religion: 'The head, the arms, the limbs, and the whole body of religious duties may be visible,' he said, 'but if secret prayer is not regarded the vital spark is gone, and there remains a breathless corpse; but when the soul of religion is alive, all the visible members are lively and active.'[16] He perceived constancy in prayer to be 'as necessary to the spiritual life as breathing is to the natural one. Prayer has been to me a kind of friendly intercourse with heaven, when I have cast away my burdens and had grace in time of need.'[17] He had been accustomed for years in Anglesey to persevere in prayer for God's mercy and grace 'in the arrangements of Providence', as he called them, 'with reference to the temporal affairs of our interest',[18] and he named his praying room in Cil-dwrn Chapel 'Peniel'. His diary is full of supplications, confessions and thanksgiving.

He desired always to keep open the channel of communication with his Father, from whom he received strength to perform his many and varied duties. He once wrote to a 'dear brother' about some controversial point or other, remarking, 'If you send an answer to me, do not raise this matter again, because I am fearful of losing the spirit of prayer.'[19] He firmly believed that 'all the promises of God were in Christ yea and amen' and would lay hold of them 'with such earnestness and importunity as if it were impossible for him to be denied — as if he could not let go his hold until he obtained the blessing'.[20] He had a firm and realistic confidence that his prayers for the out-pouring and influences of the Holy Spirit would be heard and answered, and 'He frequently said that to return thanks for the operation of the Spirit of God in the conversion of sinners was the most delightful part of a minister's duty.'[21]

On many occasions he would humble himself before God, 'agonizing for the salvation of sinners', even if it meant jeop-ardizing his health for their good. He was a 'true and faithful watchman' who 'could not think of sleep when the city was burning'.[22] He knew from experience that God could convert 'the best moralist' and subdue 'the most stubborn heart'. When he saw the huge congregations that attended his ministry in different parts of the Principality, the majority of them unconverted, their lost condition appeared before him in such a strong light that he could not help wrestling with God on their behalf.

> Sometimes he would be elevated to such a pitch of importu-nity and holy boldness, and be carried away to such a degree, as to repeat the same petition several times. Once he did so *thirteen* times; and no less than *thirteen* sinners were converted to God at that time! When the last of that number had related his experience before the church, the deacon, who had counted the repetitions and been some-what displeased, came forward and acknowledged his fault.[23]

It is almost impossible to represent him in his true character of praying for the lost. 'He manifested his tender and affectionate regard for the welfare of sinners, with such manly dignity, and in such an *inexpressible* manner, as was characteristic of Christ-mas Evans alone.'[24]

When preaching from the text Ezekiel 17:22-24, after acknowledging that the conversion of sinners is God's work alone, he unveiled the burden of his heart for the lost, 'Pray, my brethren, pray earnestly, that the God of all grace may find them out, and gather them from the forest, and fish them up from the sea, and bring them home as the shepherd brings the stray lambs to the fold.'[25] In a sermon on Acts 4:11-12 he extolled the name of Jesus 'in all its virtue and saving power', recognizing its suitability to all men's necessities, fears and dangers, before urging his brethren in the ministry to hold up the two arms of prayer and preaching that 'we may be more prosperous in his cause and service... Brethren, let us not cease to pray. Let us hold to the work of preaching the gospel. We may be made the happy instruments of the conversion of the hardest sinners in the world, while in the name of Christ we pray, and in his name we preach.'[26]

The power of his own preaching is proof enough that he had come forth 'from the ivory palaces; and the smell of myrrh, aloes and cassia, the fragrance of recent communication with God, was upon his talents'.[27] On many occasions, when he was called to preach at an Association or some other public event, he 'became mightily exercised in prayer, that I might, in the hand of the Saviour, and for his glory be made the means of converting sinners and edifying believers. "Power from on high" was occasionally vouchsafed me on these high places,'[28] preparing him to proclaim the gospel with zeal and heavenly unction. Often he spent the whole of his travelling time in prayer — it was not uncommon to hear him praying out loud as he traversed the hills and mountains — and he would not venture into the pulpit until he was sure that God was with him. In fact, he was convinced that there was an immediate connection between his devotion to prayer and the anointing that rested on his ministry. Once revived and strengthened in the inner man he would appear before the people like a giant who had just descended the Mount of God, yet with a 'meek and heavenly countenance, lighting up, charming and winning spectators; and his voice, like a silver trumpet, electrifying the whole assembly; his tongue, like the pen of a ready writer, instructing his hearers; in his hand, the sword of the Spirit, with which he cut asunder and divided between the sinner and his sins'.[29]

Though he spent many hours in the secret place before God, he was against long showy prayers from the pulpit, which he thought were forbidden in Scripture and which tended to exalt the preacher rather than Christ. 'There are many things besides grace,' he says, 'which often occasion our prayers to be long; and there are many that make long prayers in public, while they scarcely bend the knees in secret.'[30] The longest prayer in the Bible can be 'deliberately read in less than ten minutes', he would say in opposition to some prayers that were half an hour long. He was a firm believer in unity of design in public prayer and regarded the Lord's prayer as a pattern 'to collect matters within a small compass — include everything in a few words'. Prayers before sermons should contain 'specific petitions for the aid of the Spirit to preach, and that the word be blessed of God' and little else.[31] If we could exchange 'lifeless, protracted phraseology' for 'short, importunate and lively' prayers, there would be, he believed, a much greater awakening.[32] In support of his views he was fond of quoting the following anecdote of Daniel Rowland:

At an Association, which was held at New Chapel in Pembrokeshire, there was a good deal of preaching, but everything appeared exceedingly dull; at ten o'clock in the forenoon of the principal day of the meeting, one of the clergymen preached before Mr Rowland, but there was yet no movement. When Mr R. rose, before he gave out a hymn, or did anything else, he called to a preacher of the name of David — who was remarkable for short prayers and always very much to the purpose; 'David, engage in a short prayer before me, to see if thou canst rend this thick cloud; thou wilt not be longer than three or four minutes, for the long prayers that were made here at the commencement of the meeting have failed to disperse the gloom.' Upon this David began and said, 'Lord Jesus! for the sake of thy blood and thine agony, hear

me. Thy servants have been trying to winnow here the past
evening, and this morning — they can do nothing: — Lord,
there has not a single gale of heavenly wind blown yet upon
this meeting.' He then repeated the petition, saying, 'Wind,
Lord, wind, gracious Lord, for the wind is in thy fist now as
ever — Amen.' After this a peculiar tenderness descended
upon the congregation, and much weeping followed, while
Mr Rowland preached with a pleasant gale of heavenly influence.[33]

Perhaps there were no occasions when the spirit of prayer fell
on him more copiously than before the assault of some 'inward
foe or external enmity'. Then Christ followed him with the sufficiency of his grace and gave him two things in particular:
'namely, some premonition (in a dream or otherwise) that a
storm was approaching, and a spirit of prayer, with a renewed
enjoyment of his presence, until I became a prince in the confidence that the Lord Jesus was in alliance with me, like Jacob
when he met with Esau. No Esau succeeded against me; and
the omen of victory, at all times, was the spirit of prayer.'[34]
Again, 'before some calamity in connection with the cause of
Christ with which I was connected, such as chapel debts',[35] the
spirit of God descended on him and moved him to the throne
of grace, where he fervently pleaded with God that the cause
of Christ might not be harmed. This was his practice for many
years.

Once, when he was under the influence of Sandemanianism,
he 'began to whisper about abandoning the ministry on
account of the utter dryness of my affections. When things had
got to their worst pitch, and Lazarus had been buried four days,
Jesus came by, and with him the spirit of prayer was raised
again.'[36] He notices in one of his memoranda that the spirit of
prayer often descended upon him at these times like showers
of rain, turning the 'drought of summer' into 'streams on the
dry ground'.

In one of his allegories, where he compares prayer to a 'rope on board a ship that lifts and pulls down the sails to answer all winds and ebb and flow', he sums up his own attitude towards prayer, saying that a Christian's prayer life is, as it were, 'one prayer from the first breathing to the last'.[37]

Along with being a 'wrestler with God', Christmas Evans was a gentle and humble man, whose conduct was characterised by a diffident and quiet spirit. 'His fervent piety, holy zeal and unblemished life, secured for him the respect of many warm-hearted Christians,'[38] who recognised him as a 'holy man of God'. Brutus, in reference to his godliness, remarked that 'Not only was Christmas Evans a wonderfully great man, but he was God's man.'[39] He was especially careful to walk with circumspection before the world so as not to give the enemy of souls any opportunity to slander the name of Christ or to bring his cause into disrepute. With his own unstained Christian profession as a living testimony, he could freely exhort others to live soberly and righteously in this evil world, and encourage them to show their inward piety by an outward conduct that was pleasing to God; for the same God who requires a pure heart, also requires the hands and tongue to be clean:

> God hath not called us unto uncleanness but unto holiness. Let us, therefore, cleanse ourselves from all filthiness — from all manner of pollution — of the flesh and spirit, perfecting holiness in the fear of God. For it is written, 'Be ye holy, for I am holy;' holy in all manner of conversation; holy in all stations, relations and conditions of life — as husbands and wives, parents and children, masters and servants; and this always, and in all places — at home and abroad, in private and in public, in prosperity and adversity. Our conversation should be such as becometh the nature and requirements of the gospel of Christ.[40]

He endeavoured at all times to establish and maintain true discipline in himself and others, believing that the doctrine of

Christ in the profession, and the spirit of Christ governing the heart and conduct, were reasons enough to support a well-ordered lifestyle. Persons of unbecoming deportment could expect nothing less than his strong disapproval, which occasioned him much trouble from some members of the churches where he ministered. He never made any attempt to put on the airs of self-righteousness, but, with a cheerful disposition and a countenance that expressed the enjoyment of divine favour, willingly embraced people from all denominations and walks of life so long as they exhibited a love for Christ and a desire to obey his commandments. Many of his friends were Methodists or Congregationalists, and he engaged in uplifting conversations with them on his travels.

He was very zealous for the things of God and utterly sincere and honest in his dealings with others, never seeking an advantage by underhand or devious means. He thought that any departure from the truth, in word, behaviour or belief, was a disgrace both to the gospel and to a man's Christian character. At times he could be unsuspecting to a fault, and some crafty persons would treat his innocence with cruelty. Sometimes he was taken in by flattery or by an eloquent and persistent talebearer, but when he investigated the matter and discovered the truth, the injured person received his full protection and support to the disgrace of the slanderer. William Morgan, the author of the first Welsh Memoir, observes: 'I do not think that this great man knew what guile was, that is, so as to practise it; and had he attempted to assume any disguise in the presence of others, he would appear the most hideous being on earth. It was utterly impracticable for him to learn fraud of any kind; the Creator had formed him constitutionally incapable of this.'[41]

His straightforward honesty is wonderfully borne out by the following well-known anecdote. He had employed a person to sell a horse for him at a fair and after awhile he went out to see if the man had been successful:

There was a stranger bargaining for the animal, and the con-
tract was nearly completed. 'Is this your horse, Mr Evans?'
said the purchaser.

'Certainly it is,' he replied.

'What is his age, sir?'

'Twenty-three years.'

'But this man tells me he is only fifteen.'

'He is certainly twenty-three, for he has been with me these
twenty years, and he was three years old when I bought him.'

'Is he safe-footed?'

'Very far from that, I assure you, or I would not part from
him, and he has never been put in a harness since I have had
him either.'

'Please go into the house, Mr Evans,' whispered the man
whom he had employed to make the sale, 'for I shall never
dispose of the horse while you are present.'

The frank manner, however, in which Mr Evans told him
all the truth, induced the dealer to make the purchase at a
very handsome price; while he procured for Mr Evans a good
name, which is better than gold.[42]

He often expressed the hope that, by the grace of God, he had
overcome the corruptions of his heart, especially his natural
disposition towards an angry, revengeful and unforgiving spirit.
In this matter he was generally victorious, for although he
suffered greatly from the accusations and behaviour of his
opponents, he was usually ready to forgive them and to resist
vindictiveness. He took more pleasure in pardoning the offender
than in any apology offered. 'I do not think,' says William
Morgan, 'but that he would have forgiven the greatest offence,
with a thousand times more pleasure than the offender would
have sought pardon. It was only for the person who had given
offence to make some sort of confession, and in some way say
that there had been a misunderstanding; he would almost
anticipate him by saying, "Oh, do not say anything about it —
let it be buried; very likely I have been in fault also."'[43]

There was at one time a minister of another denomination

who was accused of a serious offence, which if it could have been proved, would have brought upon him a heavy punishment. This person had been engaged in a religious controversy with Christmas Evans and in the dispute had used language that, according to Christmas Evans, was both 'unfair and contemptuous'. To make matters worse the controversy had been conducted openly in the public periodicals. When Christmas Evans heard that his opponent was 'wrongfully charged', and especially when he was convinced that his imprisonment 'proceeded from political enmity and religious persecution' hidden under 'the cloak of sanctity and personal disappointment, which had produced envy', instead of enjoying the distress of his antagonist, he was deeply concerned for him and for the reputation of the dissenting body in Wales.

> When the day of the trial arrived, Mr Evans retired to his room, and earnestly besought Jesus Christ to stop the current of the flowing river, which had been filled by the above streams; he felt some confidence that he was heard. He waited with almost impatient anxiety for the news of the discharge of the prisoner, and yet with some dread, lest matters should turn against him.
>
> While he sat at the table in his own house, one of the ministers of that denomination entered, and said: — 'Mr — the prisoner is a free man.' Then without speaking a word to the person who had communicated the intelligence, with tears flowing from his eye, he fell on his knees to present the firstfruits of his joy in thanksgiving to Jesus Christ, whom he had entreated on his behalf, and addressed his Saviour in this emphatic language: 'Thanks be to thee, O Lord Jesus, for delivering through thy providence one of the ministers of the Dissenters from being destroyed — delivering him from the mouth of the lion.' After this he arose and participated with his friend in their mutual congratulations.[44]

In this matter of forgiveness he could say from his heart, 'Lord, *lay none of the sins and offences committed by any persons against me to their charge in the great Day of Judgement.* I have no wish that the law should grasp any of them, but that they should settle matters at the great mercy-seat, where I hope the multitude of my sins shall also be hid and forgotten.'[45]

In spite of his extreme poverty in Anglesey, he rarely complained about his financial straits, and was not prepared to tolerate for long others in which a spirit of ungratefulness had become a habit. He once said to a brother who was given to voice his murmurings, 'Dost thou think, brother, that thou hast ever received one good gift of God, that thou art always complaining so much?'[46] He was very generous and hospitable, often sharing his humble abode with passers-by, and always ready to give whatever he had to anyone in distress. For several years he subscribed one pound to the Bible Society, ten shillings to the Missionary Society and the same amount to the Baptist Education Society, besides contributing to the sick and needy in his own neighbourhood, according to his means. At times he felt so deeply the troubles of others that he made himself ill.

He found it hard to resist any plea for help. Once he returned home without his best top coat because he had given it to a Protestant Irish tramp who had told him he spent much of his time in reading the Bible to his illiterate countrymen. On another occasion a very poor Jew named Isaac, who had been brought up in England and could speak English well, came to him, professing faith in Christ and expressing a desire to be baptised by him. Christmas Evans, after a short examination, duly baptised him in the name of the Father and the Son and the Holy Spirit and, because of his poverty, gave him a whole suit of clothes. He later heard of him, that he continued steadfast in the Christian faith.[47]

Once a brother in Anglesey, together with his family, had been sick for some time, and in consequence was reduced to a very low state as to his circumstances. Mr Evans felt much for him, and relieved his distress to the utmost of his ability — even by giving him the *only* pound which at the time he possessed. His wife remonstrated with him for giving away the money, adding that they had none to buy food the following Saturday; to whom he replied, 'Food will come to us yet through Providence from some quarter.' The day before the market he received a letter from a friend in England, begging his acceptance of the enclosed *two pounds* for his own use. When he had read the letter he said to his wife — at the same time showing her the two pounds — 'Catherine, I told thee that Providence would return the alms-pound, for it was a loan to the Lord.'[48]

He was equally generous with his admiration and praise of other men, recognising their talents and being unafraid of them outshining him in the pulpit. He gladly sat at their feet to learn from them. He was willing to extol anyone who used his energies to promote the kingdom of God and his gifts to glorify God, irrespective of whether or not they were a member of a different denomination or from among his fellow countrymen. 'I confess it to be my duty,' he remarked, 'to love brethren of other denominations and I rejoice greatly in every virtue and success among them as among our own denomination.'[49] He said of a contemporary David Charles (1762-1834), a Calvinistic Methodist minister and the brother of the eminent Thomas Charles of Bala: 'Mr Charles was notable amongst divines. In reperusing his sermons, I feel holy sparks emanating from him, as from a great star, and melting the frost in my soul. His mode of treating the deep things of God was so able and inimitable that many of his sentences might be taken as texts to preach from.'[50] He spoke very respectfully of Bishop Beveridge, Dr Watts and Doddridge and others, and regarded Thomas Burgess, bishop of St David's, as 'God's man because he armed himself, fought against and conquered the giant'.[51]

He loved peace in the home and in the church, and with an amiable approach, 'always used his influence, wisdom and prudence to quench the spark of unhallowed fire before it burst out to a flame, and to nip the poisonous bud before it came to its full growth'.[52] Occasionally, when unduly provoked, his old nature flashed to the fore. In 1821 he was among a group of ministers who had gathered at the home of a Mr Joseph at Merthyr Tudful. David Saunders was present at the meeting and he was proud of having baptised the blind preacher, Daniel Davies, nicknamed the 'Lion of Bethesda' and a convert from Methodism. Christmas Evans was keen to meet Davies and on his arrival remarked how, in appearance, he resembled Andrew Fuller. When the host's child entered the room, Saunders rudely observed:

> 'A child always runs to its father; but you know nothing about that experience, Christmas, you never had one child.' Evans said nothing. 'That child has beautiful eyes,' went on Saunders, determined to make Evans ratty. 'It is a great thing to have good legs, legs that never swell. Your legs swell, don't they, Mr Evans?' But Evans kept his temper and tried to turn the conversation another way. Saunders was back again to the attack. 'The preachers that speak, not those that shout, are the best at Association gatherings. Those who shout end with a scream. When you get into the *hwyl*, Mr Evans, you scream.' Evans bore that, though not without wincing. When Saunders began baiting the blind preacher Davies with insults, the storm broke.
>
> 'Saunders,' said Evans, 'go and read Lord Chesterfield, and learn that the first lesson in politeness is not to insult the company in which you are. Do you imagine that our friend here does not know that he is blind. I am ashamed to have been born in the same country as you.'
>
> 'Beg pardon,' begged Saunders.
>
> 'Beg pardon, indeed,' replied Evans. 'You are too foolish and silly to be pardoned. You never know when you sin. You tell one "You have no eyes," to another "Your legs swell ... you

have no child ... you scream when you preach.'" Evans continued in merciless denunciation until the other brethren [es-
pecially John Jenkins, Hengoed] intervened.

A while later Evans had his hair cut by a barber who was
called into the house. For some years Evans had received a
rum shampoo whenever his hair was cut. This was to prevent
colds in the head. To receive pardon Saunders insisted on
rubbing the rum into Evans's hair. While doing so the quarrel restarted and it continued with intermissions throughout
their stay at Merthyr.[53]

He could also react to criticism with biting directness, which
often caused contention. Like many preachers he was accustomed to preach the same sermon on several different occasions. Once a young preacher, who had spoken in the same
service, approached him as he descended from the pulpit and
remarked sarcastically, 'Well, you have given us an old sermon
again today!'

'Why, what about it, my boy? Had you a new one?' replied
Christmas Evans, with a twinkle in his eye.

'Certainly, mine was new. Absolutely new and original.'

'Look here,' said Christmas Evans, 'I would not take a dozen
sermons like yours for this one old sermon of mine.'

'Neither would I,' joined in a listening deacon. 'I would like
to hear that sermon again, Christmas; as for yours, young man,
I have never heard it before today and I never want to hear it
again.' And there the conversation ended.

At times he was not always wise in what he said, being too
impulsive for his own good in voicing an opinion. John Jenkins,
with whom he often quarrelled, commented that he had never
known anyone so great in godliness and yet so childish.[54] During the troubles that led to his removal from Anglesey, when his
position was threatened, he referred to the Denbighshire arbi-
trators as 'merely cabbage stumps', and spoke of Samuel
Edwards, one of their number, as a 'horse-angel'. His contention with Edwards became very acrimonious. 'It is said that

C. E. fainted during the dispute. They were both in the same room and Ellis Evans said that they came out very short of breath and their spirits amazingly tender, like two giants that had expended all their energy on each other.'[55]

> He was once to preach at an Assembly in Merthyr. He was to preach last, at two o'clock, preceded by a vain, frivolous young man. In order to show respect to Mr Evans, the minister approached him and asked how much time he would allow the young man. 'A quarter of an hour,' was his reply.
>
> Having passed on this information the minister returned to Mr Evans and said, 'He won't preach unless he's given three quarters of an hour.'
>
> 'He's quite a lad!' replied Mr Evans.
>
> However, this brother began his 'three quarters of an hour' and as soon as he had announced his text our hero, who was sitting in the big pew under the pulpit, folded his arms and pretended to fall soundly asleep. In about quarter of an hour he awoke and asked in a loud voice whether the sermon was over. Having had a negative answer he slept twice more. The third time he awoke, he asked, 'Hasn't the lad finished yet?'
>
> The young man heard the hint and taking out his watch exclaimed triumphantly, 'Thank God, I have another five minutes!'
>
> 'Where is he going now?' replied Christmas Evans. 'Say, is he going to the scaffold?'
>
> If the swaggerer was not convicted of his arrogance by this shot, then his case was a hopeless one.[56]

Although there were occasions when he 'responded to attack', he tried hard not to upset deliberately or needlessly the feelings of others, saying, 'It is better to keep sarcasms pocketed, if they cannot be used without wounding the feelings of a friend.'[57]

In conversation he was friendly and knowledgeable, and at ease in the company of different classes of society. 'In the cottage and the mansion he was equally at home, and the unlettered peasant and the erudite philosopher were equally interested by his conversation.' Manuel Jones, a Methodist preacher, who met Christmas Evans as he was following his appointments to the South, enjoyed some 'religious conversation on the road' with him as the two travelled for some time together. 'He very freely related to me his experience,' recalls Jones, 'which made a deep impression on my mind, the effects of which I felt through all my journey, and in some measure I feel to this day. He was a man of holy conversation.'[58] After the labours and fatigues of a public meeting he always enjoyed the company of ministers and friends, who flocked to the house where he resided.

> If he had confidence in the persons present, he would be exceedingly agreeable and cheerful; he would listen attentively to every one that took part in the conversation, and offer pertinent remarks himself on the subject that engaged the attention of those present. If any officious person should advance anything impertinent, for the sake of showing himself, he would assume a gloomy aspect for a short time, but having silenced that individual, he would resume the conversation with fresh animation, and fill up the breaches occasioned by the intrusion with anecdotes applicable to the nature of the conversation, and all present would feel it their interest to pay the utmost attention to his eloquent remarks.
>
> It was not usual with him to speak of his fastings and prayers, and his own personal exercises in the cause of religion; but when in conversation with one or two bosom friends, he would open his heart freely; then would be seen, as through a transparent glass, the eminently pious man...
>
> He would never prolong a conversation except there was something valuable and profitable in it. He was peculiarly affectionate in his salutations to all persons, and especially to those of a sincere religious character. If a brother or sister should relate their spiritual experience, he would reply in the most encouraging manner, and make such observations as he judged suited their case.[59]

Although he had no children of his own, he enjoyed the company of children and possessed a familiar and tender disposition towards them. He could easily and quite naturally turn aside from conversing on some profound and glorious topic with another minister of the gospel, who was left with a sense of wonder at the things he had heard from him, to a small child, take him on his knee, and impart to him a word or two about the Saviour's grace and love. 'He would use no silly fondling, as some foolishly do, but would give some advice, or instruction, or some little easy verse, suitable to the temper and the age of the child; and generally what he said in this manner would be remembered after he was gone.'[60]

He was never vulgar or harsh in his conversation, but he did exercise a keen sense of humour which delighted his companions. Once when crossing one of the Merioneth mountains on a midsummer's day, he accidentally met John Herring, a talented Baptist minister from Cardigan, who greeted him with the words, '*Dear me*, this is very wonderful, to see Christmas in the middle of summer.'

'Well,' he immediately replied, 'that is not more wonderful, that I know, than to see a live herring on the top of a mountain.'[61]

His sense of the ridiculous was often used to good effect in and out of the pulpit, and with it he defused many a potentially explosive situation. One morning he came down to breakfast at a farm house, where he had the previous evening taken off a splendid pair of yellow-topped boots, bought only a day or two before at Aberystwyth and of which, it is said, he was unashamedly proud. As he was waited on by the servants, he saw to his horror that one of the girls had covered his boots from top to bottom with the daub used by farmers to ease and blacken their own clogs and shoes, thus making his boots unrecognisable. At first the look of disbelief on his face made those in his company wonder what he was about to say. Turning aside from his sense of shock, and with a flash of good-humoured inspiration, he looked at the culprit and growled, 'Well, girl, I never knew such a thing. Thou hast actually daubed my boots with the melted bottoms of your Cardiganshire corpse-candles;' and with that the 'scene concluded in convulsions of laughter'.[62]

Occasionally, in order to humble the pride of a haughty individual or to resolve a dispute that had arisen, he resorted to an illustrative style of speech, and often coupled it with a disarming humour. Once he was with two Paedobaptist ministers, both men of education and candour, who were making derogatory remarks about the institution of godfathers and godmothers in the Church of England, commenting that it was only of papistical authority. One of them addressed Christmas Evans and asked for his opinion. He replied, 'You know that I consider infant baptism papistical as well as godfathers and godmothers. Your controversy appears as unimportant in my view as that of two gentlemen having two snails, one with and the other without horns; and the proprietor of the snail without horns takes it upon him to censure the horns of the other snail; but the two snails are friends.' Upon hearing this, one of the 'snail' debaters good-humouredly burst out into a hearty laugh.[63]

On other occasions he used humour as a last resort, when reasonable arguments failed to achieve their objective, as in the case of a minister friend who was afraid of a French invasion. This good brother, who was also a tailor, expressed his concerns in the most doleful manner to Christmas Evans, who tried hard to comfort him by assuring him that God, not Bonaparte, ruled the universe. When his words of consolation failed to lift the spirits of his friend, he adopted a completely different approach. 'I will tell you, brother, what you must do,' he said gravely, as if to address the sufferer with yet more serious counsel:

When the French are about to land, you must fix your needle into one end of your yardstick, fasten the red sleeve that holds your needles in front of your hat, hang the thimble under your nose and tie your iron and sleeve board round your waist. When you hear that Boni has landed, whistle into the thimble to rouse the country; and when you meet

the army, beat the sleeve board with the iron. When they
see the red sleeve and hear the noise, Boni and his army
will be terrified and flee. You must pursue them mercilessly
with that needle protruding from your yardstick![64]

Christmas Evans would have enjoyed the story related by a
mischievous Baptist about an old Methodist christening a baby.
The minister very tenderly took the baby in his arms and at the
same time in a paternal fashion imparted a few words of advice to the young parents, 'See that you train up the child in the
way that he should go, that you surround him with the best
influences, and that you give him a good example. If you do
so, who knows but that he may become a Christmas Evans or
a John Elias! What is the name of the child?'

'*Jane*, sir,' replied the mother.[65]

As a minister he was not adept at theological debates,
although, partly because of his prominent position in the Principality, he engaged in several controversies of the day, but
more out of necessity than desire. His nature was too sensitive
for the rigours of disagreement and often, in the heat of battle,
he was wounded by criticism or abuse, making him wish that
he had never entered the fray. He preferred to be applauded
than slandered, and responded favourably to the approval of
others. He was like a woman, said Robert Jones, Llanllyfni,
'better after being praised'.[66]

He deplored the spirit of bigotry, 'with its readiness to
denounce sternly and conceitedly the opinions of others', and
was hindered in doing good by it. 'I mourned,' he said, 'to see
the prevalence of a sectarian spirit preventing good people from
assisting one another. If we offend our neighbour, there is little
hope of winning him; gentleness is best.'[67] 'Go to the field to
catch a horse,' he said to emphasise the same point, 'and how
do you think you will set about it? By cracking your whip and
chasing it with a threatening look? Instead of that, you should
approach it gently, with oats in the feeding bowl.'[68] He always

tried to treat others in a 'kind, candid and ingenuous' way,[69] and would never attempt to persuade unnecessarily those who differed from him to embrace his own beliefs. He was influenced more by the love of Christ than by the peculiarities of his own denomination.

In his early ministerial career he tended to be overly severe with those brethren who opposed him, though he never regarded them as unregenerate or in any way inferior to him, and too vigorous in the defence of his opinions. In his polemic writings there are occasions when he deals with his challengers offensively, even slanderously. Sometimes, in order to get the upper hand, he would try to confound his opponents; at other times, he would be too hasty in sharing his views, often without sufficient contemplation on the subject under discussion, and too skilful at colouring his arguments. He could, however, when the occasion demanded, be both reasonable in response and fiery in rebuke. When a deist, who also pretended to be an atheist, being aware that he was not a skilful disputer, attacked him, asking, 'What is the strongest argument in your view to prove that there is a God, and that the Scriptures proceeded from him?' he replied:

> The character given of the God of the Bible is so amiable, perfect and unblameable; so that the like was never seen in the world: — a perfect Being in justice and mercy, — just and a Saviour! I have loved the character as one fully worthy of the Creator of the world, and had I opened my eyes in the heavenly world, and heard someone say, 'It is not the God of the Bible that is here,' I would ask him, 'Who is here then?' If he is the same character as that given of the God of the Bible, he must be the same...
> The mad atheist is so blind, that he will not see the Godhead, and the eternal power in the skilful workmanship of his own body, and in the wonderful formation of the leaves, flowers and all the other glorious objects in creation, more than the mole of the earth in its abode of darkness; and because of

that, he will have to determine that there is no God in existence; as if the mole were to determine that — there is no
king, nor a royal palace, because he could not see it.

O thou atheistical mole, thou hast not travelled nor
searched sufficiently to make the decision that there is no God.
All thou canst say is, that thou dost not see nor wish to see
God. Atheist, how dost thou know, but that the being of God is
so manifest the other side of the river of death, that no doubt
is entertained by any upon the point, throughout all the vast
expanse of immortality and of eternity? The earth-mole does
not possess sufficient knowledge and information to say that
there is no Lama in Tibet without ever seeing Asia, or making a journey beyond his own village. So the atheistical worm
must travel through the gates of death, and all the regions of
the bottomless pit, and the land of destruction, and to the
heaven of heavens, and surround all the borders of time
and eternity, and comprehend all being in which the being of
God may be, ere he can successfully deny that there is a
God.[70]

His dislike for controversy was matched by a lack of taste and
aptness for intricate logical arguments. This is not to say that he
was not a thinker, for from childhood he was 'separated from
the common herd by the deeply reflective action of his mind',[71]
but he was not an original thinker or a man of independent
thought; nor are we suggesting that he was unintelligent, for in
mere intellectual power he was 'a mighty man'. His weakness
arose from a defective judgement and an inability to understand intuitively the minutiae of theological and doctrinal
issues.

He had not the comprehension of analytical power which
embraces the smallest as well as the most prominent parts
of a subject, and brings forth the whole in its entireness and
integrity. Hence he would occasionally be so wrapt up in a
one-sided view of his theme, and would pour forth so completely his energies into its investigation, under that aspect,
that, when so much had been effected, he fancied the work

was done. This was caused partly by the interference of his imagination at too early a period in his inquiries, and partly by the untrained condition of his strictly reasoning powers. He had not that native logic which so eminently distinguishes some minds... In close ratiocination, he never became mighty, and defects of this kind would occur, not infrequently, in his sermons and writings.[72]

The principal danger in the conduct of his mind was the temptation to govern all his thoughts with, what could be, an unbridled imagination; 'and there, conjuring up forms and figures and modifications from his comparatively extensive and most observant and attentive reading, he framed worlds and states of things of his own',[73] which did not always agree with reality or the doctrines of the Bible. At times he was too easily swayed by what he read, particularly if the author presented his arguments in a strong and brilliant style. The eloquence of the pen charmed and convinced him. Similarly, if the opinion of knowledgeable men, whom he respected, was stated with firm reason and powerful language, he found it hard to resist, sometimes being persuaded and led astray by them, as he was by J. R. Jones.

Finally, his friend Rhys Stephen highlights the two principal qualities of Christmas Evans's life: namely, a 'heart swelling with love to God and man', and a determination not to live for himself but for Christ Jesus, before whom 'He was ever prostrate, ever devout.' 'He was a man who feared the Lord God of heaven and earth. He walked before him with great humility all the day long. He had a deep and abiding sense of the awful character of our relations to God and eternity; and toward that God, and in reference to that eternity, he ever deported himself with reverence and fear... His love to his fellowman was manifested in the devotement of his long life to the service of his country, and to the edification of the church of God in it.'[74]

Evans's descriptive powers were perhaps never excelled. His imagination was of the imperial order, and absolutely knew no bounds; and his facility in the ready use of language was altogether wonderful. Besides this he was a man of the liveliest sensibilities, and always spoke out of a full heart, sometimes storming his hearers with his impassioned earnestness, and sometimes himself overwhelmed with the magnitude and grandeur of his theme. Add to this his pre-eminent faith and holiness of life, and we discover the secret of his astonishing pulpit eloquence — which, according to Robert Hall, entitles him to be ranked among the first men of his age.

Henry C. Fish.[1]

All the visible fire which flamed on the summit of Sinai, now breaks forth anew on Calvary; and though unseen by man, envelops in its burning the soul and the body of our glorious Substitute. Behold him rushing between you and the flames, shielding you, and quenching the flames in his blood!

Christmas Evans preaching on 1 Peter 2:24.[2]

21

'The Greatest Preacher God has ever Given to Wales'

No study of Christmas Evans would be complete without a close examination of 'the man in the pulpit', who, 'for successful popular eloquence among his own people, ranks among the most remarkable preachers of his age'.[3]

On many occasions Christmas Evans preached outdoors because the congregations were so large, and usually in the Welsh language — a language 'majestically strong and rugged, yet sweet and rhythmical, whose cadences seem to sweep the whole gamut of human thought and emotion, which has in it the terrible might of the tempest, as well as the soothing calmness of the summer breeze'.[4] According to Kilsby Jones, Welsh is 'the language of poetry, of song and of preaching',[5] and therefore ideally suited to Christmas Evans's style. Christmas Evans himself insisted that the English language, in contrast to Welsh, 'lacks fire and fervour, and is fit only for those who would make their sermons quiet and lifeless things'.[6] It is also true that he was not as confident or commanding in English, although he could be just as effective.

A minister from England, visiting Wales, met with Christmas Evans, of whom he had heard much, and with whom he was much displeased on account of what he deemed disorderly and unbecoming zeal. The Englishman preached as coldly as if he had been a Stoic philosopher, fully determined not to countenance any of the wild notions of the Welsh. When he had finished Christmas Evans commenced, and out of respect to his brother from England, he tried to speak a little broken English as well as he could; and while he was describing the glory of Christ, the greatness of his sufferings, and the infinite merits of his sacrifice in a most powerful manner, the Englishman quite forgot himself, and cried out with all his might, *'Is this my Saviour? In heaven's name, brother, lead me to know him!'* and fell down on the floor. Strange as this may appear to some, it was not at all uncommon for such effects to follow his preaching.[7]

The message he preached was the old-fashioned gospel of 'Jesus Christ and him crucified', and his main themes were the fundamental truths of the Christian faith. He proclaimed the great salvation of God in a purely evangelical sense, all the time stressing the sufficiency of Christ for redemption and man's inability to earn by his own efforts the forgiveness of sins. 'The food for the church, and for sinners,' he said, 'is found in preaching the salvation of man by the grace, merits, and the power of Christ... It is not in the duties we are to rest, but in Christ.'[8] He believed that 'Jesus Christ represented his people in his mediatorial capacity; that he fulfilled the engagements of the covenant on their behalf; that he sealed their redemption on the cross; that he arose as the first-fruits of their resurrection; that he is now in heaven interceding for them; and that ultimately he will be entitled to see the whole family of the redeemed in glory and happiness.'[9] 'Christ,' he would say, 'is the whole of our salvation, our hope and our happiness.'[10]

His aim in preaching was to arouse careless sinners out of their lethargy and to lead them to Christ. 'May these remarks,' he said at the end of one of his sermons, 'preserve you from despair under a sense of your guilt and wretchedness; drive you from all false refuges to the cross, with a penitent and grateful heart; induce you to trust, not in your own strength or wisdom or righteousness, but in the adorable name of Jesus; to live a life of faith in him, of love towards him, and of patient waiting for his mercy unto eternal salvation.'[11] He described himself as a fisher of men whose 'line should not be of fine silk but of strong thread interwoven with the hemp of truth and dipped in the spirit of prayer, for what was wanted was not something nice to look at, but a line with a hook at one end to bite'.[12] With fervour and unction, he cast that line and cried:

> Impenitent and unbelieving men, hear this blessed message of salvation! Do you intend ever to embrace the proffered mercy of the gospel? Make haste! Procrastination is ruin! Now is the accepted time! O fly to the throne of grace! Time is hastening — you will soon be swallowed up in eternity! May the Lord have mercy upon you, and rouse you from your indifference and sloth! It is my delight to invite you to Christ; but I feel more pleasure and more confidence in praying for you to God. I have besought and entreated you, by every argument and every motive in my power, but you are yet in your sins, and rushing on toward hell. Yet I will not give you up in despair. If I cannot persuade you to flee from the wrath to come, I will intercede with God to have mercy upon you for the sake of his beloved Son. If I cannot prevail in the pulpit, I will try to prevail at the throne![13]

However remote or obscure his text, he would soon lead his congregation up the hill of Calvary, and focus their minds on the cross. 'Now my hearers, let us go to Calvary,' he would say. 'What an amazing sight!'[14] Once he cried, 'O Calvary! Calvary! How could I ever pass by without looking at you.'[15] Arthur Jones of Bangor, says of him, 'His great and vigorous soul was like a man who had been born and bred in the temple, taking a walk every day, for the benefit of his health, to the hill of Calvary, the garden of Joseph of Arimathea and Mount Olivet, till he grew up the most healthy young man that ever existed.'[16] A writer in

a Welsh periodical called *The Sun (Yr Haul)*, after extolling the
uniqueness of Christmas Evans, 'A Phoenix' of 'peculiar gifts',
makes the following observations:

> In the cross of Christ he found life. By the cross of Christ he
> would live; and of the cross of Christ he would speak. Every-
> thing was too small in which this great luminary could revolve,
> but the unlimited ethereal space of the wonders of the death
> of the cross. Here his soul had room enough to rove in the
> whole circle of his ministry; and here he finds room suffi-
> ciently large for his happy soul to shine for ever in the firma-
> ment of eternal glory...
>
> Shall we not always think of the garden of Gethsemane,
> of Pilate's bar, of the crown of thorns, and Calvary's hill, when-
> ever we think of Christmas Evans? Yes! we shall gaze on the
> Son of God, as a sacrifice laid on the altar; as the Lamb that
> was slain for us; and wonder at the holy fire that consumed all
> the sacrifices from the days of Abel to that very day when it
> was extinguished by the flood of blood poured forth from the
> wounded side of the Son of Mary. These are glorious themes!
> — yes, sublime indeed, when exhibited by a man of Christ-
> mas Evans's talents![17]

When preaching from the text: 'But God forbid that I should
glory save in the cross of our Lord Jesus Christ,' he unveils the
mysterious glory of the cross — 'where the greatest wealth and
the greatest poverty met, the most astounding weakness and
the greatest strength, the heaviest curse and the highest love,
the deepest agony and the greatest power' — before crying
out: 'I feel some absorption in the cross, and some secret at-
traction, yet overpowering, that unfits my heart to love the world
as of old. I feel as if nails held me by my heart to the cross of
Christ, and every nail dipped in the oil of free love, so that I
would not draw any of them out, for they agree with my heart.'[18]

Christmas Evans had not only understood these doctrines
in an intellectual sense, enabling him to impart truth to his hearers, he had also been profoundly moved by them in his own

heart. He had experienced for himself the deep things of the gospel, and his sermons, effectual and thrilling as they were, were an overflow of that experience. 'Not only had he heard of the bread of angels and of the corn of heaven, but this bread and this corn were his daily food; not only had he heard of the river of God, the streams whereof maketh glad the city of our God, but the crystal waters of this river were his constant drink.'[19] A preacher, he thought, rather than being just a dry and passive mouthpiece, should be filled to overflowing with his subject, overcome by it almost, and aroused by the influences of the Holy Spirit, so as to produce a meaningful and lasting impression on those who listen. His object was not only to enlighten the understanding, but to warm the heart that all should *feel* as well as *see* the glories of Christ.

Thus, when he stepped into the pulpit 'His soul was kindled and inflamed by the live coals from the altar... His words and thoughts became radiant with fire and metaphor; they flew forth rich, bright, glowing, like some rich metal in ethereal flame.'[20] He was like the fiery volcano of 'Etna or Vesuvius, pouring the lava of his own eloquence in a torrent of liquid fire on the heads of his hearers, until their feelings kindled and burned with the intensest glow'.[21] He spoke with the whirlwind and the storm, with words that broke rocks into pieces, his one eye flashing as his whole being was stirred to the depths by the truths he uttered; and his hearers, dissolved by the Spirit's hallowed influence, were carried away to the gate of heaven. 'He transported them,' says one, 'beyond the region of argument, and leaving all their cavils and prejudices immeasurably behind, rapt them away to the third heaven of ecstasy!'[22] At times this 'glorious dramaturgical Boanerges',[23] as he has been described, preached with such impassioned earnestness, being so full of the love and power of God, that he seemed quite overwhelmed with the greatness and magnitude of what he was saying, and trembled like an aspen leaf.

This passion, which cleared away everything before him, and the divine anointing, which made the truth shine so brilliantly, 'often rendered him superior to himself, clothed him with a superhuman energy, till he seemed a messenger from the other world. The man was lost in his theme. Art was swallowed up in the whirlpool of excited feeling. The audience were swept irresistibly along by the current of the discourse; acknowledging by tears and groans the preacher's hold upon their hearts; and sometimes losing all self-control, and bursting into the most extravagant expressions of wonder and delight.'[24] The power of the world to come was felt through the whole assembly. The ungodly, with expressions of terror and dismay, expected at that moment a summons to the bar of God; the humble and penitent rose to their feet, triumphantly extolling the sufficiency of Christ's sacrifice to cleanse their guilty consciences; proud men were brought low and dissolved by the holy fire; and all were made to look beyond the preacher to Christ and to hear 'no voice but the voice of God piercing the hearts of sinners'.[25]

At times, however, the noise of the greater part of the congregation was offensive to persons of refined taste; and sometimes he was under the necessity of retiring, leaving the field or the street where he had been preaching, full of people, some in the greatest agony of mind, crying out for mercy; others praying, others singing, and a great many jumping; while many spectators were gazing, some with great approbation, firmly believing that God was among them, that his arm was made bare in the conversion of sinners, and that nothing less than Almighty power could accomplish such mighty works. Although he did not justify all the proceedings in such powerful revivals, yet many have been added to the Lord, whose lives and conversation corresponded with their profession.[26]

Sometimes, after preaching with 'holy fire', and while there were tears flowing and 'Amens' resounding, he waited quietly for several moments to allow the people to recover their composure before continuing.

Those who know little about 'the movings of God's Spirit on the soul' have accused him of preaching only to the affections, and explained the secret of his power in terms of the fiery, impetuous and emotional nature of the Welsh people; but such ideas fail to take into account Christmas Evans's own walk with God, the anointing that rested upon his ministry and the number of lives that were changed for good through his preaching. He was eminently a man of faith, holiness and prayer. It has already been mentioned that while travelling to preaching engagements, he spent many hours in prayer, wrestling with God on behalf of sinners and pleading for an outpouring of his Spirit on the word he was about to preach; so that frequently within a few minutes of entering the pulpit he attained a rare degree of inspiration — 'It was as if a strong wind blew, increasing rapidly into a tempest; at last the heavy drops of rain fall, followed by heavy showers, and down, down it comes, pattering for a while, until the whole land is covered as with a deluge.'[27]

Kilsby Jones, in the masterly essay he wrote to the *Homilist* on the *Characteristics of Welsh Preaching*, supplies a fitting tribute to Christmas Evans's style:

> It was his tremendous passion, in conjunction with a peerless imagination, that gave Christmas Evans so much power over a congregation. To see his huge frame quivering with emotion, and to watch the lightning flash of his eye — that lustrous black eye of which Robert Hall said it would do to lead an army through a wilderness — and to listen to the wild tones of his shrill voice as he mastered the difficult prosopopoeia, was to feel completely abandoned to the riotous enthusiasm of the moment. Abstractions, dry as the bones which Ezekiel of old saw in the valley, he could clothe with sinews, flesh and skin, and breathing life into them, make them stand on their feet. Of scenes enacted centuries ago in the glens and on the hills of Judea his fire and fancy enabled him to furnish so vivid a representation that all sense of the distance both of time and place was entirely lost; and though he was frequently

guilty of the grossest anachronisms, yet so admirably sustained were the parts assigned to the different characters, and so life-like and natural were the sentiments put into their mouths, that the discrepancy, however glaring, did not damage the effect. So genuine was the fire that burned within him, and so completely did he throw the whole of his impassioned soul into his descriptions, that even the fastidious critic was 'taken captive', and compelled to become his admirer.[28]

It has been said that the Welsh are gifted with a rich and unbounded imagination which for generations has been quickened and developed amid the wild scenery of mountains and hills. 'The Welsh nature,' says one writer, 'is exceptionally sensitive to mysteries, and has a keen appreciation of the superhuman. When the light of the Gospel was excluded this expressed itself in superstitions, wild or pathetic, but when the Gospel came that nature so sensitive to every touch of the mysterious was captivated and enraptured by the wondrous story of the incarnation and of the cross.'[29] Throughout his ministry Christmas Evans was 'captivated and enraptured by the wondrous story', expressing it with an imagination of genius that thrilled his listeners. Imagination was the principal power of his soul, uniting and absorbing, and sometimes overshadowing all his other talents, bold in its course, prolific and adventurous in flight, gripping in magnetism. 'He was often illogical, but he had a gorgeous and excursive fancy which invested his sermons at times with a charm and a power that were wholly resistless.'[30] Owen Thomas of Liverpool thought his imagination to be 'one of the most fruitful that ever belonged to a man'.[31]

He had the ability of turning whatever he saw into a flight of fancy and of impressing on the mind some spiritual lesson from it. Once, along with Brutus and Evan Jones (Castleton), he turned into a public house in Caernarfonshire to shelter from the rain. In the parlour was a map of the Battle of Waterloo, which absorbed his attention:

'Boys,' he said, 'look at this map.'

They went to the other side of the room and told him it was a map of the Battle of Waterloo.

'Who do you see here?' he said.

'We see Wellington among his officers,' they replied, 'and those with their hats in their hands are receiving his instructions.'

'Well,' he said, 'Wellington in the great Battle of Waterloo is similar to the Prince of our salvation in heaven. The great General of Zion on the immortal hill looks at the tribes of Israel in the wilderness fighting with Ammon, Amalek and Moab, along with the forces of darkness; and it is he who orders and controls the awful battle. The English, Scottish, Prussians, Hanoverians, etc., were not just fighting at Waterloo; but they were all fighting against Boni and the French, who were conquered by Wellington. In our battle the Anglicans, Baptists, Wesleyans, Methodists and Independents are fighting against one enemy and receiving directions from the glorious General in heaven. Who else do you see?' said Christmas Evans.

'We see Sir Thomas Picton,' they replied.

'He was the Saint Peter of the battle,' said he. 'Who is next?'

'The Marquis of Anglesey.'

'Oh,' said Christmas Evans, 'he was the Saint Paul of the battle because he fought against wild beasts.'

He continued in a similar vein as each name was mentioned, while leaning against his elbow on the table. When his friends told him that they saw Boni escaping, the table wing collapsed and Christmas Evans tumbled to the floor. They hurried to him and helped him up. After he had regained his composure, he said, 'I fell to rise again; Boni fell at Waterloo and his overthrow was eternal — he never rose again. The head of the dragon was crushed at Calvary and it will never recover from the bruise it received from the bloody heel.'[32]

The brilliance of his imagination gave rise to comparisons with Milton and Johann Paul Richter,[33] while its creativity, coupled with a copious vocabulary and flowing eloquence, earned him the title *The Golden-Mouthed Chrysostom of Wales*.[34] Some, recognising that many of his sermons were sacred poems, called him *The Poet of the Pulpit*; and others, on account of his allegorical illustrations, which he used with greater success than any other Welsh preacher, compared him with John Bunyan. 'Christmas Evans in the pulpit more nearly approached the great Dreamer than any pulpit master of whom we have heard,' writes Paxton Hood. 'Many of his sermons appear to have been long-sustained parables and pictures alive with allegorical delineation of human character.'[35]

Dr Jenkyn, in the *Homilist*, compares Christmas Evans's mind to 'a large museum' that was filled with things that were 'brilliant and ingenious'; and describes his imagination as

> ... a huge, ornate, splendid airship. He would preach always from the car of this airship and had in his possession an ample supply of the best and purest theology. Before mounting the airship he would discourse with his hearers in an ordinary way, expounding matters to them, but once inside he would untie the ropes and ascend smoothly and splendidly before their eyes, and from this position he would shoot at them from the 'ten cannons of Sinai', or, if circumstances demanded, he would pour on them showers of blossoms or a diadem of roses, all perfumed with the fragrance of the ivory palace. It is true that the airship had no helm but he was masterly enough to prevent it from losing itself in a cloud and disappearing from the congregation's view.[36]

The descriptions he unveiled before his congregations were both beautiful and terrifying — they were striking representations that came alive and were easily intelligible to his hearers. He had the power to make the Bible live and move, to reproduce Biblical events in modern garb, to embody and personify, to recount imaginary conversations between characters to illustrate his chosen theme. With 'a genius for observing people and places and characteristics', he presented them to his congregations in a lively and dramatic form. 'His best-known sermons are really dramas — comedies and tragedies ... with Christmas Evans himself as playwright and actor.'[37] His allegories and parables were of intense human interest; the figures and illustrations he described were taken from everyday life, frequently from industry or commerce; the names of his central characters, the scenery he pictured so vividly and naturally caught hold of the common people, and made them think they were part of the events that were being so graphically unveiled before them. If the text were the devilish swine of Gadara, he would make you believe you were watching the fiendish, bristling herd rushing headlong over the cliff — you would hear their piercing squeals, see the splashing waters engulf them, and stand aghast at the expressions of shock and despair on the keepers' faces.

> If he were describing the nature and requirements of the law of God, ten thousand at least of his hearers would imagine themselves at the foot of Mount Sinai, beholding the mountain enveloped in flames, and hearing the thunders rolling, that they could hardly persuade themselves they were on the top of one of the Welsh hills, hearing Christmas Evans preach. And no one but himself could instantly transport them from that grand and awful scene to the province of Judea, in the land of Canaan, to behold the Son of God in the garden of Gethsemane, weltering in his blood, and behold him on Calvary, with his hands and feet nailed to the cross, and his side pierced with a spear.
>
> His hearers could evidently see the clouds darkening, the storms gathering, and terrors setting themselves in battle array before the Son of God, in storms sufficiently heavy and terrific to sweep all the human race to eternal misery. The shaking of the earth, the rending of the rocks, the opening of the graves, the darkening of the sun, were not only spoken of, but brought before their eyes; and the voice of the centurion, 'Truly this was the Son of God,' reverberated in their ears, and melted the hearts of many.[38]

Rhys Stephen, in his sermon on the death of Christmas Evans, observes that 'He was capable of making any impression on the minds of his hearers that he thought proper.'[39]

He certainly left an impression on one old lady, a Mrs Griffith, who remembers Christmas Evans from the days of her youth, about 1825:

> I never heard him mention Paul except as 'old Saul of Tarsus'. He often mentioned the huge, old, red dragon. He pictured Christ going to the cross with the golden sack on his back... He encouraged people to look through the lattice, as the Bereans did, in order to see more clearly. He would call Calvary 'the little mountain of Golgotha'... Christmas used to hold a fellowship meeting at Capel Newydd on a working day and he would do all the speaking, almost. Many came there from different parts and the elderly sisters would return home with 'their aprons full'. A sermon, like a stocking, needed quirks, said Christmas, and a few wedges to keep it steady. After being away, he preached at Sardis and drew tears from the eyes of the hardest as he told them about his father dying and saying that he did not know what would become of Christmas, his little boy. He would speak of the golden tongs lifting the sinner from the burning fire. He used to say that a nursing shawl would fade after the mother had nursed many children but that the nursing shawl of Zion was none the worst for wear.[40]

It has rightly been said that he possessed an overflow of imagination, which meant that he often described everything and everyone in his stories down to the smallest detail. 'Thus Nicodemus was not merely a man of the Pharisees, a ruler of the Jews, but Evans gave him a flowing white beard, a wealth of snow-white hair and a purple robe; and described him making his way furtively at midnight through wind and driving rain to the upper room at Jerusalem.'[41] Occasionally his pictures lacked taste and refinement, but for boldness of creation, for deep feeling and fancy, for forcefulness of detail they were unique and unequalled by any of his contemporaries.

> When he stood up on the platform in the open air, or in the pulpit, and when his heart was thoroughly warmed, and his whole spirit transported, that some brilliant metaphor or some pregnant illustration attracted his attention, beguiled him till he had in two or three sentences exhausted it; then came another and another, still more bright and still more beauteous; and, haply among their gorgeous combinations and ever-varying flashes and coruscations, he lost himself, descending at length a worn man to the matter-of-fact before him and the people. Even then he had possessed them as well as himself, and for weeks and months to come, his text lived in their minds surrounded by the brilliant halo of his magical representations.[42]

At times his fancy, like a high-spirited racehorse, ran riot and was not disciplined with sufficient sobriety or judgement. He took his pictures too far, working out his illustrations and similes 'to rags and tatters' until they bordered on the extravagant, even the ridiculous, although the sheer realness and unction of the preacher kept the truth firmly in view.

> The wish was that [his imagination] might be less the master and more the servant; less addicted to throw out illustration and metaphor and allusion till by its very affluence it had sometimes entirely overlaid the subject in hand, instead of waiting submissively until that subject had been laid bare before the people...
>
> That which so many excellent preachers have not at all, or have so sparingly that it is painful to witness a trial of its power, he had in very excess itself. So far from hunting down a metaphor was he, that it cost him all his care and courage to save himself from being hunted down *by* metaphors; and it was easily perceived, when he got into the heart and heat of his discourse, that he would, in a few minutes, reject, or give a very summary reception to, as many of them as would make an ordinary man's fortune for life.[43]

At the meetings where he was to preach some brother would generally introduce the divine service, while he sat in the pulpit looking over his notes, which he rarely had before him in preaching. He commenced by giving out one stanza to sing, and never more than one. The singing over, he rose slowly, with a firm and majestic step, took a respectful view of the congregation and then, holding the Bible close to his eye, which seemed at times particularly prominent, he read his text loudly enough to be heard distinctly, before placing the sacred word on the pulpit. The opening to the sermon was short but striking and as he proceeded he appeared 'like a conqueror, having nothing now to do but to divide the spoil and give to every one his portion'.[44] He finished promptly, before the solemn impressions made on the minds of the congregation were lost, offered a short but powerful prayer for the Spirit of God, through the merits of Christ, to bless the work, and then concluded the service by giving out from memory, in the most ardent tones, a single verse of a hymn, usually one of William Williams's. He never sat down until the people had finished singing.[45]

He never preached down to a congregation, as if he knew more than they did, but gave them credit for observation, comprehension and intelligence; nor did he go to the opposite extreme of being overbearing or too intellectual and thus losing them in the 'intricacies of doctrine'. He studied his subject carefully and wisely, interpreted Scripture by Scripture, and brought forth in a familiar manner the deep things of God, so that even the poorest and least educated among his listeners could hear him with understanding and delight. One who had every opportunity of forming a correct opinion of his preaching, observes: 'He divided his subject systematically, and altogether naturally, so that his sermon appeared as a body complete in all its parts... It was no hardship to follow him through the different parts of his discourse, for they all had a bearing on each other... His talents were such as to enable him to cast a

ray of light upon the darkest points in the Christian system.'[46]
Whether he was in the wildest glens of Caernarfonshire before
the illiterate, or at the great Associations when men of prominence and learning were present, he preached in the same clear
and distinct manner; and, as one says, 'The sound of heaven
was heard in his sermons ... for the conversion of thousands
unto God.'[47]

Surprisingly Christmas Evans did not employ much physical
movement when preaching. At the beginning of his career he
attempted a few strokes and motions in way of actions, but
they were awkward and clumsy, and his friends advised him to
abandon them. Consequently he only used to stretch forth a
hand occasionally or point a finger or shrug his shoulders or
shake his head, gesticulations that were always easy, appropriate and forcible; and which, if not graceful, at least comple-
mented his manner of speaking.[48] His appearance in the pulpit
was fine and commanding — he stood erect, his forehead high,
countenance holy and his one eye fiery and penetrating —
'forcibly striking the mind with the idea of a great man, a man
who felt the importance of the work in which he was engaged,
and was conscious from whence aid sufficient for the work was
derived; so that in him humility and dignity were blended'.[49]
Such a bodily presence added immense interest to the scene
and increased the expectations of the congregation. He had
studied the rules of rhetoric and elocution, which helped to
repress awkwardness and to induce calmness and
self-possession.

His powerful voice, tender rather than harsh, did not possess the variation of tone common to many Welsh preachers,
nor did he vary the speed of his utterance; rather he 'spoke
right on, his words following in rapid succession one after the
other, as if there were a crowd of them at the gates pressing on
for utterance, until the flow of speech was amazing and
astounding to the hearer. Sometimes the preacher would shout

at a high pitch of voice, somewhat approaching a scream.'[50]
'He had a kind of loud squeak,' says Mrs Griffith, 'which would
ignite everything once he had warmed to his subject. He
preached on the cemetery wall in Amlwch, and out came the
loud squeak, "Arise, dry bones."'[51] Usually he spoke in a moderate tone, with strength and good volume; not melodiously,
except when his voice was elevated to a higher key than
normal, or when his feelings, moved by the inspiration of the
moment, were carried away with the heavenly gale, far beyond
himself; then his voice would be touched with the sweetest
pathos and display 'such a peculiar, indescribable twist that one
would think it was not his own voice. It was so penetrating,
electrifying and agreeable, yet so powerful, that it operated upon
the body as well as the mind. The writer positively asserts that
he has felt that peculiar sensation which he cannot describe,
while sitting under his ministry.'[52]

Once 'that peculiar sensation' was experienced at a minister's meeting. He was preaching with little or no effect in a church
that had for many years been hardened by Sandemanianism,
when all of a sudden, before he was aware of it, the Spirit of
God began to move. Tears rolled down the cheeks of his hearers and several cried out most bitterly for mercy. At this his own
heart was touched and completely melted down. He stopped
preaching for a moment and then cried out, *'Let thy kingdom
come! Let thy kingdom come!'*, repeating the petition several
times, louder and louder, 'until he gave his voice that peculiar
convoluted tone which no human being can describe or hear
unmoved. Not one of the ministers present will ever forget the
unaccountable sensation they felt.' They had never heard such
a sound before and it rang in their ears for a considerable length
of time. The rest of the congregation were deeply moved, the
effect on many beyond words, and from that time a wonderful
work of God commenced in that place.[53]

Christmas Evans has been criticised, and in many cases rightly so, for his use, or over-use, of humour in the pulpit. He had a very keen natural tendency to humour and of seeing and por-traying the ridiculous, and with it he used to send congregations into hysterics. He possessed a satirical laugh and the ability to flash suddenly before his hearers a gleam of something absurd. At times his use of humour, though enjoyed by many, bordered on indecorum in the house of God, and brought too much of the theatre into the place of worship. This tendency in our preacher, a defect certainly, was nonetheless one of the reasons for his popularity, and although he tried to keep it in check, he allowed it more rein than other Welsh preachers. John Elias never resorted to humour in the pulpit, but condemned its use, along with Henry Rees, Daniel Rowland and Robert Roberts, Clynnog. Williams of Wern only used humour in the first year of his ministry, abandoning it soon after; whereas John Jones, Talsarn, at times employed a 'noble humour' that had a 'most delicious flavour', but not as frequently or with such effect as Christmas Evans.

There were times before preaching when he experienced a kind of 'stage fright', which so gripped him that he was reluc-tant to stand before a congregation. Sometimes, if he felt he did not have the congregation's sympathy, he could not con-tinue with his sermon. Once, when he was announced to preach in his old neighbourhood of Llandysul, 'and expecting some persons to be present whom he knew would be disposed to question his deliverances, he was so unnerved by the prospect, that he could not be prevailed upon to fulfil his engagement, unless a local brother minister would go and *stand by him*'.[54] At times, as a result of these panic attacks, he utterly failed in his preaching, much to his own dismay. In Merionethshire, once, he abruptly left the pulpit and went to the nearest house. The minister of the place hurried after him, and asked what had disturbed him. In agony of spirit he cried out, 'Why did all the people look at me? For I could see nothing but eyes, brother, nothing but *eyes*, peering at me as if I were something more than man. I cannot preach today; *the people look to me and not to Christ*.' He was eventually persuaded to return, but preached most unhappily.[55]

Similarly, if he had been 'disturbed in his mind' or detained unnecessarily by the first preacher, he occasionally failed in his preaching. Such a failure was so apparent to his sensitive nature, no doubt exaggerated thereby, that it 'made him ill, and it was only an intimate friend or a dexterous brother that dared approach him very soon after'. These times he generally blamed on 'his own inaptitude in the science of religious teaching; and with occasional bitter reference to the second causes, he principally visited it upon his own spirit, and with much entreaty and supplication he sought forgiveness for the past and strength and guidance for the future'.[56] After preaching half his sermon without any unction at one of the assemblies in the South, he gave up and admitted, 'I experience this at home every month. The Lord strips me of everything and makes me nothing, so that I may know that I am Christmas.'[57]

On occasions, if he was expected to preach again in the same neighbourhood after a failure, he could not be persuaded by all the powers and authorities to re-appear. One day, after preaching very unsatisfactorily in the morning, and being announced to appear again in the afternoon, he escaped to a farm house which he well knew, 'But by the time he reached there, every man, woman and child had gone to hear Christmas Evans! And to complete his adversity, having got into the farmyard, he was there imprisoned by a fierce dog, who would not allow the preacher to escape until the family returned *after* the service was over, to witness and to help him out of his predicament!'[58]

However, these failures and weaknesses, common to every public speaker, were far outweighed by the gifts and authority he possessed, causing many to speak of him as 'The greatest preacher God has ever given to Wales'. The aim of this chapter has not been to defend that opinion, but to set before the reader 'the man in the pulpit', where Christmas Evans earned a name that, according to David Jones (Cardiff), 'was a power in itself that excelled all other names throughout the Principality'.[59]

However excellent the written sermons of Welsh ministers might appear in any language whatever, the effect is nothing, comparatively, to that produced by the living speakers. Their superiority as preachers may be ascribed, measurably, to their pathetic, warm and masterly manner of delivery, and their prepossessing appearance and compass of voice, which enable them to command the attention of thousands. Much of the original force and beauty of their sermons, therefore, are lost in translating.

J.Davis.[1]

The Rev. Christmas Evans was an eminent servant of Christ and the most eloquent preacher in the Principality for the last fifty years.

Obituary, 1838.[2]

22

Sermon Extracts

The sermons of Christmas Evans are considered in Wales 'of unrivalled excellency, especially as it regards the ingenuity and splendour of their imagery, and the appropriateness and force of their application'. They are said to have shocked congregations like electricity. In them the author displays an 'extraordinary knowledge of human nature'[3] and a captivating eye for detail, with a style and language that are strongly symbolic, and all related in dramatic terms. The thoughts are not very deep, but, as intended, they enlighten the understanding and warm the heart.

Many who heard him speak testify to the fact that they could never find him in his published sermons or works — they heard the man but not the preacher or the orator. While it is true that the written sermons lack 'the almost superhuman energy' and passion of the 'live performances', and fail to exhibit, in any efficient manner, his stunning pulpit rhetoric and the original force and beauty of his deliveries, they nevertheless, if read aright, give a glimpse of the power and gifts he possessed, and portray his burning conviction and unshakeable faith in God's word.

410   *Christmas Evans*

The Fall and Recovery of Man

One of the greatest sermons preached by Christmas Evans was
The Fall and Recovery of Man, nicknamed by some, either
because of its subject matter or because it was first delivered in
a cemetery, *The Graveyard Sermon*.[4] It is probably correct to
assign its origin to the preacher's early years in Anglesey and to
say that it was preached by him on several occasions before it
became well known. It was certainly often repeated by him in
the course of his itinerancy, with considerable variation. It is
regarded by many as Christmas Evans's finest sermon. Robert
Hall, after its translation into English, pronounced it to be one
of the best sustained allegories in the language. It secured a
very wide circulation, with a large reading public as far away as
America, where it was reprinted several times. It is included in
the seven volume work *The World's Great Sermons* published
in 1909, the only sermon by a Welsh preacher, and is listed as
discourse number twenty-seven in the book *The Great Sermons
of the Great Preachers*, standing alongside sermons by such
men as Jonathan Edwards, Martin Luther, John Knox, George
Whitefield, John Wesley and John Bunyan.

Part of the sermon was translated into English by Dr Raffles
of Liverpool, who had been given the substance of it by Samuel
Breeze during one of his visits to Bristol, and has been used
down the years as *A Specimen of Welsh Preaching*. One morning at breakfast Dr Raffles read to Christmas Evans his own
version of the sermon and then exclaimed, 'Did you actually
say all *that*?' 'Oh yes,' replied Christmas Evans, 'I did say all
that, but I could never have put it into such English.'[5] Below is
one of the early translations, which has been 'everywhere justly
admired as one of the finest productions of sanctified genius';
but first we relate the story behind its introduction into the English language:

'At a meeting of ministers in Bristol, the Rev. Mr — invited several of his brethren to sup with him. Among them was the minister officiating at the Welsh meeting-house in that city. He was an entire stranger to all the company, and silently attentive to the general conversation of his brethren. The subject on which they were discoursing was the different strains of public preaching. When several had given their opinion, and had mentioned some individuals as good preachers, and such as were models as to style of composition, &c. Mr — turned to the Welsh stranger, and solicited his opinion. He said he felt it a privilege to be silent, when such men were discoursing, but that he felt it a duty to comply with his request. "But," said he, "if I must give my opinion, I should say that you have no good preachers in England. A Welshman would set fire to the world while you were lighting your match."'

'The whole company requested the good man to give them some specimen of the style and manner of preaching in Wales. "Specimen," said he, "I cannot give you. If John Elias were here, he would give you a specimen INDEED. I cannot do justice to the Welsh language! Your poor, meagre language would spoil it; it is not capable of expressing those ideas which a Welshman can conceive; I cannot give you a specimen in English without spoiling it." The interest of the company was increased, and nothing would do but something of a specimen. "Well," said the Welshman, "if you must have a piece, I must try, but I don't know what to give you — I recollect a piece of Christmas Evans. He was preaching on the depravity of man by sin — of his recovery by the death of Christ, and he said:

> Brethren, if I were to represent to you, in a figure, the condition of man as a sinner, and the means of recovery by the cross of Jesus Christ, I should represent it something in this way: Suppose a large graveyard, surrounded by a high wall, with only one entrance, which is by a large iron gate, which is fast bolted. Within these walls are thousands and tens of thousands of human beings, of all ages and classes, by one

epidemic disease bending to the grave. The grave yawns to swallow them, and they must all die. There is no balm to relieve them, no physician there. They must perish. This is the condition of man as a sinner. All have sinned, and the soul that sinneth shall die. While man was in this deplorable state, Mercy came down and stood at the gate, looked at the scene and wept over it, exclaiming, 'Oh that I might enter! I would bind up their wounds; I would relieve their sorrows; I would save their souls!'

While Mercy stood weeping at the gate, an embassy of angels, commissioned from the court of heaven to some other world, paused at the sight, and heaven forgave that pause. Seeing Mercy standing there, they cried, 'Mercy, Mercy, can you not enter? Can you look upon that scene and not pity? Can you pity and not relieve?'

Mercy replied, 'I can see;' and in her tears she added, 'I can pity, but I cannot relieve.'

'Why can you not enter?' inquired the heavenly host.

'Oh,' said Mercy, 'Justice has barred the gate against me, and I cannot, must not, unbar it.'

At this moment Justice himself appeared, as it were to watch the gate. The angels inquired of him, 'Why will you not suffer Mercy to enter?'

Justice replied, 'My law is broken and it must be honoured! Die *they*, or Jesus must!'

At this there appeared a form among the angelic band like unto the Son of God, who, addressing himself to Justice, said, 'What are thy demands?'

Justice replied, 'My terms are stern and rigid; I must have sickness for their health. I must have ignominy for their honour. I must have death for their life. *Without the shedding of blood there is no remission.*'

'Justice,' said the Son of God, 'I accept thy terms. On me be this wrong. Let Mercy enter, and stay the carnival of death.'

'When,' said Justice, 'will you perform this promise?'

Jesus replied, 'Four thousand years hence, upon the hill of Calvary, without the gates of Jerusalem, I will perform it in my own person.'

The deed was prepared and signed in the presence of the angels of God. Justice was satisfied, the gate was opened and Mercy entered, preaching salvation in the name of Jesus. The deed was committed to the patriarchs, by them to the kings of Israel and the prophets — by them it was preserved until Daniel's seventy weeks were accomplished. Then, at the appointed time, Justice appeared on the hill of Calvary, and Mercy presented to him the important deed. 'Where,' said Justice, 'is the Son of God?'

'Behold him,' answered Mercy, 'at the foot of the hill, bearing his cross.' And then she departed and stood aloof at the hour of trial. Jesus ascended the hill, while in his own train followed his weeping church.

Justice immediately presented him with the deed, saying, 'This is the day when this bond is to be executed.'

When he received it, did he tear it in pieces, and give it to the winds of heaven? No! He nailed it to his cross, exclaiming, 'It is finished.' Justice called on holy fire to come down and consume the sacrifice. Holy fire descended. It swallowed up his humanity, but when it touched his deity it expired! And there was darkness over the whole heavens and an earthquake shook the mountain; but the heavenly host broke forth in rapturous song, 'Glory to God in the highest, on earth peace and good will to men.'

'This,' said the Welshman, 'this is but a specimen of Christmas Evans.'[6]

The Triumph of Calvary

The following extract is taken from a sermon Christmas Evans preached on Isaiah 63:1-6 and is another example of the celebrated *Specimens of Welsh Preaching*:

After the prophets of ancient times had long gazed through the mists of futurity at the suffering of Christ and the glory that should follow, a company of them were gathered together on the summit of Calvary. They saw a host of enemies ascending the hill arrayed for battle and most terrific in their aspect. In the middle of the line was the Law of

God, fiery and exceeding broad and working wrath. On the right wing was Beelzebub with his troops of infernals; and on the left Caiaphas and his Jewish priests, and Pilate with his Roman soldiers. The rear was brought up by Death, the last enemy. When the holy seers had espied this army, and perceived that it was drawing nigh, they started back and prepared for flight. As they looked around, they saw the Son of God advancing with intrepid step, having his face fixed on the hostile band. 'Seest thou the danger that is before thee,' said one of the men of God.

'I will tread them in mine anger,' he replied, 'and trample them in my fury.'

'Who art thou?' said the prophet.

He answered, 'I that speak in righteousness, mighty to save.'

'Wilt thou venture to the battle alone?' asked the seer.

The Son of God replied, 'I looked and there was none to help, and I wondered there was none to uphold; therefore mine own arm shall bring salvation unto me, and my fury it shall uphold me.'

'At what point wilt thou commence thy attack?' inquired the anxious prophet.

'I will first meet the Law,' he replied, 'and pass under its curse; for lo! I come to do thy will, O God. When I shall have succeeded at the centre of the line, the colours will turn in my favour.'

So saying he moved forward. Instantly the thunderings of Sinai were heard, and the whole band of prophets quaked with terror. But he advanced undaunted amidst the gleaming lightnings.

For a moment he was concealed from view, and the banner of wrath waved above in triumph. Suddenly the scene was changed. A stream of blood poured forth from his wounded side, and put out all the fires of Sinai. The flag of peace was now seen unfurled, and consternation filled the ranks of his foes. He then crushed, with his bruised heel, the Old Serpent's head, and put all the infernal powers to flight. With his iron rod he dashed to pieces the enemies on the left wing, like a potter's vessel.

Death still remained, who thought himself invincible, having hitherto triumphed over all. He came forward, brandishing his sting, which he had whetted on Sinai's tables of stone. He darted it at the conqueror, but it turned down and hung like the flexible lash of a whip. Dismayed, he retreated to the grave, his palace, into which the conqueror pursued. In a dark corner of his den, he sat on his throne of mouldering skulls, and called upon the worms, his hitherto faithful allies, to aid him in the conflict, but they replied, 'His flesh shall see no corruption.' The sceptre fell from his hand. The conqueror seized him, bound him, and condemned him to the lake of fire; and then rose from the grave, followed by a band of released captives, who came forth after his resurrection to be witnesses of the victory he had won.[7]

Behold I Stand at the Door and Knock

Those who had often heard Christmas Evans said he never preached more powerfully than the evening he spoke from Revelation 3:20. 'The thousands present were fairly carried away by the rich imagination and fervid eloquence of the greatest preacher that God has ever given to Wales.' After he had spoken for three quarters of an hour, he shut his Bible and said:

Oh, my dear brethren, why will you pay no heed to your best Friend? Why will you let Him stand knocking, night and day, in all weathers, and never open the door to Him? If the horse-dealer or cattle-drover came you would run to open the door to him, and set meat and drink before him, because you would expect to make some money by his visit. But when the Lord Jesus stands knocking at the door of your heart, bringing to you the everlasting wealth, which he gives without money and without price, you are deaf and blind; you are so busy that you cannot attend. Markets and fairs, pleasures and profits occupy you; you have neither time nor inclination for such as He. Let Him knock! Let Him stand without, with the door shut in His face, what matters it to you? Yet it does matter to you.

Oh, my brethren! I will relate to you a familiar parable, and so tell you how it is with some of you, and, alas! how it will be in the end. I will tell you what happened in a Welsh village, I need not say where. I was passing through that village in early spring, and saw before me a beautiful house. The farmer had just brought his load of lime into the yard; his horses were sleek and all appeared prosperous about him. He went in, closed the door, and sat down to his dinner. As I came up a stranger stood knocking at the door. There was a friendly look in his face that made me say as I passed, 'The master's at home; they won't keep you waiting.'

Not long after I was again on that road, and as soon as I came in sight of the house I saw the same stranger knocking. At this I wondered, and as I came near I saw that he stood as one who had knocked long. As he knocked he listened. Said I, 'The farmer is busying making up his books, or counting his money, or eating and drinking. Knock louder, Sir, and he will hear you. But,' I added, 'you have great patience, Sir, for you have been knocking a long time. If I were you, I would leave him tonight and come back tomorrow.'

'He is in danger and I must warn him,' replied he; and knocked louder than ever.

Sometime afterwards I went that way again; there the man still stood, knocking, knocking, knocking! 'Well, Sir,' said I, 'your perseverance is the most remarkable I have ever seen! How long do you mean to stop?'

'Till I can make him hear, I hope,' was his answer; and he knocked again.

Said I, 'He wants for no good thing. He has a fine farm, flocks and herds, stack-yards and barns.'

'Yes,' he replied, 'for the Lord is kind to the unthankful and to the evil.'

Then he knocked again, and I went on my way, wondering at the goodness and patience of that mysterious stranger.

Again I visited that district. It was December. The weather was very cold. There was an east wind blowing, and the snow fell thickly. It was getting dark, too, and the pleasantest place, as you all know, at such a time, is the fireside. As I passed by the farm-house I saw the candle-light shining through the windows, and the smoke of a good fire coming out of the chimney. But there was the man still outside — knocking, knocking! And as I looked at him I saw that his hands and feet were bare and bleeding, and his visage as that of one marred with sorrow — 'so marred more than any man, and his form more than the sons of men'. My heart was very sad for him, and I said, 'Sir, you had better not stand any longer at that hard man's door. Let me advise you to go over the way to that poor widow's door. She has many children, and she works for her daily bread; but she is hospitable and will make you welcome.'

'I know her,' he said. 'I often converse with her; her door is ever open to me, for the Lord is the husband of the widow, and the father of the fatherless.'

'Then go,' I replied, 'to the blacksmith's yonder. I see the cheerful blaze in his smithy; he works early and late. His wife is a kind-hearted woman. They will treat you like a prince.'

He answered solemnly, '*I am not come to call the righteous, but sinners to repentance.*'

At that moment the door opened, the farmer came out cursing and swearing, carrying a cudgel in his hand, with which he smote him, and then angrily shut the door in his face. This excited my anger fiercely. I was full of indignation to think that a Welshman should treat a stranger in that fashion. I was ready to burst open the door and maltreat him in return. But the patient stranger laid his hand upon my arm, and said, 'Blessed are the meek; for they shall inherit the earth.'

'Sir,' I exclaimed, 'your patience and your long-suffering are wonderful; they are beyond my comprehension.'

He then looked at me tenderly — I shall never forget that look! and said, 'The Lord is long-suffering, full of compassion, slow to anger, not willing that any should perish, but that all should come to repentance.' And again he knocked as he spoke.

It was dark; the smithy was shut, and they were closing the inn; having failed to get him away from the door I at length sought shelter for the night, wondering more and more at the patience and pity of the man. In the village inn I learned from the landlord the character of the farmer, and, late as it was, I went back to the patient stranger and said, 'Sir, come away; he is not worth all this trouble. He is a hard, cruel, wicked man. He has robbed the fatherless, he has defamed his friend, he has built his house in iniquity. Come away, Sir. Make yourself comfortable with us by the warm fireside. This man is not worth saving.' With that he spread his bleeding palms before me, and showed me his bleeding feet and his side which had been pierced; and I beheld it was the Lord Jesus.

'Smite him, Lord!' I cried in my indignation; 'then perhaps he will hear thee.'

'Of a truth he *shall* hear me. In the day of judgment he shall hear me when I say, "Depart from me, thou worker of iniquity into everlasting darkness, prepared for the devil and his angels."' After these words he vanished, and I saw Him no more. The wind blew, the snow and sleet fell, and I went back to the inn.

'There has been much knocking in the depth of the night at my chamber door, Christmas,' cried my landlord. 'Get up! Get up! You are wanted by a neighbour who is at the point of death! It is that farmer of whom we spoke last evening.'

Away I hurried along the road to the end of the village, to the farm-house where the stranger had been knocking. But as I got near I heard the voice of the farmer's agony, 'Oh, Lord Jesus, save me! Oh, Lord Jesus, have mercy upon me! Give me but a day — but an hour — for repentance! Oh, Lord, save me!'

His wife was wringing her hands, his children were paralysed with fear. 'Pray! Pray for me!' he cried. 'Oh, Christmas, cry to God for *me*! He will hear *you*; *me* He will not hear!' I knelt to pray; but it was too late — He was gone — *gone to his own place!*[8]

The Hind of the Morning and the Chariot of Mercy

Two extracts follow from a sermon Christmas Evans preached at Caerphilly and in the surrounding neighbourhood during the excitement that accompanied his settlement there. He delivered it on many occasions for several weeks and months, during which time he wrote it out. The text is: 'Whom the heaven must receive until the times of restitution of all things.' (Acts 3:21).

> Behold the *Hind of the Morning* on that dreadful mountain! It is the place of skulls, where Death holds his carnival in companionship with worms, and hell laughs in the face of heaven. Dark storms are gathering there — convolving clouds, charged with no common wrath. Terrors set themselves in battle array before the Son of God; and tempests burst upon him which might sweep all mankind in a moment to eternal ruin. Hark! Hear ye not the subterranean thunder? Feel ye not the tremor of the mountain? It is the shock of Satan's artillery, playing upon the Captain of our salvation. It is the explosion of the magazine of vengeance. Lo, the earth is quaking, the rocks are rending, the graves are opening, the dead are rising, and all nature stands aghast at the conflict of divine mercy with the powers of darkness. One dread convulsion more, one cry of desperate agony, and Jesus dies — an arrow has entered into his heart. Now leap the lions, roaring, upon the prey; and the bulls of Bashan are bellowing; and the dogs of perdition are barking; and the unicorns toss their horns on high; and the devil, dancing with exultant joy, clanks his iron chains and thrusts up his fettered hands in defiance towards the face of Jehovah![9]

Christ might have ridden in a chariot of fire all the way from Bethlehem to Calvary; but he preferred riding in a chariot of mercy, whose lining was crimson and whose ornament the malefactor's cross. How rapidly rolled his wheels over the hills and the plains of Palestine, gathering up everywhere the children of affliction, and scattering blessings like the beams of the morning!...

Now we see the chariot surrounded with enemies — Herod, Pilate and Caiaphas, and the Roman soldiers, and the poplace of Jerusalem, and thousands of Jews who have come up to keep the Passover, led by Judas and the devil. See how they rage and curse, as if they would tear him from his chariot of mercy! But Jesus maintains his seat and holds fast the reins, and drives right on through the angry crowd, without shooting an arrow or lifting a spear upon his foes. For in that chariot the King must ride to Calvary — Calvary must be consecrated to mercy for ever. He sees the cross planted upon the brow of the hill and hastens forward to embrace it. No sacrifice shall be offered to Justice this day, but the one sacrifice which reconciles heaven and earth. None of those children of Belial shall suffer today. The bribed witnesses and clamorous murderers shall be spared — the smiters, the scourgers, the spitters, the thorn-plaiters, the nail-drivers, the head-shakers — for Jesus pleads on their behalf: 'Father, forgive them! they know not what they do. They are ignorant of thy grace and truth. They are not aware of whom they are crucifying. Oh, spare them! Let Death know that he shall have enough to do with me today! Let him open all his batteries upon me! My bosom is bare to the stroke. I will gather all the lances of hell in my heart!'

Still the chariot rushes on, and 'fiery darts' are thick and fast, like a shower of meteors, on Messiah's head, till he is covered with wounds and the blood flows down his garments and leaves a crimson track behind him. As he passes, he casts at the dying malefactor a glance of benignity, and throws him a passport into Paradise, written with his own blood; stretches forth his sceptre, and touches the prison-door of death, and many of the prisoners came forth, and the tyrant shall never regain his dominion over them; rides triumphant over thrones and principalities and crushes beneath his wheels the last enemy himself, and leaves the memorial of his march engraven on the rocks of Golgotha![10]

Searching for the Christ Child

Herod ordered the wise men to go and search diligently for the young child. The Magi immediately complied, according to the king's instructions:

I see them approaching some village, and when they came to the gate they inquired, 'Do you know anything of the young child?'

The gateman came to the door; and, supposing them to have asked the amount of the toll, said, 'O, three halfpence an ass is to pay.'

'We do not ask what is to pay,' replied they, 'but do you know anything of the young child?'

'No; I know nothing in the world,' answered he; 'but there is a blacksmith's shop a little further on; inquire there, and you will be very likely to obtain some intelligence concerning the object of your inquiry.'

The wise men proceeded on as directed and when they came to the blacksmith's shop, they asked, 'Do you know anything of the young child?'

A harsh voice answered, 'There is no such thing possible for you as having the asses shod now; you shall in two hours hence.'

'We do not ask you to shoe the asses,' said they, 'but inquire for the young child, if you know anything of him?'

'Nothing in the world,' said the blacksmith, 'but inquire at the tavern that is on your road and probably you may hear something of him there.'

On they went and stood opposite the door of the tavern and cried, 'Do you know anything of the young child?'

The landlord, thinking they had called for the porter, bid the servant to attend, saying, 'Go, girl; go with a quart of porter to the strangers.'

'We do not ask for either porter or ale,' said the wise men, 'but something about the young child that is born.'

'I know nothing in the world of him,' said the landlord, 'but turn to the shop on the left hand; the shopkeeper reads all the papers and you will be likely to hear something respecting him there.'

They proceeded accordingly towards the shop and repeated their inquiry, 'Do you know anything of the young child here?'

The shopkeeper said to his apprentice, 'Reach half a quarter of tobacco to the strangers.'

'We do not ask for tobacco,' said the wise men, 'but some intelligence of the young child we require.'

'I do not know anything of him,' replied the shopkeeper, 'but there is an old Rabbi living in the upper end of the village; call on him and very probably he will give you every information you desire respecting the object of your search.'

They immediately directed their course towards the house of the Rabbi; and having reached it, they knocked at the door and being admitted into his presence, they asked him if he knew anything of the young child. 'Come in,' said he, and when they had entered and were seated, the Rabbi referred to his books and chronicles and said he to the wise men, 'There is something wonderful about to take place; some remarkable person has been or is to be born; but the best thing for you is to go down yonder street, and there is living there, by the river side, a son of an old priest; you will be sure to know all of him.'

Having bid the old Rabbi a respectful farewell, on they went; and having reached the river's side, they inquired of the bystanders for the son of the old priest. Immediately he was pointed out to them. There was a 'raiment of camel's hair about him and a leathern girdle about his loins'. They asked him if he knew something of the young child. 'Yes,' said he, 'there he is: behold the Lamb of God, that taketh away the sin of the world! Here he is; he will bruise the dragon's head and will bring in everlasting righteousness to everyone that believeth in his name.'[11]

Satan Walking in Dry Places

Christmas Evans's description of Satan walking 'about like a roaring lion, seeking whom he may devour', has been considered inimitable. The sermon from which it is taken was originally preached by him early in his Anglesey ministry and with few alterations he continued to preach it until his death. 'It carried revival on its wings into many villages throughout the Principality and under its pleading many conversions occurred.'[12]

I see the wicked spirit like a winged dragon, having a long tail, drawing circles and flying in the air, in search of a dwelling place. Having cast his fiery looks upon a certain neighbourhood, he spied a young man in the bloom of his days and in the strength of his powers, sitting on the box of his cart, going for lime. 'There he is,' said the old hellish dragon; 'his veins are full of blood and his bones are full of marrow; I will cast the sparks into his bosom and will set all his lusts on fire; I will lead him on from bad to worse until he commits every sin. I will make him a murderer and will plunge his soul for ever beneath the boiling billows of the great fiery furnace.' With this I see him descending in all the vehemence of his character, but when close by the lad, the dragon heard him sing,

> When on the cross the Saviour hung,
> The midday sank in midnight gloom;
> When guilty sinners were redeemed,
> The midnight burst in midday bloom.

Upon which the dragon cried out, 'This place is too dry for me,' and away he flew.

I see him again, a second time, hovering in the air and seeking for a resting place. In a flowery meadow, by a river of clear water, he saw a maiden, eighteen years of age, among the kine, picking up some beautiful flowers here and there. 'Behold her,' said Apollyon, full of destruction and carnage; 'I will poison her mind and lead her astray from the paths of the Almighty enemy; I will make her a harlot and will ultimately cast her over the precipice until she sinks for ever in the furnace of divine wrath.' He hastened down; and, approaching the maiden, found her singing the following stanzas, in a heavenly, transporting frame of mind, and with a voice that might almost melt the rocks:

> Unto the righteous will arrive,
> A day of rest serene,
> When to their joy they see the Lord,
> Without a veil between.

> Then from the grave I shall arise,
> And take my joyful stand,
> Among the saints who dwell on high,
> Received at God's right hand.

'This place is too dry for me,' says the dragon, and off he flew.

From the meadow the dragon ascended like a great balloon, with renewed rage, blowing smoke and fire from his mouth and threatening damnation to all creation. 'I will have a place to rest and dwell in,' said Apollyon, 'in spite of the purpose, covenant and grace of God!' With this he espied an aged woman, sitting at the door of her cottage and spinning on her little wheel. 'Ah, she is ripe for destruction,' said the dragon; 'I will give her a taste of the burning hearths of damnation and will cast her into the lake that burneth with fire and brimstone.' With this he decended on the eaves of the cottage and heard the old woman, with a trembling voice, but with some heavenly feelings, repeat the following beautiful passage: 'For the mountains shall depart and the hills be removed, but my kindness shall not depart from thee, neither shall the covenant of my peace be removed, saith the Lord that hath mercy on thee!' 'This place is too dry for me,' said the dragon, and he is off again.

It might have been thought that all these disappointments would discourage him from prosecuting his infernal designs farther; but not so. He was determined, if possible, to find a dwelling place. For this purpose he arose again to mark some spot where he might lodge and find a welcome. He saw in a small village a neat and decent house of refreshment. 'There,' said he, 'will I dwell and lead to bondage every one that shall cross the threshold, and make them fast in eternal fetters.' He flew down like lightning, entered the house and walked into the parlour; but there he found a company of ministers of the New Testament, returning from an Association, who were talking about the victory of Calvary, and exchanging appointments with each other. The wicked spirit could not stay within the sound of their voices, but retreated with hasty steps, muttering and growling as he went along, 'This place is too dry for me, I will return to my house from which I came.'[13]

Reconciliation and Forgiveness for the Prodigal

The extract below is taken from *The Allegories of Christmas Evans*:

> Shoni sulked at his wages and turned his back on his master's house, after having served there many years. After rambling from place to place, Shoni decided to go to town for a stroll, to see what was going on there. When walking along the street who should meet Shoni unexpectedly but his old master. When Shoni saw him he became rather shy and his answers were curt, and he showed plainly that he was in no humour to chat with him at any length.
>
> 'Well, well, Shoni,' said the master, 'this won't do. If we are to part, let us part friends. Come along with me.'
>
> Away went the master and Shoni towards Cross Street, and they went into the sign of the 'Lion of the Tribe of Judah', and having sat down, the master called for a couple of glasses of wine from the winepress of Eschol, which had been pressed in the winepress of Calvary. They were served with the very best quality, and before Shoni had drunk very much of it, he was on his feet, the tears like lustrous pearls trickling down his cheeks, and his right hand extended towards his master, exclaiming loudly, 'Master! Friends from this time out, friends until the grave, dear Master. Friends to the great eternity. Home with you, dear Master. From this time out I'll spend my life in your service — forevermore, forevermore! Is my sin forgiven, dear Master?'
>
> 'Yes, dear Shoni; come back, come back. *And their sins and iniquities he will remember no more*. Welcome, welcome home. Your old living awaits you still!'[14]

Parable of the High-Minded Bone

There arose a fierce contention in the human body. Every member sought another place than the one it found itself in or was fitted for. After much controversy, it was agreed to refer the whole matter to a man whose name was Solomon

Wise-in-his-own-conceit. He was to arrange and adjust the whole business and to place every bone in its proper position. He received the appointment gladly, and was filled with joy and confidence. He commenced with finding a place for himself. His proper post was the heel, but where do you think he found it? He must needs be the golden vessel in which the brains are deposited.

Natural consequences followed. The coarse heel bone was not of the right quality, or of the suitable dimensions to contain the brains, nor could the vessel intended for that purpose form a useful or comely part of the foot. Disorder ensued in foot, head, face, legs and arms. By the time Solomon Wise-in-his-own-conceit had reconstructed the body, it could neither walk, nor speak, nor smell, nor hear, nor see. The body was, moreover, filled with intolerable agony and could find no rest, every bone crying for restoration to its own place, that is to say, everyone but the heel bone; that was mightily pleased to be in the head and to have the custody of the brains.

Sin has introduced similar disorders amongst men and even amongst professors of religion and into many congregations. In the church of Christ there is a fitting place for every member of Christ and every gift of his grace, in order to their cooperation, so that they cannot work apart nor occupy each other's places.[15]

The Smiting of the Rock

The text is 1 Corinthians 10:4: 'For they drank of that spiritual rock that followed them, and that rock was Christ':

Who can describe the distress throughout the camp; and the appearance of the people, when they were invited to approach a flinty rock, instead of a fountain or a stream to quench their thirst? What angry countenances were there, what bitter censures, and ungrateful murmurings, as Moses went up to the rock, with nothing in his hand but a rod!

'Where is he going,' said they, 'with that dry stick? What

is he going to do on that rock? Does he mean to make fools of us all? Is it not enough that he has brought us into this wilderness to die of thirst? Will he mock us now by pretending to seek water in these sands, or open fountains in the solid granite?'

But see! He lifts the rod; he smites the rock; and lo, it bursts into a fountain; and twelve crystal streams roll down before the people! Who can conceive the sudden transport? Hear the shout of joy ringing through the camp, and rolling back in tumultuous echoes from the crags and cliffs of Horeb!

'Water! Water! A miracle! A miracle! Glory to the God of Israel! Glory to his servant Moses!' It was a resurrection day to Israel, the morning light bursting upon the shadow of death. New life and joy are seen throughout the camp. The maidens are running with cups and pitchers to the rock. They fill and drink; then fill again, and haste away to their respective tents, with water for the sick, the aged, and the little ones, joyfully exclaiming, 'Drink, father! Drink, mother! Drink, children! Drink, all of you! Drink abundantly! Plenty of water now! Rivers flowing from the rock!' Now the oxen are coming, the asses, the camels, the sheep, and the goats — coming in crowds to quench their thirst, and plunging into the streams before them. And the feathered tribes are coming, the turtle-dove, the pigeon, the swallow, the sparrow, the robin, and the wren; while the croaking raven and fierce-eyed eagle, scenting the water from afar, mingle with them around the rock.

Brethren, this is but a faint emblem of the joy of the church in drinking the waters that descend from Calvary, the streams that gladden the city of our God.[16]

The Raising of Lazarus

Here Christmas Evans perceives 'four strong men on their journey towards Lazarus's grave for the purpose of raising him to life':

One of these men, who was eminent for his piety, said, 'I will descend into the grave and will take with me a bowl of the salt of duties, and will rub him well with the idea that he can do whatever he chooses.' Having said this, he entered the grave and commenced his rubbing process.

I watched his operations at a distance and after a while inquired, 'Well, are there any symptoms of life there? Does he arise, does he breathe, my brother?'

'No such thing,' replied he, 'he is still quiet and I cannot salt him to will it — and besides this, his smell is rather heavy.'

'Well,' said the second, 'come you out; I was afraid that your means would not answer the purpose; let me enter the grave in your stead.' The second entered, carrying in his hand a whip of the scorpions of threatening; and, said he, 'I will make him feel.' He directed his scorpion and fiery ministry at the dead corpse; but in vain, and I heard him crying out, 'All is unsuccessful; dead he is after all.'

Said the third, 'Make room for me to enter and I will see if I cannot bring him to life.' He entered the grave and took with him a musical pipe; it was melodious as the song of love and the sweetest singing; but there was no dancing in the grave.

The fourth said, 'Means of themselves can effect nothing, but I will go for Jesus, who is the resurrection and the life.' Immediately he left to seek Christ and speedily returned, accompanied by the Saviour.

And when the Lord came, he stood in the door of the sepulchre and cried out, 'Lazarus, come forth!' and the dead body was instantaneously instinct with life.

Let our confidence be in the voice of the Son of God. And let us turn our faces toward the wind and say, 'O breath, come from the four winds and breathe upon these slain that they may live!'[17]

A man's private letters often let you into the secrets of the heart.

C.H.Spurgeon.[1]

Letters, unlike biographies, are likely to include the ordinary, but in some respects that is to our advantage, for as Pascal says, 'Man's virtue must not be judged by great occasions, but by his ordinary life.'

Iain H.Murray.[2]

23
Letters

A Short Apology to an Unidentified Recipient

The first letter is reproduced without adjustment or correction.

Llangefni, 27 April, 1813

Sir

I am very sorry that I was from home when you have sent to me to get signatures to the Petition to Parliament for the protection of the Baptist Mifsion in India. I have had but one Lords day to make known unto the people the nature of the Businefs. If I had time enough I might got one thousand signatures. We are not acquainted of any way of sending the Petition up to London but to you.

Sir your Humble Servant

Christmas Evans[3]

A Letter on Infant Baptism to William Williams

On 28 October, 1817, Christmas Evans wrote a letter on infant baptism to William Williams of Grafton Street, London, who was often solicited by many of his brethren in the ministry, as

well as those among whom he laboured, to print the letter —
and 'Being unwilling that the Church of Christ should lose anything that came from the pen of so great a champion in Israel,
— I now comply with their request. And may the King in Zion
bless what is here stated, for his own glory, and that the Pope's
idol of Infant Baptism may fall, as Dagon did, before the Ark of
God! So prays yours to serve in the gospel of Christ, W. W.,
May 3, 1822.' The following are extracts:

Dear Brother Williams,
    My delay in not writing to you before this has not been
owing to any want of love, regard, or attachment towards
you, but to my creeping snail-like nature after my Master's
business, and some weak struggling in his great cause. The
visit you paid us was the occasion of much joy and pleasure; and we all observed, among many good qualities attached to you, one particularly fine, viz. your paying more
regard to please Jesus Christ than any of those that oppose
him in his ordinance...
    Brother, what a deep matter of regret it is that Satan is
honoured among Christians, being attired in the mantle of
infant sprinkling; and he is worshipped in that garb, alas!
among Christians, instead of Father, Son and Holy Ghost,
whose authority is to be honoured and submitted unto in
gospel baptism! 'Tis no wonder that Dr Gill termed it the
ground-work and pillar of popery. It changes the face of the
Christian church, by fixing the list of membership and Christianity in bowl sprinkling and not in regeneration, new creation, personal religion, and a creditable profession of love to
Jesus: thus it builds the wall of the Christian church with
untempered mortar...
    Dear brother, baptism, according to Christ's commission,
is a third thing in the religion of the New Testament; it does
not appear there but upon the third stage, according to the
practice of the apostles as well as the commission: but
paedo-baptism is the first thing in religion. The bowl appears
first on the stage, before the atonement and the divine influence. The sprinkling bowl achieves great things without the

aid of the gospel or the Spirit. It will cast out the devil from the innocent mortal, throw the babe over the walls of the covenant and the Christian church (at least) with its own hand. Thus it pretends to snatch thousands from the grasp of the wicked one, and by the power of its own arm, with a drop of water, throws them into the kingdom of heaven.

What a daring error this must be that pretends to such mighty things! When these high pretensions are realized in the minds of parents, it is not to be wondered at that they are so eager to throw their dear little offspring into the anti-Christian basket, to swing them to the skirts of paradise; for they can do all this without any exercise of mind upon God and the spiritual world. It is not surprising at all that they choose this expedient, rather than committing them by faith and prayer to the Saviour; laying them down on the carpet of divine purpose and sovereign grace, at his feet; wrapping them up in the linen of his promises, which are given to Christian parents to tranquillize their thoughts concerning their children, and to draw out their hearts in prayer for them; for they announce the purpose of the Saviour to pour the spirit of the new birth upon their seed, and to call their offspring unto himself, to succeed their parents as subjects of divine approbation and partakers of his favour and likeness...

It deserves our minutest attention, that in the whole body of the history of the administration of [gospel] baptism, during the time of the superintendence of the inspired ministers until the beginning of the third century, the celebration of it is always in conjunction with some energy and power from the spiritual world, regenerating sinners unto the faith, love and obedience of the gospel...

I must draw to a close, dear brother. I greet your brethren in Grafton Street, although I have never seen them. I wish them to be moved by the great impulse of the love of Jesus. May you and I be directed more and more unto the love of God, and unto the patient waiting of Christ, with our loins girded, our candles lighted, and our watch awakened, still waiting the noise of his feet. I hope to see you again in Anglesey, and indeed in London also. May we be blessed with more of the spirit of Jesus Christ to mortify us unto self-love, self-righteousness, and self-pleasure, and quicken us unto Christ as the very end of life...

May the Lord's blessing descend upon your wife, children and church... I earnestly beg a remembrance in your prayers.

Your unworthy but affectionate brother,

C. E.
Llangefni, Anglesey,
Oct.28, 1817.[4]

A Letter in Answer to the Question: Can a Man Come to Christ if he Will?

The following undated letter respecting the role of the will and understanding in salvation was published in a Welsh Magazine. Part of it is reproduced here:

Man's inability to repent of his sins, believe the gospel, and love the Lord his God with all his heart, is highly criminal, *because he will not.* How can a man love any object against his will? How can a man love the object which he really hates?

Let the case be represented in the following manner: John the Jacobin was a dear lover of equality, and hated all laws and every kind of government. One day he formed a plan to blow up the royal palace and to destroy the queen, the best and most amiable young lady that ever sat upon a throne or wore a crown; but he was caught in the very act, was committed to prison, and kept there for a long time, until he almost starved to death. He was almost naked and very filthy; he was poor and wounded, sick and sore.

While he was in this deplorable condition, a messenger from the queen requested him to get up, walk out and come to the royal palace without delay. He told him the danger of procrastination; that in a very short time he would be tried for his rebellion, would undoubtedly be found guilty, and must die the death if he did not give the queen his heart, love her sincerely, and be united to her in marriage. Moreover, said he, whatever you do, don't play the hypocrite; the queen does not want you to marry her, except you love her.

'Marry the queen!' said John. 'I don't believe a word of it. There is no reality in your message, sir; it is too good to be true. Love the queen! How can I, sir? No, sir! I hate her. I hate her government. I hate the law that forbids me to do my own will.'

The day of trial soon arrived. The prisoner appeared at the bar. He had a most impartial trial and every indulgence granted him that his case required. He was found guilty of high treason and the sentence of condemnation was pronounced upon him. He that believeth not is condemned already. He was removed from court to prison to await the hour of execution. He confessed to the jailer that justice was done to him according to the law, 'but I don't like the law,' said John. 'I hate it now as much as ever.'

At this juncture another messenger from the queen appeared before him, informing him that her majesty loved him so ardently and sincerely that she had suffered the greatest degradation, shame and pain on his account; that she had actually suffered the punishment due to him — had rendered to the government and law of the realm that honour and satisfaction equivalent to their demands.

At his side was her majesty's maid of honour, bearing testimony to the truth of these declarations. 'Here is water to wash you,' she said. 'I am ready to wait upon you. Here is bread to strengthen you, here is oil to anoint you, here is wine to refresh you, here is everything that can make a sick man well, a poor man rich, and a miserable man happy.'

'Oh Lord,' said John, 'can all this be true?'

'Yes, verily,' said the messenger of peace, drawing out a large parchment from his pocket, 'here is the queen's affidavit on the subject.'

'Oh, what manner of love is this!' said the prisoner. 'Has she suffered thus for me — wretched, ragged, filthy me — for me a rebel and a traitor? Does she love me? Yes, she does. I believe it. I have no more doubt of it than I have of my own existence. All that grieves me now is that I don't love her enough.'

Something similar to this is the conversion of sinners to God.[5]

A Letter of Consolation

On 5 November, 1834, Christmas Evans wrote to the poet
Robert ap Gwilym Ddu, who had recently lost his daughter.

> She was not sent away in fear, but it was the sight of Jesus
> that moved her. She was not obliged to die until she was
> made content to leave her father and mother; the lifeline
> was not severed, but it was undone like a silk thread. Jesus
> was willing for her to die, and she was too; don't you, then,
> be unwilling. Pray that you will be allowed to depart with
> such signs of peace with God through the blood of the cross.
> The religion of Jesus does not make us unfeeling Stoics in
> the face of losing our loved ones, but it moderates our grief
> with submission to the will of God.[6]

A Letter in Support of Josiah Jones

Although Christmas Evans was at times severe towards persons of doubtful character, never tolerating duplicity in any who
professed Christ, he was always prepared, particularly in his
latter years, to vindicate those who had been wrongly accused;
and on many occasions he manifested much good sense and
compassion towards such persons. In this letter, which is given
verbatim, he offers his support for Josiah Jones, who had been
falsely accused of immorality.

Caernarfon April 25 1836
Dear brother in the Gospel
    Without compulsion from any but entirely from the dic-
tates of conscience I was moved to write the following lines,
to show all that happens to read them which is my judgement
concerning the accusation brought against you by a whore
in this town, which you may show as my testimony, which
may induce them that have some confidence in my judgement and integrity, to believe that you are falsely accused
as I do.

To them I say that I feel for you Josiah Jones, I have a compassionate feeling towards you, and do sympathize with you under your severe trial.

I believe that a plot is formed between some vain pretenders of religion with the whore to break his character — The evidence comes only from a common whore, and so lame and self-contradictory that impartial men in the town cannot believe it. I look upon it as a diabolical conspiracy against the name and happiness of Mr. Jones.

He lived in the town in love with his neighbour and carried on a respectable trade as a printer, and was paying well, and clearing his way as an honest man, behaved as a religious man in his family among large company of workmen. There is no proof that he has been quietly of any immorality during the many years he resided in this town. My brother you are welcome to show this testimony of mine to all the friends at Merthyr Tydfil or elsewhere. Let them know that I have lived a nearest neighbour of him in this town near four years

affectionately

Christmas Evans[7]

A Letter on Church Discipline

Christmas Evans maintained the strictest discipline in his churches and was very particular in admitting new members, making certain that he received only truly converted persons. He used to say 'that it was a sign of death in the pot of the sons of the prophets, when they were not careful enough in receiving members to examine whether they were truly converted or not. The gospel requires faith and repentance, and fruits meet for repentance, in all candidates for baptism and church membership.'[8] His views on Associational union and church discipline are shown in a letter he wrote to a friend on 5 August, 1836, while at Caernarfon. It is evident that his aim was to keep the spirit of unity through the bond of peace while maintaining the purity of the church and ministry. He draws on his own years of

experience as a pastor to impart Biblical advice, displays a keen
insight into human behaviour and depends utterly upon God
for all things:

BELOVED BROTHER:
   I write to you, August 5, 1836, in the seventieth year of
my age, and in the fiftieth of my ministry. After conversing
much with ministerial brethren, earnestly desiring to see our
Associational union brought into action by representatives
of the churches, with a view to promote,
   I. A determination. 1) To bear each other's burden more
efficiently in the denomination to which we belong. I lament
the deficiency in this point, and ardently wish to see it effectually remedied. 2) To watch over and promote a holy conversation among all the members and all the preachers in a
more efficient manner, to prevent persons of unbecoming
conversation from obtaining privileges in any church, when
they have been excluded in another, for that would occasion
spots and blemishes to appear on the bright countenance of
the ministry. The Associational union, in which all the
churches of the same faith and order join, should be a
defence of the independence of the churches through their
representatives: it should also operate as a sort of check
upon independency, lest it should become opposed to the
general good, and frustrate the co-operation of the whole
body. *That they all may be one*, is the motto.
   II. Respecting church discipline. We cannot be certain
that we are doing right by administering the same punishment to all offenders, even for the same offence; for the
general character weighs heavily in the balance of discipline. Also a distinction should be made between the
seducer and the seduced; and between being overcome, or
falling into sin, and living habitually in sin, and following it as
a slave following his master. The denial of Peter, from weakness, and without previous deliberation, was very different
from the betraying of Judas, and his intentional selling of
Christ...

III. There are two things, brother, which we ought to avoid in the exercise of discipline. 1) We should avoid too great severity on the one part, and 2) too much leniency on the other part. Wisdom is necessary here to distinguish the different characters, those who require severity, and those who claim tenderness: the two are to be found blended in the principle of evangelical discipline...

IV. I have witnessed danger, and have sustained some harm myself, and seen harm done in churches, by exercising tenderness towards some persons, in the vain hope of their reformation. Receiving verbal testimony or mere fluent acknowledgements from their lips, without waiting for fruit in action also: some having been often accused, and as often turning to the refuges frequented by them. I never exercised tenderness towards such as these, without being repaid by them afterwards, if they had opportunity. Shimei-like, they would curse me after having shed the best oil of tenderness on their heads...

V. I perceive that the Scriptures make a difference between one that falls into sin, and one wallowing in it; between one overtaken by a party of marauders, and dragged into the camp, and made drunk at supper, and one like Judas, going to the party, and being secretly one of them, having pistols as they had: such are hypocrites. I have many times been the advocate of the fallen, and in a variety of instances have observed this operating beneficially for the church. Sometimes I have found those who had been spared upon their own verbal contrition, blessing God for his long forbearance of them, and also their spiritual brethren, who had in a manner set their bones...

VI. We should be careful that discretion and love be in exercise, though in strife and contention it be not always an easy matter to do this. When the beasts of dissension get loose from the caravan, Satan sometimes drives them through the streets of Zion, that they may enter the houses of the inhabitants; and like the lioness that escaped from the keepers at Shrewsbury, and attacked the foremost horse in the carriage; so contentions frequently attack the leaders, in order to stop the carriage of the ministry as it travels on in the labours of the pulpit. In the midst of the noise of strife, the man of God must raise his voice to heaven for courage and tenderness, so that the oil of Christ's love to the souls of men may be found in the oil-flagon of reproof, which is poured on the head; for if anger and revenge enter in, they will drop, like the spider in Germany, into the pot, and that will prevent the salutary effect of the oil, because the poison of wrath is mixed with it. The righteousness of God cannot be fulfilled in this manner in the discipline...

VII. You cannot be conscious, brother, of the great difficulty there is not to speak unadvisedly with our lips, as did Moses whilst drawing water for the rebellious Israelites. The rebellion of the people had embittered his spirit, so that his obduracy stood like a cloud between the people and the tenderness of the Lord, when he was showing mercy upon them by giving them water. Moses upbraided their rebellion instead of showing mercy, as the dispensation of God now required; a dispensation which contained in it a secret intimation of the great mercy to be shown by the death of Christ on the cross...

There are two things, brother, which you should observe: First, you will be called upon to attend to causes of contention; and you will find persons so hardened, that you will not be able to obtain weapons in all the armoury of God's word that will terrify them and make them afraid of entering their old haunts; such are persons without faith, and without the fear of God and the love of Christ influencing their minds...

Secondly, for your own encouragement, brother, I remark that you will have to attend to the exercise of discipline, and to treat with persons that may be alarmed, and made to tremble at the word of God, and not rush on presumptuously in their evil course... They are afraid that any storm or rock of offence should come in the way of the gospel ship, for their treasure is on board of it, and they have an interest in it. They dread the thought of walking unwatchfully and licentiously, lest they should be robbed of their riches, and forfeit the fellowship of God in prayer, lose the light of his countenance, and his peace in the means of grace, and lest they should be deprived of their confidence in the merits of Christ and a good conscience. They have denied themselves, and

have pulled out the right eye, lest they should not be acceptable before God. They dread harbouring in their bosoms the
old guilt and former doubts. They are cautious not to give a
night's lodging to such miscreants as anger, revenge, lust
and things which are on the earth; for they know that these
are robbers, and if they have any indulgence they will steal
away the *title deeds* of assurance to the inheritance; they
are well aware, also, that they will sustain the loss of a pure
conscience, which has been purged by the blood of Christ,
and which, as a golden chest, is a preserver of our confidence immovable unto the end. It is possible, brother, to
manage and discipline such professors. They have something to lose, consequently they will not flee from their refuge, lest they should be destroyed. *Keep that which thou
hast...*

May the spiritual gift be kindled in you, brother. Grace be
with you for ever and ever.

Affectionately

Christmas Evans
Caernarfon, August 5, 1836.[9]

A Letter on Forgiveness

Two days after the above letter was written Christmas Evans
wrote to a minister on the spirit of forgiveness so frequently
urged in the Scriptures, exhorting Christians not to take the
doctrine of election to extremes, but to pray earnestly for their
enemies according to Scriptural principles. His motive, as
always, was the glory of God and the salvation of sinners.

BELOVED BROTHER,
I have but little time to write upon the subject, and I do
not find my thoughts freely gushing forth on this point, and
the fountain bubbling up as it were within me; nor do I find
my ideas collected on this topic. There are many Scriptures,
all of which are given for our instruction, especially in the
devotional book of Psalms, which seem to contain requests
that the Lord would retaliate upon his enemies, and the

enemies of his people; and with these the request of Paul in 2 Timothy iv.14, appears to coincide: 'The Lord reward him according to his works.' Hundreds of such petitions of God's people might be cited.

It must be observed, that there are some things in such expressions for examples and instructions to us, and some things above our line, and beyond our circle.

I. That which is above the line of our duty in them is: those individuals, when uttering such prayers, were under divine inspiration, and so were led to speak correctly respecting the principles and designs of those against whom those petitions were uttered, and they knew by divine inspiration what God intended to do with such persons; therefore, it was God that spoke by them. 'They were holy men of God speaking as they were moved by the Holy Ghost.' In this they were above the line of imitation to us.

II. They are, notwithstanding, replete with instruction; and there are some things in them for our examples.

1. To establish in our minds a persuasion that there is still a woe belonging to persons of such conduct, even in our days, as well as in theirs; the same woe is to the enemy of God now as was then.

2. Though we cannot recognise them by inspiration, yet we have a rule by which to judge of their conduct, and a balance in which their conversation can be weighed. *By their fruits ye shall know them.*

3. That it is the duty of the people of God to importune him constantly to disarm his and their enemies, and stop the current of the destruction and devastation they make.

4. Not knowing by inspiration that they are vessels of wrath, and objects of the righteous judgement of God for ever, the light of the gospel urges us to pray for a stop on their ungodliness, not by damning them, but by slaying the enmity, and reconciling the enemies, giving them repentance for their sins, and faith in Christ for their remission, that they may know the truth, and recover themselves from the snare of the devil, who like fish are caught in it.

5. Here, again, streams out still another and a different ray of this light. If some person attempted to injure me in my character, by slander, calumny and falsehood; I have no inspiration by which I may know that such a one sins the sin unto death, and that God has abandoned him to irrecoverable delusion; therefore I must, according to the nature of the gospel, and the grace of God, pray for my enemy; not that he should take him to heaven in his enmity and ungodliness, but that he would grant him repentance, and make him sensible of his crime, and then forgive him for Christ's sake. I do not expect forgiveness myself of God for the sake of the blood of Christ, but in connection with repentance and sorrow under a sense of my sins. I perceive it necessary, and have been enabled to pray for my greatest enemies, that they may be saved in the same way that I myself expect to obtain forgiveness, even in connection with repentance and faith in the blood of Christ. Our hearts must be brought into such a state in respect of our enemies, that we can say, we would rather they should be brought to heaven in God's gracious method, than that they should perish under the righteous judgement of Jehovah.

6. Though this be the state of a Christian's mind before God in reference to his enemies, yet he is not bound to manifest his pardon to them, until they turn to him, and profess their contrition and show signs of sorrow of heart for their offence. To discover pardon to a transgressor without his giving any evidence of repentance, may be of great injury to him by hardening him in his impenitence, as well as being unscriptural. Jesus prayed for his enemies on the cross, but he manifested forgiveness to them only through faith in his blood, upon their repentance or change of their minds towards God, when they were pierced in their hearts on the day of Pentecost.

Affectionately

Christmas Evans.
Caernarfon, August 7, 1836.[10]

A Letter on the Spirit and Manner of the Ministry

Below is a letter that Christmas Evans wrote, probably towards the end of his life, to a young preacher. In it he draws on his own wealth of experience to highlight the qualities necessary for a successful ministry; 'and they may be regarded as having been earnestly put into practice by him in the ablest period of his own eminent labours'.[11] In many ways the letter is a biographical sketch of how he approached the task of sharing the gospel — a task he regarded as second to none—and offers insights into his thoughts on such topics as the usefulness of gaining knowledge, the composition and division of sermons, the necessity of prayer and the right use and training of the voice.

DEAR BROTHER, —
1. *Consider, in the first place, the great importance, to a preacher, of a blameless life.* You must, like Timothy, 'flee youthful lusts', as you would escape from beasts of prey; for there are kinds of beasts, living in the wilderness of man's corruption, that will charm, by means of their beauteous colours, those that walk among their haunts; there is no safety but by keeping from them, and adhering to such as live by faith, and watch, and pray. It will be well for you, while you travel through the coppice of youth, to keep from all appearance of evil. May you have grace to pass through the coppice of forbidden trees, without cutting your name into the bark of one of them, or you may be upbraided, at critical times, by those who may wish to prove that you are not better than themselves; even the *iota*, inserted by your hand, may be produced after many years.
2. *I remember the words of Luther, that reading, prayer, and temptation are necessary to strengthen, and to purify the talents of a minister.* Read, to extend your general knowledge, especially as to the plan of redemption, according to the Scriptures, in all its parts, from the election to the glorification; that you may, like a spiritual watchmaker, know all the relative

cog-wheels, and be able to open them in the pulpit, and to connect them all by faith, hope and charity, that they may occupy their own places, and exhibit their true results on the dial-plate; thus proving yourself a workman that needeth not be ashamed, rightly dividing the word of truth. Be not like that thrasher, who presumptuously took his watch to pieces in the barn, and could not put it together again, but was obliged to carry it home in his handkerchief. The messengers of God, described in the book of Revelation, are full of eyes behind, and before.

You must use prayer to fetch strength out of Christ, like the homer to carry home the manna in, or the water-pot of the woman of Samaria. Without the prayer of faith, the preacher will have 'nothing to draw with' from the well that is deep, — even *the deep things of God.*

Temptation is requisite, to prove the nature of the metal of the preacher's character, and doctrine, — 'approved of God'. The piece of gold, in every true minister's ministry, must be tried in some furnace, prepared by Divine Providence. He must, therefore, do the work of an evangelist, fulfil his ministry, endure hardness, and affliction, and thus prove himself a good soldier of Jesus Christ.

3. *Avail yourself, in the morning of your days, of every opportunity to acquire knowledge useful for the ministry.* Let it be your constant aim, to turn every stream and rivulet of knowledge in the right direction, to facilitate the work of the ministry, for the good of souls, and the glory of God; as the bee, in all her excursions amongst the flowers of the gardens, and the hedges, gathers honey to enrich the hive, as the common treasury of the industrious race. Always have a book to read, instead of indulging in vain conversations. Strive to learn English, as you cannot have academical training. Learn your own mother tongue well. Learn to write a good hand by frequent practice. Avoid vain conversation instead of growth in knowledge. Remember this, that you cannot commit some loved sin in private, and perform the work of the ministry in public, with facility and acceptance. For a preacher to fall into sin, be it a secret one, and to live in it, is as fatal, ultimately, as the cutting of Samson's hair. Be strong in the grace that is in Christ Jesus against all corruption.

4. With regard to the composition of your sermons: first, *let the matter be evangelical*. The doctrine of the Gospel is a mould from heaven, and not changed. It puts its own impress and shape on the professor that is melted into it, so that his justification, sanctification, and all his salvation, flow from the merits of Christ; and all through God's grace, and not of yourselves. The gospel, as a glass, should be kept clean and clear in the pulpit, that the hearers may see the glory of Christ, and be changed to the same image. Every duty is to be urged by evangelical motives. 'Let us have grace,' etc. Hereby we can serve God in all the duties of the kingdom of heaven. The whole is summed up in living by faith, which worketh by love, to him that died for us, and rose again for our justification.

Secondly, *let your divisions be natural to the text*. Take care that your interpretations accord with the contexts. Two or three general heads; avoid many. Four or five remarks you may make on each head; see that they are fairly in the truth of the text.

Thirdly, *I am not inclined to make inferences, or applications, from the whole*. When the preacher has expended his strength or ingenuity in endeavouring to impress, and apply the truth to the minds of his hearers, application seems to me to be doing again what has been effected already. The blacksmith does not put the horseshoe in the fire, after he has nailed it to the hoof; and the cook does not spread the cloth again, when dinner is over.

Fourthly, *beware of long sermons, as well as long prayers*. When there is but one preacher, he should not preach for more than an hour; when there are two, both should not be more than an hour and a half, that the worship may close within two hours; whenever this time has passed, coolness and fatigue ensues. To put three ministers to preach (in one meeting) is a modern corruption, and likely to make some progress in Wales; while the English, generally, have but one sermon in one service. They excel us herein; for we do not read that, on the day of Pentecost, Peter, James and John, preached after each other; but Peter, '*one* of the twelve', delivered that successful sermon. When we lose sight of the Scriptures, and common sense, we are driven to extremes, though it be with kindly purpose of respecting strange ministers, by putting them to preach.

5. *Attend, also, my young brother, to your outward appearance in the pulpit*. Beware of a proud, haughty appearance, with wandering eyes, and unfeeling countenance, so that the people utterly fail to see the man of God in you. We must, in order hereunto, have something like unto Moses, when he had been on the mount with God, that will indicate seriousness, love to souls, a spirit of prayer, zeal for Christ, and longing for the salvation of men; like unto those who have felt the fear of perdition ourselves, and the infinite value of salvation by God's grace; and that we wrestle with God in order to be useful to souls. These things must be imprinted on our appearance and deportment, having transformed us, in some measure, to a heavenly form and habit. Our outward conversation should be consistent herewith, or men will despise us as hypocrites, without the fear of God.

6. *Avoid, my dear brother, all foolish bodily gestures*.

7. We come now to the part of the subject upon which you are most anxious to have my thoughts: that refers to *the delivery of your sermons*. It is difficult to put general rules or rhetoric into execution. After reading all that has been said by Blair, Williams, Fuller, and the Archbishop of Cambray (Fenelon), who have spoken at length of Cicero and Demosthenes, it is easy, by endeavouring to follow them, to lose the spirit of the work, and thus, by seeking the form, to forfeit the life. Preach the gospel of the grace of God intelligibly, affectionately, and without shame — all the contents of the great box, from predestination to glorification. It was the closing and concealing of this box that occasioned the opening of the venomous Mohammedan box, as well as that of Popery, together with all the vain legality that is to be found among Protestants, established and dissenting. It may be said, that they seek justification; but it is by the deeds of the law. The locking up, and the losing, of the doctrine of grace, through the merits of Christ, utterly destroyed the Jewish Church; for it was in the chest, which they locked up by their false interpolations of Scripture, that the 'things which belong to their peace' were contained; 'but now,' says the Redeemer, 'they are concealed from their eyes;' shut up under unbelief. 'The things that pertain to their peace' belong also to our peace, as Gentiles. The Deity of Christ, etc.; Redemption, etc. Excuse this digression, for the river of God's throne moved me along.

We were upon the best mode of delivering sermons for edification. It is not easy to reduce the rules of prudence into practice. I have seen some men, of the highest powers, who understood Greek better than their mother-tongue, attempting to preach according to rule, and to them the pulpit was like unto Gilboa; they neither affected themselves, nor their hearers. The difficulty was, the bringing of their regulations into natural practice. I saw one of those men, the most eminent for learning and genius, who found the right way, under the influence of a mighty fervency that descended upon him in the pulpit, so that his voice became utterly different from what it used to be, and his tongue at liberty, as though something was cut that had hitherto restrained his tongue and affections from natural exercise.

Here you have the sum and substance and mystery of all rules:—

1. *Let the preacher influence himself; let him reach his own heart, if he would reach the hearts of others; if he would have others feel, he must feel himself.* Dry shouting (or vociferation) will not do this. The shout of a man who does not himself feel the effect of what he says, hardens, instead of softening; locks, instead of opening the heart.

2. *The elevation and the fire of the voice must accord with the fervency of the matter in the heart.* A person said to me once, 'Mr Evans, you have not studied Dr Blair's Rhetoric.' That man, with his rules, was always as dry as Gilboa. 'Why do you say so,' replied I, 'when you just now saw hundreds weeping under the sermon? That could not be, had I not first of all been influenced myself, which, you know, is the substance and mystery of all rules for speaking.' Wherever there is effect, there is life; and rules, without life, have no power. Now, brother, follow the natural course of affection and voice. Raise not the voice while the heart is dry; but let the heart and affections shout first; let it commence within.

Take this comparison: — Go to the blacksmith's shop; he first puts the piece of iron in the fire, and there is no sound of striking the anvil; he collects together the coals for heat; then he tells the boy, 'Blow!' while he masterfully manages the shovel, adjusting the coals, and asking sundry questions. He calmly looks at the fire heating the iron, and does not yet take hold of the hammer, nor order his assistants to use the sledge; but at length, seeing that the iron has attained the proper malleability, he takes it out, covered with sparkling fire, puts it on the anvil, handles the hammer, and orders his workman to take the larger one, and fashions it according to his pleasure; and so on, all day long. Here, observe, he does not beat the iron in order to make it hot, for without first heating it, the beating process is in vain. Equally vain is the hammer of vociferation, unless the matter is brought home with warmth into our hearts. We have often sought to produce effect, and to influence our hearers, much as though the smith merely put the iron in fire, and barely warmed it; it is contrary to the nature of things to use the hammer while the material is not duly tempered. Thus I have frequently, brother, found myself in preaching.

You have, above, the mystery of all effective speaking, in Parliament, at the bar, and in the pulpit; remembering the difference in the subjects and the sources of heat. In the pulpit, we speak of the deep things of God; and we are to pray for, and to expect warmth from the Divine Spirit. You complain that you cannot get your voice into a manageable key, and yet to speak with liveliness and power. Many, with a bad voice, well-governed, have become powerful speakers; while others, with a good voice, have, in consequence of not mastering a natural key, and not being able to move themselves, been most ineffective speakers. I would direct you to fix your voice at its natural pitch, which you may easily do; you may then, with facility, raise and lower it according to the subject in hand. If you commence in too high a key, you cannot keep it up long.

First, you cannot modulate it as the occasion may require; and you fall into an unpliable, tedious monotony, and all natural cadence and emphasis is lost. Without attuning the voice into the natural key, effective oratory is impossible.

Secondly, remember, not to speak in your throat or nostrils. If the former, you must soon become hoarse, and harsh loudness follows; the glory and vivacity are then departed, and instead of facility and cheerfulness, you have the roarings of death — the breath failing, with forced screams, and harsh whisperings.

Thirdly, raise your voice to the roof of your mouth; do not close your teeth against it, neither imprison it in the nostrils, but open your mouth naturally, and keep your voice within your lips, where it will find room enough to play its high and its low intonations, to discourse its flats and sharps, to utter its joys and sorrows. When you thus have your voice under control, instead of you being under its control, dragging you about in all disorder, you will find it your servant, running upon your errands, up and down, all through the camp, alternating in energy, and pliability, to the end of the sermon; and not becoming cold and weak, scarcely bearing you through, like Bucephalus, Alexander the Great's horse, which, mortally wounded, just brought his master out of the battle and then expired.

Fourthly, remember not to press too much upon your breath, when you have attained the natural use of it, by using very long sentences, without pausing at proper places, which (pauses) will add to the effect, as well as preserve the voice; so that you will be, like the smith, ready to strike the duly-tempered metal, prepared to give the suitable emphasis at the end of the paragraphs. Let the matter raise the voice, do not attempt by the voice to elevate the subject.

Fifthly, use words easily understood, that the people's affections may not cool, while the mind is sent to a dictionary, to understand your terms. The great work, the exploit of a minister, is to win the heart to believe in Christ, and to love Him.

Sixthly, bear in mind, also, the necessity of keeping the voice free, without (affected) restraint; give every syllable and every letter, its full and proper sound. (It is one of the peculiarities and excellencies of the Welsh language, and proves its Eastern origin.) No letter has to complain that it is (condemned to be) mute and neglected, and has no utterance. In English, many letters have this complaint; but in Welsh, every letter, even as the knights at the round table of

King Arthur, has, without preference, its own appropriate and complete sound.

Seventhly, remember also to enunciate clearly the last syllable in every Welsh word; that will cause your most distant hearer to understand you; while, without this, much of what you say must be inevitably lost.

Eighthly, in order to all this, carefully attend to the manner of the best and ablest preachers and imitate, not their weaknesses but their excellencies. You will observe, that some heavenly ornament and power from on high are visible in many ministers when under the Divine irradiation, which you cannot approach to by merely imitating their artistic excellence, without resembling them in the spiritual taste, fervency and zeal which Christ and his Spirit 'work in them'. This will cause, not only your being like unto them in gracefulness of action and propriety of elocution, but will also induce prayer for the anointing from the Holy One, which worketh mightily in the inward man. This is the mystery of all effective preaching. We must be endowed with power from on high: here is the grand inward secret. Without this, we (often) perceive that it is impossible, with all academic advantages, to make good preachers of young men from any college, in the Church of England, or among the dissenters, in the English or the Welsh language. A young preacher must have the mystery of being 'constrained' by 'the love of Christ'; 'the gift of God' must be kindled in him; and He alone, by the Spirit, can sustain that gift by the Holy Spirit...

'Who is sufficient for these things?' May the Lord give you, brother, a good understanding in all things; and preserve in you the heavenly gift by the Holy Ghost! May it be rekindled where it is, and contributed where it is not! Without it, we can do nothing for the glory of God, or the good of souls.

Affectionately,

Christmas Evans[12]

Appendix
1

A Sketch of Daniel Rowland's Preaching

The following sketch by Christmas Evans was prepared through T. Thomas, vicar of Llanbeblig, for the author of the *Ministerial Records*, and 'deserves the more attention, because it is the sketch of a Welshman, an eye-witness, a keen observer, a genuine admirer of his hero, and one who was himself in after days a very extraordinary man':

> Rowland's doctrine was Calvinistic; his mode of speaking was axiomatic, in sentences, neat, accurate and pregnant with sense. His mode was peculiar to himself — inimitable. Methinks I see him now entering in his black gown through a little door from the outside to the pulpit, and making his appearance suddenly before the immense congregation. His countenance was in every sense adorned with majesty, and it bespoke the man of strong sense, eloquence, and authority. His forehead was high and prominent; his eye was quick, sharp, and penetrating; he had an aquiline or Roman nose, proportionable comely lips, projecting chin and a sonorous, commanding, and well-toned voice.
>
> When he made his appearance in the pulpit, he frequently gave out with a clear and audible voice Psalm 27:4 to be sung. Only one verse was sung before sermon, in those days

notable for divine influences; but the whole congregation joined in singing it with great fervour. Then Rowland would stand up, and read his text distinctly in the hearing of all. The whole congregation were all ears and most attentive, as if they were on the point of hearing some evangelic and heavenly oracle, and the eyes of all the people were at the same time most intensely fixed upon him. He had at the beginning of his discourse some stirring, striking idea, like a small box of ointment which he opened before the great one of his sermon, and it filled all the house with its heavenly perfume, as the odour of Mary's alabaster box of ointment at Bethany; and the congregation being delightfully enlivened with the sweet odour, were prepared to look for more of it from one box after the other throughout the sermon.

I will borrow another similitude in order to give some idea of his most energetic eloquence. It shall be taken from the trade of a blacksmith. The smith first puts the iron into the fire and then blows the bellows softly, making some inquiries respecting the work to be done, while his eye all the time is fixed steadily on the process of heating the iron in the fire. But as soon as he perceives it to be in a proper and pliable state, he carries it to the anvil, and brings the weighty hammer and sledge down on the metal, and in the midst of stunning noise and fiery sparks emitted from the glaring metal, he fashions and moulds it at his will.

Thus Rowland, having glanced at his notes as a matter of form, would go on with his discourse in a calm and deliberate manner, speaking with a free and audible voice; but he would gradually become warmed with his subject and at length his voice became so elevated and authoritative, that it resounded through the whole chapel. The effect on the people was wonderful; you could see nothing but smiles and tears running down the faces of all. The first flame of heavenly devotion under the first division having subsided, he would again look on his scrap of notes and begin the second time to melt and make the mind of the people supple, until he formed them again into the same heavenly temper. And thus he would do six or seven times in the same sermon.

Rowland's voice, countenance, and appearance used to change exceedingly in the pulpit, and he seemed to be greatly

excited; but there was nothing low or disagreeable in him —
all was becoming, dignified, and excellent. There was such
a vehement, invincible flame in his ministry, as effectually
drove away the careless, worldly, dead spirit; and the people
so awakened drew nigh, as it were to the bright cloud — to
Christ, to Moses, and Elijah — eternity and its amazing
realities rushing into their minds.

There was very little, if any, inference or application at
the end of Rowland's sermon, for he had been applying and
enforcing the glorious truths of the gospel throughout the
whole of his discourse. He would conclude with a very few
striking and forcible remarks, which were most overwhelming
and invincible; and then he would make a very sweet, short
prayer, and utter the benediction. Then he would, full of
perspiration, make haste out of the pulpit through the little
door. His exit was as sudden as his entrance. The vast
congregation was left in a very heavenly frame, enjoying
the light of the Lord's countenance, and magnifying his Holy
Name with all the powers of their souls, and all this in such a
manner as it is impossible to describe on paper. Rowland
was a star of the greatest magnitude that appeared the last
century in the Principality; and perhaps there has not been
his like in Wales since the days of the apostles.[1]

Appendix
2

An Apology for Welsh Jumping

The revivals of the eighteenth century were accompanied by a new practice which came to be known, derogatorily, as *Welsh Jumping*. Scores of people, who were touched by the power of God's Spirit and brought into the kingdom of light, gave full vent to their feelings in loud exclamations of *gogoniant* (glory) and 'hallelujah', and would literally jump for joy while praising God for his saving grace. They expressed 'the unmixed, fresh, irresistible joy of salvation. Energy, emotion, understanding, memory, natural senses, spiritual desires, all — and more besides — were transported to hitherto unimaginable heights of reality in the enjoyment of God.'[2]

This practice, it seems, first began in 1762 at Llangeitho under the energetic and fervid preaching of Daniel Rowland, who, entertaining some doubts respecting its propriety, neither encouraged nor discouraged it, but remained silent on the matter. Some of his contemporaries, however, were outspoken in their approval of it; men such as William Williams, Pantycelyn, who regarded the public demonstrations of praise at Llangeitho as a 'blessed summer's day'. 'It is come! It is come!' he cried in response to the outpourings of joy.[3] Others, particularly among the English brethren, were uneasy at the thought of 'American enthusiasm', and feared that the revival would be ridiculed and harmed by such expressions of religious fervour. John Thornton, an evangelical philanthropist, in his opposition to these *Jumpers*, wrote several times to Rowland, urging him to put a stop to the practice. Rowland had no desire to say anything on the subject, but felt constrained by Thornton's importunity to reply, which he did in the following manner: 'You English blame us, the Welsh, and speak against us and say, "Jumpers, jumpers". But we, the Welsh, have something also to allege against you; and we most justly say of you, "Sleepers, sleepers".'[4] According to Rowland's son, Thornton never mentioned the matter again to his father.

Christmas Evans's first real encounter with this phenomenon was in 1788 at Timothy Thomas's church, when many new converts expressed their joy 'in ecstatic bodily movements, arm-wavings and enthusiastic singing and laughing'. At the time he was greatly surprised by such animation in divine worship. However, in later years he came to view similar manifestations as a work of God and in November, 1829, before a number of English brethren, he made the following apology, which he wrote in his diary:

> I observed that I could find no account of it among the Welsh until the time of Harris and Rowland, Calvinistic Methodists, who flourished in Wales about the same time as Whitefield and Wesley in England. The preaching of these men was the means of producing a religious revival throughout all the Principality, which had sunk into a state of deep lethargy, since the time of the great awakening under Vavasor Powell, about one hundred years before...
>
> Mr Rowland and Mr Harris were both of the communion of the Episcopal church and, as such, there was not so much enmity against them at first; but after they had come out, and when the people understood that they were preachers of the cross of Christ, considerable persecution arose against

them from the multitude; but it was now too late — for the gates of the city were opened — the leaven was put in the meal — the fire had been kindled — the sword was drawn from the scabbard, and many had been wounded (spiritually), and were ready to open the door for the gospel in spite of every danger. Harris, Rowland and the two Williamses had been clothed with power from on high, and the hammer of their ministry was sufficiently heavy to break in pieces the northern iron. Several laymen of powerful minds were also raised up about this time, such as Mr David Morris and others, who were valuable auxiliaries to carry on the work. By their ministry, this praising and jumping in religious enjoyment began in Wales, which has not wholly left it on certain occasions until this day.

As an apology for them, granting at the same time the possibility of extremes even in a good cause in the present state; and that graceless persons may feel something from these strong powers, as of the powers of the world to come, in the miraculous gifts of the Holy Ghost in the Apostolic age, observe:

1. That it appears to me like the residue of the Spirit and the powers of the world to come, which were necessary to open a way for the gospel through the darkness and obduracy of paganism in the days of the Apostles.

2. It is no argument of importance against it, that many graceless persons felt a considerable degree of influence at the time as well as others; for so it was in the case of Saul, king of Israel, and some besides named in Scripture.

3. There is no essential difference between religious enjoyment in Wales, and that which is now experienced in America; and that which accompanied the preaching of Whitefield in England, and even in Scotland, and that which also followed the ministry of President Edwards in America, when whole towns and neighbourhoods echoed with the sound of persons praying and praising God, as if a bursting-cloud shower of the Spirit of grace and prayer had descended upon them. Persons under the ministry of Whitefield wept, cried for mercy and even fainted by the power of his influence.

4. And such powers are absolutely necessary for the spread of the gospel in every country, and in every land; and therefore the Millennium is described in the Bible as a period remarkable for the outpouring of the Holy Ghost — 'that a nation shall be born at once' — and 'the flowing of the nations shall be to the mountains of the Lord's house'. It is these powers that have driven, as it were, the gospel into every nook of the mountains of Wales, as well as into its cities, towns and villages; while in England, with all the advantages of education, the gospel, in a manner, is hidden in a corner; and it had not run through the country and searched out and taken possession of all the inland parts of this spiritual Africa, and that for the want of these gales of divine influence and powers peculiar to the gospel; and it can never be spread through every part of England as it is in Wales without these powers.

Common preaching will not do to rouse sluggish districts from the heavy slumbers into which they are sunk. Indeed, formal prayers and lifeless sermons are like bulwarks raised against these powers in England; and this evil genius has also entered the Principality under the pretence of order. Five or six stanzas will be sung as dry as Gilboa, instead of one or two verses, like a new song, full of God, of Christ and grace, and the Spirit, until the heart is attuned for worship. The burying-grounds are kept in fine order in Glamorganshire, and green shrubs and herbs grow on the graves, but all this is of little value, for the inhabitants of them are all dead — so is every form of godliness, where its power is not felt. Order without life is exceedingly worthless.

You exhibit all the character of human nature, leaving every bud of the flower to open in the beams of the sun, except in divine worship; on other occasions you appear to have as much fire in your affections as the Welsh have. If you are noticed in a court of law, the most efficient advocate, such as Erskine, will give you the greatest satisfaction; but you are contented with a preacher, speaking so lifelessly and so low, that you can hardly understand the third part of what he says; and you will call this decency in the sanctuary. Tomorrow I shall see you answering fully to the human character, in your own actions; when the speakers on the platform will be urging the claims of Missions, you will then beat the boards, and manifest so much life and cheerfulness, that not one of you will be seen to take up a note-book, nor any other book, while the speaker shall be addressing you. A Welshman might suppose, by hearing your noise, that he had been silently conveyed to the midst of one of the meetings of the *Welsh Jumpers*, with this difference, that you would perceive many more tears shed, and hear more 'calves of the lips' [Hosea 14:2] offered up, in the rejoicing meetings of Wales. But you will use your heels well on such occasions, and a little of your tongues. But even in Wales, in certain places — that is, places where the fervent gales are not enjoyed which fill persons with fear and terror and joy in approaching the altar of God — you may see, while hearing a sermon, one looking into his hymn book, another into his note book, and a third turning over the leaves of his Bible, as if he were going to study a sermon in the sanctuary, instead of attending to what is spoken by the preacher as the mouth of God. If there is joy and gladness pertaining to many, the light of God's countenance in the sanctuary should develop it; until a fire is kindled, and he speak with his tongue, making melody unto the Lord in his heart, and praising him with his lips.

5. It is vain to urge objections against these powerful gales of divine influence, and allege that it is under the ministry of the illiterate preachers of Wales only they are experienced. Harris, Rowland and the two Williamses were not so, for they had been brought up for the established church. Whitefield and Edwards were men of education, and they preached the doctrine which in England is considered evangelical.

6. It is also beside the point to affirm that only persons of no weight, that is, ignorant boys and girls, are in the habit of thus rejoicing and praising God in his temple; for it is certain, that those who express their joy in this manner, possess so much sound, experimental knowledge, as to make them eminent in that respect. I have listened to many of them in the midst of their enjoyment, and have often been delighted while they repeated true, evangelical and substantial stanzas, replete with profound sentiment; for in such seasons, they could find out the very best, which made impressions on their memories, and these rapturous powers developed them, as if the tongue were moved by the heat and force of the fire within. And many other things of an evangelical and gracious character they will utter on these joyful occasions, with such heavenly eloquence that would be inimitable, and impracticable even for themselves to utter with the same effect, without enjoying these meltings of spirit.

This enjoyment is accompanied by many tears and much tenderness of heart; nor are persons of a dry spirit and hard heart ever regarded as fit subjects for this work of praise, in these blessed seasons of Christian enjoyment. It does not accord with any, but with him whose heart melts like wax, and runs in the form and mould of the gospel.

7. There is no way in which churches or particular persons, may enjoy this heavenly ecstasy, but by walking with God, and by cultivating a spirit of watchfulness and prayer, which show its pure and holy character. It awakens watchfulness against all evil tempers, improper expressions, and wicked actions, lest the sense of it should be lost. Such a frame of mind cannot be expected by living in sin. These individuals come to the house of God with an earnest desire for this enjoyment, and dreading lest there should be something in them which would cause God to deny them this unspeakable privilege.

It is an exceedingly easy matter for a minister to manage a congregation while Christian enjoyment keeps them near to God. They are diligent and zealous, and ready for every good work. But it is very easy to offend this joyous spirit — or give it what name you please, enthusiasm, religious madness, or *Welsh jumping* (its English name) — and make it hide itself. A quarrel and disagreement in the church will occasion it to withdraw immediately. Indulging in sin, in word or deed, will soon put it to flight. It is like unto the angel formerly, who could not behold the sin of Israel without hiding himself; so is the angel of the religious life in Wales, which proves him to be a holy angel, though he has the name of a

Welsh Jumper. My prayer is, that this angel be a guard upon every congregation, and that none should do anything to offend him. It is an exceedingly powerful assistant to accompany us through the wilderness. But the individual who has not felt its happy influences, has nothing to lose; hence he does not dread a dry meeting and a hard prayer, for they are all the same to him; but the people of this enjoyment pray before prayer, and before hearing, that they may meet with God in them.

8. The seasons when these powers are vouchsafed to the churches of Wales, are to be noticed. It is generally at a time when the cause of religion is at a low ebb — all gone to slumber; this happy spirit of enjoyment, like the angel of the pillar of fire, appears when there is distress and everything at the worst. Its approach to the congregation is like the glory of God returning to the temple of old; it creates a stir among the brethren — they have a new prayer, and a new spirit given them to worship God. This will lay hold of another — some new strength and light will appear in the pulpit, until it will be imagined that the preacher's voice is altered, and that his spirit is become more evangelical, and that he preaches with a more excellent savour than usual. Tenderness will descend upon the members, and it will be seen that Mr Wet-eyes and Mr Amen have taken their place among them. The heavenly gale will reach some of the old backsliders, and they are brought with weeping to seek their forfeited privilege. By this time the sound of Almighty God will be heard in the outer court, beginning to move the hearers like a mighty wind shaking the forest. In those seasons of refreshing from the presence of the Lord, some churches will receive, in the course of the year, additions of one hundred, others a hundred and fifty, and some others upwards of two hundred new members.

Sometimes the gale seems as if it blew upon the outer court — upon the hearers, and the young people from ten to fifteen years of age — when nothing extraordinary appears in the light and effect of the ministry, nor in the church; but afterwards making its way through the outer court to rouse the inner court, until a great concern is awakened for the state of the soul.

But observe: The revival that begins in the church and proceeds from thence to the world, and not that which commences outside of the church, is more frequent and more efficient in its converts, for the pangs of labour are to begin in Zion.

9. Again, it may be remarked that the happy effects which follow these powerful revivals, evince their nature. They are certain, where they are strong, to bend the oaks of Bashan — men of strong and sturdy minds, and haughty hearts — to attend the ministry of the word; they will bring all the ships of Tarshish, the merchants of this world, into the harbour of hearing; the power of the day of the Lord will raze all the walls of bigotry to the foundations. The thoughts of eternal realities, and the spirit of worship, are by these powers diffused abroad, and family worship is established in scores of families, where a few months before no regard was had unto it. The door of such a district, thus opened by the powers of the world to come, shall not be closed against the hearers of the gospel, until a goodly number of souls are there converted unto God. Where the living waters flow, dead fish are made alive by its virtues.

10. Since the first appearing of these mighty powers at Llangeitho, under the ministry of Mr Rowland, they have been showers of blessing, which are poured down on the congregations of the Baptist and Congregationalists as well as the Calvinistic Methodists; and sometimes one of these denominations are favoured with them, whilst the others are destitute. These refreshing seasons were, at times, experienced in a very powerful manner at Llangeitho, for about fifty years; that is, all the period of Mr Rowland's ministrations in that church. About two thousand persons assembled there for communion once a month, from the several counties of Wales, even in winter, and about three thousand in the summer season; which rendered it the most extraordinary place in Europe, and beyond a doubt, hundreds of those who assembled there, on such occasions, are now in heaven singing the new song. If to live on the merits of Christ, to fear God, and praise him, and lead a sober and righteous life, is an evidence of a godly state, then this was visible at that time, at Llangeitho.

This is the apology I made in Bristol (England), in the house of Mr Cousner, before Mr Winter, minister of Counterslip, and others, November, 1829. The English brethren acknowledged that their views were altered to a considerable degree respecting the *Welsh jumping*. I expressed my desire that England should be blessed with it; and added, that they are not likely to fill England with the gospel without some portion of it; and that, if they shall experience these powers, many of their forms will be abolished; for they will not favour the English nor the Welsh, but must have their own way.[5]

Appendix
3

Changes in the Exercise of Singing in Divine Worship

Christmas Evans was very much in favour of treasuring hymns in the memory and of singing them from the heart without musical accompaniment. He feared that the emphasis placed on reading music and singing in tune, and the 'hymn practice' that was encouraged by some Baptist ministers, were dampening the enthusiasm of the old style of singing. In writing about the 1828 revivals in America and Wales, he made the comment: 'The sound of an organ praising God, instead of persons with broken hearts ... would be sufficient cause for these visitations to withdraw without much ceremony, and never to return.'[6] When he was a minister in Caernarfon, the singing was led by a young girl. On one occasion she failed to marry words to music, and when Christmas Evans saw a member of his congregation take a hymn book out of his pocket, he said, 'You won't have those in heaven. Put it back in your pocket.'[7] His concern was that mere form would replace spiritual life, and with that in mind he observed:

> I have had an opportunity of noticing the effects of the new method of singing, which has been for some time practised in several of the Baptist churches, and brought to such a

degree of favour in some congregations, so that the old tunes were forgotten. Yet the practice that everyone should sing with his book in his hand did not prevail in them all; but the old method of committing hymns to memory still continued as heretofore, and by this means the evil was in a great measure counteracted.

But I perceive that singing in the heart, and making melody to the Lord, was soon lost, and some proud and selfish spirit crept in, so that the spirit of conviction withdrew from the assemblies to a lamentable degree. Instances are not infrequent of persons convinced by hearing the old, lively and enlivening singing; for there was something in it inimitable, like the sound of Almighty God, and like the sound of many waters. I hope the Welsh will be able to retain that which makes them excel all other nations. Fiery preaching, like that of Whitefield's and singing of the same strain, full of heavenly life, and the spirit of worship, are the principal excellencies of the Welsh; this, more than anything else, has been the means of preserving the Welsh language amongst them as a nation. *There is a savour of something evangelical and heavenly* experienced by reading the poetical works of Williams of Pantycelyn; and I regret to perceive it losing ground in the Baptist churches; and it is the wonder of the earth, in my view, to what an extent it has been lost amongst the Calvinistic Methodists, where, ere this, it has prevailed in so eminent a manner. Prosperity follows it, wherever it is, and blight and barrenness ensue in those places from which it withdraws.[8]

Appendix
4

Terms of Communion

Throughout his ministry Christmas Evans tried very hard to promote a genuine and lasting unity between members of different denominations. Although a decided Baptist and a forceful advocate of the distinctive tenets of that group, he was not of the strictest sect and, when the occasion demanded a defence of his beliefs, he was 'especially alive to the importance of not fighting the battles of God in the spirit of the devil'. A catholic spirit pervaded the whole of his life, and he avowed it not only as a part of his duty to love good and eminent men from other denominations, but delighted in admiring whatever was notable among them.

All through his career he baptised by immersion. When he baptised in the River Frogwy, for instance, he put one hand on the shoulder of the candidate and the other he raised, declaring, 'This is how I understand the New Testament, so this is how I administer the ordinance.'[9] Mrs Griffith, quoted before, says that at one time he baptised everyone in Anglesey and she particularly remembers him baptising in Ceidio Lake, near Llanerchymedd. He was always thankful to the Lord 'for placing me in the ministry among the Baptists because their beliefs

and religious exercises leave the great banner of Christ's commission unchanged'.[10]

In 1816, in answer to a pamphlet on mixed communion by
Robert Hall, Christmas Evans wrote a thirteen page document
entitled the *Terms of Communion*. At the time 'the English custom [among Baptist churches] was to practise open communion; that is, to invite Christians who had not been baptised by
immersion to partake of the Lord's Supper on exactly the same
terms as Baptist believers'. In Wales, however, only Baptists —
those who had been baptised by immersion — 'were allowed
to commune in a Baptist church. Communion there was a closed
one. And that was the bone of contention between the two'
great preachers. Christmas Evans could not understand 'why
Baptist churches should open their communion doors to include those who would not acknowledge the authenticity of
their baptism'.[11]

In his reply to Hall's pamphlet he expresses the desire 'That
all the people of God should exert themselves together, as
members of one communion, to promote the cause of Christ in
the world… How easily we could carry on our missionary cause
— the building of meeting houses — and our academical institutions — should all Israel be thus united; nothing could with-
stand our efforts.' He asserts that nothing avails in procuring
admittance to the kingdom of heaven 'but a personal profession of faith and repentance', and that 'the concurring voice of the
Scriptures is that baptism is the door to Christian communion'.

He goes on to acknowledge that 'it is our duty to make all
sacrifices in our power, towards uniting all the people of God in
one communion' and thereby effect the most beneficial results
among the churches. The two principal barriers among Christians 'are the *immersion* of believers' and 'the *sprinkling* of in-
fants'; therefore let Christians of both descriptions labour willingly
to remove these 'two remarkable separating walls' and so promote unity. Then, in characteristic style, he pictures his attempt

to destroy the barrier of '*the immersion of all believers on the profession of their faith, as an initiating ordinance to communion in the kingdom of Christ* ':

> I took my pickaxe in my hand and went up to this barrier. Pausing a little, to examine the wall, I perceived something divine emanating from it! But, being resolute, I said, 'Certainly it is better to pull thee down, than that thou shouldst be the occasion of keeping thousands from communion, whom I expect to meet in heaven!'
>
> Directly I lifted my pickaxe to break down the barrier; but I imagined in one moment's time, that twelve queens, of heavenly extraction, confronted me, hard by the wall, exclaiming, with loud but heavenly voices, 'Mortal man, hold thy hand! What art thou about to do? Wilt thou presume to sacrifice what is not thine own? Art thou so full of temerity as to attempt the demolishing of this barrier which heaven erected, and which was sanctioned by the Messiah to be the visible wall of separation, between his kingdom and the world? and that, not only during one century, but to the end of time? Know, vain man, that he expects to find this barrier in good repair at his second coming. Look more minutely at the sacredness of this wall! Is it not easy for thee to see the name of the Triune Jehovah, engraved by a heavenly hand, on the front of it — *Baptising them in the name of the Father, and of the Son, and of the Holy Ghost*: — this was not stolen, but given by the commission of heaven itself!...
>
> 'Should this separating wall be razed, we must put on our mourning garments; and all the court of heaven will be offended, at the sight of such an injury done unto a divine erection! Beside, look about thee, mortal worm!'
>
> I did so; and, behold, by my side, stood fifty or sixty princesses of the blood, personifying the Scriptures which speak of baptism. These were preparing suits of mourning garments for themselves, and exclaimed, as with one voice, 'If thou wilt injure that barrier with thy pickaxe and hammers, we must walk in black all our days!'
>
> Their expostulation pierced my soul; my heart failed within me; and I said, 'Heavenly family, and visitants from the

invisible world, I will cast away my pickaxe and hammers!' and as they dropped from my hand, I exclaimed, 'I will never touch this sacred wall of separation, for the sake of any man living; let my veneration be what it may for his talents and piety.' The impossibility of my making any sacrifice, without incurring the displeasure of the heavenly visitants, now appeared, in a very striking manner, to my mind; and they concluded their address by saying, 'Mortal! *Buy the truth, and sell it not!*' Proverbs xxiii.23.

Notwithstanding, I was not convinced that no sacrifice could be made on the other side. I, therefore, humbly desired the queens and princesses of the heavenly regions to go along with me. Immediately we went to the other separating wall, commonly called *Paedobaptist Barrier*. Then I said, 'Dear brethren, I have been attempting the pulling down the Baptist *Barrier* on my side, and to sacrifice it for the promotion of general communion among the godly; but these heavenly personages, who are with me, prevented me, by asserting, that the wall was not of *human invention*, but according to the "counsel of God". Luke vii.30. Brethren, cannot you make a sacrifice of your barrier without offending the noble ladies of the court of heaven? They are of opinion, they say, that something may be done on your side. They allege, that there is no written patent, in the Volume of Inspiration, for your wall, any more than the Samaritans had for the erection of their temple; and that, though they took the name of Jehovah, and engraved it upon the front of their temple, yet it was not put there by any written order from Jehovah!' They, however, refused, and pleaded for their barrier...

'Dear brethren,' I replied, 'it was not from any blind attachment to the barrier, on my side, that I refused to destroy it, but because it is according to the written patent in the books, and because we shall be judged according to what is written in them; therefore demolish your barrier, that we may be in one communion! If you put your pickaxe to it, these princesses will smile at the downfall. They allege, that there will be no mourning, no putting on of sackcloth, by any positive command, any moral duty, or by an example of Christ or his apostles; and that none of the sister Scriptures, from

the first of Genesis to the last of the Revelation; yea, no part
of the Bible will grumble at the downfall of it... Pray indulge
no undue attachment to what is not written; but sacrifice it
for the communion of the godly!' Still they refused...

He concludes by urging all to 'make sacrifices towards promoting general communion; but we must go to our own fields to
get victims' — the fields of bigotry, men's-tradition,
human-invention, commandment-of-men, Judaism, carnal-
relation, relative-holiness — rather than to the premises of the
great Lord of the soil. The 'field of his positive commands, the
field of the spirituality of his kingdom, Christ's-baptism field,
practice-of-the-apostles' field, necessity-of-the-new-birth field,
written-word field, Jerusalem-above field, spiritual-seed field'
should all be left untouched as the union must not be advanced
at the expense of sacred doctrine.[12]

Appendix
5

The Graveyard sermon

The Specimen of Welsh Preaching quoted in the chapter *Sermon Extracts*, though free from some of the objections on the ground of taste that might be raised against the original, omits much of Christmas Evans's characteristic imagery. We therefore insert a different version of the same passage that was 'taken from the lips of the preacher and rendered into English by one of his frequent hearers and intimate friends'.[13] 'Delivered with all his energy of spirit,' says David Phillips, who heard the substance of this passage from Christmas Evans, 'and with all the volume and power of his wondrous voice, it produced of necessity an overpowering sensation in those who were privileged to be his hearers, and to whom the Welsh was their vernacular tongue... All the stores of his energy, and the resources of his voice, which was one of great compass, depth and sweetness, seemed reserved for the closing portions of the picture, when he delineated the routed and battered hosts of the pit retreating from the cross, where they had anticipated a triumph, and met a signal and irretrievable overthrow.'[14]

Methinks I find myself standing upon the summit of one of the highest of the everlasting hills, permitted thence to take a survey of our earth. It shows me a wide and far-spread burial-ground, over which lie scattered in countless multitudes the wretched and perishing children of Adam. The ground is full of hollows, the yawning caverns of death, whilst over it broods a thick cloud of fearful darkness. No light from above shines upon it, nor is the ray of the sun or moon, or the beams of the candle, seen through all its borders. It is walled around. Its gates, large and massive, ten thousand times stronger than all the gates of brass forged amongst men, are one and all safely locked. It is the hand of Divine Justice that has locked them, and so firmly secured are those strong bolts which hold these doors, that all the created powers even of the heavenly world, were they to labour to all eternity, could not drive so much as one of them back. How hopeless the wretchedness to which the race are doomed, and into what irrecoverable depths of ruin has the disobedience of their first parent plunged them!

But behold, in the cool of the day there is seen descending from the eternal hills in the distance, the radiant form of Mercy, seated in the chariot of the divine promise, and clothed with splendour, infinitely brighter than the golden rays of the morning when seen shooting over mountains of pearls. Seated beside Mercy in that chariot is seen another form like unto the Son of Man. His mysterious name is the 'seed of the woman', and girt around him shines the girdle of eternity radiant with the lustre of the heaven of heavens. 'He has descended into the lower parts of the earth.'

I see Mercy alight from the chariot, and she is knocking at the huge gate of this vast cemetery. She asks of Justice, 'Is there no entrance into this field of death? May I not visit these caverns of the grave and seek, if it may be, to raise some names at least of the children of destruction, and bring them again to the light of day? Open, Justice, open; drive back these iron bolts and let me in, that I may proclaim the jubilee of deliverance to the children of the dust.'

But I hear the stern reply of Justice from within those walls; it is, 'Mercy, surely thou lovest Justice too well to wish to burst these gates by force of arm, and thus obtain entrance by mere lawless violence. And I cannot open the door. I cherish no anger towards the unhappy wretches. I have no delight in their eternal death, or in hearing their cries as they lie upon the burning hearth of the great fire kindled by the wrath of God in the land that is lower than the grave. But I am bound to vindicate the purity, holiness and equity of God's laws; for "without shedding of blood there is no remission".'

'Be it so,' said Mercy, 'but wilt thou not accept of a surety who may make a sufficient atonement for the crime committed and the offence given?'

'That will I,' said Justice, 'only let him be duly allied to either party in this sad controversy, a kinsman, near alike to the injured Lawgiver and to the guilty tenants of the burial-ground.'

'Wilt thou, then,' said Mercy, 'accept of the puissant Michael, prince among the hosts of heaven, who fought bravely in the day when there was war in heaven, and also vanquished Apollyon upon the summit of the everlasting hills?'

'No,' said Justice. 'I may not, for his goings forth are not from the beginning, even from everlasting.'

'Wilt thou not then accept of the valiant Gabriel, who compelled Beelzebub to turn and seek safety in flight from the walls of the heavenly city?'

'No,' cried Justice, 'for Gabriel is already bound to render his appointed service to the King Almighty; and who may serve in his place while he should be attempting the salvation of Adam's race? There needs,' continued Justice, 'one who has, of right belonging to him, both omnipotence and eternity, to achieve the enterprise. Let him clothe himself with the nature of these wretches. Let him be born within these gloomy walls, and himself undergo death within this unapproachable place, if he would buy the favour of heaven for these children of the captivity.'

But while this dialogue was held, behold a form fairer than the morning dawn, and full of the glory of heaven, is seen descending from the chariot. Casting, as he passes, a glance of infinite benignity upon the hapless tenants of that burial-ground, he approaches, and asks of Justice, 'Wilt thou accept of me?'

'I will,' said Justice, 'for greater art thou than heaven and the whole universe.'

'Behold, then,' said the stranger, 'I come; in the volume of the book has it been written of me. I will go down, in the fulness of time, into the sides of the pit of corruption. I will lay hold of this nature, and take upon me the dust of Eden, and, allied to that dust, I will pour into thy balances, Justice, blood of such worth and virtue that the court of heaven shall pronounce its claims satisfied, and bid the children of the great captivity go free.'

Centuries have rolled by, and the fulness of time is now accomplished; and see, an infant of days is born within the old burial-ground of Eden. Behold a Son given to the dwellers of the tomb, and a spotless Lamb, the Lamb of God, is seen within that gloomy enclosure. When the hour came at which the ministers of the Divine Justice must seize upon the victim, I see them hurrying towards Gethsemane. There, in heaviness and sorrow of soul, praying more earnestly, the surety is seen bowed to the earth, and the heavy burden he had assumed is now weighing him down. Like a lamb, he is led towards Golgotha — the hill of skulls. There are mustered all the hosts of darkness, rejoicing in the hope of their speedy conquest over him. The monsters of the pit, huge, fierce and relentless, are there. The lions, as in a great army, were grinding fearfully their teeth, ready to tear him to pieces. The unicorns, a countless host, were rushing onwards to thrust him through, and trample him beneath their feet. And there were bulls of Bashan, roaring terribly; the dragons of the pit are unfolding themselves, and shooting out their stings, and dogs many are all around the mountain. 'It is the hour and power of darkness.'

I see him passing along through this dense array of foes, an unresisting victim. He is nailed to the cross; and now Beelzebub and all the master-spirits in the hosts of hell have formed, though invisible to man, a ring around the cross. It was about the third hour of the day, or the hour of nine in the morning, that he was bound as a sacrifice, even to the horns of the altar. The fire of divine vengeance has fallen, and the flames of the curse have now caught upon him. The blood of the victim is fast dropping, and the hosts of hell are shouting impatiently: 'The victory will soon be ours.' And the fire went on burning until the ninth hour of the day, or the hour of three in the afternoon, when it touched his Deity — and then it expired. For the ransom was now paid and the victory won. It was his. His hellish foes, crushed in his fall, the unicorns and the bulls of Bashan retreated from the encounter with shattered horns; the jaws of the lions had been broken and their claws torn off, and the old dragon, with bruised head, dragged himself slowly away from the scene, in deathlike feebleness. 'He triumphed over them openly,' and now he is for ever the Prince and Captain of our salvation, made perfect through sufferings. The graves of the old burial-ground have been thrown open; and from yonder hills gales of life have blown down upon this valley of dry bones, and an exceedingly great army have already been sealed to our God, as among the living in Zion.[15]

Notes

Preface
1. EWH, p. 355.
2. D. M. Lloyd-Jones, *The Puritans: Their Origins and Successors* (The Banner of Truth Trust, Edinburgh, 1987), pp.170-171.
3. Lewis Drummond, *Spurgeon: Prince of Preachers* (Kregel Publications, Grand Rapids, 1992), p.329.
4. B. A. Ramsbottom, *Christmas Evans* (The Bunyan Press, Luton, 1985), p.8.
5. DP, p.vi.
6. RS, p.x.

Introduction: 'A Great Cloud of Witnesses'
1. C. Silvester Horne, *A Popular History of the Free Churches* (James Clarke & Co., London, 1903), p.309.
2. Edward Morgan, *John Elias: Life, Letters and Essays* (The Banner of Truth Trust, Edinburgh, 1973), p.ix.
3. EWH, p.176.
4. Morgan, *John Elias*, p.ix.
5. TR, p.20.
6. 'Thousands of our people,' says Penry, 'know Jesus Christ to be neither God nor man–priest nor prophet–almost never heard of him. O desolate and forlorn condition! Preaching itself, in many parts, is quite unknown. In some places, a sermon is read once in three months.' Ibid.
7. These tracts, written by a fictitious Martin Marprelate, and printed secretly by Robert Waldegrave and John Hodgkins in 1588-89, are humorous and violent attacks on the failings of the Church of England. 'Their main importance lies in the fact that they spread alarm in official circles concerning

secret printing presses and led to more repression of Puritans.' Peter Toon, *The New International Dictionary of the Christian Church* (Zondervan Publishing House, Grand Rapids, 1978), p.633.

Penry's exact connection with these 'Tracts' has never been satisfactorily established.

8. TR, p.25.

9. Ibid., p.28.

10. David Jones, *Life and Times of Griffith Jones of Llanddowror* (Tentmaker Publications, Clonmel, 1995), p.122.

11. Geraint H. Jenkins, *Literature, Religion and Society in Wales 1660-1730* (University Press of Wales, Cardiff, 1978), p.151.

Its success was immeasurable. 'The flames of Rees Prichard's candle burned strongly on Welsh hearths for over two centuries and his work counts as much in the religious history of Wales as the hymns of Williams, Pantycelyn.' Ibid., p.154.

12. HWB, pp.26-27.

13. DWB, p.1093.

14. Howell T. Evans, *The Making of Modern Wales* (The Educational Publishing Co., Cardiff, n.d.), p.80.

15. *The Book of the Three Birds* is a dialogue between three birds: an eagle represents Oliver Cromwell, the dove a Puritan reformer, and the raven an Episcopalian, perhaps Archbishop William Laud (1573-1645).

16. HW, p.282.

17. Evans, *The Making of Modern Wales*, p.77.

18. One of the reasons for his expulsion was his refusal to obey Archbishop Laud's injunction to read, after the morning service, the *Book of Sports*, a proclamation authorizing Sunday sports.

19. GHJ, p.73.

20. EWH, p.190n.

21. Hughes published Prichard's *The Welshman's Candle* (1681), a Welsh version of Bunyan's *The Pilgrim's Progress* (1688), and he was responsible for the printing of 8000 Bibles in 1678 and a further 10,000 in 1690. HW, p.289.

22. R. Tudur Jones, *Vavasor Powell* (Orphans Press, Leominster, 1975), p.7.

23. TR, p.102.

24. In his book *The Bird in the Cage, Chirping* he meets the accusations of his opposers who had defamed his character as one of the administrators of the Propagation Act. He also urges all followers of Christ to stand firm amidst the approaching persecution.

25. TR, p.105.

26. F. R. Webber, *A History of Preaching in Britain and America* (Northwestern Publishing House, Milwaukee, 1952), part 2, p.558.

27. GHJ, p.75.

28. Jones, *Vavasor Powell*, p.26.
29. For a brief comment on the influence and spread of his circulating schools see chapter four: *The Gospel in North Wales.* In our present chapter we concentrate on his preaching.
30. Jenkins, *Literature, Religion and Society in Wales*, p.14.
31. Estimates as to the numbers that attended his preaching range from 500 to 4000.
32. Eifion Evans, *Daniel Rowland and the Great Evangelical Awakening in Wales* (The Banner of Truth Trust, Edinburgh, 1985), p.26.
33. Jones, *Life & Times of Griffith Jones*, pp.151-152.
34. GHJ, p.183.
35. Jones, *Life and Times of Griffith Jones*, p.164.
36. Hugh J. Hughes, *Life of Howell Harris, the Welsh Reformer* (James Nisbet & Co., London, 1892), (Reprinted by Tentmaker Publications, Hanley, 1996), p.42.
37. In all Williams published 'at least ninety-two volumes, booklets, pamphlets, essays and sermons'. GHJ, p.422.
38. Ibid., p.355.
39. Richard Bennett, *Howell Harris and the Dawn of Revival* (Evangelical Press of Wales, Bridgend, 1987), p.42.
40. Geoffrey F. Nuttall, *Howel Harris 1714-1773: The Last Enthusiast* (University Press of Wales, Cardiff, 1965), p.54.
41. Hughes, *Howell Harris*, p.206.
42. Tom Beynon, *Howell Harris: Reformer and Soldier (1714-1773)* (The Calvinistic Methodist Bookroom, Caernarfon, 1958), p.2.
43. TR, p.334.
44. Bennett, *Howell Harris*, p.182.
45. Arnold Dallimore, *George Whitefield: The Life and Times of the Great Evangelist of the 18th Century Revival* (The Banner of Truth Trust, Edinburgh, 1989), vol.1, p.246.
46. Hughes, *Howell Harris*, p.2.
47. Evans, *Daniel Rowland*, p.1.
48. GPW, p.66.
49. Evans, *Daniel Rowland*, p.1.
50. John Owen, *A Memoir of Daniel Rowlands of Llangeitho* (The Banner of Truth Magazine, Issues 215-216, 1981), p.61.
51. Owen, *Daniel Rowlands*, p.49.
52. GHJ, p.349.
53. Owen, *Daniel Rowlands*, p.59.
54. Hughes, *Howell Harris*, p.201.
55. Evans, *Daniel Rowland*, p.7.
    For a superb sketch of Daniel Rowland's preaching see *Appendix 1.*
56. HWB, p.193.

57. Peter Sager, *Wales* (Pallas Athene, London, 1996), p.158.
58. SM, pp.137-138.

Chapter 1 – Troubled Youth and Conversion
1. DP, pp.207-208.
2. Jeremy Taylor (1613-1667) was an Anglican bishop, a literary genius and an eloquent preacher.
3. DP, pp.237-238.
4. William Edwards, *Christmas Evans*, New Biographical Series–No.46 (The Religious Tract Society, London, n.d.), p.16.
5. Thomas Phillips, *The Life, Times, Contemporaries, Personal Appearance, Innocence, Wit, Pulpit Talents, and Labours of Christmas Evans* (W.Jones, Cardiff, 1878), p.4.
6. The storms at the end of November, 1766, brought havoc to the lower Cardiganshire and North Carmarthen areas: sheep were drowned; soil and chalk were washed away from the fields; the harvest, stored in barns, was destroyed; furniture was carried away in the floods and many had to escape for their lives through the windows of their houses in the middle of the night; the bridges of Newcastle Emlyn and Cardigan were swept away and all the houses of Llanybydder were flooded. CENN, p.1.
7. There is an oak tree near the village of Tre-groes, planted in 1938, that marks the approximate site of Christmas Evans's birth.
8. Glanmor Williams, *Welsh Baptists in an Age of Revolution 1776-1832* (The Baptist Quarterly, vol.33, No.5, January 1990), pp.204-205.
9. DME, p.3.
10. DWB, p.758.
11. A, p.102.
12. Edwards, *Christmas Evans*, p.3.
13. GPW, pp.149-150.
14. DP, p.18.
15. RS, pp.5-7.
16. Ibid., p.2.
17. It is surprising that Joanna trusted her son into the hands of James Lewis, especially as she must have been aware of his doubtful character and intemperance.
18. ER, p.26.
19. RS, p.2.
20. Ibid., p.3.
21. GPW, p.150.
22. DME, p.5.
23. GHJ, p.384.

'Under the influence of Thomas Perrot, who succeeded the founder of the academy in 1718, the Carmarthen seminary became increasingly liberal in character. Indeed, it acquired a reputation as a nursery of hetero-doxy. Many disaffected Calvinist students were searching for a less exacting and rigorous theology, and by allowing them the freedom to exercise their own independent judgements, Perrot enabled some of them to desert orthodox paths and to espouse the cause of Arminianism ... From the 1730s onwards, students and ministers who found Calvinist doctrines unpalatable drifted towards Arminianism. Between 1750 and 1780 many of them, believing that Christ was not divine and was subordinate to God, were converted to Arianism. After 1780 Unitarianism became the logical culmination of this odyssey.' Ibid., pp.314,315.

24. DNB, vol.X, p.1009.
25. David Lloyd (1724-79) was 'an eloquent preacher, wrote poetry in Welsh, was a master of Latin, Greek and Hebrew and spoke French and Italian fluently'. In his day he was 'the greatest religious genius and the greatest influence in the cause of religious freedom in Cardiganshire, if not in the whole of Wales'; in Lord Aberdare's view 'He was the only Welshman who up to that time had won a European reputation.' DWB, p.577.
26. David Williams, *A History of Modern Wales* (John Murray, London, 1969), p.167. The term Arianism is derived from Arius, a bishop of Alexandria, whose doctrine of the Trinity was condemned at the Council of Nicea in AD325. He taught that God the Son was the first creature of the Father and that there was a time when God the Son did not exist. Consequently, in his view, the Son is not of the same nature as the Father and does not possess the divine attributes in equality with the Father. In his own words, Arius said, 'If the Father begat the Son, he that was begotten had a beginning of existence; and from this it is evident that there was a time when the Son was not. It therefore necessarily follows that he had his subsistence from nothing.' *The New International Dictionary of the Christian Church*, General Editor: J.D.Douglas (Zondervan Publishing House, Grand Rapids, 1990), p.67. Jehovah's Witnesses are the modern-day Arians. When David Davis was ordained nearly all of the sixteen ministers present were Arians.
27. The Socinians of the sixteenth century were anti-trinitarian, denying the deity of Christ. Their thought gave rise to modern Unitarianism. In the eighteenth century many of the Independent Churches in Wales drifted towards Unitarianism, which 'resulted in a definite severance in the year 1771, from which period the progress of Independency in Wales has been steady and often rapid'. Horne, *A Popular History of the Free Churches*, pp.308-309.
28. DME, p.34.
29. PH, p.44.
30. TR, p.442.
31. DME, p.35.

32. TR, p.442.
33. RS, p.6.
34. ER, pp.32-33.
35. SM, pp.245-246.
36. Ibid., p.191.
37. RS, pp.100-101.
38. CENN, p.9.
39. RS, p.7.

Chapter 2 — Early Pilgrimage

1. F. R. Webber, *A History of Preaching in Britain and America*, part 2, p.579.
2. DP, p.19.
3. William Beveridge (1637-1708), bishop of St Asaph (1704-8), 'was a man with an unquenchable thirst for learning and a deep desire to nurture a sense of holiness and devotion among his flock'. GHJ, p.178. His *Thesaurus Theologicus* was published posthumously in 1711.
4. ER, p.39.
5. DME, p.31.
6. Ibid.
7. DP, p.22.
   There is another account of how Christmas Evans lost his right eye. He was returning home from a fair at Llandysul with, among others, Timothy Davis and a servant David Evans. Christmas Evans made some patronising and provocative comments to David Evans who in retaliation hit him with a small piece of wood, thus causing the injury.
8. DP, p.22.
9. RS, pp.7-8.
10. PH, p.42.
11. JD, p.4.
12. Jan Morris, *The Matter of Wales: Epic Views of a Small Country* (Penguin Books, London, 1986), p.111.
13. SM, p.287.
14. DP, pp.22-23.
15. RS, p.8.
16. SM, p.247.
17. William Perkins may have been a student at Carmarthen Academy under Evan Davies in 1745.
18. DWB, p.747.
19. DME, p.32.
20. DP, pp.21-22.
21. David Davies (1763-1816) was three years older than Christmas Evans. He was ordained in 1790 as the assistant minister of the church at Llangeler, where he was so successful that a larger chapel (Saron) had to be built in

1792 to accommodate the growing congregation. In 1795 he received a call to the pastorate of Mynydd-bach (Swansea) and its branches. Here again he met with remarkable success and in 1803 he built Ebenezer Chapel in the town. Five years later he relinquished the mother-church of Mynydd-bach and confined himself to Ebenezer and Sketty. He died on the 26 December, 1816. DWB, p.114.

Davies is regarded as 'one of the most powerful pulpit orators in his own or any other age', with a voice of 'thrilling and impassionate tones'—in no respect inferior to George Whitefield, according to competent judges who frequently heard both. TR, pp.434, 437. A well-known Welsh minister says of him, 'In his best days he was one of the chief, if not the chief, of all the Welsh preachers.' Ibid., p.438. Another remarks that he exhibited the 'happy combination of the fire of the Methodists and the learning of the Dissenter', and, together with his celebrated contemporaries, aroused the whole country: 'New interests were formed, and new chapels erected in every direction; and a wide-spread revival, which commenced in the year 1807, and lasted for two or three years, vastly increased the membership of the churches.' Thomas Rees, *Miscellaneous Papers on Subjects Relating to Wales* (John Snow & Co., London, 1867), p.74. During his pastorate of twenty-six years he admitted 2000 members to the communion of the churches under his charge.

Among Welsh Independents he is an historical figure. Others have described him as a 'father' to Independency in the same way as his contemporary Thomas Charles was a 'father' to Methodism. His ministry was certainly varied and widespread: he was a tireless itinerant; he planted churches, trained preachers and gained a reputation as an accomplished hymn writer, composing eighty-one Welsh hymns in all. He also started to publish a useful edition of the Bible in Welsh with explanatory notes appended to each chapter, but died before the work was completed. In his later years he was affectionately known as *The Great Revivalist of Swansea*.

22. DP, p.24.
23. RS, p.12.
24. DP, pp.24-26.

Chapter 3 — Inspired but Depressed
1. EWH, p.357.
2. DP, p.26.
3. An apology for *Welsh Jumping* was written by Christmas Evans in 1829. See *Appendix 2*.
4. DP, p.26.
5. DME, p.45.
6. RS, p.15.
7. Ibid., p.14.

8. DME, p.50.
9. RS, p.20.
10. DME, p.46.
11. RS, p.16n.
12. DME, p.48.
13. PH, p.51.
14. RS, p.16.
15. DP, pp.28-29.
16. GPW, p.153n.
17. 'The effect of that sermon on the congregation is compared to the explosion of powder shattering the rock. Some fainted, others screamed, and all felt terrified, as if they were summoned to stand in the presence of their Judge.' TR, p.403.
18. GPW, p.153.
19. Morgan, *John Elias*, p.407.
20. GPW, p.107.
21. Evans, *Daniel Rowland*, p.329.
22. DNB, vol.X, p.982.
23. DWB, p.451.
24. Evans, *Daniel Rowland*, p.230.
25. Rees, *Miscellaneous Papers*, p.39.
26. When Peter Williams was only 5 years of age he was 'taken by his mother on horseback to Llanddowror to hear Griffith Jones preach'. GHJ, p.348.
27. Jones, *Life & Times of Griffith Jones*, p.181.
28. Williams, *A History of Modern Wales*, p.150.
29. Evans, *Daniel Rowland*, p.298.
30. Peter Williams, in conjunction with David Jones, Pontypool, published 4000 copies of John Canne's *Bible* 'with additional marginal references and explanatory notes of his own at the foot. Alterations were also made by Williams in the text. The patronage of the Methodist Association had been promised for this work, but was suddenly withdrawn on the eve of publication, with the result that Williams lost about £600 by the transaction.' DNB, vol.XXI, pp.436-437.
31. Ibid., p.437.
    Thomas Rees makes a similar comment: 'His expulsion, in the seventieth year of his age, after faithfully and signally serving the connexion for nearly fifty years, and often at the peril of his life, was, to say the least, an act of the basest ingratitude. Multitudes among the members of the Methodist body disapproved of it; but being the act of parties whom they had placed in power, they were all implicated in it.' TR, p.386.
32. Evans, *Daniel Rowland*, p.311.
33. PH, p.169.
34. RS, p.20.

35. DP, p.24.
36. RS, pp.20-21.
37. Ibid., pp.21-22.
38. DP, p.28.

Chapter 4 — The Gospel in North Wales

1. HWB, p.193.
2. Hughes, *Howell Harris*, pp.59, 66.
3. Ibid., p.123.
4. Beynon, *Howell Harris*, p.105.
5. Evans, *Daniel Rowland*, p.235.
6. Beynon, *Howell Harris*, p.35.
7. Evans, *Daniel Rowland*, pp.235-236.
8. Thomas Rees, *The Growth of Nonconformity: An Argument for Disestablishment* (Swansea, 1883), pp.7-8.
9. Helen C. Knight (Compiler), *Lady Huntingdon & her Friends* (Baker Book House, Grand Rapids, 1979), p.45.
10. *George Whitefield's Journals* (The Banner of Truth Trust, Edinburgh, 1985), p.231.
11. HW, p.307.
12. Jones, *Life & Times of Griffith Jones*, p.79.
13. GHJ, p.377.
14. Owen, *Daniel Rowlands*, p.60.
15. Madam Bevan died in 1779 and was buried alongside Griffith Jones. In her will she bequeathed her estate of £10,000 to the circulating schools to ensure their continuation. However, two of her relatives, Elizabeth Stepney and William Lloyd, who were trustees, challenged the will and the whole fund became tied up in the Court of Chancery for thirty-one years. 'From this set-back there was to be no recovery. Deprived of essential financial aid, the circulating school system withered and died.' GHJ, p.378.
16. Thomas Charles was not the founder of the Sunday Schools as they were in existence around Neath and Swansea, amongst sparse congregations of nonconformists, as early as the latter part of the seventeenth century. A century later, Morgan John Rhys urged the churches to adopt the system as a means of spreading a knowledge of the Scriptures and of the Welsh language, and Edward Williams established schools in Oswestry and other nearby places. Thomas Charles, by his organising skills and success in providing reading material, simply placed the schools on a firmer footing.
17. R. M. Jones and Gwyn Davies, *The Christian Heritage of Welsh Education* (Evangelical Press of Wales, Bridgend, 1986), p.21.
18. The need for Welsh Bibles was long-standing and 'seemingly insatiable: when limited supplies of the 1748 edition of the Welsh Bible reached Anglesey, poor people nearly scratched out the eyes of Thomas Ellis, vicar

of Holyhead, as they surged forward and fought to acquire a copy; similarly, there was such an extraordinary demand for the Scriptures among the parishioners of the vale of Conwy that poor people borrowed money in order to buy copies'. GHJ, p.379.

19. After Thomas Charles had placed the Bible in Mary Jones's grasp, and witnessing the tears of joy and gratitude, he turned to his friend David Edwards, a much respected Methodist preacher at Bala, and said, 'Is not such a sight as this enough to melt the hardest heart? A girl, so young, so poor, so intelligent, so familiar with Scripture, compelled to walk all the distance from Llanfihangel to Bala (about fifty miles there and back) to get a Bible! From this day I can never rest until I find out some means of supplying the pressing wants of my country that cries out for the Word of God.' M.E.R., *Mary Jones and her Bible* (Gospel Standard Trust Publications, Harpenden, 1994), p.108.

20. SM, pp.83-84.

21. Evans, *The Making of Modern Wales*, pp.131-132.

22. Iain Murray, *Thomas Charles of Bala* (The Banner of Truth Magazine, 13th Issue, November 1958), pp.14-15.

23. PH, p.229.

24. D. Densil Morgan, *Smoke, Fire and Light: Baptists and the Revitalisation of Welsh Dissent* (The Baptist Quarterly, vol.32, 1987-88), p.225.

25. The growth of Baptist membership manifested itself in surges. The first took place in 1774. 'The second was in 1789 when 603 were baptised, compared with only 150 but a few years earlier. The third surge took place in 1795 when 822 new members were received into fellowship, and the fourth and most spectacular of all, in 1807 when 1368 converts were baptised.' Ibid, p.229.

26. Glanmor Williams, *Welsh Baptists in an Age of Revolution, 1776-1832* (The Baptist Quarterly, vol.33, No.5, January 1990), pp.207, 208.

27. C.E., *Early Records of Baptist Churches* (Baptist Magazine, vol.9, 1817), p.56.

Chapter 5 — Lleyn: A New Man and a New Ministry

1. SM, p.207.

2. 'Also in 1789, agreement was reached to divide the Welsh Association into three, not because of any disagreement in doctrine or discipline, but with a view to the spread of the Gospel, and the convenience of the churches. It was an unwise decision and did not help the infant churches of North Wales. In the new arrangement, the Northern Association had 9 churches, the South Western 18, and the South Eastern 19.' Childs, *Christmas Evans and the Demonstration of the Spirit*, p.68.

3. ER, p.56.

4. CENN, 21.

5. DP, p.38.
6. William Burkitt (1650-1703), an evangelical churchman and a close friend of William Gurnal, wrote *Expository Notes, with Practical Observations on the New Testament,* which was published posthumously in 1724.
7. *Barcud* was a play on words and means 'a hawk'.
8. RS, p.23.
9. DBMW, p.194.
10. RS, p.24.
11. Ibid., pp.23-24.
12. Ibid., p.25.
13. David Jones (1741-92), a convert of Howel Harris, was a fiery Baptist preacher, who, in Christmas Evans's estimation, helped to dispel the darkness that overshadowed the Baptist movement.
14. *The Life and Death of Mr Vavasor Powell,* which includes his autobiography, was published in English in 1671, but it was the Welsh translation, published in 1772, coupled with the oral traditions concerning Powell that were alive in mid-Wales at the end of the eighteenth century, that fired Christmas Evans's imagination. In 1791 Howel Harris's *Autobiography* was published in English and within the year there was a Welsh translation. This too influenced 'the one-eyed preacher', although probably not until after his Lleyn ministrations.
15. DP, p.43.
16. DWB, p.856.
   Richardson also promoted John Elias's reputation as a preacher by sending him to preach in his stead at a monthly meeting held at Bryn-du in Anglesey, where the service was so successful that the congregation felt that a great and bright light had dawned on them.
17. PH, p.190.
18. GPW, p.156.
19. DWB, p.876.
20. GPW, pp.139-140.
21. Ibid., pp.140-141.
22. Ibid., p.141.
23. Ibid., p.116.
24. Ibid., p.117.
25. Ibid., p.156.
26. While working on a farm owned by John Prichard, the father of Richard Jones of Wern, Roberts became seriously ill, suffering severely with acute rheumatism for about two months. By the time he rose from his bed, his muscles had contracted, causing curvature of the spine, which made him several inches shorter. After awhile his muscles recovered but his spine remained curved for the rest of his life.
27. DME, pp.63-64.

28. RS, p.26.
29. CENN, p.116.
30. DP, p.44.
31. RS, p.98.
32. The validity of this story is questionable in view of the fact that the men with whom Christmas Evans travelled north were mature and knowledge-able ministers of the Gospel, who would have felt responsible for 'the lad from the South'.
33. RS, p.99.
34. DME, pp.61-62.
35. DP, p.45.
36. GPW, pp.154-155.
37. DP, p.42.
38. DME, pp.64-65.
39. Several of Christmas Evans's contemporaries, men such as David Davies, John Elias, William Williams, Ebenezer Morris, and other ministers of national fame, also made preaching excursions throughout Wales. 'These visits of the great preachers aroused the whole country. The spirits of the ministers were fired, the churches were revived, and multitudes who never attended a place of worship were attracted by the fame of the preachers to go and hear them, and were so affected that they afterwards became regu-lar hearers and church members. The universal prevalence of Dissent in Wales is principally to be ascribed, under God, to the repeated excitements and the religious interest awakened by the itinerant preaching of our great preachers.' Rees, *Miscellaneous Papers*, p.90.
40. DP, pp.46-47.
41. Christmas Evans was the first Baptist minister to become well-known throughout Wales and his fame travelled far beyond Wales and the United Kingdom. For instance, 'his career is said to have given a powerful stimu-lus to the American Evangelist D. L. Moody'. E. W. Price Evans, *Christmas Evans, 1766-1838*, (The Baptist Quarterly, vol.9, 1938-39), p.195.
42. DBMW, p.194.
43. RS, p.29.
44. Ibid., pp.28-29.
45. Ibid., pp.26-27.
    Christmas Evans has confused his dates. In 1829 he was not in Caer-philly, but pastor of the Tabernacle Church, Cardiff. His Caerphilly minis-try began in 1826 and ended in 1828.

Chapter 6 — Anglesey: Pastor of 'The Dark Isle'

1. JD, p.16.
2. DP, p.50.
3. Ibid., p.51.

4. In later years, the wife of John Elias, Christmas Evans's contemporary and fellow-worker on the island from 1799, suffered personal loss from one of these 'lootings'. Elizabeth Elias dealt in drapery and millinery and the goods for sale were shipped from Liverpool to the little harbour of Porth Amlwch. In April 1818 the *Marchioness* was carrying goods from Liverpool to Anglesey when it was 'driven by a storm and was wrecked on Dulas beach. Pirates and thieves ran to the wreck and completed the work of the storm by taking away everything movable from the ship.' Morgan, *John Elias*, p.77.

5. The early Baptists met in a house (Cae Garw, Rhostrehwfa) which was owned by Robert Williams, one of the first to be baptised in Anglesey in 1779. Williams moved to a cottage which stood in the lower corner of the present cemetery at Cil-dwrn and the Baptist congregation used it as a place of worship. In 1781 the cottage was demolished and the first Cil-dwrn chapel was built. It was 'a simple building, rather low yet solid, with a few seats in the form of a half moon facing the pulpit. The chapel and house were built at the same time with a thatched roof and a floor of clay and straw.'

Although the official name of the church at Llangefni is Ebenezer, it is more usually called Cil-dwrn on account of Robert Williams's habit of giving sweets to the people who came to his cottage to do their shopping. It appears that his cottage was a sort of shop for the neighbourhood and that he gave sweets as a *cil-dwrn* (tip/bribe) to his customers. Hywel M. Davies (the present minister at Cil-dwrn), *Capel Cildwrn 1779-1998* (unpublished paper, translated 1998).

6. TMB, p.104.
7. CENN, p.56.
8. Ibid., p.57.
9. Ramsbottom, *Christmas Evans*, p.40.
10. C.E., *Early Records of Baptist Churches*, p.56.
11. DBMW, p.193.
12. DP, pp.52-53.
13. C.E., *Early Records of Baptist Churches*, p.56.
14. CENN, p.56.
15. DME, p.71.
16. CENN, p.58.
17. R. Evans, *Life and Times of the Rev. David Jones* (Llanelly, 1885), p.69.
18. TMB, p.202.
19. RS, p.39.
20. SM, p.288.
21. Robert Hall (1764-1831), an English contemporary of Christmas Evans, was educated at the famous Nonconformist Academy run by John Ryland. He began his ministry as co-pastor with Dr Evans of the Baptist Church in Broadmead, Bristol, and quickly established a reputation as an eloquent

preacher and a master of the stately, periodic style of pulpit oratory. In 1791, after a painful breach with Dr Evans, he moved to Cambridge, where he succeeded Robert Robinson in the pastorate. He suffered two periods of mental breakdown after which he had a profound religious experience, which he described as his 'conversion'. In 1807 he moved to Harvey Lane Baptist Church in Leicester and exercised a wide and influential ministry there. He returned to Broadmead Chapel and died five years later.

Silvester Horne, in *A Popular History of the Free Churches*, remarks: 'At the height of his power he produced such effects upon his hearers as perhaps no other preacher of modern times has equalled. He was known to draw an audience to its feet and hold it thus spell-bound for as long as half an hour. On great occasions ... he rose to superb heights of eloquence, and his sermons in advocacy of the missionary cause show how the majestic idea of the Kingdom of God had captured his imagination.' (p.391). When Christmas Evans heard him speak he longed to be able to preach in the same tone.

22. Edwin Charles Dargan, *A History of Preaching, vol.2, From the Close of the Reformation Period to the End of the Nineteenth Century 1572-1900*, (Baker Book House, Michigan, 1970), p.500.

In *The Autobiography of William Jay* (The Banner of Truth Trust, Edinburgh, 1974) the expression 'a continent of mud' is applied by the author to Dr Owen's works (p.124). In O.G.Gregory's work on the life of Robert Hall it is said to refer to Dr Gill's works. It is probable that there has been a misapplication either by Jay or by the minister from whom he received the anecdote. It is inconceivable, is it not, that Hall should refer to the works of one of the finest theologians in such a derogatory manner?

According to Lewis Drummond, Charles Spurgeon, with tongue in cheek, also called Gill's systematic theology 'a continent of mud'. Gill was one of Spurgeon's predecessors at the New Park Street Baptist Church and Spurgeon greatly admired both the man and his works. *Spurgeon: Prince of Preachers*, pp.64, 182, 183.

23. DWB, p.563.
24. SM, pp.81-82.
25. E. W. Price Evans, *Christmas Evans, 1766-1838* (The Baptist Quarterly, vol.9, 1938-9), p.202.
26. RS, p.185.
27. SM, p.201.
28. Ibid., p.289.
29. GPW, p.181.
30. CENN, p.58.
31. ER, pp.148-149.
32. Ramsbottom, *Christmas Evans*, p.41.

Chapter 7 — Associational Preaching

1. GPW, pp.234-235.
2. DWB, p.855.
3. TR, p.389.
4. CENN, p.75.
5. RS, p.38.
6. DME, p.75.
7. CENN, pp.74-75.
8. TMB, p.87.
9. Webber, *A History of Preaching in Britain and America*, part 2, pp.543-544.
10. GPW, pp.158-159.
11. JD, p.19.
12. DP, p.56.
13. JD, p.18.
14. A, p.109.
15. EWH, p.216.
16. A, pp.101-107.
17. Christmas Evans, *Alegorïau* (Hughes and Son, Wrexham, n.d.), p.14.
18. DME, p.239.
19. During the time of Christmas Evans, the Northern Association branched into three regions: Anglesey, Arfon and Denbighshire.
20. DP, p.204.
21. Men such as Samuel Breeze, Titus Lewis, Joshua Watkins, Joseph Harris, J. P. Davies (Tredegar), John Herring, J. Evans (Pen-y-garn), John Jones (Newtown), David Evans (Dolau).
22. DP, p.205.
23. HWB, pp.197-201.
24. SM, pp.254-255.
25. Ibid., p.255.
26. G. Holden Pike, *The Life and Work of Charles Haddon Spurgeon*, vol.1 (The Banner of Truth Trust, Edinburgh, 1991), p.379.
27. DP, p.57.
28. Ibid.

Chapter 8 — The 'Frigid Zone' of Sandemanianism

1. Lloyd-Jones, *The Puritans*, pp.185-186.
2. Childs, *Christmas Evans and the Demonstration of the Spirit*, p.81.
3. Evans, *Daniel Rowland*, p.339.
4. Ibid., p.340.
5. DNB, vol.VII, p.1296.
6. Sandemanian 'opinions and practices chiefly consist in their weekly administration of the Lord's Supper; their love feasts, of which every member is required to partake; their kiss of charity used on this occasion; their

weekly collection before the Lord's Supper for the support of the poor and
other expenses; mutual exhortation, abstinence from blood and things
strangled; washing each other's feet, which they understand as a literal
precept, &c.; they maintain a plurality of elders, pastors, or bishops in each
church; in discipline they are very strict and severe.' Evans, *Life and Times
of the Rev. David Jones,* p.58n.

In addition, infant baptism was reintroduced; the conditions of membership were very strict, one stipulation being that the church could control
the use of members' private money. The sect was very exclusive and inter-
marriage was common.

7. DNB, vol.VII, p.1296.
8. Ibid., p.1297.
9. Childs, *Christmas Evans and the Demonstration of the Spirit,* p.80.
10. Andrew Fuller, *Strictures on Sandemanianism in Twelve Letters to a Friend*
    (Thomas Williams, London, 1811), p.27.
11. The Sandemanian churches in America survived until 1890, and in Great
    Britain in the 1970s it was reported that two congregations remained, one
    in Edinburgh and one in London.
12. Fuller, *Strictures on Sandemanianism,* p.37.
13. TMB, p.115.
14. A. G. Fuller, *The Principal Works and Remains of the Rev. Andrew Fuller*
    (Henry G.Bohn, London, 1852), pp.56-57.
15. Fuller, *Strictures on Sandemanianism,* p.17.
16. Lloyd-Jones, *The Puritans,* p.174.
17. DP, pp.72-73.
18. Ibid., p.73.
19. Lloyd-Jones, *The Puritans,* p.186.
20. PH, p.71.
21. Jones had been baptised by Henry Davies, minister of Llangloffan, in
    June, 1788. He joined the church at Ramoth and within a year became its
    pastor.

    'J. R. Jones of Ramoth was orthodox enough, accepting the five basic
    Calvinistic tenets. He accepted too, although somewhat cautiously, the doc-
    trine of the three separate persons in the Trinity but did not accept the
    teaching about the eternal filiation of Christ. He also followed McLean in
    his definition of faith... He no more liked the ways of the Methodists than
    did the reformers of South Wales... He, like them, stood firmly by the Scrip-
    tures and rejected the interference of the trustees of the Particular Baptist
    Fund but he lacked their tolerance, accepting McLean's argument for una-
    nimity in the church.. He had no room for the authority of a Quarterly
    Meeting or an Association; the gathered church was complete in itself...
    Ministers were not paid but drew upon church funds according to their
    needs.' TMB, pp.120-121.

22. Childs, *Christmas Evans and the Demonstration of the Spirit*, p.71.
23. DP, p.66.
24. DWB, p.488.
25. Ibid.
26. PH, p.73.
27. DP, p.66.
28. RS, p.42.
29. CENN, p.39.
30. Ibid., p.36.
31. Ibid., p.38.
32. Ibid.
33. RS, pp.42-46.
34. CENN, p.39.
35. Childs, *Christmas Evans and the Demonstration of the Spirit*, p.74.
36. RS, p.44.
37. After the Ramoth church had separated, others followed: 'Harlech, Bryndeunydd and Trawsfynydd in Merioneth; Cricieth and Llanllyfni in Caernarfon; and Rhosllannerchrugog in Denbighshire. The churches in Dolgellau, Glyn Ceiriog and Rhuthun were split, some members in favour of the new system, others against. By 1800 the schism was complete and McLean's association established in the country.' CENN, pp.43-44.
38. DWB, p.488.
39. DP, p.65.
40. When a young man, Robert Morgan, tried to contribute to the debate in a rather flustered manner, the reaction of Christmas Evans was to whisper frivolously, 'Can you see the boat in distress?' CENN, p.42.
41. DP, p.61.
42. CENN, p.42.
43. Ibid.
44. DP, p.62.
45. Ibid., pp.63-64.
46. Ibid., p.67.
47. CENN, p.43.

Chapter 9 — 'A Cold Heart Towards Christ'

1. Lloyd-Jones, *The Puritans*, p.187.
2. Robert Oliver, *Christmas Evans* (Reformation Today, Jan./Feb. 1976), p.24.
3. CENN, p.40.
4. Edmund Francis was a Sandemanian Baptist minister who was ordained as Christmas Evans's assistant on 1 December, 1795. He remained a Sandemanian for the rest of his life. 'In or very shortly after 1801 he had founded "Scotch Baptist" churches at Caernarfon and Llanllyfni, under his own pastorate.' He 'supervised the publication of the hymnary edited

by J. R. Jones of Ramoth, and in 1829 he published Welsh translations of three of the works of Archibald McLean'. DWB, p.269.

5. RS, pp.48-49.
6. Ibid., pp.50-53.
7. GPW, pp.159-160.
8. RS, p.55.
9. DME, p.83.
10. RS, p.57.
11. DP, p.64.
12. RS, p.60.
13. DP, p.65.
14. TMB, p.123.
15. By 1796, the approximate date of Christmas Evans's defection to Sandemanianism, the membership at Llangefni had risen to about 200 and met in several places on the island.
16. DP, p.60.
17. Childs, *Christmas Evans and the Demonstration of the Spirit*, p.79.
18. DWB, p.517.
19. Childs, *Christmas Evans and the Demonstration of the Spirit*, p.79.
20. Ibid., p.80.
21. RS, p.72.
22. PH, p.76.
23. CENN, p.48.
24. DP, p.65.
25. CENN, p.48.
26. Ibid., pp.48-49.
27. Childs, *Christmas Evans and the Demonstration of the Spirit*, p.80.
28. DP, p.74.
29. Ibid., p.99.
30. DP, pp.75-77.
31. DBMW, p.246.
32. CENN, p.44.

Chapter 10 — A Deeper Walk with God

1. *New King James Version* (Thomas Nelson, Nashville, 1991).
2. DP, p.72.
3. Ibid., p.71.
4. RS, p.60n.
5. DP, pp.68-69.
6. Ibid., p.69.
7. RS, p.49.
8. Ibid., p.48.
9. Sabellianism, so named after Sabellius, a presbyter of Ptolemais AD250,

who, in his desire to maintain the absolute unity and indivisibility of God, denied that the distinctions (persons) within the Godhead were ultimate or permanent. His doctrine attempted to defend monotheism against tritheism by insisting that Father, Son and Holy Spirit are not three distinct persons, but three different manifestations and names of the same divine person, who appears to people in different modes at different times. In the Father he reveals himself as Creator, in the Son as Redeemer and in the Holy Spirit as sanctifier; in the Old Testament he manifests himself as the Father, in the gospels as the Son, and after Pentecost as the Spirit. Sabellianism was condemned by the council of Rome in AD260, and Sabellius was excommunicated by Pope Calixtus.

10. DP, pp.69-70.
11. Ibid., p.69.
12. Ibid., p.71.
13. Ibid., p.214.
14. Ibid., p.215.
15. DME, pp.106-107.
16. CENN, p.66.
17. MS from Cil-dwrn Chapel WSE/195.
18. DP, p.85.
19. Ibid., pp.85-86.
20. CENN, p.83.
21. SM, p.260.
22. DP, p.78.
23. Ibid., pp.78-82.
24. Ibid., p.82.
25. CENN, p.68.
26. Ibid., pp.68-70.
27. Ibid., pp.79-80.
28. Ibid., pp.70-71.

Chapter 11 — Times of Refreshing

1. SVS, p.288.
2. Eifion Evans, *Two Welsh Revivalists: Humphrey Jones, Dafydd Morgan and the 1859 Revival in Wales* (Evangelical Library of Wales, Bridgend, 1985), p.26.
3. C.E., *Early Records of Baptist Churches*, p.57.
4. JD, p.68.
5. CENN, p.71.
6. C.E., *Early Records of Baptist Churches*, p.57.
7. The gallery at Cil-dwrn was built without altering the height of the roof, which meant that the ceiling above the gallery was very low.
8. DP, pp.83-84.

9. SM, pp.181-182.

10. DBMW, p.311.

11. In Caernarfonshire, for instance, from 1811-1816 meeting houses were built at Rhoshirwaun, Llanllawen, Galltraeth, Pwllheli and Garn; and in Denbighshire at Llanrwst, Glanwydden, Llandudno, Llanefydd, Cefn-mawr, Llangollen and Glyn Ceiriog. C.E., *Early Records of Baptist Churches*, p.58.

12. DBMW, p.310.

13. DP, pp.94-96.

14. Ibid., pp.96-97.

15. RS, pp.66-67.

16. JD, p.65.

17. CENN, pp.61-62.

18. DP, pp.87-88.

19. CENN, p.62.

20. JD, pp.84-85.

21. DP, p.87.

22. JD, p.85.

23. DBMW, p.275.

24. CENN, p.77.

25. Ibid., p.78.

26. Ibid., pp.78-79.

27. Ibid., p.77.

28. William Cobbett (1762-1835) was an essayist, radical politician and agriculturist. See DNB vol.IV, pp.598-601.

29. Thomas Paine (1737-1809), a deist and radical revolutionary, was the author of *The Rights of Man* (1791, 1792), which was an answer to Edmund Burke's *Reflections on the Revolution in France* (1790), a classic statement of conservative values. 'Paine is the only English writer who expresses with uncompromising sharpness the abstract doctrine of political rights held by the French revolutionists. His relation to the American struggle, and afterwards to the revolution of 1789, gave him a unique position, and his writings became the sacred books of the extreme radical party in England.' DNB vol.XV, p.78.

30. TMB, pp.131-132.

31. CENN, p.77.

'Almost all those who reacted positively to the French Revolution came from the ranks of those influenced by Arminianism or Arianism.' HW, p.338.

'By 1800 most Welsh Baptists would have agreed with the English Baptist preacher, Robert Hall, when in his famous sermon of that year he denounced modern infidelity, by which he meant the principles of the French Revolution.' Williams, *Welsh Baptists in an Age of Revolution 1776-1832*, p.212.

32. CENN, p.77.
33. HW, p.339.
   Although Rhys was a Baptist minister he published the work of the atheist
   Volney; he was actuated by a hatred of the Roman Catholic Church and
   believed that the Revolution had ensured its overthrow in France; his Re-
   publican ideas, which he had imbibed in Paris, were almost treasonable to
   Pitt's government; and he emigrated to America at the beginning of the
   trials for treason of members of the radical London societies with which he
   was associated.
34. TMB, p.111.
35. Five issues of his Welsh magazine (*Cylch-grawn Cynmraeg*) appeared
   between 1793-4 from three different presses, and 'their contents are proof
   of his zeal for education, freedom of conscience, social reform and the
   Welsh language'. HW, p.339.
36. DWB, p.846.
37. CENN, p.62.
38. Ibid., p.79.
39. Evans, *Christmas Evans, 1766-1838*, p.203.
40. DP, pp.212-214 & CENN chapter 9.
41. CENN, p.76.
42. RS, pp.68-69.
43. Ibid., p.68.
44. C.E., *Early Records of Baptist Churches*, p.58.
45. CENN, p.76.
46. DME, p.123.
47. DWB, p.355.
48. Ibid., p.356.
49. RS, pp.202-203.
50. Ibid., pp.73-74.
51. Phillips, *Christmas Evans*, p.19.
52. Ibid.
53. *Seren Gomer* 'marked a stage common to many European peoples in
   encouraging an awareness of nationality. It was also vital in the creation of
   an informed public opinion on religious, moral, social and political issues.
   The practice of regular reading which it encouraged involved a quantum
   leap forward for the transition of a society, in which knowledge was transmitted by tradition, folk-lore and even superstition, to one in which
   up-to-date information was more thoroughly and systematically acquired
   by a process of regular reading.' Williams, *Welsh Baptists in an Age of
   Revolution 1776-1832*, p.210.
54. RS, pp.74-75.
55. DME, p.124.
56. Ibid., pp.130-131.

Chapter 12 — 'Begging' Tours

1. R.Morris, *Christmas Evans* (Simpkin, Marshall & Co., London, 1870), pp.11-12.
2. The chapels built during this period, 'with very rare exceptions, exhibited no architectural taste whatever. They were plain, unsightly buildings, more like barns or warehouses than places of worship. The comparative small-ness and poverty of the congregations partly accounted for this; and it was no easy matter to persuade the descendants of people who had been com-pelled for generations to worship God in caves, barns, and obscure cottages, that neat and costly places of worship were necessary and be-coming. The least architectural ornaments ... were regarded by many as sinful innovations and signs of pride, unbecoming the humble worship-pers of God.' TR, pp.454-455.
3. CENN, p.81.
4. RS, p.76.
5. CENN, pp.81-82.
6. GPW, p.165.
7. DP, p.89.
8. Ibid., pp.88-89.
9. Ibid., p.92.
10. JD, pp.150-151.
11. DP, p.89.
12. DME, p.124.
13. JD, p.152.
14. DP, pp.90-92.
15. DME, p.160.
16. CENN, p.85.
17. RS, p.77.
18. DP, pp.92-93.
19. DME, p.149.
20. DP, p.93.
21. CENN, p.80.
22. TMB, p.198.
23. DME, pp.148-149.

Chapter 13 — Controversy

1. DP, pp.209-211.
2. TMB, p.37.
   Henry Gregory 'was very cruelly harassed and tormented by the unfeel-ing and barbarous persecutors'. On one occasion all his cattle were taken away by the authorites, except one, which they left '*to furnish milk for the children*'. Soon, however, when Gregory was away from home, the au-thorities returned and took away the last cow. TR, p.160.

3. DWB, p.286.
4. Williams, *Welsh Baptists in an Age of Revolution*, p.206.
5. Hughes, *Life of Howell Harris*, p.279.
6. TR, p.421.
7. W. T. Owen, *Edward Williams 1750-1813: His Life, Thought and Influence* (University of Wales Press, Cardiff, 1963), p.120.
8. GPW, p.167.
   In fact, the Arminians had no sympathy with theological liberalism and were far removed from the unorthodoxy that had emerged from the Carmarthen Academy.
9. DP, pp.98-99.
10. GPW, p.168.
11. Gwynfor Jones, *Christmas Evans—1766-1838* (The Evangelical Magazine of Wales, Bridgend, Dec.1973/Jan.1974), p.9.
12. DBMW, p.289.
13. CENN, pp.140-142.
14. Jones, *Christmas Evans—1766-1838*, p.9.
15. Williams, *Welsh Baptists in an Age of Revolution*, p.207.
16. DBMW, p.290.
17. CENN, pp.148-149.
18. DP, p.100.
19. Morgan, *John Elias*, p.141.
20. Ibid.
21. RS, p.84.
22. CENN, p.150.
23. Ibid., p.151.
24. Ibid., p.152.
25. Ibid., p.153.
26. RS, p.84.
27. CENN, p.154.
28. GPW, p169.
29. Jones, *Christmas Evans—1766-1838*, p.10.
   Owen Jones in GPW (p.169n.) argues that Thomas Jones's 'bitter epithet of reproach' was applied to Christmas Evans's opinion and 'not to the person at all', which is what 'Jones himself says in a letter published January, 1820', a few months before his death. Christmas Evans understood the epithet to apply to himself.
30. Cantre'r Gwaelod is a place that lies under Cardigan Bay and, according to legend, was submerged following the negligence of the drunken floodgate keeper.
31. CENN, p.155.
32. DME, pp.221-222.
33. Fuller, *Works and Remains of Andrew Fuller*, p.19.

34. J. W. Morris, *Memoirs of the Life and Writings of the Rev. Andrew Fuller* (1816), p.265.

Fuller gives three reasons for his shift away from hyper-Calvinism to a more evangelical Calvinistic position: 'First, his close study of the Bible with its many admonitions to the lost to repent and be converted; second, his reading of the lives of Eliot and Brainerd, who were uninhibited in their addresses to those poor benighted heathens; and finally, his discovery of Jonathan Edwards's *Inquiry into the Freedom of the Will*.' Timothy George, *Faithful Witness: The Life and Mission of William Carey* (Inter-Varsity Press, Leicester, 1991), p.55.

35. Morris, *Memoirs of Andrew Fuller*, p.270.

The principal teaching of Fuller's *The Gospel Worthy of All Acceptation* is unfolded in six propositions:

'1. Unconverted sinners are commanded, exhorted, and invited to believe in Christ for salvation.

2. Everyone is bound to receive what God reveals.

3. The gospel, though a message of pure grace, requires the obedient response of faith.

4. The lack of faith is a heinous sin which is ascribed in the Scriptures to human depravity.

5. God has threatened and inflicted the most awful punishments on sinners for their not believing on the Lord Jesus Christ.

6. The Bible requires of all persons certain spiritual exercises which are represented as their duty. These include repentance and faith no less than the requirement to love God, fear God, and glorify God. That no one can accomplish these things apart from the bestowal of the Holy Spirit is clear. Nonetheless the obligation remains. In this respect "man's duty and God's gift" are the same thing, seen from different perspectives.' George, *Faithful Witness*, pp.56-57.

36. Childs, *Christmas Evans and the Demonstration of the Spirit*, p.80.

37. Fuller, *Works and Remains of Andrew Fuller*, p.110.

38. Although Edward Williams (1750-1813) described himself as a moderate Calvinist, he was closer to being an Amyraldian, a position Fuller repudiated. Amyraldianism, named after the seventeenth century French theologian Moise Amyraut, is a system of Reformed theology based on the premise that God wills all to be saved if they believe. Other later Reformed theologians such as Charles Hodge and B.B.Warfield regarded Amyraldianism as an inconsistent mixture of Arminianism and Calvinism.

39. TR, p.433.

40. RS, p.83.

41. Thomas Jones entered the debates of Higher Calvinism and Arminianism with vigour and is noted for his skill at steering Methodism safely between the two camps. He strongly opposed Arminianism and although he was

critical of hyper-Calvinism, he was not able to embrace fully the 'Modern Calvinism' of his friend Edward Williams.
42. Owen, *Edward Williams*, p.124.
43. DP, p.98.
44. Ibid., p.99.
45. Ibid., pp.216-218.
46. Ibid., p.103.
47. RS, pp.108-109.
48. DP, p.99.
49. Ibid., p.101.
50. GPW, p.170.
51. Williams, *Welsh Baptists in an Age of Revolution*, p.207.

Chapter 14 — Sorrows and Trials
1. SM, p.152.
2. RS, p.97.
3. Ibid., pp.98-100.
4. JD, p.89.
5. RS, pp.104-105.
6. Ibid., p.102.
7. Ibid., pp.102-103.
8. Ibid., p.103.
9. DP, pp.175-176.
10. RS, pp.103-104.
11. Ibid., p.104.
12. C.E., *Early Records of Baptist Churches*, p.57.
13. JD, p.87.
14. Ibid.
15. DP, p.102.
16. CENN, pp.89-90.
17. RS, pp.105-106.
18. Ibid., pp.106-107.
19. Ibid., p.108.
20. CENN, p.91.
21. Ibid., p.92.
22. Ibid.
23. Ibid., pp.92-93.
24. Ibid., p.93.
25. Ibid., p.94.
26. Ibid., p.95.
27. Ibid., p.94.
28. Ibid., p.95.
29. Ibid., p.96.

30. ER, p.150.
31. Ibid., pp.150-151.
32. DME, pp.220-221.
33. DP, pp.103-104.
34. RS, p.174.
35. Ibid., pp.174-175.
36. PH, p.162.
37. ER, pp.151-152.
38. DP, p.104.
39. RS, p.110.
40. DP, pp.104-105.
41. Ibid., p.105.
42. Ibid.
43. CENN, pp.96-97.
44. Ibid., p.97.
45. Ibid., p.97-98.
46. DP, pp.105-106.
47. RS, p.111.
48. Ibid., pp.111-112.
49. DP, pp.208-209.

Chapter 15 — Caerphilly: The Best Years

1. SM, p.163.
2. CENN, pp.101-102.
3. Ibid., p.102.
4. RS, p.249.
5. Ibid., pp.250-252.
6. TMB, p.167.
7. DWB, p.783.
8. DME, pp.226-227.
9. CENN, p.101.
10. RS, p.112.
11. DME, p.227.
12. RS, p.113.
13. DP, p.110.
14. CENN, p.104.
15. Ibid., p.105.
16. RS, p.114.
17. PH, p.266.
18. RS, pp.120-121.
19. Ibid., p.122n.
20. GPW, p.173.
21. DP, p.111.

22. RS, p.135.
23. Ibid., p.136.
24. Evans, *Daniel Rowland*, p.351.
25. ER, p.159.
26. *Isaac Mann Autograph Collection*, Osborn MSS 46, ALS to Managers of Particular Baptist Fund, January 4, 1829, Cardiff.
27. DP, p.111.
28. RS, p.116.
29. Ibid., p.124.
30. Ibid., pp.124-125.
31. Ibid., p.126.
32. Ibid.
33. RS, pp.114-115.
34. Ibid., p.115.
35. ER, p.160.
36. Ibid., pp.159-160.
37. CENN, pp.105-106.
38. Ibid., pp.106-107.
39. RS, p.113.
40. DME, pp.228-229.
41. ER, p.158.
42. RS, p.114.
43. ER, p.160.
44. Evans, *Christmas Evans, 1766-1838* (The Baptist Quarterly, 1938-39), vol.9, p.199.
45. RS, pp.129-130.
46. DWB, p.375.
47. RS, p.130.
48. DP, p.111.
49. Ibid., pp.111-112.
50. RS, pp.128-129.
51. DP, p.112.
'Christmas Evans retained close links with Tonyfelin after 1828. Even in 1838, the year in which he died, he was sent £5 by Tonyfelin towards the Baptist cause at Caernarfon. When the new hall in Tonyfelin was built in 1928 it was named "The Christmas Evans Memorial Hall" to remember this very gifted preacher.' H. P. Richards, *Tonyfelin Welsh Baptist Church, Caerphilly, 1784-1984* (D. Brown & Son Ltd, Cowbridge and Bridgend, 1985), p.32.

Chapter 16 — Cardiff: Vale of Contention
1. SM, p.193.
2. *Isaac Mann Autograph Collection*, Osborn MSS 46, ALS to William Paxon, 1829 January 3, Cardiff.

3. DP, p.114.
4. Ibid., pp.114-118.
5. Ibid., p.118.
6. *Isaac Mann Autograph Collection*, Osborn MSS 46, ALS to William Paxon, 1829, January 3, Cardiff.
7. *The Baptist Quarterly*, Calendar of Letters, No.164, 1828, November 7.
8. CENN, p.109.
9. RS, p.138.
10. *Isaac Mann Autograph Collection*, Osborn MSS 46, ALS to William Paxon, 1829, January 3, Cardiff.
11. Ibid., ALS to Managers of the Particular Baptist Fund, 1829, January 4, Cardiff.
12. DP, p.118.
13. The 1828 revival in Wales began in Carmarthenshire and spread throughout the counties of the south. It has been estimated that about '280 were added to the church at Llanddeusant, and about 2000 to the Calvinistic Methodist churches' in Carmarthenshire at that time. 'Many notable men amongst the Congregationals commenced their ministerial careers as a result of this revival.' Eifion Evans, *Revival Comes to Wales: The Story of the 1859 Revival in Wales* (Evangelical Press of Wales, Bridgend, 1986), p.17.
14. DP, pp.119-120.
15. Ibid., pp.121-122.
16. Ibid., p.122.
17. Ibid., pp.122-123.
18. Ibid., p.138.
19. Ibid., pp.138-139.
20. Evans, *Life and Times of the Rev David Jones*, p.79.

R. Evans has some very complimentary things to say about Christmas Evans, but he is harsh in his opinion when he focuses on his departure from Cardiff: 'Christmas Evans was a preacher and nothing else. He never could lead — he never could understand people, nor rule to their satisfaction. He would rule with a rod of iron, ever and anon going to extremes. He was lax to a fault in business qualifications, and he was too ready to make friends, and then discard a large part of them. He failed for want of understanding human nature. He was an autocrat in the North, but not in the South. In the North he practised the Presbyterian form of government, which could not be tolerated in the South. In Anglesey he was king; in Glamorganshire only a subject, open to be governed by the many. Church discipline was in Anglesey vested in the minister, and he practised it for forty years; but in the South every church had the sole government of its own affairs, both in discipline and order. In the North — the government was synodical; in the South — congregational.' *Life and Times of the Rev David Jones*, pp.57-58. The author is obviously taking a very one-sided view and basing his opinion on the two unhappy years that Christmas Evans spent in Cardiff.

21. DP, p.137.
22. Evan Jones (1793-1855) moved to Castleton in September 1823 and his ministry was very successful in that place. He remained there until his death.
23. DP, p.137.
24. William Jones (1790-1855) became pastor of Bethany English Church, Cardiff, in 1816 and held that position until his death. He is best remembered for his literary and historical writings and, like Christmas Evans, translated a large portion of Dr Gill's *Commentary on the New Testament* into Welsh.
25. RS, p.140.
26. DP, p.137.
27. Francis Hiley (1781-1860) was a mighty Baptist preacher.
28. John Jenkins (1779-1853) was inducted at Hengoed in 1809 and remained there for the rest of his life. He travelled throughout Wales preaching and selling his books. In the Fullerian controversy he came to prominence as an exponent of the higher Calvinism. Christmas Evans, along with John Evans (Pen-y-garn) and David Evans (Maes-y-berllan), had preached at his ordination in 1806.
29. DME, pp.53-54.
30. RS, p.139.
31. ER, pp.165-166.

Chapter 17 — 'The Old Field Marshal'
1. SM, p.35.
2. DP, p.124.
3. RS, p.161.
4. DP, pp.124-125.
5. GPW, p.179.
6. Ibid., pp.179-180.
7. Ibid., pp.180-181.
8. DP, p.141.
9. Ibid., pp.140-141.
10. DME, pp.236-238.
11. DP, pp.142-143.
12. Ibid., p.142.
13. CENN, p.113.
14. RS, p.144.
15. DP, p.143.
16. Ibid., pp.143-144.
17. Ibid., pp.144-145.

18. RS, p.145.
19. Ibid.

Chapter 18 — Caernarfon: An All Round Ministry
1. DP, p.146.
2. Ibid., p.148.
3. Ibid., pp.147-148.
4. See chapter 22 *Sermon Extracts*
5. DP, p.153.
6. Ibid., p.152.
7. RS, p.148.
8. Ibid.
9. TMB, p.177.
10. DP, pp.150-151.
11. CENN, p.114.
12. DP, pp.156-157.
13. Ibid., p.157.
14. Ibid., p.154.
15. Ibid., p.150.
16. RS, p.147.
17. DME, p.245.
18. DP, p.150.
19. RS, p.147.
20. SM, pp.278-279.
21. JD, p.93.
22. DP, p.156.
23. DME, p.243.
24. A, pp.89-90.
25. SM, p.85.
26. Ibid., p.86.
27. ER, p.115.
28. DP, p.155.
29. CENN, p.116.
30. JD, p.131.
31. Ibid., p.150.
32. DME, pp.243-244.
33. CENN, p.87.
34. Ibid., p.115.
35. JD, p.109.
    'The emergence of the temperance movement from the 1830s was rightly
believed to be one of the strongest pillars of the Baptists and other Nonconformists.' Williams, *Welsh Baptists in an Age of Revolution 1776-1832*,
p.209.

36. EWH, pp.308-309.
37. CENN, p.115.
38. RS, p.149.
39. DP, p.151.
40. Ibid., p.154.
41. SM, p.278.

Chapter 19 — 'Wheel about, Coachman, and Drive on'
1. SM, p.207.
2. A, p.16.
3. JD, pp.156-157.
4. DP, p.179.
5. The three men were Lewis of Llanwenarth, Davies of Felin-foel and Thomas of Aberduar. Lewis and Davies both died before Christmas Evans.
6. DP, pp.161-162.
7. ER, pp.177-179.
8. CENN, p.118.
9. DP, p.163.
10. Ibid., pp.163-164.
11. SM, p.285.
12. RS, p.153.
13. Ibid.
14. DP, p.164.
15. DWB, p.112.
16. TMB, p.187.
17. ER, p.191.
18. In one of his last sermons on the prodigal son, perhaps even his last, after repeating the son's confession to his father, Christmas Evans said, 'Methinks I hear the father answering him, "Stop! Stop! Stop! None of that, my boy! Hold your peace! None of that talking about where or what you will be on my premises. If I will that you be as a hired servant, as a hired servant you must be; if I will make of you a door-keeper, a door-keeper you must be; or if I will that you have a place at the head of my table, *there* you must be; not as you will, but *as I will, says the Lord of Hosts!* Amen! Amen!"' J. Bolton, *Gospel Ministers and Places* (The Friendly Companion, 1897), pp.18-19.
19. DP, p.165.
20. CENN, p.119.
21. RS, pp.153-154.
22. Ibid., pp.154-155.
23. CENN, p.120.
24. *Baptist Magazine* (1838), p.352.
25. DP, p.166.
26. CENN, p.120.

27. Ibid.
28. DP, p.167.
29. CENN, p.120.
30. GPW, pp.177-178.
31. CENN, p.121.
32. DP, p.169.
33. Ibid., pp.168-169.
34. GPW, p.206.

Chapter 20 — 'No Ordinary Person'
1. Phillips, *Christmas Evans*, pp.30-32.
2. Warren Wiersbe, *Great Christians you Should Know* (Inter-Varsity Press, Leicester, 1984), p.72.
3. ER, p.123.
4. DME, p.111.
5. Ibid.
6. JD, p.98.
7. DP, pp.172-173.
   There are two oil paintings of Christmas Evans. The first was finished around 1829 and paid for by the students of Bristol Baptist College. The second was painted because of the persuasion of his friend William Williams during his Caernarfon pastorate and was owned by his wife. Both show him at his best. CENN, p.125.
8. JD, pp.98-99.
9. PH, p.110.
10. CENN, pp.86-87.
11. Ibid., p.86.
12. DME, p.152.
13. Ibid., pp.112-113.
14. Edwards, *Christmas Evans*, p.13.
15. DP, p.86.
16. JD, p.55.
17. RS, p.102.
18. Ibid., p.101.
19. CENN, p.134.
20. JD, p.38.
21. Ibid.
22. Ibid.
23. Ibid., pp.38-39.
24. Ibid., p.39.
25. SM, p.114.
26. SVS, pp.337-338.
27. DP, p.174.

28. RS, p.102.
29. JD, p.55.
30. DP, pp.201-202.
31. Ibid., p.201.
32. Ibid., p.203.
33. Ibid., pp.202-203.
34. RS, p.101.
35. Ibid.
36. Ibid.
37. A, p.113.
38. JD, p.20.
39. CENN, p.135.
40. SM, p.95.
41. DP, p.185.
42. SM, p.294.
43. DP, p.181.
44. Ibid., pp.181-183.
45. Ibid., p.183.
46. Ibid., p.173.
47. Ibid., p.94.
48. Ibid, p.180.
49. Christmas Evans, *Alegorïau*, p.11.
50. Phillips, *Christmas Evans*, pp.19-20.
51. CENN, p.136.
52. JD, p.56.
53. ER, pp.128-130.
54. CENN, 127.
55. Ibid., p.95.
56. Christmas Evans, *Alegorïau*, pp.10-11.
57. DP, p.189.
58. JD, p.99.
59. DP, pp.192-193.
60. Ibid., p.188.
61. Phillips, *Christmas Evans*, p.22.
62. DME, p.163.
63. DP, p.189.
64. CENN, p.86.
65. EWH, p.364.
66. CENN, pp.127-128.
67. DME, p.221.
68. Christmas Evans, *Alegorïau*, pp.11-12.
69. SM, p.292.
70. DP, pp.189-191.

71. RS, p.157.
72. Ibid., pp.158-159.
73. Ibid., p.70.
74. Ibid., pp.161-162.

Chapter 21 — 'The Greatest Preacher God has ever Given to Wales'

1. Henry C. Fish, *Masterpieces of Pulpit Eloquence Ancient and Modern* (Hodder & Stoughton, London, 1869), vol.2, pp.595-596.
2. SM, p.90.
3. Dargan, *A History of Preaching*, vol.2, pp.496-497.
4. EWH, p.32.
5. Vyrnwy Morgan, *The Life and Sayings of Kilsby Jones* (Elliot Stock, London, 1896), p.114.
6. Webber, *A History of Preaching in Britain and America*, part 2, p.581.
7. JD, p.79.
8. DP, pp.219-220.
9. Ibid., p.199.
10. SVS, p.331.
11. SM, pp.61-62.
12. TMB, p.188.
13. SM, p.138.
14. SVS, p.258.
15. Sulwyn Jones, *Christmas Evans* (The Evangelical Magazine of Wales, Bridgend, Feb.1986), p.14.
16. JD, pp.100-101.
17. Ibid., pp.99-100.
18. A, p.10.
19. DP, p.197.
20. PH, pp.326-327.
21. William Rees, *Memoirs of W.Williams of Wern* (John Snow, London, 1846), p.103.
22. SM, p.298.
23. GPW, p.324.
24. SM, p.298.
25. JD, p.77.
26. Ibid., pp.28-29.
27. GPW, p.205.
28. Morgan, *Life and Sayings of Kilsby Jones*, p.97.
29. EWH, p.183.
30. R. Morris, *Christmas Evans* (Simpkin, Marshall & Co., London, 1870), p.19.
31. CENN, p.129.
32. Ibid., pp.129-130.

33. Johann Richter, known as Jean Paul, was a contemporary German writer, whose 'sentiment, ingenuity, whimsical style, and lavish detail' made his novels extremely popular; and whose 'sustained attention to contemporary life was a new feature'. His work foreshadowed the 'village story' of later decades. *The New Encyclopædia Britannica* (London, 1981), vol.10, p.1174.

34. John Chrysostom (c.347-407) was a famous preacher, a Church Father, and an archbishop of Constantinople. His eloquent and heart-searching sermons and exposition of the Bible in the cathedral at Antioch earned him the name *chrysostomos*, 'golden-mouthed'.

35. PH, p.41.

36. Christmas Evans, *Alegorïau*, p.13.

37. DWB, p.222.

38. JD, pp.22-23.

39. Ibid., p.23.

40. CENN, pp.76-77.

41. Webber, *A History of Preaching in Britain and America*, part 2, pp.580-581.

42. RS, p.161.

43. Ibid., pp.160-161.

44. JD, p.76.

45. 'He was always considerably put out if some officious brother gave out a hymn, especially if a long one, after his sermon. His feeling was, that, from the reading of his text to the close of the service, it was his own to conduct.' RS, p.122n.

46. DP, pp.194-195.

47. Ibid., p.198.

48. While he was alive, and more so after his death, a few of Christmas Evans's countrymen attempted to imitate his style and manner of preaching. There was the shrug of the shoulders, the shaking of the head, the hurried exclamation of *Bendigedig!* — but all without the vigour and inspiration of the master.

49. JD, pp.75-76.

50. GPW, p.205.

51. CENN, p.76.

52. JD, p.78.

53. Ibid., p.78-79.

54. DME, p.74.

55. RS, p.165.

56. Ibid., pp.165-166.

57. CENN, p.133.

58. DME, pp.173-174.

59. Evans, *Life and Times of the Rev David Jones*, p.78.

Chapter 22 — Sermon Extracts

1. HWB, p.193
2. *The Evangelical Magazine and Missionary Chronicle, 1838*, Vol.XVI (Thomas Ward and Co., London, 1838), p.437.
3. SVS, p.3.
4. *See Appendix 5.*
5. PH, pp.91-92.
6. HWB, pp.193-195.
7. SVS, pp.198-200.
8. EWH, pp.351-355.
9. SM, pp.141-142.
10. Ibid., pp.143-144.
11. DP, pp.247-249.
12. ER, p.86.
13. DP, pp.244-247.
14. A, p.24.
15. RS, pp.187-188.
16. SM, pp.40-41.
17. DP, pp.249-251.

Chapter 23 — Letters

1. Iain H. Murray (editor), *Letters of Charles Haddon Spurgeon* (The Banner of Truth Trust, Edinburgh, 1992), p.12.
2. Iain H. Murray (editor), *D. Martyn Lloyd-Jones: Letters 1919-1981* (The Banner of Truth Trust, Edinburgh, 1994), p.xx.
3. *Isaac Mann Autograph Collection*, Osborne MSS 46, ALS to unidentified recipient, 1813, April 27, Llangefni.
4. *Letter from the Rev. CHRISTMAS EVANS, of Anglesey, to the Rev. Wm WILLIAMS, of Grafton Street, London*, Regent's Park College, Angus Library, Oxford, Tract II, 2.b.13f (ii).
5. JD, pp.146-149.
6. CENN, p.117.
7. NLW, MSS.
8. JD, pp.80-81.
9. DP, pp.223-230.
10. Ibid., pp.231-234.
11. RS, p.85.
12. Ibid., pp.85-96.

Appendices

1. J. C. Ryle, *Christian Leaders of the 18th Century* (The Banner of Truth Trust, Edinburgh, 1978), pp.203-205.
2. Evans, *Daniel Rowland*, p.320.

3. GHJ, p.366.
4. Owen, *Daniel Rowlands*, p.35.
5. DP, pp.126-137.
6. Ibid., p.120.
7. TMB, p.185.
8. DP, pp.157-159.
9. CENN, p.136.
10. Ibid., p.135.
11. Ibid., p.84.
12. Christmas Evans, *The Decision of a General Congress Convened to Agree on 'Terms of Communion' Occasioned by the Rev Robert Hall's Pamphlet on that Subject* (London, 1816).
13. SM, p.48.
14. DP, pp.236, 237.
15. Ibid., pp.238-242.

Index

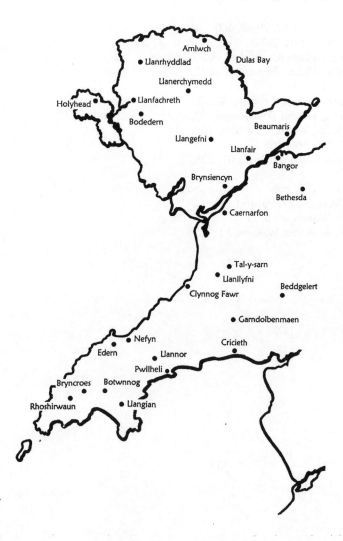

Amlwch

● Llanrhyddlad   Dulas Bay

Llanerchymedd

Holyhead ●   ● Llanfachreth

● Bodedern   Beaumaris

Llangefni ●
                ● Llanfair
                            ● Bangor

Brynsiencyn ●

                ● Caernarfon

                            ● Bethesda

                        ● Tal-y-sarn
                      ● Llanllyfni
                                ● Beddgelert
            Clynnog Fawr ●

                        ● Garndolbenmaen

        ● Nefyn   Cricieth ●
    Edern ●   ● Llannor
            Pwllheli ●
Bryncroes ●   Botwnnog
Rhoshirwaun ●   ● Llangian

Holyhead

Pen-sarn   Holywell
                    Flint
Bangor
Bethesda   Denbigh
Caernarfon   Llanrwst
              Betws-y-coed   Ruthin

            Snowdon   Wrexham
                        Llangollen
            Blaenau Ffestiniog
            Maentwrog   Glyn Ceiriog
Pwllheli   Talsarnau   Bala

            Dolgellau
            Cadair Idris
                Llanbryn-mair   Llanfair Caereinion
            Machynlleth   Montgomery
                        Newtown
Aberystwyth   Llanidloes
                Llangurig
            Lledrod   Presteigne
        Llangeitho   Tregaron
Llangrannog   Mydroilyn
    Pen-parc Tre-groes
Cardigan   Llangeler Llandysul   Hereford
  Newport   Llanfihangel-ar-arth
Llangloffan Newcastle Pentre Llanllwni
Fishguard   Emlyn -cwrt Pencader   Llandovery   Talgarth
  Little Newcastle   Trefeca
Whitchurch   Pen-y-banc   Brecon
St David's   Blaen-waun   Llandeilo
    Llanddowror   Llangynidr
    Laugharne   Carmarthen   Abergavenny
                                    Tredegar   Blaenafon   Monmouth
Pembroke   Llanelli   Dowlais Rhymni   Abersychan
                    Hirwaun Merthyr   Pontypool
            Neath   Aberdare Tudful   Argoed Pontnewydd
                Swansea Aberavon   Hengoed   Caerllion
                        Pontypridd   Bedwas   Newport
                    Taff's Well Caerphilly
                Llanharan Tongwynlais   Castleton
                Bridgend Whitchurch
                    Cardiff
                Cowbridge